# RECLAIMING THE LOCAL
# IN LANGUAGE POLICY
# AND PRACTICE

# RECLAIMING THE LOCAL IN LANGUAGE POLICY AND PRACTICE

*Edited by*

## A. Suresh Canagarajah

Routledge
Taylor & Francis Group
New York   London

First published by Lawrence Erlbaum Associates, Inc., Publishers
10 Industrial Avenue
Mahwah, New Jersey 07430

Reprinted 2008 by Routledge

Routledge

270 Madison Avenue
New York, NY 10016

2 Park Square, Milton Park
Abingdon, Oxon OX14 4RN, UK

Cover design by Kathryn Houghtaling Lacey

**Library of Congress Cataloging-in-Publication Data**

Reclaiming the local in language policy and practice / edited by A.
    Suresh Canagarajah.
        p.   cm. — (ESL and applied linguistics professional series)
    Includes bibliographical references and index.
  ISBN 0-8058-4592-5 (cloth : alk. paper)
  ISBN 0-8058-4593-3 (pbk. : alk. paper)
  1. Mass media policy.  2. Local mass media.  3. Communication,
    International.   I. Canagarajah, A. Suresh.   II. Series.
  P119.3.R43   2004
  302.23—dc22                                    2004046927
                                                      CIP

10   9   8   7   6   5   4   3   2   1

# Contents

## PART 2: INTERROGATING LANGUAGE POLICIES

## PART 3: REFRAMING PROFESSIONAL LIVES

## PART 4: IMAGINING CLASSROOM POSSIBILITIES

# Series Editor Foreword

The many issues associated with rapidly expanding globalization have become the mainstay of publications in language policy and practices, language teaching, applied linguistic research, and a myriad of attendant areas that have do to with the spread and influence of English around the world. Although the effects of globalization around the world are being discussed in such diverse circles as brokerage companies, law firms, international businesses, and education and although the spread of English has come to largely benefit those in positions of power, relatively little has been said about changes at the local level caused by globalization, directly or indirectly.

This book is unique in the sense that it focuses specifically on the outcomes of globalization in and among the communities impacted by these changes. Locally, the effects of global homogeneity, as they relate to language, are most immediately felt in terms of how language is used and studied, how knowledge and expertise are constructed, and how local policies are established and carried out. Canagarajah focuses on the great risk that local language practices, discourses, and values will be engulfed by the sweeping economic and political forces brought about by globalization. This book sets out to portray the local perspectives on the resulting changes that are in many cases outside the control of those most directly affected by them. Taken together, this collection of chapters gives voice to the communities, groups, and individuals that would not be otherwise heard.

The enormous forces of the global tidal wave highlighted in the volume underscore the importance of preserving the local, be it in the cases of language hybridity, loss, and discoursal multimodality. The rapid spread of English and "modern" ways of teaching can be felt from Brazil to Brunei to the Mexican borderlands and profoundly affect all that is involved: the individual language teachers, teaching practices, school-age learners, and the perceptions of self in another language.

This book not only identifies the urgent local concerns caused by the increasing linguistic and social homogeneity in the representations of literacy and expertise, but also brings to the foreground the rising issues of exacerbated power inequality. Canagarajah and the contributing authors describe the devaluation and pejorization of local knowledge and practices for the sake of the imported notions of "progress" and "innovation." They illuminate the contradictions and paradox that the local contains complex values of diversity, multilingualism, and plurality that can help to reconceive the multilingual society and education for postmodern times. Taken together, the chapters approach the task of reclaiming the local by means of negotiating with the present and the global to make space for the local. The perspective is forward-looking, emphasizing the need to engage with global realities, rather than avoiding engagement with other cultures and communities or hiding away from change. Collectively, the contributions to this book make a much-needed statement about the consequences of political, social, and linguistic displacement of the local. Although in the past few years, the voices of the local scholars and teachers have been listened to with greater attention, the danger of disappearance of local traditions and ways of speaking and doing has not lessened. The local is celebrated and treasured in this book that reflects a diversity of concerns, perspectives, issues, or points of contention arising with globalization. The ultimate purpose of this collection is to demonstrate that "progress," "modernization," and "global village-ness" can come at a high human, social, and cultural cost that may never be recovered.

—*Eli Hinkel*
*Series Editor,*
*ESL & Applied Linguistics Professional Series*
*Seattle University*

# Preface

The contributions in this collection insert the place of the local in theorizing language policies and practices in applied linguistics. The authors make a case for local social practices, communicative conventions, linguistic realities, and knowledge paradigms for actively informing language policies and practices for classrooms and communities in local contexts. They engage with the dominant paradigms in our discipline to not only show why it is important to take account of the local to relate to the needs of local communities, but also to critically inform language practices and policies pertaining to other communities. The chapters are primarily addressed to researchers and graduate students in applied linguistics. The authors' intent to complicate the dominant discourse on language policies and practices presupposes a knowledge of the state of the art in applied linguistics. However, the articles are written with such clarity that nonspecialists can still follow and appreciate the arguments these authors are making.

The strengths and limitations of this collection derive from the fact that these articles were originally a response to a call for articles for a special topic issue (see *Journal of Language, Identity, and Education [JLIE]*, Vol. 4). Because we had space for only four articles in this issue of *JLIE*, others who had interesting proposals came together to work toward this book. The call brought together scholars from different parts of the world who saw the need for complicating dominant disciplinary constructs in the light of local conditions. It was exhilarating to discover that scholars in communities as diverse as Brazil, Hong Kong, Iran, India, and Malaysia realized the limitations of dominant applied linguistic constructs and were working on promoting local knowledge. However, scholars from many other communities (who didn't have access to journals and academic communication relating to the "center") didn't respond to the call for articles. Therefore, this collection does not attempt to be geographically representative. Furthermore, the chapters relate to the research interests of the authors and don't attempt a coverage of all the subjects relevant to applied linguistics. Although we have research relating to second language acquisition, sociolinguistics, literacy, and language planning in this volume, the majority of the articles are case studies of specific contexts and communities, and have a bias toward situations of language teaching. However, these studies are relevant beyond their specific contexts in terms of initiating a discussion of the local knowledge relating to other communities and contexts, on subjects vastly different from those covered here. The studies also offer models for scholars interested in local knowledge elsewhere.

## ACKNOWLEDGMENTS

We are thankful to Lawrence Erlbaum Associates, Inc. (the publishers of *JLIE*) for responding favorably to the idea that the special topic issue should be expanded into a larger, book-length project. Naomi Silverman has been a demanding but sympathetic Sponsoring Editor, representing Lawrence Erlbaum Associates, Inc., who has pushed this project forward in positive directions. The Series Editor, Eli Hinkel, has read our various drafts at different stages of the project to shape the coherence of this book. The reviewers for Lawrence Erlbaum Associates, Inc.—Natalie Kuhlman, San Diego State University; Timothy Reagan, University of Connecticut; Jim Tollefson, University of Washington; and Alastair Pennycook, The University of Technology, Sydney—read the manuscript closely to offer valuable suggestions that enhance the organization and rigor of the articles. We are also thankful to the copyeditor, Tina Hardy, for "cleaning up" the textual peculiarities of contributions coming from diverse regions of the world!

—*Suresh Canagarajah*

# Introduction

Suresh Canagarajah
*Baruch College of the City University of New York*

"We suffer increasingly from a process of historical amnesia in which we think that just because we are thinking about an idea it has only just started" says Stuart Hall (1997, p. 20) in reference to the current excitement about processes of globalization. It may be true that the first documented use of the term "globalization" in the dictionary dates to 1961.[1] But the phenomenon is by no means new. It could be argued that globalization started when the first ships from Europe arrived in my part of the world (i.e., South Asia) in the 15th century. Some may go even further to see—in the development of maps and maritime travel, the collapse of Christendom, global exploration, the rise of the nation-state, and the creation of citizenship, passports, and diplomacy—certain forms of translocal connections developing between communities (Robertson, 1992). Whenever it may have started, the current heightened discourse relating to globalization (what Robertson, 1997, calls "globe talk" and what Abu-Lughod, 1997, calls "global babble") is both a blessing and a curse. This discourse is welcome because it has enabled us to reexamine our assumptions about social life and to redefine knowledge; it is limiting because we are getting carried away with notions of global homogeneity and promoting practices and relationships that are even more reductive than before.

Arjun Appadurai (2000) captures the dilemma well when he says that there is a disconnect between the *knowledge of globalization* and the *globaliza-*

---

[1]Kilminster (1997, p. 257) gives this date as the first occurrence in the Webster Dictionary (quoted in Block & Cameron, 2002, p. 2).

*tion of knowledge*. This can be understood in many interesting ways (although Appadurai himself doesn't explicate it for us). To begin with, we talk of globalization as ushering in a new life of border-free, unrestricted, fluid relationships between communities; but knowledge itself is narrowly constructed, splintered along different communities, devoid of effective attempts at developing an intercultural understanding or a fair exchange of ideas. Another expression of this disconnect is that certain discourses of globalization make us assume a pluralistic model of a world where all communities enjoy relative autonomy, with empowered local identities, values, and knowledge; but the way knowledge is spread belies this notion, displaying a one-sided imposition of homogeneous discourses and intellectual traditions by a few dominant communities. In both cases, what is lacking is a greater negotiation between global processes and local conditions, leading to the construction of a diversified knowledge tradition that benefits from the richness of practices and values in the human community. Therefore, we need to develop a more contextualized and critical understanding of what globalization means.

It is the view of the authors in this volume that the local is getting shortchanged by the social processes and intellectual discourses of contemporary globalization. We point to ways in which the negotiation of the global can be conducted by taking greater account of the local and respecting its value and validity. In providing a more pronounced place for the local in disciplinary discourses, we envision a shift in our practices of knowledge-making. The local shouldn't be of secondary relation or subsidiary status to the dominant discourses and institutions from powerful communities, whereby the global is simply applied, translated, or contextualized to the local. Making a space for the local doesn't mean merely "adding" another component or subfield to the paradigms that already dominate many fields. It means radically reexamining our disciplines to orientate to language, identity, knowledge, and social relations from a totally different perspective. A local grounding should become the primary and critical force in the construction of contextually relevant knowledge if we are to develop more plural discourses. In other words, what we envision is a "globalization from below" (to adopt a phrase from Appadurai, 2000), where we conceive and conduct globalization from a different vantage point. It is such an approach that will enable us to realize the potential of globalization to construct more democratic relationships.

Consider the ways in which the local is shortchanged in current discourses in our field of applied linguistics. There are generally two attitudes characteristic of our response to globalization. One encourages the spread of certain homogeneous codes, discourses, and communicative practices in all communities as universally relevant or applicable. For example, ELT (English Language Teaching) textbooks teach service-exchanges typical of those in American settings, giving the assumption that this is the established mode of discourse for this mode of interaction in any community (see Cameron, 2000). Preferred forms of language acquisition are based on activities and talk that lead to the exchange of information (as practiced in task-based language teaching, or TBLT, approaches popular in the West) because experts assume that such methods universally assure effective mastery of a language (see Block, 2002). Such "McCommunication" pedagogies (to use Block's term) orientate to the learner as a rational, free agent of communication; they ignore the diverse constraints and motivations that learners have to negotiate to communicate effectively. Furthermore, in language policy planning, the need for English in other communities is assumed to be beyond dispute as it is considered natural that people everywhere would want to arm themselves with a powerful language for global relationships. That the local languages may have an equal or greater role to play in educational and social development is often ignored (see Bruthiaux, 2002). What is ironic is that if such biased orientations were already there in our field before, they are now promoted with even greater vigor under the name of globalization. If they were discussed with some diffidence, hesitance, and qualification earlier, now they are treated as self-evident and promoted unconditionally.

The alternate discourse of globalization envisions empowering the local, but it assumes that globalization guarantees this by virtue of its new modes of social relations and communicative interaction. This discourse goes to the other extreme of exaggerating the democratic nature of globalization. In discussing computer-mediated learning and communication as reflective of globalization, Warschauer (2000) argues that local dialects of English are more widely used in the Internet, challenging the power of standard or "native" dialects of English. His main argument in "The Changing Global Economy and Future of English Teaching" is that "globalization will result in the further spread of English as an international language and a shift of authority to nonnative speaker and dialects" (2000, p. 511). He concludes his reflections optimistically: "If English is imposing the world on our students, we as TESOL professionals can enable them, through English, to impose their voices on the world" (2000, p. 530). We can understand how the fluidity in cultural practices and communication generated by recent technology encourages such utopias of empowerment for non-native speakers and dialects. However, this attitude has to be tempered by a recognition of more fundamental and intractable features characterizing the new media—that is, the dominant styles of interaction reflective of male and Eurocentric cultures (see Murray, 2000; Selfe & Selfe, 1994), the monopoly of certain software developers in shaping cyber communication, and the increasing digital divide that leaves a good segment of the world's population electronically deprived (Faigley, 1997). In terms of language, gatekeeping procedures in most institutions still prioritize "standard English" (i.e., dominant dialects of "native speaker" communities). The place of the local is then not guaranteed in globalization; it has to be achieved through socially informed struggle and strategic negotiation.

The chapters in this volume critically analyze the implications of the global in diverse communities to propose strategic modes of intervention for the local in language policies and practices. Seeing globalization compelling many disciplines (including those related to language studies) to redefine their traditional paradigms, the authors in the volume argue for a space for the local in knowledge construction activities. We intend to build on the new vistas opened by globalization and the new forms of representation achieved by the local to reorientate language studies.

This project grew out of a special issue of the *Journal of Language, Identity, and Education* (Vol. 4, Fall 2002) on the topic "Celebrating Local Knowledge on Language and Education." The project generated such wide interest among scholars in our field that we couldn't limit the contributions to a single journal issue. We decided then to publish the present collection as separate from the journal issue. Still, this volume doesn't aim to be exhaustive. It presents case studies in specific fields and communities that raise broader questions with ramifications for other contexts. The terms *local* and *global* are relative to the different contexts shaping the studies in the various chapters. In some cases, the local may refer to a classroom; in others, to a minority group within a country or a whole community in the geopolitical periphery. Similarly, the global can refer to something large as the dominant discourses and institutions of the western hemisphere or, more particularly, to the nation-state in relation to the various subcultures and communities constituting it. Furthermore, the scope is also wide: the local is discussed in relation to identities, values, relationships, language, and knowledge. Whatever the domain of discussion, the authors bring an edge to their orientation: they articulate the case of the local before it gets silenced, distorted, or reproduced by the global.

## DISCIPLINARY REORIENTATION

Before we proceed to consider the ramifications of the issues raised by the authors in this volume for rethinking our disciplinary orientation in applied linguistics, it is useful to consider how some of the fields in the humanities and social sciences are redefining their approaches in relation to globalization. To take the teaching of literature first, Paul Jay (2001) argues that literary study in Europe and the United States has always been tied to developing a national consciousness. As a result, the literary canon has been parochially defined, constituting authors and texts that affirm dominant national values. One way to take account of globalization is to add texts from other communities beyond one's border to develop a global literary awareness. But Jay is not satisfied with this measure alone. He argues that even the traditional texts belonging to the canon—those written by Shakespeare, Pope, Wordsworth, or Eliot—should now be read differently. In the context of an expanded historical and geopolitical framework, these texts can be interpreted to show how such influences manifest themselves in the texts and broaden their implications. On the other hand, if the translocal context is kept out of the literary text, it is important to examine the diverse political and aesthetic motivations for this authorial choice. In accommodating this revised interpretive approach, literary study becomes more interdisciplinary and socially situated.

Or let us consider anthropology. The traditional aim was to capture the cultural practices and values of a community in their pristine purity, undistorted by external influences, in a remote geographical corner isolated from the inroads of "civilization." In the context of globalization, the project becomes different. No community is isolated from others. There is complex cultural contact between even the remotest communities all the time. Cultures are characterized by inveterate mixing that makes any question of distinctiveness elusive. Cultures are therefore not preconstucted but always in a state of becoming—in strange, hybrid, diffuse, and deterritorialized forms. In fact, cultures themselves travel, contaminating other cultures or choosing new habitations—as we can see in the spread of diaspora communities. So the anthropological project, as redefined by Clifford (1992), is the study of "traveling cultures," one that encompasses the global shaping of the local and the local coloring of the global.

Similarly, in sociology, Robertson argues for a reorientation. He defines the new task as "both the universalization of particularism and the particularization of universalism" (1997, p. 80). This means not only moving beyond the treatment of the nation-state or unitary social institutions and communities as the primary units of analysis. The revision paradoxically involves both widening and localizing social inquiry. Although bringing translocal forces into the analysis of society, Robertson argues that inquiry should become particularized to the point of accommodating the place of individuals and other local institutions. In doing this, the traditional treatment of social units as homogeneous will also be revised as greater diversity becomes visible. The character of discourse communities, like disciplinary circles in the academy (physicists, historians, etc.), is a case in point. Although constituted by local members and featuring local practices, they are also part of an international community of like-minded scholars with other overarching values. Paradoxically, discourse communities are local and global at the same time.

Although the examples from these disciplines show a move toward engaging more intensely with the global and local forces shaping different areas of inquiry, postcolonial scholars have argued that this is not enough. They propose that this global–local negotiation should be conducted with an edge; that is, from the consciously adopted standpoint of the local. Scholars like Bhabha (1994) and Mignolo (2000) emphasize that the "locus of enunciation" makes a difference in knowledge construction. Aligning ourselves with the interests of the marginalized, and conducting our thinking with a grounding in local contexts and social practices, do make a difference in our perspectives on things. By orientating to local–global negotiations from the viewpoint of the powerful or the position of geopolitical centers, one will most likely enunciate traditional discourses that confirm the status quo. Appadurai (2000) thinks along the lines of Bhabha and Mignolo when he urges scholars in his discipline of area studies to accommodate knowledge from alternate institutions and sources to initiate a "globalization from below." Although academic knowledge is made from the center, top-down, unilaterally, leading to hegemonic thinking that fails to create a true global awareness and understanding, Appadurai envisions a new form of grass-roots level knowledge-making. He identifies nongovernmental organizations (NGOs) and their subgroups, transnational advocacy networks (TANs), as having the capacity to contribute to knowledge in this manner. These agencies are able to muster experiences and observations from local life in diverse geographical settings. They enjoy considerable potential for knowledge dissemination in the popular consciousness in the many communities in which they work. They also bring with them a critical social awareness that is not compromised by the national interests of any single state or the hegemonic interests of powerful organizations like the World Bank, IMF, or WTO. Although this may be a controversial proposal, the point is that new ways of making grounded knowledge from periphery contexts should be explored further.

## THIS VOLUME

It is important to keep in mind such activities of disciplinary reorientation as we move to the first section of this volume where we reexamine some of the central constructs in our own field of applied linguistics. In the opening chapter, after providing a historical and theoretical orientation to the notion of local knowledge, I illustrate how certain familiar constructs in our field (like linguistic identity and speech community) can be redefined by understanding the work of applied linguists in South Asia. These linguists are redefining familiar disciplinary constructs to suit their local contexts by rediscovering linguistic practices traditional to their region. I proceed to bring out the paradox that the locally grounded precolonial forms of orientating to language practices provide fruitful avenues for explaining the reality of overlapping communities, fluid linguistic identities, and deterritorialized cultures of postmodern society. We have underestimated the knowledge traditions of minority communities in our effort to systematize knowledge from the perspectives and contexts of the powerful. It may not be the case that local knowledge can always explain any and every phenomenon in contemporary life; it is simply that knowledge from hitherto suppressed traditions serve to constructively challenge and reconstruct dominant paradigms, exposing their biases and vested interests. Local practices thus have a critical effect on global paradigms, fostering more balanced inquiry practices.

In the second chapter, Rakesh Bhatt deconstructs the notion of "standard language/s." Although we have seen many recent critiques of this concept, the fact that the locus of enunciation for this chapter is postcolonial India should make a difference. Bhatt argues that in order to give validity to local appropriations of English and their accompanying hybrid communicative practices, we have to free ourselves from the discourses upholding standard languages which still provide a condescending treatment of the Englishes used by speakers of other languages. Bhatt shows how dominant disciplinary constructs relating to acquisition, use, and norms should be pluralized to accommodate local practices. In the next chapter, Dominique Ryon considers how sociolinguistics conducted from traditional positivistic assumptions may exacerbate the death of local languages, affecting the ecology of linguistic diversity. She shows the ideological slant in language death studies that ignores local resistance and assumes assimilation into the dominant language of the nation-state as the norm. To represent local interests, sociolinguistics has to tap alternate kinds of data from other loci of enunciation—such as the poems, folk songs, and in-group publications that Ryon collects from Louisiana to contest the notion that Cajun French is dying.

In the fourth chapter, Lynn Mario de Souza deconstructs the dominant model of literacy to expose its grapho-centric (or word-based) bias. This model has been propagated globally by the colonization activities of Europe, leading to the suppression of diverse alternate literacies. In an attempt to recover these local literacies, de Souza explicates the logic of a multimodal literacy tradition, as practiced by the Kashinawá in Brazil. The texts of this community feature the complex integration of diverse symbol systems—that is, words, pictures, icons, color, and spatial arrangement. These texts assume alternate cultural practices that even to translate this model of literacy sympathetically for modern grapho-centric educational purposes leads to distorting both the medium and the message. Ironically, such local traditions of literacy provide useful heuristics to understand the new texts emerging in postmodern communication, especially in the multimodal, polysemiotic, and hypertextual examples in cyberspace. To cope with these emergent "multiliteracies" (see Cope & Kalantzis, 2000) and redefine existing literacy paradigms, local practices from precolonial times provide useful hints. de Souza's study confirms the paradoxical power of local traditions to contribute constructively to translocal knowledge, the possibility I theorize in the opening chapter.

In the next section, we move on to issues of language planning and policy. The biggest shift under the influence of globalization discourse is that the nation-state (the basic unit of language planning hitherto) is now of reduced relevance for such purposes. We need policy frameworks that accommodate domains both larger and smaller than the nation-state (as we saw earlier in the case of sociological reorientations). Our policies have to be mindful of the porous borders that open up each country to people, goods, and ideas that shuttle across communities. On the other hand, we are also now increasingly sensitive to pockets of language groups—immigrants, minorities, and "virtual communities" of cyberspace—who were previously swept under the carpet of national unity and homogeneous community.

The chapters by Kanavillil Rajagopalan, and Maya David and Subra Govindasamy, are complementary in illustrating both sides of a related dilemma. Rajagopalan discusses local resistance in Brazil to the inroads made by the global language English, whereas David and Govindasamy discuss attempts to reaccommodate English when the dominant nationalistic policies in Malaysia had excluded it in favor of the indigenous language. With hindsight, local scholars in Malaysia now realize that their "Malay-Only" policy has done a disservice to local people as it has denied them the resources (of English) to lay a claim for global opportunities of advancement. This extreme nationalist policy failed additionally because it didn't recognize that the local itself is not unitary and homogeneous. The local in Malaysia constitutes Tamil and Chinese language groups (immigrants with a long history in this country) who feel discriminated by the dominant Malay group's monolingualist policy. The chapter grapples with the complexity of now reviving the use of English to negotiate the conflicts *between* local groups and *with* the global (without sacrificing the native languages) to truly empower each community. Paradoxically, to empower the local involves wisely appropriating the global. Such examples from history should be instructive to Brazilians as they position themselves against English. Rajagopalan wrestles with ways of maintaining the power of local Portuguese in Brazil without isolating the community from English. Unfortunately, Brazilian linguists, who adopt an apolitical and detached orientation to language policy (and prefer not to intervene in linguistic processes as they believe in the positivistic tradition of their discipline), only exacerbate the polarization of positions that prevents a productive negotiation of the local and the global there.

Chapter 7, by Sharon Utakis and Marianne Pita, discusses a case of transnational policy formation in education. Such policy needs are already a pressing concern for Dominicans when it is only "virtual" for Malaysians and Brazilians in postmodern life. Even the latter communities are begin-

ning to realize that local education for their children should enable them to
relate to transnational conditions. For Dominican families, whose community life literally encompasses New York City and the Dominican Republic
(DR), the local is already global. A meaningful language policy in education
for the Dominican community in New York should go beyond the assimilationist assumptions motivating even well-intentioned bilingual programs
for immigrants in the United States. If the first language is permitted only
as a transition on the path to the nationally dominant English, this is a rec-
ipe for the making of monolinguals with unitary linguistic identities. What
the Dominican families want for their children is an educational grounding
in *both* languages so that their children can shuttle between New York and
DR with balanced bilingual competence.

In the next section of the book, we consider the challenges facing transnational professionals. As in other sectors of employment in the New Economy, language teachers are also shuttling between communities for
professional training and work. What teaching philosophies and pedagogical practices should they adopt in their new domains of employment?
Should they simply follow the dominant policies and practices of the host
communities where they teach, and suppress the other professional values
they bring with them from their previous experience? But Said (1993) and
Bhabha (1994), among other postcolonial scholars, have reminded us that
the strength of migrants, exiles, and other transnationals is their "double
vision" or "in-betweenness" that enables them to adopt a critical orientation
toward both home and host community. In this light, David Block considers
how teachers from France in England may make a critical contribution as
they articulate their "local" values based on more teacher-fronted and
form-focused learning in a context where task-based learning is sometimes
taken to extremes. The next chapter, by Angel Lin, Wendy Wang,
Nobuhiko Akamatsu, and Mehdi Riazi, also analyzes the ways in which the
language learning experience of these four non-native teachers at home
and abroad may serve to reconceive English as a pluralized global language
informed by local norms, functions, and pedagogies. The aim of the authors is to reconfigure the profession by going beyond traditional distinctions like standard and local English, native and non-native speaker
teacher, or English as a second language (ESL) and English as a foreign
language (EFL) teaching.

Both these chapters are considerably longer than the others for a good
reason. The authors are creatively experimenting with new modes of research inquiry and representation to articulate the local experiences of
their subjects. Too often, under the impersonal and positivistic modes of research practice and reporting, the unique experiences and identities of participants get filtered out. To let marginalized voices speak in the profession,
we need new modes of research and writing. Block's biographical research

that taps the stories of teacher trainees and the introspective narratives of Lin and her colleagues introduce new strategies to represent the local in mainstream academic discourses.

In the final section, we explore classroom contexts of language teaching. We forget often that the classroom is an important site of policymaking at the microsocial level. The values and practices inculcated in the classroom have the power to reconfigure language relations in the wider society. So Peter Martin and Jasmine Luk show how local identities, knowledge, and discourses need to be brought in to negotiate the learning of unfamiliar codes and content in ELT. They complicate dominant teaching practices that valorize communicative methodologies and "English-Only" instruction to show the place that needs to be given to local discourses and identities if teaching is to be productive. In the final chapter, Elisabeth Mermann-Jozwiak and Nancy Sullivan provide a nice conclusion to the volume as their classroom is situated literally in the "borderlands"—that is, between the languages and cultures of the Unites States and Mexico. They also remind us that the classroom constituting Mexican American and Anglo-American students is itself often a contact zone of the global and local and of different cultural groups—analogous to the larger postmodern society where communities jostle against each other. That classrooms today are contact zones (see Pratt, 1991) is true even of classrooms in Martin's Brunei and Luk's Hong Kong, where different cultures have to be negotiated in the textbooks, discourses, and content. In such classrooms, then, the local is a microcosm of the global. Delving deeply into the local sensitizes students to the challenges involved in navigating global diversity. To undertake this cultural education, Mermann-Jozwiak and Sullivan encourage students to become ethnographers as they sample the codes and cultures of the minority community through fieldwork and the study of multicultural literary texts. As they share their results, the students are able to examine their own biases about others in their locality. Both minority and majority group students come off with a critical understanding of their own identities in a multilingual world.

## A DISCIPLINARY SHIFT IN PROGRESS

Where does such research lead us? I like to end this editorial introduction with a concrete example of programmatic changes in ELT policy and practice. I present this as a vision of the things to come in our field in the face of globalization and the empowerment of the local. Although the reorientations and redefinitions in some of the other areas in applied linguistics are still being discussed, the pedagogical changes in ELT are already affecting practice in many circles today. The chapters by Bhatt, de Souza, and Lin

and her colleagues, and those in the final section of the volume on pedagogy, point to the type of changes I articulate next.

The pedagogical changes in ELT are initiated by developments in
postmodern social relations, economy, and communications that are altering the character and status of English language. Consider how the following developments may affect language pedagogy:

- With the rise of postcolonial communities, the ownership of English is changing. There are more speakers in the world today who use
English as an additional language compared to those who have used it
traditionally as their "native language" (i.e., those of British ancestry).
Not only are "non-native" speakers more in number; English is also
used increasingly in multilingual contexts both inside and outside traditionally homogeneous English-speaking countries (i.e., in England,
North America, and Australia). There is statistical backing to the claim
that native speakers may have "lost their majority in the 1970's"
(Graddol, 1999, p. 58). Projecting that by the year 2050 native speakers
of English will be 433 million whereas those who have nativized the language will be 668 million, Graddol argues in "The Decline of the Native
Speaker" that "in future [English] will be a language used mainly in
multilingual contexts as a second language and for communication between non-native speakers" (1999, p. 57). This development marks the
deterritorialization of the English language. English has gained a life
beyond its land of origins, acquiring an identity and currency in new
geographical and social domains, as it gets localized for diverse settings
and purposes.

- A general fluidity and mixing in languages, cultures, and identities is becoming a fact of life. This is partly occasioned by the need to
shuttle between communities in postmodern society. Transnational life
makes borders porous as ideas, goods, and people flow with greater mobility. Further, diaspora communities have established a social life in
lands beyond their traditional homes, and are enabling different languages and cultures to exist side by side. Following this general
deterritorialization of cultures and de-centering of identities, we now
acknowledge the difficulty in defining people and communities in exclusive ways. For example, we are unable to categorize certain individuals or communities as "non-native" to English. Cultural values and
practices associated with English or the Western civilization now form
the local cultures and identities of many communities. These developments are also shattering the traditional separation of codes and discourses, engendering greater linguistic hybridity.

- New literate competencies are demanded by what is called "the
New Work Order" (see Gee, 2000). In the Fordist industrial context of

the past—characterized by a strict division of labor, and hierarchies reflecting mental and physical work—literacy requirements and linguistic capital were divided unequally along the workforce. As Bernstein (1971) described it some time back, the boss used the expanded code (featuring relatively complex syntax and abstract vocabulary), and the worker the restricted code. But in the post-Fordist era of computerized workplaces in the new economy, all work involves engagement with knowledge, information, and communication (see Gee, 2000). The division between blue-collar and white-collar workers has become blurred as everyone has to make informed decisions at work. Information technology has turned all of us into knowledge workers. The new workplace also requires a diversity of capabilities and aptitudes. Skills of planning and implementation are required for almost everybody. Computer literacy is universally needed. Professionals have to move from one domain of work to another with ease, as and when they are required. Thus each worker has to deal with multiple textualities and discourses.

• The expanded market of the "New Economic Order" and transnational industrial production networks have also created greater interaction between people from diverse linguistic backgrounds. Industrial production spans many communities today. A Canadian construction firm (that I know of) gets its designs drawn by engineers in Sri Lanka, imports its hardware from China, and employs immigrants from South America for physical labor. There is communication between different language groups in this context of work. Even if they interact in English, we have to acknowledge that they bring different dialects to this interaction. The transnational production relationships and marketing networks require multilingual competencies from today's workers.

• Finally, the new media of communication, such as the Internet, encourage greater hybridity and fluidity in communication. To be literate in the Internet, for example, requires competence in not only different modalities of communication (sound, speech, video, photographs) and different symbol systems (icons, images, spatial organization, and charts, in addition to words) but also multiple registers, discourses, and languages. Texts are becoming multivocal. For example, in a web text describing the breakthrough in DNA (in academic register) we will now simultaneously have a sound byte from scientist Watson (in casual spoken register), a box on the side giving the legal uses of DNA (in legalese, or the passionate oral rhetoric of attorney Barry Scheck), with another link giving the testimony of someone who was recently released from death penalty because of evidence from DNA (possibly a sound byte in African-American English or Spanish), concluding with a description of new uses of DNA by researchers in Germany or Japan (sound bytes in their languages, captioned in English). Thus we now have the resources to present multiple discourses and languages within the boundaries of the same text.

These developments in linguistic and textual hybridity are by no means new. De Souza's chapter (4) shows that multimodal literacy was already practiced in precolonial Brazil. My article (chap. 1) on South Asian definitions of identity and community shows that precolonial India was comfortable with shifting linguistic identities and fluid community relations. What's new is that these conditions have now begun to make their presence felt in the West in a more pronounced way, and also gained more intense expression at a global level. However we may account for these developments, it is becoming clearer to everyone that there are new competencies required for communication and literacy in today's world. We readily recognize in the context of the developments described earlier that teaching literacy in a single language (English) and a single dialect of that language (Standard American English) fails to equip our students for real-world needs. Not only speakers of the *outer* or *expanding* circle (in the Kachruvian paradigm), but those in the *inner* circle of traditional English-speaking communities have to now be proficient in negotiating multiple dialects, registers, discourses and, if possible, languages, to function effectively in a context of postmodern globalization. These changes have motivated ELT professionals to reconsider our assumptions of language acquisition and pedagogical practice (see Holliday, in press).

The changing priorities in the teaching of English can be tabulated in the following manner (see Fig. I.1):

| FROM: | TO: |
| --- | --- |
| "target language" | repertoire |
| text and language as homogeneous | text and language as hybrid |
| joining a community | shuttling between communities |
| focus on rules and conventions | focus on strategies |
| correctness | negotiation |
| language and discourse as static | language and discourse as changing |
| language as context-bound | language as context-transforming |
| mastery of grammar rules | metalinguistic awareness |
| text and language as transparent and instrumental | text and language as representational |
| L1 or C1 as problem | L1 or C1 as resource |

FIG. I.1.   Shifts in pedagogical practice.

It is important to realize that rather than focusing on a single language or dialect as the target of learning, teachers have to develop in the students the competence in a repertoire of codes to manage postmodern communication. Although joining a new speech community was the objective of traditional language learning, now we have to train students to shuttle between communities by deploying relevant codes. Furthermore, in a context of diverse norms and conventions in the system of English language, it is important to understand the relativity of notions of correctness. If what is nonstandard in one community could be standard in another, it is more important to teach students how to negotiate appropriate usage for the different contexts. It is possible to bring vernacular features into mainstream communication with appropriate ways of flagging one's intention to represent one's identity or special rhetorical purposes—as minority scholars Geneva Smitherman (2003) and bell hooks (1989) do with African-American vernacular in their academic publications. It is for this reason that we have to now focus more on strategies of communication rather than on grammatical rules. With effective discourses strategies, speakers and writers may employ features of their sociolect or even personal coinages for special rhetorical purposes. It is possible for certain vernacular or nonstandard items to get mainstreamed over time as they gain wider social acceptance—as we see in many examples in the history of English language. For this purpose, we have to teach language as changing rather than static. But, too often, the underlying assumption of language teaching is conservative and prescriptive. Other matters of pedagogical common sense like the context-bound nature of language have to be modified by the realization that effective discourse strategies can be instrumental in changing the context. When Smitherman and hooks strategically use street speech in scholarly writing, they are reconstructing the academic context as more open for minority community participation. Such pedagogical shifts are important at a time when the notion of language as transparent has been challenged by the awareness that speakers and communities represent their identities, values, and cultural practices through this rich semiotic system. In this endeavor, the first language or culture of a speaker may not be a hindrance but a resource (as the chapters in the final section of the volume illustrate).

To sustain these new pedagogical practices, we are seeing the development of macroeducational changes in the professional discourse and infrastructure relating to ELT. The microlevel changes in day to day classroom practice need to be complemented by suitable research and scholarship informed by a revised set of priorities. I see this shift as one from a hierarchical approach in professional structuring to a more leveled approach (see Fig. I.2):

| | Hierarchical Approach: | Leveled Approach: |
|---|---|---|
| Norms: | Native and nativized Englishes | Global English as a plural system |
| | Native and non-native speakers | Experts and novices in each variant |
| | "Native" norms as target | Local norms of relevance |
| Expertise: | Established knowledge | Local knowledge |
| | Unilateral knowledge flow | Multilateral knowledge flow |
| | Researcher and scholar generated | Practitioner generated and collaborative |
| Curriculum: | Innovation and change | Continuity |
| | Top-down | Ground-up |
| Pedagogy: | Methods-dominated | Postmethod practices |
| | Skills-based | Project-based |
| Materials: | Authenticity | Relevance |
| | Published in the center | Locally generated |

FIG. I.2.  Shifts in professional discourse and structure.

There is an emerging consensus that we need to relate to language norms differently. Giving up distinctions based on native and nativized Englishes (where the latter is still given second-class treatment, although it is increasingly accepted as systematic and rule-governed like the former), we have to relate to Global English as a plural system with heterogeneous grammatical and discourse conventions. This will influence us to give up treating "native" English as the norm that needs to be taught and used universally. In fact, this way of orientating to English will also influence us to abandon the distinction native or non-native speaker. In a context of locally developed Englishes, all speakers are "native speakers" of this pluralized Global English. But we can make a distinction between speakers based on expertise (rather than birth) in each variety of English. Although I am an expert speaker of Sri Lankan English, I am a novice speaker of Australian English. For effective communication in the Australian speech community (if the need arises), I may have to develop more competence in that variant through natural or classroom acquisition. The development of more complex negotiation skills, broader language repertoires, and metalanguage abilities (discussed earlier) will see to it that speakers of different varieties can communicate without breakdown.

Although the superiority of native varieties has led to a dichotomized approach to language teaching (where professional expertise from the "center" is treated as authoritative), the pluralized approach to English language will encourage multilateral knowledge flow. Local knowledge from the many postcolonial communities can offer valid contributions to pedagogical practice. Also, the insights of practitioners—especially in communities distant from research and scholarly centers—should be given an important place in knowledge formation in the field. The role of language consultants also will change. Traditionally, personnel from cultural and educational institutions in the West arrogated to themselves the right to travel to other countries to initiate curriculum change. With a few months of stay and observation, they enjoyed the power to dictate changes in a top-down manner, often influenced by the pedagogical fashions of the center. In the leveled approach, we have to consider negotiating with existing curricular traditions to generate changes from the ground up. This would involve active partnership between donors and local agents in educational development. As for authoritative methods, thankfully, recent pedagogical literature articulates a "postmethod" consciousness (see Kumaravadivelu, 1994; Prabhu, 1990). We now hold that there is no "best method" that assures successful learning; we even doubt the validity of the concept of methods, as pedagogical practices are eclectical, contextual, and contingent. This reorientation can empower local teachers to focus on the learning strategies that work for their own students in the light of the purposes and objectives that define their teaching. The reality of multiliteracies and postmodern work conditions, which encourages shuttling between different discourses according to the shifting domains of work, has also challenged the traditional compartmentalization of skills. In the place of skills-based teaching, many are moving to project-based pedagogies which focus more on carrying out specific communicative objectives, acquiring the discourses and skills relevant to the project in the process of accomplishing it (Cole & Zuengler, 2003; Warschauer, 2000). In the case of teaching materials, again, the current emphasis on authenticity is misdirected. Authentic materials are composed from a corpus of language features typical of native-speaker communication. These materials come from center publishers for the pragmatic reason that they have the resources to mass-produce textbooks for other communities. But if authenticity is defined in terms of the shifting purposes and identities of the speakers, it has to be contextually negotiated. Teachers are adopting many strategies to collect texts that are locally meaningful—that is, students' bilingual journals, recording and transcriptions of local communication, documentation of oral histories, and collection of interview and narrative data from families by student ethnographers. Through these activities, many teachers have developed teaching materials that are relevant to the local community.

## CONCLUSION

The disciplinary reorientation articulated for ELT above is an example of globalization from below. Rather than imposing one variety (usually that of the dominant community) as universally applicable, we are trying to pluralize the norms. The developments in postmodern social and communicative life are tapped to create a significant space for local codes, identities, knowledge, and teaching traditions. Teachers are trying to diversify students' skills and competencies so that communication can effectively take place among individuals who are ready to negotiate differences. We need a similar articulation in other areas of language policy and practice. As we negotiate the social, educational, and communicative challenges ushered in by the intensified forms of contemporary globalization, we have to remember to treat the local as an equal partner in the new discourses and practices that are developing. The following chapters help us to stand globalization on its head, conducting inquiry from the standpoint of local communities, to develop more inclusive and egalitarian language policies and practices.

## REFERENCES

Abu-Lughod, J. (1997). Going beyond global babble. In A. D. King (Ed.), *Culture, globalization, and the world system* (pp. 131–138). Minneapolis, MN: University of Minnesota Press.

Appadurai, A. (2000). Grassroots globalization and the research imagination. *Public Culture, 12,* 1–20.

Bernstein, B. (1971). *Class, codes and control* (Vol. 1). London: Routledge and Kegan Paul.

Bhabha, H. K. (1994). *The location of culture.* New York: Routledge.

Block, D. (2002). "McCommunication:" A problem in the frame for SLA. In D. Cameron & D. Block (Eds.), *Globalization and language teaching* (pp. 117–133). London: Routledge.

Block, D., & Cameron, D. (2002). Introduction. In D. Cameron & D. Block (Eds.), *Globalization and language teaching* (pp. 1–10). London: Routledge.

Bruthiaux, P. (2002). Hold your courses: Language education, language choice, and economic development. *TESOL Quarterly, 36,* 275–296.

Cameron, D. (2002). Globalization and the teaching of "communication skills." In D. Cameron & D. Block (Eds.), *Globalization and language teaching* (pp. 67–82). London: Routledge.

Clifford, J. (1992). Traveling cultures. In L. Grossberg, C. Nelson, & L. Treichler (Eds.), *Cultural studies* (pp. 96–112). New York: Routledge.

Cole, K., & Zuengler, J. (2003). Engaging in an authentic science project: Appropriating, resisting, and denying "scientific" identities. In R. Bayley & S. Schecter (Eds.), *Language socialization in bilingual and multilingual societies* (pp. 98–113). Clevedon, England: Multilingual Matters.

Cope, B., & Kalantzis, M. (Eds.). (2000). *Multiliteracies: Literacy learning and the design of social futures.* London: Routledge.

Faigley, L. (1997). Literacy after the revolution. *College Composition and Communication, 48*, 30–43.

Gee, J. P. (2000). New people in new worlds: Networks, the new capitalism and schools. In B. Cope & M. Kalantzis (Eds.), *Multiliteracies: Literacy learning and the design of social futures* (pp. 43–68). London: Routledge.

Graddol, D. (1999). The decline of the native speaker. *AILA Review, 13*, 57–68.

Hall, S. (1997). The local and the global: Globalization and ethnicity. In A. D. King (Ed.), *Culture, globalization, and the world system* (pp. 19–40). Minneapolis: University of Minnesota Press.

Holliday, A. (in press). *The struggle to teach English as an international language*. Oxford, England: Oxford University Press.

hooks, b. (1989). *Talking back: Thinking feminist, thinking Black*. Boston: South End Press.

Jay, P. (2001). Beyond discipline? Globalization and the future of English. *PMLA, 116*, 32–47.

Kumaravadivelu, B. (1994). The postmethod condition: (E)merging strategies for second/foreign language teaching. *TESOL Quarterly, 28*, 27–48.

Mignolo, W. D. (2000). *Local histories/global designs: Coloniality, subaltern knowledges, and border thinking*. Princeton, NJ: Princeton University Press.

Murray, D. (2000). Protean communication: The language of computer-mediated communication. *TESOL Quarterly, 34*, 397–422.

Prabhu, N. S. (1990). There is no best method—Why? *TESOL Quarterly, 24*, 161–176.

Pratt, M. L. (1991). Arts of the contact zone. *Profession, 91*, 33–40. New York: MLA.

Robertson, R. (1992). *Globalization*. London: Sage.

Robertson, R. (1997). Social theory, cultural relativity, and the problem of globality. In A. D. King (Ed.), *Culture, globalization, and the world system* (pp. 69–90). Minneapolis: University of Minnesota Press.

Said, E. (1993). *Culture and imperialism*. New York: Alfred Knopf.

Selfe, C., & Selfe, R. J., Jr. (1994). The politics of the interface: Power and its exercise in the electronic contact zone. *College Composition and Communication, 45*, 480–504.

Smitherman, G. (2003). The historical struggle for language rights in CCCC. In G. Smitherman & V. Villaneuava (Eds.), *From intention to practice: Considerations of language diversity in the classroom* (pp. 7–39). Carbondale: Southern Illinois University Press.

Warschauer, M. (2000). The changing global economy and the future of English teaching. *TESOL Quarterly, 34*, 511–536.

# Part I

# REDEFINING
# DISCIPLINARY CONSTRUCTS

# Chapter 1

# Reconstructing Local Knowledge, Reconfiguring Language Studies[1]

Suresh Canagarajah
*Baruch College of the City University of New York*

> *It is when a discourse forgets that it is placed that it tries to speak for*
> *everybody else.*
> —*Stuart Hall* (1997a, p. 36)

## INTRODUCTION

The term *local knowledge* has been with us for some time, its more conspicuous example being the title of Geertz's (1983) book. However, it has acquired its critical edge only in the last decade or so, with the scholarship of movements like postcolonialism and cultural studies. Although I problematize this term later to grapple with its complexity, it is good to start with some familiar assumptions. The term has acquired different currency in different domains of discourse:

- In the anthropological sense, it refers to the beliefs and orientations emerging from the social practices of a community through its history (see Geertz, 1983). These beliefs have their own rationale and validity, though they may differ from the knowledge forms valued at the global level.

---

[1]This is a revised and substantially expanded version of an article that appears in the *Journal of Language, Identity and Education, 1*(4), pp. 243–259.

• In the social sense, it contrasts with the official knowledge informing the policies and procedures of various institutions (legal, fiscal, political). People generally develop extra-institutional (or "vernacular") discourses in their everyday life about how to negotiate these relations in their own terms (see Barton & Hamilton, 1998).[2]

• In the academic sense, it refers to knowledge that diverges from what is established or legitimized in the disciplines (see Foucault, 1972). The beliefs that don't fall within the established paradigms continue to circulate unofficially at the local level among smaller circles.

• In the professional sense, practitioners develop a knowledge of accomplishing their work in ways that are not acknowledged or recommended by the authorities and experts. Perhaps this is how many of us in language teaching best know this term. The knowledge generated in our daily contexts of work about effective strategies of language learning and teaching may not enjoy professional or scholarly recognition (see, for example, Canagarajah, 1993; Pennycook, 1989, p. 613).

In all these domains, there are certain common assumptions that characterize the term. Local knowledge is context-bound, community-specific, and nonsystematic because it is generated ground-up through social practice in everyday life.

## A STORY OF DENIGRATION

> *I think the global is the self-presentation of the dominant particular. It is*
> *a way in which the dominant particular localizes and naturalizes itself*
> *and associates with it a variety of other minorities.*
> —*Stuart Hall* (1997b, p. 67)

Despite recent efforts to perceive local knowledge in nonpejorative terms, in many circles it is still treated as received wisdom and unexamined beliefs that are parochial, irrational, or backward. Even the sometimes romanticized orientations to local knowledge—such as magic, folklore, or myth— show a subtle inequality with scientific knowledge. What has led to this low estimation of local knowledge?

Perhaps there is something fundamental in processes of knowledge construction that explains this bias. Generalization, systematization, and model building involve a certain amount of abstraction that filters out the

---

[2]This is analogous to the notion of local literacies or vernacular literacies, in which even those without formal education develop their own ways of interpreting institutional texts and effectively managing social relations through their unorthodox practices (see Barton & Hamilton, 1998).

variability of experience in diverse contexts. The more we move beyond the surface level contingencies of performance, the closer we are supposed to be in defining the invariable deep structures of competence (as we know well in our own field of linguistics). Eventually, the phenomenon we are describing is removed from its locality, the structure is reduced of its social and cultural "thickness," and the particularity of experience informing the model is suppressed as unruly or insignificant. Furthermore, such activities of knowledge formation are not innocent, nonpartisan, or value-free. There is the question as to whose perspectives are to shape interpretation and analysis. The establishment of operative knowledge in any society thus always involves contestation. What is left out is the local knowledge that constitutes the perspectives and practices of the disempowered. At any rate, the orthodoxy will itself generate opposition and deviation at the local level through the sheer process of individuals attempting to define their independence. Thus we can find pockets of local knowledge that characterize the beliefs and practices of minority communities in different historical periods. In precolonial South Asia, for example, we can identify the hidden oppositional discourses of the untouchables against the upper-castes, the lay against the priestly circles, and the vassals against the landowners (see Adas, 1992; Khare, 1984; Scott, 1990). These are just a few manifestations of the interconnection between knowledge and power in human history.

But the most systematic and concerted campaign to denigrate local knowledge at the global level begins with the movement of modernism. Inspired by the values of enlightenment and resulting in empirical science, this movement has led to the suppression of diversity. The values that were important for this movement were universality, standardization, and systematicity, all for the end of predictability, efficiency, and eventually, progress (see Dussel, 1998). From this perspective, variability, contingency, and difference were a problem. As modernism established geopolitical networks and a world economy that fostered its vision of life, all communities were pressed into a uniform march to attain progress. Those who stubbornly insisted on maintaining their own vision of "progress" or "reason" faced the danger of being isolated, impoverished, and discriminated. Some read in this history a process of time conquering place (see Bhabha, 1994, pp. 212–235; Kaplan, 1998; Mignolo, 2000). Constructs like worldview, reason, and culture are measured according to their "maturity" in time. The distinction between being civilized and primitive is based on time. Localities are ranked hierarchically according to the phases they have to pass through to reach the advanced stage representing modernity. All that a community has to do is jettison the idiosyncrasies associated with its locale—the vestiges of one's stubborn backwardness—and adopt the values that define progress.

The parallel movement of colonialism may be considered to have spread the values of modernism beyond Europe in a more direct and invasive fashion.[3] The local knowledge of colonized communities began to be suppressed with missionary zeal in the name of civilization. In spreading the enlightenment values, European powers set up their institutions of governance, jurisprudence, health, and education here that systematically suppressed local knowledge in diverse domains. In what has come to be labeled "a denial of coevalness," European nations refused to acknowledge that the divergent cultural practices of other communities could have a parallel life of equal validity (see Mignolo, 2000). There are recorded instances of public debates between British educators and local Hindu pundits in my hometown in Sri Lanka, where the former attempted to prove the error in local knowledge in fields like astronomy, geography, and medicine (see Chelliah, 1922). There was no effort made to understand that the local *ayurvedic* (i.e., homeopathic and holistic) medical tradition, for example, was based on different values and rationale, and that there was no common point of reference to compare it with the Western system (see Shiva, 1990, pp. 250–255). By default, the comparison was done in the terms of the powerful (i.e., the Western therapeutic or allopathic orientation), and local knowledge was made to appear silly.

It should be clear at this point that the science of modernism is not a value-free, culture-neutral, pure rationality that is of universal relevance. This orientation to knowledge in objective and impersonal terms draws from certain specific cultural traditions (i.e., Judeo-Christian, Renaissance; see Huff, 1993; Merton, 1970). The reason why this form of science developed in Europe at this time can also be accounted for in terms of 17th-century sociohistoric conditions in Europe (see Adas, 1989; Hessen, 1971; Jacob, 1976; Porter, 1995). Modernist knowledge is therefore a form of local knowledge—local to communities in Europe. It is not hard to understand this paradox of a global knowledge that is in fact local to a specific community. If we acknowledge that *all* knowledge-producing activities are context-bound and collaborative, scientific knowledge also had to have a shaping influence from its locality of production. However, enlightenment is one of the most ambitious attempts of a local knowledge to extend its dominion in global proportions. Its modus operandi was to absorb other forms of knowledge on its way and suppress recalcitrant beliefs as it presented itself as valid for everyone (see Hall, 1997a). To the extent that this strategy of hegemony is successful, we fail to recognize its local, contextualized character. We accept it as ours. It may sound surprising, then, that the challenge for local knowledge is not from global knowledge, universal

---

[3]We may postpone for the moment the debate whether modernism motivated colonization or vice versa (see Dussel, 1998).

knowledge, or transcendental knowledge. It is simply from another form of local knowledge, that is, that which belongs to the more powerful communities. It is precisely for this reason that the inequality between intellectual traditions has to be interrogated without presumptions about the universal validity or legitimacy of any single form of knowledge. There is something unethical about one tradition of local knowledge lording it over other forms of local knowledge.

## THE RISE OF THE LOCAL?

> [L]ocality itself is a historical product and ... the histories through which
> localities emerge are eventually subject to the dynamics of the global....
> There is nothing mere about the local.
> —Arjun Appadurai (1996, p. 18)

Has all this changed in the postmodern conditions of present time? After all, is not postmodernism essentially anti-enlightenment in values? Do not celebrated contemporary notions like hybridity, pluralism, and multiculturalism provide a space for the local from diverse backgrounds?

It is an interesting irony that the success of modernism in integrating all the communities into the global whole intricately has created greater visibility for the local. Technological advances have brought the world closer, developing a keener awareness of previously remote communities. The advances of media have channeled the voices and images from localities far and wide into one's very home. Internet and other modalities of communication mingle diverse codes and discourses from different localities. The industrial work-space has been decentered to include a network of communities which provide labor, expertise, and resources for production. The need for expanded business opportunities has sent multinationals scurrying to previously unknown localities to market their products with sophisticated cultural understanding. Even the nation-building agendas and border-drawing activities undertaken during colonialism to suit Euro-centric norms and interests have led to uprooting many communities (some of which were already transplanted for reasons of labor, trade, and slavery), leading to diasporas which pluralize life everywhere. We live in a world where languages and cultures jostle against each other and mix fluidly, irrespective of which locality from which they come. Can we then say that space is gaining over time—in a reversal of the dialectic unleashed by modernism?

But we have to be careful not to exaggerate these changes. We have to treat postmodern globalism as not representing a revolutionary shift from earlier conditions, but a revised continuation of the modernist project of globalization. Whether its origins are 30 years ago (Harvey, 1990) or 300 years back (Giddens, 1990), or even before from premodern times (Robertson, 1992), globalization has worked to the disadvantage of local knowledge. The contemporary postmodernist movement simply adopts a different strategy to carry out the interests of the status quo. If modernist globalization tried to eradicate local knowledge, postmodern globalization incorporates it in its own terms. If modernism suppressed difference, postmodern globalization works through localities by appropriating difference. This strategy of accommodating local knowledge is necessitated partly because of the consequences of modernity—which, as we saw earlier, did create a space for the local. In addition, the resistance generated against modernism by different localities has to be managed strategically with a different modus operandi if the status quo is to be maintained. Therefore, what we now see are more complex relations between time and space. We see interesting paradoxes where some parts of the East appear to be practicing the modernist project of technological progress more successfully than the West.

However, power is still not shared equally in the new dispensation. The nations and institutions that orchestrate the representation of the local are still a handful, not very different from the powers of the colonial period (see Amsden, 2002). Despite the myriad symbols that pluralize contemporary cultural and communicative life, economy still shows sharp disparities between the rich and the poor (see Jameson, 1998; Miyoshi, 1998). Therefore, the local finds representation only according to the purposes and forms permitted by the powerful. As Hall (1997a) puts it, postmodern globalization "is now a form of capital which recognizes that it can only, to use a metaphor, rule through other local capitals, rules alongside and in partnership with other economic and political elites. It does not attempt to obliterate them. It operates through them" (p. 28).

Consider, for example, the way fashionable postmodernist discourses of pluralism work these days. Although the notion of hybridity gives life to the local with one hand, it takes away its radical potential by hyphenating it with other Western and global cultural constructs. The specificity and particularity of the local is lost in being fused or recycled with other elements from Western society. Furthermore, postmodern discourses like multiple subject positions (in describing identity), heteroglossia (in describing codes), and multiculturalism (in describing community), complicate and muddle difference, defining these social constructs in less materially grounded terms. Scholars from non-Western communities point to the irony that just when they gain hope that there is going to be an appreciation of their identity and values, they feel cheated to find that the currently popular discourses reduce the significance of their particularity (see Moya, 1997). In fact, even current forms of postcolonialism in the West are treated by many periphery scholars as blunting the critical edge of local knowledge (see Bahri, 1997).

Features of the postcolonial that are celebrated in academia and popular discourse are picked according to the interests of the dominant communities, in a way that does not disturb their hegemony. These fashionable movements relate to non-Western cultural and literary products in terms of the standpoint of the West.

Although we enjoy greater opportunities today for the celebration of the local, we cannot be complacent that postmodern globalization truly liberates the local by virtue of the cultural and technological changes we see around us. In a recent issue of *TESOL Quarterly*, which explores the implications of globalization for language teaching, many of the authors said they consider the Internet and computer-mediated communication as validating periphery Englishes, empowering non-native students, and democratizing social relations (see Murray, 2000; Warschauer, 2000). Although these scholars do make some obligatory qualifications, they are largely enthusiastic about the possibilities of revolutionary learning and communication. But we have to critically engage with postmodern conditions to make a space for local knowledge in terms of disempowered communities. There is work to be done in developing transformative pedagogies that would lead to more egalitarian relations in society and education.

## REDISCOVERING THE LOCAL

> *We are all Caribbeans now in our urban archipelagos ... Perhaps there's no return for anyone to a native land—only field notes for its reinvention.*
> —*James Clifford* (1988, p. 173)

Despite the designs of the global in the past centuries, we can take heart in the fact that local knowledge has not been totally eradicated. The local has negotiated, modified, and absorbed the global in its own way. As Appadurai (1996) has pointed out, the local realizations of the global have not always followed the expectations of the metropole. Dominant discourses have been taken over selectively and, sometimes, superficially to facilitate a convenient coexistence with local cultures. I have described elsewhere how successive orthodoxies in our field, such as communicative approaches and task-oriented pedagogies, have been translated by local teachers and students in Sri Lankan classrooms to suit the styles of teacher-fronted instruction practiced from precolonial times (see Canagarajah, 1999). ELT professional discourse in local communities represents a fascinating mix of the center and periphery, the new and the old.

This realization presents both good news and bad news for our project of recovering the local. Although local knowledge has not completely died, it is also not pure. Local knowledge has not been waiting undistorted and whole for scholars to come and discover it. It has been going through many locally initiated and globally enforced changes all this time. For example, the local has been changing its positionality in relation to the changing practices of the global. It has done so partly to resist the global, partly for its own survival. Furthermore, after the long history of globalization, almost no community can claim today that it is not integrated into the global network of communication, travel, or trade, and transformed in the process. It is but realistic to adopt the position that the local is a relational and fluid construct. We have to identify the many changes the local has been going through if we are to develop a suitable project to reconstruct it now for our purposes.

Paralleling the appropriation of the global by the local, the global has absorbed local knowledge and resources for its own purposes. If the former is a mixing initiated from the ground up, the latter works top down. Consider the claim by Basem Ra'ad (2001) that the linguistic resources of Etruscan and Caananite civilizations were absorbed by first Greek and then Latin, eventually leaving no trace of the minority cultures. The provocative thesis by Martin Bernal (1987) regarding the AfroAsiatic roots of classical culture points to another example of how the local has been taken over by the more powerful without proper acknowledgment. In fact, the residue left after the looting by the global is increasingly hard to recover. Rather then proceeding further into local communities to recover local knowledge, paradoxically, we have to sometimes burrow deeper into the global to extricate recycled bits of the local.

More problematic is the possibility that the very geographical ground of the local has been shifting during globalization. With communities uprooted for many reasons, or willingly crossing their traditional borders, their shared culture and history have become transnational. Diaspora communities do not have a consolidated physical locality on which to build their local knowledge. In the case of quintessential diasporas—such as the Kurdish or Sikh communities, which don't have an autonomous traditional homeland (see Cohen, 1997)—their locality is paradoxically translocal. The local knowledge of these communities is at best a shared intersubjective reality, constituted by commonly cherished discourses and practices. More recent exiles—such as my own Sri Lankan Tamil community, with more people living in cities like Toronto and London than in their homeland of Jaffna for which a separatist struggle is being waged—are also constructing new, expanded, mediated forms of locality through literature, news media, and the arts. As Appadurai (1996) puts it, "The many displaced, deterritorialized, and transient populations that constitute today's ethnoscapes are engaged in the construction of locality, as a structure of feeling, often in the face of the erosion, dispersal, and implosion of neighborhoods as coherent social formations" (p. 199).

If we can grant the possibility that the local is still being "constructed" (as Appadurai, 1996, puts it)—that it is not something of the past, preexisting and rooted in a specific geographical domain—we can also consider the local knowledge constructed by many virtual or invisible communities in cyberspace and other media of contemporary communication (see Clifford, 1994). In fact, many exile communities such as the Tibetans and Tamils enjoy a stronger sense of identity and richer knowledge base on the Internet. Consider also other subcultural groups and special interest circles (of alternative lifestyle or narrowly defined social causes) who are developing their "virtual neighborhoods" and shared knowledge in cyberspace.

In such novel domains of postmodern communication, we will readily acknowledge that locality is a discourse. But even for other more geographically rooted traditional communities, the local is largely discursive. Both insiders and outsiders to the community have formed notions, values, and attitudes about the "local" which now become part of local knowledge. The sediments of texts, talk, poetry, art, memory, desire, dreams, and many unstated assumptions that people have developed through history about their community now define the local. I marvel at the different apologetic traditions local scholars in my Tamil community have had to develop from time to time to resist the thrusts of modernism. They have argued that (a) local intellectual traditions are a precursor to the values of enlightenment thinking, and anticipate it; (b) they transcend modernism and have the answers for the problems created in the West; and (c) they operate on a totally different rationale and do not relate to modernism in any way (see Paranirupasingham, 1991; Suseendirarajah, 1991). Such theorizations show how the discourse on local knowledge is relational—defined in relation to global knowledge, perhaps based on what is strategic for local interests at different periods. How do we work through these periodic layers of interpretation in history to understand local knowledge? Is there any possibility of ever reaching an "authentic" indigenous knowledge as we work through these interpretations of an interpretation? Therefore, we must not think of local knowledge as transparent or grounded, which can be unproblematically recovered without interpretive effort from a foundational source.

Moreover, as the global holds sway among all communities in the world, we have lost any neutral or objective position from which to perceive the local. We are increasingly interpreting the local through global theoretical lenses. This is inescapable if we grant the epistemological dominance Western intellectual paradigms have held for centuries. As we conduct knowledge worldwide largely in terms of enlightenment values, even local scholars (often trained in Western academic institutions) have to use the dominant tools in their field for celebrating the local. The local can be defined, once again, only in relation to global knowledge, as did the apologists of earlier times. We can understand the superhuman interpretive effort it would take to work against the dominant paradigms that cast local knowledge in a negative light. One has to break the available hermeneutic molds to empower local knowledge.

An additional challenge in reconstructing local knowledge for contemporary purposes is that it has remained for centuries in an undertheorized state, in the form of unreflected assumptions or everyday practices. In fact, because many traditional communities are largely oral in character (even when they have had a written tradition like my Tamil community), valuable stocks of local knowledge are lost even for the local people. Passing on knowledge from mouth to mouth through successive generations places constraints on the extent to which local wisdom can be developed in a sustained and critical manner. Remember, also, that these marginalized communities have not always enjoyed the material resources to develop their knowledge in explicit and formal terms, or to preserve them adequately.

Given the fluid and relational character of local knowledge as articulated earlier, it should be easy to understand that it is not a unitary or homogenous construct. The local is as multiple and diverse as the global (as evident from the changes in modernism and postmodernism described earlier). There are diverse practices, discourses, and ideological tendencies that constitute local knowledge. Even in precolonial education, for example, the Tamil community has had different pedagogical traditions (Jeyasuriya, n.d; Sirisena, 1969). Yes, we did have a product oriented guru-shishya method which featured some of the rigid forms of teacher-fronted education. But we also had the more nonformal and practice-oriented apprentice system of education that now resonates well with such fashionable pedagogies as the legitimate peripheral participation of Lave and Wenger (1991). This diversity is similar to the gurukkal and pathsala traditions in the Hindu Indian culture and the madrasseh and makkab traditions of the Islamic world.

It is not surprising, then, that the local can contain chauvinistic tendencies. In fact, the onslaught of the global has been forcing the local to retreat further into more stubborn and unreasonable positions in a desperate attempt to maintain its independence. The educational enterprises of fundamentalist circles in the Islamic world today, of developing controlled forms of religious schooling in their madrassehs, result in suppressing secular and critical thinking. Understandably, this is done to safeguard traditional values and protect students from encounters with other threatening intellectual traditions. Unfortunately, this strategy leads to an extreme form of localism. Celebrating local knowledge, therefore, does not mean holding up a mythical form of classical knowledge as possessing the answers to all contemporary questions or representing resources that are always progressive and radical. Local knowledge has to be veritably reconstructed—through an ongoing process of critical reinterpretation, counterdiscursive negotiation, and imaginative application.

## TOWARDS A PRACTICE OF LOCALIZING KNOWLEDGE

> *But how is theory appropriated and resisted, located and displaced? How*
> *do theories travel among the unequal spaces of postcolonial confusion and*
> *contestation? What are their predicaments? How does theory travel and*
> *how do theorists travel? Complex, unresolved questions.*
> —*James Clifford* (1989, p. 179)

It should be clear from the aforementioned characterization that what we mean by local knowledge is not a philosophical paradigm or a body of ideas (these are not unproblematically available for us now). Celebrating local knowledge refers to adopting a practice. We treat our location (in all its relevant senses: geographical, social, geopolitical) as the ground on which to begin our thinking. Local knowledge is not a *product*, constituted by the beliefs and practices of the past. Local knowledge is a *process*—a process of negotiating dominant discourses and engaging in an ongoing construction of relevant knowledge in the context of our history and social practice. What is important is the *angle* from which we conduct this practice—that is, from the locality that shapes our social and intellectual practice. This is nothing new. As we discussed earlier, all knowledge is local. We can interpret other knowledge constructs and social formations only from our local positionality. This is our hermeneutic bias. The difference is that although we previously adopted a positionality based on Western or modernist paradigms that were imposed on everybody, we are now going to think from the alternate position of our own locality, which is more relevant for our community life and speaks to our interests. Ideally, this epistemological practice envisions not just changing the *content* of knowledge, but the *terms* of knowledge construction. Rather than merely replacing one set of constructs with another, this practice aims to relentlessly critique and democratize knowledge construction.

In some ways, what I am developing here is an amplification of what has already been put forward by minority scholars in regard to oppositional discourse practices. Remember the *politics of location*, articulated by feminist scholars, borrowing a metaphor from Adrienne Rich (1986). Being sensitive to the situatedness of one's own subjectivity compels one to sympathetically understand the struggles experienced by others in other contexts, while also appreciating the differences (see Kaplan, 1998). Standpoint epistemology is another articulation in feminist circles of the importance of knowledge-making from one's locality (Hartsock, 1990). The power of location is widely appreciated by minority ethnic scholars as well. bell hooks's (1989) imploration to "talk back" to dominant discourses with an awareness of one's roots is one such articulation. In more recent scholarship, especially in heavy-duty philosophical discourse, postcolonial theorists like

Homi Bhabha (1994) and Walter Mignolo (2000) speak of the *locus of enun-ciation.*[1] In other words, the context from which we speak shapes the knowledge we produce. To exemplify the difference location will spell for scholarly discourse, we might say that although postmodernism is a critique of enlightenment from a Euro-centric positionality (and may have its own usefulness), a more radical critique informed by colonialism, race, and geopolitics (as articulated in this chapter) can be expected to come from the standpoint of colonized communities.

This practice of localized knowledge construction involves several important components. I describe them as forming a deconstructive and reconstructive project. These two projects inform each other. They constitute an ongoing engagement with knowledge that must be ready to deal with the new questions raised in the process. Such a practice involves the following:

- Deconstructing dominant and established knowledge to understand its local shaping—Our own local positionality provides a demystifying perspective from which to conduct this critique. This activity involves much more than showing that the dominant constructs are biased toward the culture and history of western communities. Appreciating the rationale and validity of dominant constructs in their contexts of origins, we are able to translate with greater awareness the features that are useful for other localities. Thus, this involves a *reconstructive* activity as well. We must interpret established knowledge for local needs and interests. Although this process of appropriation has occurred somewhat unconsciously in the past, now we undertake this enterprise more reflectively.

- Reconstructing local knowledge for contemporary needs—Any knowledge construct has to be constantly reinterpreted to speak to current conditions. As new questions emerge in the changing social and geopolitical domains, we have to consider how local knowledge would relate to them. Similarly, this reconstructive process can creatively redefine the disciplinary paradigms of the mainstream. We should not underestimate local knowledge to be of relevance only for local needs. However, this reinterpretation is effective when it is accompanied by a *deconstructive* project as well. We have to critique traditional knowledge to unravel the limiting influences from feudal, caste, religious, and other chauvinistic contexts of production. Of course, the ways in which colonialism has distorted its character also need to be critically addressed.

---

[1]It is not my intention to go into the subtle differences in the way these theorists orientate to location or epistemology. I am more interested in developing a synthetic view of the emerging practice of local knowledge for the project in this volume.

We must note that this reflexive practice is well served by the "double vision" or "in-betweenness" of which postcolonial people are gifted (Bhabha, 1994). Compelled to become aware of nonlocal discourses from the history of colonization, while also enjoying a local subjectivity, we have a dual consciousness that provides a critical vantage point for this intercultural engagement. This consciousness also enables us to move beyond the myopic entrapment of the local. Celebrating local knowledge should not lead to ghettoizing minority communities, or forcing them into an ostrich-like intellectual existence. A clear grounding in our location gives us the confidence to engage with knowledge from other locations as we deconstruct and reconstruct them for our purposes. This engagement should extend to a sympathetic understanding of suppressed knowledge traditions from other colonized communities as well. In a sense, such an epistemological practice would lead us beyond the global and local dichotomy. We cannot indulge in an easy reversal of former hierarchies to posit one tradition of local knowledge as superior to others. Although we start from an awareness of geopolitical inequalities (which are historically real), our intellectual practice leads to translocal engagement of wider relevance.

Before I illustrate in the next section how this project works, I must point out that scholars from different postcolonial regions are theorizing such localized epistemological practices under different labels and metaphors these days. Ioan Davies (1998), working from the African context, used the metaphor of *fetishization*: "an alternate reading of fetish is not that of fake, but of a double meaning.... By living in the slippage between the dominance and the subordination of the surface, a mutation is being created with new languages and new possibilities" (pp. 140–141). This description may serve as a rough gloss for what Bhabha (1994) calls "inbetweenness" as he works from the Indian context. Hannerz's (1997) notion of *creolization*, borrowed from the linguistic process of mixed languages (whereby the colonial is transformed in the shape of the local), is employed by Caribbean scholars to describe local appropriations of dominant knowledge (see Glissant, 1990/1997). Moreiras (1998), theorizing from a Latin American context, uses the label *Second Latin Americanism* (to distinguish it from previous colonial descriptions of the region) for "a kind of contingent epistemic performativity ... an epistemic social practice of solidarity, with singular claims originating within whatever in Latin American societies still remains in a position of vestigial or residual exteriority, that is, whatever actively refuses to interiorize its subalternatization with respect to the global system" (p. 97). We can discern in Moreiras's prose the struggle to capture the local that eludes the all-embracing grasp of the global. Mignolo (2000) comes up with a huge collection of neologisms to capture localized epistemic practice by reviewing the thinking of a range of postcolonial scholars: that is, border thinking, double critique, transculturation, pluritopic thinking, new mestiza consciousness, barbarian theorizing, and even "bilanguaging love."

## AN EXAMPLE—REDEFINING SPEECH COMMUNITIES AND IDENTITIES

> *We need to explode the myth of pure and autonomous communities,*
> *reject the earlier mechanistic and territorial models of community and*
> *present new perspectives on the concepts of space and time which can*
> *address the dynamic flows that make community life. There is a need to*
> *take a more processual view of power and agency, to note that*
> *communities are not just dominated by rigid structures and fixed*
> *boundaries but are like a "happening."*
> —*Papastergiadis* (2000, p. 200)

There are many examples of local scholars redefining linguistic constructs without possessing a sophisticated awareness of the feverish theoretical activity going on in academia. South Asian linguists, for example, are grappling with notions of speech community and membership that are true to their locality and history. An exploration of this activity shows that there are serious social ramifications behind the enterprise of localizing knowledge.

Consider the implications of some of the central constructs in our field to characterize linguistic identity and speech community. These constructs are loaded with a unilingual and homogeneous ethos. Although the now discredited notions such as native speaker or mother tongue speaker require us to identify ourselves according to our parental language or language of infancy, even the alternatives such as L1 and L2 force us to identify a single language as receiving primacy in terms of our time of acquisition or level of competence (see Singh, 1998). In South Asian communities, such as mine, we grow up with two or more languages from childhood, developing equal competence in all of them, fluidly moving between each of them in our everyday life according to the different domains of family (regional dialect of Tamil), school (English), neighborhood (Muslim dialect of Tamil), and governmental institutions (Sinhala). Our hybrid identity is partly a reflection of our speech communities, which accommodate multiple languages and language groups. But the dominant definitions in our discipline still insist on identifying speech community according to homogeneous constructs—if not language or dialect (Hockett, 1958), at least in terms of attitudes (Labov, 1972), values, and usage of a language (Bauman & Sherzer, 1974; Hymes, 1972). There is little tolerance for multiple languages to exist side by side, without speakers assimilating to one or the less powerful language dying out. But in South Asia, even the smallest pockets of immigrant groups maintain their language for generations (see, for examples, Khubchandani, 1997). Furthermore, although bilingualism is acknowledged, mainstream linguistics is still squeamish about hybrid languages that show considerable mixing. In many South Asian locales, the very boundary between languages is fluid, calling into question our ability to separate one language from another (see Khubchandani, 1997, for examples). One can imagine the difficulty for people in my region to identify themselves as native speakers of "a" language. People may identify themselves as speakers of different languages very fluidly, based on the different contexts of interaction and competing claims on their affiliation.

Consider now the implications when mainstream disciplinary constructs enter social and academic discourse in South Asia. In a very subtle way, these constructs have begun shaping social reality here with damaging results. Khubchandani (1997) observes the following in relation to India: "Until as recently as four or five decades ago, one's language group was not generally considered as a very important criterion for sharply distinguishing oneself from others.... Following Independence, language consciousness has grown, and loyalties based on language-identity have acquired political salience" (p. 92).

We can imagine how exclusive categories of identification can lead to ethnic and linguistic sectarianism. Such conflicts also result from resources not being shared adequately. As speech communities are defined homogeneously, the linguistic and literacy needs of many "hidden" minority communities go unmet. In fact, the dominant constructs become handy for elites in the region to define their groups as the majority or the sole group and monopolize educational and economic resources.

If we position ourselves in such a non-Western linguistic locale, the ideologies informing our dominant disciplinary constructs become easy to deconstruct. In relatively more homogeneous Western communities, where nations have traditionally been defined on the basis of language groups, the notion of unitary language identification makes good sense (see Kandiah, 1998; Singh, 1998). In such communities, there is also a traditional bias that linguistic diversity is a problem (Graddol, 1999, p. 68). Because they do not have a long history of engaging in linguistically and culturally plural life, these communities have not developed complex sociolinguistic constructs for dealing with life at that level. Although there is increasing recognition of difference in contemporary Western communities, there are still attempts to micromanage diversity in terms of English-only ideologies or other forms of institutionalized frameworks (such as quota systems).

More abstract influences on the dominant linguistic constructs also become visible from a localized perspective. Khubchandani (1997) detects a bias toward temporal metaphors in linguistics: "... even studies of various spatial aspects of speech behavior—such as regional dialects, bilingualism, diglossia, language contact and borrowings—are framed in terms of temporality" (p. 85). Because of this bias, he finds that "the impact on language systems of various ecological factors ... [have] been treated only peripherally" (p. 86). Other South Asian scholars have pointed out that, in fields such as Second Language Acquisition, ecological factors like codeswitching, mixing, and speech accommodation have not been sufficiently studied, as unilateral temporal progression toward the target language is the focus (see Sridhar, 1994). Interestingly, as discussed earlier, the project of modernism favored time over space. Furthermore, the modernist emphasis on efficiency and uniformity through numerical abstraction also influences the use of these constructs to categorize people, filtering out the complex diversity of linguistic life. We thus become sensitive to some ulterior motivations in the applications of these definitions. Postcolonial scholars point out that constructs like linguistic identity and speech community were put to use in the colonial period in lands like India to categorize people for purposes of taxation, administrative convenience, and political control (Mohan, 1992).

South Asian linguists are attempting to rediscover the local knowledge pertaining to interaction strategies and language negotiation that traditionally motivated people to manage their multilingual life harmoniously (see Annamalai, 1998; Dasgupta, 1998; Pattanayak, 1998). To describe this stock of knowledge, they have to resort to atypical metaphors and models. Using the Sanskrit term *Kshetra*, Khubchandani (1997) treats region as the primary level of traditional analysis in the Indian context. Not coterminous with any existing political or administrative boundaries, *Kshetras* "can be visualized as a rainbow; here different dimensions interflow symbiotically into one another, responsive to differences of density as in an osmosis" (Khubchandani, 1997, p. 84). Thus speech communities are, for Khubchandani, regions that accommodate different mix of languages. He comes up with seven regions that characterize the more than hundred languages in India, producing contextually shifting identities. How people live together with this dynamic multilingualism and engage in harmonious civic life, he terms *organic pluralism* (which he distinguishes from the *institutional pluralism* of the West, which is centrally stratified). This model is characterized by the two features of synergy and serendipity:

> Individuals in such societies acquire more *synergy* (i.e., putting forth one's own efforts) and serendipity (i.e., accepting the other on his/her own terms, being open to unexpectedness), and develop positive attitudes to variations in speech (to the extent of even appropriating deviations as the norm in the lingua franca), in the process of "coming out" from their own language-codes to a neutral ground. (Khubchandani, 1997, p. 94)

These constructs capture the expectation among local people that linguistic interactions need to be constantly negotiated. Social life begins with the assumption that one is going to engage with people from different languages on an everyday basis, and that one's interactional moves have to be made with that expectation. The mix of languages and fluidity in interactions do not have to be confusing. They are not confusing to the local people. They have been living with this reality for generations. While maintaining these differences, they still manage to develop a "superconsensus" that facilitates social cohesion (Khubchandani, 1997, p. 84). Khubchandani has to resort to romantic-sounding metaphors like rainbow, symbiosis, osmosis, synergy, and serendipity to describe a multilingual reality that lacks a suitable language in mainstream linguistics.

What is interesting about this activity of localized knowledge-making is that it leads to redefining the dominant constructs in the field and, possibly, revisioning conditions in other communities—not excluding the West. As we know now, there is a crisis in the terms used to define linguistic identity in the West. The revisions being made in the census of the United States are just one instance of fumbling attempts to grapple with diversity (see Anderson, 1988). There are even greater challenges in formulating policies about language and education that would do justice to the diverse communities now populating the United States (see Ricento & Burnaby, 1998). New strategies of interpersonal communication and literacy are being developed in everyday life as people from different languages and dialects of English interact with each other. A meaningful challenge to the rise of monolingualist and racist ideologies in the West would come from suitable models for policymaking and social regulation that show that harmony, unity, and progress are possible alongside an accommodation of diversity. The knowledge from other localities that account for their multilingual life can enhance the activities of scholars in the West. After all, these are communities that have experienced a longer history of multilingualism and multiculturalism. I am not saying that postcolonial linguists offer ready-made constructs for use in the West. In fact, some of the limiting features of local linguistic identity—such as caste-based dialects and identities—need to be more reflexively analyzed. But the theorization of many local scholars (referred to in this section) shows interesting examples of the deconstructive and reconstructive practice that can help redefine notions like language identity and speech community in our field.

## CONCLUSION

The earlier example serves to prove the importance of maintaining an ongoing conversation with local knowledge—if not to respect the aspirations and wholeness of marginalized communities, then at least for our common academic pursuit of broadening knowledge construction practices. The local will always have a questioning effect on established paradigms, deriving from the nonsystematized, unorthodox, and simply messy features of its existential practice. An ongoing conversation with local traditions is a healthy dialectic for mainstream knowledge. Already, situated scholarship has exposed how fields central to our interest have had a questionable formation in colonial history: the orientation to language and language teaching as a value-free, instrumental, pragmatic activity in ELT is rooted in the history of teaching English for purposes of colonization (see Pennycook, 1994; Phillipson, 1992); the narrow literary canons now being questioned were formed for the purpose of teaching English in colonies like India and forming a docile citizenry (see Viswanathan, 1989). Similar motivations have been uncovered in fields like anthropology (see Asad, 1973) and area studies (Moreiras, 1998). As many disciplines are redefining their assumptions these days, especially under the changes initiated by postmodern globalization (see Appadurai, 2000, for anthropology; Jay, 2001, for literary studies; Robertson, 1997, for sociology), it is important to consider how knowledge from diverse localities can inform new epistemological practices. Ironically, the benefits of this negotiation are clearer for the "hard" sciences. Research agencies like the National Institutes of Health (Stolberg, 2001), Center for Disease Control (Hitt, 2001), and Memorial Sloan-Kettering Cancer Center (Rosenthal, 2001), are now experimenting with herbal medicine and folk medical practices from non-western cultures to tap their resources for purposes in the West.

Paradoxically, local knowledge can motivate conversations between different localities, answering questions that transcend one's own borders. It is possible to talk about common subjects and explore related questions while having a starting point that is specific to one's locality. It is when we acknowledge the localness of each of our own knowledge that we have the proper humility to engage productively with other knowledge traditions. The assumption that one's knowledge is of sole universal relevance does not encourage conversation. It is possible to develop a pluralistic mode of thinking where we celebrate different cultures and identities, and yet engage in projects common to our shared humanity. Breaking away from the history of constructing a globalized totality with uniform knowledge and hierarchical community, we should envision building networks of multiple centers that develop diversity as a universal project and encourage an actively negotiated epistemological tradition.

**REFERENCES**

Adas, M. (1989). *Machines as the measure of men*. Ithaca, NY: Cornell University Press.
Adas, M. (1992). From avoidance to confrontation: Peasant protest in precolonial and colonial Southeast Asia. In N. Dirks (Ed.), *Colonialism and culture* (pp. 89–126). Ann Arbor: University of Michigan Press.

Amsden, A. H. (2002, January 31). Why are globalizers so provincial? *The New York Times*, p. A25.

Anderson, M. J. (1988). *The American census: A social history*. New Haven, CT: Yale University Press.

Annamalai, E. (1998). Nativity of language. In R. Singh (Ed.), *The native speaker: Multilingual perspectives* (pp. 148–157). New Delhi, India: Sage.

Appadurai, A. (1996). *Modernity at large: Cultural dimensions of globalization*. Minneapolis: University of Minnesota Press.

Appadurai, A. (2000). Grassroots globalization and the research imagination. *Public Culture, 12*, 1–20.

Asad, T. (Ed.). (1973). *Anthropology and the colonial encounter*. London: Ithaca Press.

Bahri, D. (1997). Marginally off-center: Postcolonialism in the teaching machine. *College English, 59*, 277–298.

Barton, D., & Hamilton, M. (1998). *Local literacies: Reading and writing in one community*. London: Routledge.

Bauman, R., & Sherzer, J. (Eds.). (1974). *Explorations in the ethnography of speaking*. New York: Cambridge University Press.

Bernal, M. (1987). *The fabrication of ancient Greece, 1785–1985. (Vol. 1 of Black Athena: The Afroasiatic roots of classical civilization)*. New Brunswick, NJ: Rutgers University Press.

Bhabha, H. K. (1994). *The location of culture*. New York: Routledge.

Canagarajah, S. A. (1993). Up the garden path: Second language writing approaches, local knowledge, and pluralism. *TESOL Quarterly, 27*, 301–306.

Canagarajah, S. A. (1999). *Resisting linguistic imperialism in English teaching*. Oxford, England: Oxford University Press.

Chelliah, J. V. (1922). *A century of English education*. Vaddukoddai, Sri Lanka: Jaffna College.

Clifford, J. (1988). *The predicament of culture: Twentieth-century ethnography, literature, and art*. Cambridge, MA: Harvard University Press.

Clifford, J. (1989). Notes on theory and travel. *Inscriptions, 5*, 177–188.

Clifford, J. (1994). Diasporas. *Cultural Anthropology, 9*, 302–338.

Cohen, R. (1997). *Global diasporas*. Seattle: University of Washington Press.

Dasgupta, P. (1998). The native speaker: A short history. In R. Singh (Ed.), *The native speaker: Multilingual perspectives* (pp. 182–192). New Delhi, India: Sage.

Davies, I. (1998). Negotiating African culture: Toward a decolonization of the Fetish. In F. Jameson & M. Miyoshi (Eds.), *The cultures of globalization* (pp. 125–145). Durham, NC: Duke University Press.

Dussel, E. (1998). Beyond Eurocentrism: The world system and the limits of modernity. In F. Jameson & M. Miyoshi (Eds.), *The cultures of globalization* (pp. 3–31). Durham, NC: Duke University Press.

Foucault, M. (1972). The discourse on language. In *The archeology of knowledge* (pp. 215–237). New York: Pantheon.

Geertz, C. (1983). *Local knowledge: Further essays in interpretive anthropology*. New York: Basic Books.

Giddens, A. (1990). *The consequences of modernity*. London: Polity.

Glissant, E. (1997). *Poetics of relation*. (B. Wing, Trans.). Ann Arbor: University of Michigan Press. (Original work published 1990)

Graddol, D. (1999). The decline of the native speaker. In D. Graddol & U. H. Meinhoff (Eds.), *English in a changing world* (pp. 57–68; AILA Review 13). Guildford, England: AILA.

Hall, S. (1997a). The local and the global: Globalization and ethnicity. In A. D. King (Ed.), *Culture, globalization, and the world system* (pp. 19–40). Minneapolis: University of Minnesota Press.

Hall, S. (1997b). Old and new identities, old and new ethnicities. In A. D. King (Ed.), *Culture, globalization, and the world system* (pp. 41–68). Minneapolis: University of Minnesota Press.

Hannerz, U. (1997). Scenarios for peripheral cultures. In A. D. King (Ed.), *Culture, globalization, and the world system* (pp. 107–128). Minneapolis: University of Minnesota Press.

Hartsock, N. (1990). Rethinking modernism: Minority vs. majority theories. In A. R. J. Mohamed & D. Lloyd (Eds.), *The nature and the context of minority discourse* (pp. 17–36). New York: Oxford University Press.

Harvey, D. (1990). *The condition of postmodernity.* Cambridge, England: Blackwell.

Hessen, B. (1971). *The social and economic roots of Newton's Principia.* New York: Howard Fertig.

Hitt, J. (2001, May 6). Building a better blood sucker. *The New York Times Magazine,* pp. 92–96.

Hockett, C. F. (1958). *A course in modern linguistics.* New York: Macmillan.

hooks, b. (1989). *Talking back: Thinking feminist, thinking black.* Boston: South End Press.

Huff, T. (1993). *The rise of early modern science: Islam, China, and the West.* Cambridge, England: Cambridge University Press.

Hymes, D. (1972). Models of the interaction of language and social life. In J. J. Gumperz & D. Hymes (Eds.), *Directions in sociolinguistics: The ethnography of communication* (pp. 35–71). New York: Holt, Rinehart & Winston.

Jacob, M. (1976). *The Newtonians and the English revolution: 1689–1720.* Ithaca, NY: Cornell University Press.

Jameson, F. (1998). Notes on globalization as a philosophical issue. In F. Jameson & M. Miyoshi (Eds.), *The cultures of globalization* (pp. 54–80). Durham, NC: Duke University Press.

Jay, P. (2001). Beyond discipline? Globalization and the future of English. *PMLA, 116,* 32–47.

Jeyasuriya, J. E. (n.d.). The indigenous religious traditions in education. In *Educational policies and progress during British rule in Ceylon* (pp. 4–23). Colombo: Associated Educational Publishers.

Kandiah, T. (1998). Epiphanies of the deathless native user's manifold avatars: A postcolonial perspective on the native speaker. In R. Singh (Ed.), *The native speaker: Multilingual perspectives* (pp. 79–110). New Delhi, India: Sage.

Kaplan, C. (1998). *Questions of travel: Postmodern discourses of displacement.* Durham, NC: Duke University Press.

Khare, R. S. (1984). *The untouchable as himself: Ideology, identity, and pragmatism among the Lucknow Chamars.* Cambridge, England: Cambridge University Press.

Khubchandani, L. M. (1997). *Revisualizing boundaries: A plurilingual ethos.* New Delhi, India: Sage.

Labov, W. (1972). *Sociolinguistic patterns.* Philadelphia: University of Pennsylvania Press.

Lave, J., & Wenger, E. (1991). *Situated learning: Legitimate peripheral participation.* Cambridge, England: Cambridge University Press.

Merton, R. (1970). *Science, technology, and society in seventeenth-century England.* New York: Howard Fertig.

Mignolo, W. D. (2000). *Local histories/global designs: Coloniality, subaltern knowledges, and border thinking.* Princeton, NJ: Princeton University Press.

Miyoshi, M. (1998). "Globalization," culture, and the university. In F. Jameson & M. Miyoshi (Eds.), *The cultures of globalization* (pp. 247–273). Durham, NC: Duke University Press.

Mohan, K. (1992). Constructing religion and caste: Manipulating identities. *Social Science Research Journal, 1,* 1–12.

Moreiras, A. (1998). Global fragments: A second Latin Americanism. In F. Jameson & M. Miyoshi (Eds.), *The cultures of globalization* (pp. 81–102). Durham, NC: Duke University Press.

Moya, P. (1997). Postmodernism, realism, and the politics of identity: Cherrie Moraga and Chicana feminism. In C. T. Mohanty & M. J. Alexander (Eds.), *Feminist geneologies, colonial legacies, democratic futures* (pp. 125–150). New York: Routledge.

Murray, D. (2000). Protean communication: The language of computer-mediated communication. *TESOL Quarterly, 34,* 397–422.

Papastergiadis, N. (2000). *The turbulence of migration.* Cambridge, England: Polity Press.

Paranirupasingham, S. (1991, October). *Tiru poo kailasapathy avarkaLum poRu-Laaraaichiyum.* [Mr. P. Kailasapathy and the search for Truth.]. Paper presented in the Academic Forum of the University of Jaffna, Sri Lanka.

Pattanayak, D. P. (1998). Mother tongue: An Indian context. In R. Singh (Ed.), *The native speaker: Multilingual perspectives* (pp. 124–147). New Delhi, India: Sage.

Pennycook, A. (1989). The concept of "method," interested knowledge, and the politics of language teaching. *TESOL Quarterly, 23,* 589–618.

Pennycook, A. (1994). *The cultural politics of English as an international language.* London: Longman.

Phillipson, R. (1992). *Linguistic imperialism.* Oxford, England: Oxford University Press.

Porter, T. M. (1995). *Trust in numbers: The pursuit of objectivity in science and public life.* Princeton, NJ: Princeton University Press.

Ra'ad, B. L. (2001). Primal scenes of globalization: Legacies of Canaan and Etruria. *PMLA, 116,* 89–110.

Ricento, T. & Burnaby, B. (Eds). (1998). *Language and politics in the United States and Canada: Myths and realities.* Mahwah, NJ: Lawrence Erlbaum Associates.

Rich, A. (1986). *Blood, bread, and poetry: Selected prose, 1979–1985.* New York: Norton.

Robertson, R. (1992). *Globalization.* London: Sage.

Robertson, R. (1997). Social theory, cultural relativity, and the problem of globality. In A. D. King (Ed.), *Culture, globalization, and the world system* (pp. 69–90). Minneapolis: University of Minnesota Press.

Rosenthal, E. (2001, May 6). Chairman Mao's cure for cancer. *The New York Times Magazine,* pp. 70–73.

Scott, J. C. (1990). *Domination and the arts of resistance.* New Haven, CT: Yale University Press.

Shiva, V. (1990). Reductionist science as epistemological violence. In A. Nandy (Ed.), *Science, hegemony, and violence* (pp. 232–56). Delhi, India: Oxford University Press.

Singh, R. (Ed.). (1998). *The native speaker: Multilingual perspectives.* New Delhi, India: Sage.

Sirisena, U. D. I. (1969). Editorial introduction. In *Education in Ceylon: Part 1* (pp. xxv–xvii). Colombo, Sri Lanka: Ministry of Education and Cultural Affairs.

Sridhar, S. N. (1994). A reality check for SLA theories. *TESOL Quarterly, 28,* 800–805.

Stolberg, S. G. (2001, May 6). The estrogen alternative. *The New York Times Magazine,* pp. 108–110.

Suseendirarajah, S. (1991, March). PantiTamaNiyin peerum pukaLum vanTa vaaRu [Accounting for the name and prestige of Panditamani]. Paper presented at the Academic Forum, University of Jaffna, Sri Lanka.

Viswanathan, G. (1989). *Masks of conquest*. New York: Columbia University Press.
Warschauer, M. (2000). The changing global economy and the future of English
  teaching. *TESOL Quarterly, 34*, 511–536.

# Chapter 2

# Expert Discourses, Local Practices, and Hybridity: The Case of Indian Englishes[1]

Rakesh M. Bhatt
*University of Illinois, Urbana–Champaign*

## INTRODUCTION

The transformation of English in postcolonial contexts—from a colonial idiom to various indigenous ones—was inevitable for it to represent faithfully the ethos of its cultural context of use, and to enable speakers of English in multilingual contexts to use it as an additional resource for linguistic, sociolinguistic, and literary creativity (Baumgardner, 1996; Bhatt, 2001a; Canagarajah, 1999; Kachru, 1982, 1983, 1986; Rahman, 1999). This process of transformation, worldwide, has resulted in the emergence of many new Englishes, each peculiar to its own locality and its own culture. Indian English[2] is one instance of the transformation—recording, reflecting, and creating various complexes of sociocultural nuances indigenous to local contexts of use (Bhatt, 1995, 2001a, 2001b, 2002a, 2002b; Kachru, 1983, 1986). The codification of these Englishes, however, has been challenged, and continues

---

[1]Many thanks to Suresh Canagarajah and Barbara Hancin–Bhatt for their comments and suggestions.
[2]I am using "Indian English" here as a cover term for all the varieties of English spoken in India.

ogeny refers to the processes by which variation and diversity are controlled in preference

**26**                                                                        BHATT

hery, and Global–Local. This is, of course, the dialectic by which the

This chapter focuses on the nature of sociolinguistic struggle between the center and the peripheries over practices, meanings, and identities of Englishes. Restricting the exploration to the use of English language in India, I first examine the historical function of expert discourses that suppress variation in their attempts to impose control (hegemony) and order (homogeny) on English language acquisition and use.[3] Of course, local communities have always responded creatively to this imposition by adopting different strategies of resistance and negotiation. However, new varieties of expert discourse have been constructed by the globally powerful, according to the changing social and political conditions in history, to control the "unruly" local life of English. I then present evidence of local practices to demonstrate creativity and systematicity in the so-called English linguistic "chaos." The examination of currently evolving hybrid codes and discourses provides an understanding of how Indian English speakers and writers navigate sociolinguistically between their regional riches and the homogenized global norms. This understanding will enable us to develop a pluralistic orientation to norms in English language in specific and linguistic communication in general.

## PLANNING ENGLISH, PLANNING INEQUALITY

The history of the spread of English in India is generally traced to an ordinance issued in 1835 that laid the blueprint of a colonial linguistic ideology designed to devalue the cultural capital and values of the colonized. The ordinance based on the recommendation of T. B. Macaulay (1957/1835), entitled *Minute on Indian Education*, decreed that English should be the medium of all schools and universities in India. The motivation behind this was to create "a class who may be interpreters between us and the millions we govern, a class of persons, Indian in blood and colour, but English in taste, in opinion, in morals and in intellect" (quoted in Sharp, 1920, p. 116). The logic of this language-in-education policy—restricting the distribution

---

[3]*Hegemony* is the process by which dominant groups win universal acceptance for their version of things. Ideally, rather than eradicating oppositional views, hegemony works by accommodating them in a way that the dominant group's view still enjoys superiority and legitimacy. *Homogeny* refers to the processes by which variation and diversity are controlled in preference for uniformity in language norms that favor the dominant groups.

(crucially, access) of English to a small number of Indians—was governed essentially by a colonial ideology of race and skin color. The assumption clearly is that the acquisition of English by the colonized may not change their biology (blood and skin color), but could create a new culture (taste, opinions, morals, and intellect) that could interface with the civilized colonizers (cf. also Viswanathan, 1989). Such colonial projects are not specific to India, but are noticed elsewhere. Portuguese colonialism, for example, "tried to eradicate the African languages in institutional life by inculcating Africans through the educational systems in Portuguese only with myths and beliefs concerning the savage nature of their culture" (Macedo, 2000, p. 16). Similarly, French colonization, motivated by a "mission civilatrice," called on the services of the French language to civilize the colonized whose languages were not adequate. This point is summed up well by l'Abbé [Abbot] Grégoire in the following way: "Enfin les nègres de nos colonies, dont vouz avez fait des hommes, ont une espèce d'idiome pauvre [...] qui, dans tous les verbes, ne connait guère que l'infinitif" (quoted in De Certeau, Julia, & Revel, 1975, p. 302). [Translation: Finally, the Negroes of our colonies, whom you've made into men, have a type of poor language which, for all the verbs, hardly know anything other than the infinitive.][1]

The colonial project in India did produce linguistic-cultural alterations, as Macaulay had envisioned. The alterations have led to the formation of a social-linguistic apartheid,[2] its reproduction being assured by the creation of a "class of person," as Ramanathan (1999) notes, "the Indian middle class, with [...] relatively easy access to English [that now] represents an inner circle of power and privilege that for a variety of reasons remain inaccessible to particular groups of people in India ... [that are pushed] into outer circle" (p. 211). The English-linguistic apartheid is sustained in structures where English is not only available but, most importantly, accessible. Although English is available to everyone, the linguistic hierarchy is maintained through the distribution of different types of language. The middle class has access to "standard" varieties that approximate the global norm; the lower classes speak less prestigious varieties. Agnihotri and Khanna (1995) further confirm this:

> The most significant consequence of sustaining English in India has been a major social division between the select elite and the "Englishless" masses. Even within the educated English-knowing group there is a split between those for whom English is the medium of instruction in prestigious public

---

[1]Thanks to Errol O'Neill for bringing this to my attention. He kindly provided the English translation of the quote.

[2]This system of legalized segregation, unique to South Africa, is used here in a metaphorical sense to refer to sociolinguistically-based inequality (i.e., English-speaking vs. vernacular-speaking) of different class groups within a society. This inequality can be pervasive and unalterable like apartheid.

(i.e., private) schools and those who largely study English as a subject in ordinary government schools. The route to power, prestige and riches, even today, lies through English. (p. 15)

The power of English—as the language of opportunity and social mobility—is now globally accepted in India, especially as part of the "Three Language Formula."[6] The pedagogy in the past—colonial and postpartition—has, unfortunately, standardized English in India, ignoring local practices and oftentimes denigrating them to the status of Pidgin ("Babu" or "Butler" English) varieties (cf. Hosali & Aitchison, 1986; Mehrotra, 1997, 2000). In colonial India, where education was the only source of the cultural capital necessary for the accumulation of both economic and political power, the principal medium of that initiation was Standard British English. The most important instrument of the reproduction of this variety of English was the educational system, because it is in schools that the production of hegemonic ideologies hides behind a number of legitimating forms such as the claim by dominant classes that their interests represent the interests of the entire community, the claim that conflict only occurs outside of the sphere of the political (i.e., economic conflict is viewed as non-political), and the presentation of specific forms of consciousness, beliefs, attitudes, values and practices as natural, universal, or even eternal (Giroux, 1981, p. 24). It is important to realize, therefore, that language standardization has played an intranational role—that is, to stratify the local community—during colonial times. As we turn to the effects of language standardization from an international perspective in postcolonial times (i.e., from the angle of global–local conflicts), we must see how such planning efforts are connected to intranational versions in colonial times. Thus, efforts in postcolonial India to democratize English language pedagogy are confronted with "expert" discourses (which I have also called *venerable discourses* in my other publications, within the general framework of the "fellowships of discourse"—a la Foucault, 1972) to refer to a body of statements that denigrate local practices and promote the global norm.

---

[6]To equalize the burden of language learning among the different linguistic regions and, at the same time, foster nationalism (sociocultural integration), three important sociolinguistic trends were identified in postcolonial India:
  1. Socialism—recognition of the importance of mother tongues for equal access to education for everybody.
  2. Nationalism—rediscovery of the importance of indigenous languages.
  3. Nationism—selection of an official language of the Union for political integration.
These trends were codified by the education commission in India in terms of "Three Language Formula" that required a child to be introduced to at least three languages during the course of his or her school education:
  1. The regional language or the mother tongue where the latter is different from the regional language.
  2. Hindi or, in Hindi-speaking areas, another Indian language.
  3. English or any other modern European language.

## The Venerable Fellowships of Discourse

The rise of postcolonial Englishes and their generally growing popularity in different local and regional linguistic markets—for example, the celebrated use of noncanonical linguistic forms in the literary, television, film, and advertising domains—challenges the homogeny and hegemony of Standard English. The implications of this are far-reaching: The more linguistic capital the postcolonial English speakers possess by virtue of creating their own intellectual and cultural property, the more they are able to exploit the system of differences to their advantage, thus threatening the structure of the symbolic power relations. Even the previously disenfranchised (the lower classes) are appropriating the English language, infusing it with their values and interests. The Indian middle class also finds that there are more creative ways of integrating English with the local languages to manage the sometimes conflicting demands of global and national life. When such local appropriations occur, the expert discourse—a strategic and regulatory system of ideological management—serves to neutralize language variation by providing the tools, the rhetorical methods, and the theoretical-methodological constructs needed to naturalize and essentialize[7] the standard language and to marginalize the nonstandard varieties as deviations from the norm.

For the most part, the expert discourses on English language learning, teaching, and use have been generally concerned with questions related to the notions of epistemology, authenticity, and authority (Bhatt, 2002a). With respect to epistemology, these discourses construct (or manufacture) the proper knowledge relating to new varieties of English. Furthermore, they define which varieties are authentic and which are not. Through such strategies, they spell out who has the authority to make grammaticality judgements. These expert discourses recall Foucault's (1972) postulation that the production of discourse in any society is at once controlled, selected, organized, and redistributed according to a number of procedures whose role is to avert its powers and its dangers, to master the unpredictable event. As such, the preservation, reproduction, and the distribution of power is serviced by the same institutions that produce it, enabling "fellowships of discourse," the function of which is as follows: "... to preserve or to reproduce discourse, but in order that it should circulate within a closed community, according to strict regulations, without those in possession being dispossessed by this very distribution" (Foucault, 1972, p. 225).

---

[7]To *naturalize* is to make the views of the dominant group on language norms be treated as objective, universal, and beyond debate—that is, to make them appear natural. *Essentialize* is to reduce a construct (i.e., community, culture, language) to a core set of characteristics that identify it. By essentializing something, we deny the internal contradictions, complexity, and variability in that construct.

The discourse "fellowships" of the global English language (a la Crystal, 1997) privilege homogenization and centralization of language use and, as I have argued elsewhere (Bhatt, 2002a), contest the functional view that diversifies and decentralizes language practices. Contemporary fellowships of expert discourse on English language are constituted by researchers and scholars in leading Anglo–American educational, professional, and cultural institutions in the language-related fields, those who disseminate their knowledge through prestigious scholarly journals and books, and professional conferences and statutory bodies. The key to the operation of these fellowships is the control of "standard language." Thus, an ideology of standardization is recruited to delimit language by imposing ordered and reasoned patterns of correct usage through codification of form and function, and by minimizing variation in the grammatical structure and lexis while maximizing the allocation of social and linguistic roles (cf. Bhatt, 2001a; see also Mugglestone, 1995). The ideology of standardization is discursively introduced in expert discourses. The cumulative effect of these expert discourses is that the architecture of existing power configurations as well as the parameters of structural changes in those configurations appear normal, obvious, and, in fact, desirable. Oftentimes we lose sight of the fact that these discourses enable a view of standard language as worth something independent of its market, as if it possesses intrinsic virtues (Pyles & Algeo, 1982); but in practice they depend on the market, that is, these are the means through which the dominant groups derive power from and exert control over the instruments of reproduction and competence (*inter alia*, the school system, the lexicographers, the grammarians).

The codification of these discourses is enabled by the kind of intellectual imperialism whereby a particular model of language, possessed by an ideal native speaker–hearer in a completely homogeneous speech community, assumes a paradigmatic status in the linguistic sciences as a whole (Chomsky, 1986). It is this foundational assumption that is behind dichotomies such as standard–nonstandard, native–non-native, language–interlanguage, and target–fossilized. Although the first two dichotomies have become so naturalized in the field that they are now common sense, the latter two need more examination. Treating different varieties of nativized Englishes as merely a transitory "interlanguage" in a new speaker's path to acquiring the target language denies legitimacy to such varieties. Even when such varieties are shown to have become stabilized and systematized as to serve as the norms for postcolonial communities, experts consider them merely "fossilized" forms, that is, errors that have become habitualized. Such discourses reveal what Vivian Cook (1999) has explained as the "comparative fallacy" in the field. That is, we judge a multilingual speaker's identity, competence, and language in reference to monolingual speakers and their varieties. We deny the autonomy, creativity, and independence of a multilingual person to develop the codes and conventions that serve his or her unique needs. We also treat the linguistic competence of a multilingual person as made up of isolated competencies of native-like fluency in each different language (i.e., the notion of ambilingualism). In this case, as in others in life, we must recognize that the sum is more than its parts.

When these discourses are naturalized, they begin to influence areas of practical application—such as language teaching. The ESL–ELT profession thus recognizes, unproblematically, "ambilingualism"[8] as the goal of second language acquisition, "fossilization" as the ultimate fate of second language learners, and "interlanguage" as the variety spoken by non-native speakers (cf. Bhatt, 2002a; Sridhar, 1994). Such discourses produce a habit of thought: soon after being introduced, these constructs are understood as mathematical axioms above debate; the assumptions shared are not propositions to be defended or attacked (cf. Bhatt, 2001a, 2001b). The ESL–ELT "expert" discourse thus contributes to what Foucault (1980) has called the "régimes of truth," the discursive formations that rationalize and naturalize the historical structures of power asymmetries in English language use in postcolonial contexts.

The undesirable consequences of the expert discourses appear in different forms of attitudinal internalizations among native and non-native English teachers. One set of attitudes appears in the writings of Helen Johnson (1992), in her article entitled "Defossilizing." She portrays the ESL learner, from the native speaker perspective, in the following manner:

> We have all come across them at one time or another. Easily *recognizable* by their inability to move in any direction except sideways and *by the glazing of their eyes* when you mention the present perfect tense. I am, of course, referring to students *suffering from chronic "intermediate-itis,"* students whose fluent and extensive output consists almost entirely of communication strategies and very little grammar—*the "fluent-but-fossilized"* ... Every method has its *Frankenstein's monsters, grotesque parodies* of whatever it is the teaching has emphasized, and these *tediously inaccurate chatterers* are the *unfortunate creations* of the communicative approach. (emphasis added; p. 180)

What is unfortunate is that even well established varieties of World Englishes that ESL students bring to class from their own communities are treated by uninformed teachers as fossilized forms. In the name of defossilizing, they then begin to impose their own varieties on the students, eradicating the dialects of the students.

The other perspective, still more unfortunate, is the view that "a non-native cannot aspire to acquire a native-speaker's language competence"

---

[8]By "ambilingualism" is meant the orientation to competence in two different languages as separate and independent of each other. A more complex orientation would perceive the competence of the bilingual as featuring an integrated proficiency where the whole is more than the constituting parts.

(Medgyes, 1992, p. 340). Ironically, even non-native teachers of English subscribe to this view—as it is evident in Medgyes, who is a champion of non-native teachers in many of his other works. This attitude, produced and reproduced in the works of, among others, Quirk (1990, 1996), Davies (1989, 1991, 2001), Selinker (1972, 1993), and Honey (1983, 1997), is more clearly present in Medgyes's later work where the verbal deprivation theory (of Bereiter, Engelman, Osborn, & Reidford, 1966) is attitudinally reconstituted in the following way (Medgyes, 1994): "... we [non-natives] *suffer* from an inferiority complex caused by *glaring defects* in our knowledge of English. We are in *constant distress* as we realize how little we know about the language we are supposed to teach" (emphasis added, p. 40). It is ignored that multilinguals may possess unique insights into English, deriving from a comparative orientation, that monolingual native speakers cannot possess.

With respect to English language learning and teaching in India, the dominant discourse has arguably been very successful in securely reproducing the structure of "class difference," as envisioned in *Minute on Indian Education* (Macaulay, 1957/1835). The reproduction of social classes is now based on technical, linguistic-theoretic dichotomies in second language acquisition (SLA) and English language teaching (ELT) such as standard–nonstandard, native–non-native, language–interlanguage, and target–fossilized. Even where Indian English speakers meet the criterion of functional bilingualism, these dichotomies are used by the profession as an alibi for maintaining linguistic ethnocentrism disguised as concern over intelligibility among the English-using population (Bhatt, 2002a; Lippi-Green, 1997; Nelson, 1992; Smith and Nelson, 1985). The middle class can use these dichotomies to exert their power over lower classes to classify their varieties of English as nonstandard, fossilized, interlanguages. By using these dichotomies to classify English speakers in the intranational context, local people give life to these biased expert discourses that sustain the geopolitical hegemony of standard English.

However, marginalized communities and interests are not always passive in the face of expert discourses. They go on producing counterdiscourses to contest the validity of expert discourses. The acquisition and use of postcolonial Englishes carry the possibility of altering the structures of power by shifting the focus from authenticity to appropriacy and appropriation (Kramsch & Sullivan, 1996). In other words, local communities are deviating from the need to learn and use "authentic" English, as spoken by "native" speakers in the West. They have moved on to argue for the use of English that is "appropriate" for their local context (in the light of the norms and values that are important to the Indian community) and, even more recently, for their right to take on this language and make it their own without any regard to native speaker norms (i.e., appropriation). As Seidlhofer (2001) puts it, they have moved on from "parochial domesticity and exclusive native speaker norms to global inclusiveness and egalitarian license to speak in ways that meet diverse local needs" (p. 135). This possibility of subversion carried out by new (postcolonial) Englishes, however, meets another obstacle: the "new didacts" who present what I have tentatively termed a neo-colonial discourse on English language use in India.

## Neo-Colonialism and the New Didacts

Colonial expert discourses were actively engaged in teaching the virtues of the English language (and culture) to the indigenous people while devaluing local symbolic systems as vernacular (languages and cultures). Neo-colonial expert discourses represent what Kachru (2001, p. 9) has called the "genres of guilt and atonement." He argues that it is in the genre of atonement that "other constructs emerge: those of the natives of the Anglophone Asia. *The native mind is constructed as unthinking, without initiative and devoid of linguistic and literary visions ...*" (Kachru, 2001, p. 9; emphasis added). The construction of the local as unthinking, unimaginative, and incapable forms the core of the neo-colonial expert discourse. Phillipson and Skutnabb–Kangas (1996), the new didacts, exemplify the nature of this discourse most clearly in their article "Is India throwing away its language resources?" They declare the following:

> We have been observing the Indian language scene for many years, and recently spent two months in India analyzing language policy. And we are worried.... We can exemplify why we are worried. We have met people from all parts of India whose family history reflects loss of the mother tongue in a short period of time. Grandparents are unable to communicate with their own grandchildren because of the shift to English that English-medium schooling, urbanization and geographic mobility have facilitated. In this way the cultural resources and heritage of Kannada, Kashmiri, Malayalam, Marathi, Tamil, Telugu and countless other languages are being lost. At the individual level, the loss of inter-generational communication and continuity is a personal tragedy. (Phillipson & Skutnabb–Kangas, 1996, pp. 23–25)

This new form of linguistic colonialism, expressed in terms of expert discourse, produces and reproduces an attitude that Indians are incapable of managing their own linguistic affairs. These condescending statements in fact betray their knowledge (or lack thereof) of the historical-sociolinguistics of Indian multilingualism in general, and, more specifically, the role various Englishes play in different social, economic, and political marketplaces in India. In the context of the Phillipson and Skutnabb–Kangas quote, cited earlier, two fallacies related to their understanding of Indian multilingualism need to be examined, albeit briefly. They are as follows: (a) that the hegemony of English (as a language of wider communication) in India is the same as earlier Persian and Sanskrit hegemonies, and (b) that English bilingualism in India is subtractive and replacive.[9] I close this section by discussing these two fallacies.

First, let's discuss the fallacy of English hegemony. In the mid-19th century, English in India took over almost all the functions hitherto assigned to Persian and, before that, to Sanskrit. The use of Sanskrit, or the Deva Bhasha—language of the Gods—was tied to caste ideologies, accessible only to the high caste (elite) Brahmins, whereas others spoke Prakrit. That is, Sanskrit was permitted to be used exclusively by the high castes, confined in the hands of the Brahman, never to be used by the common masses. The written records, the plays of Kalidas and Magh, also show this robust diglossic use of Sanskrit with Prakrit: the kings and the nobles used Sanskrit, whereas women and the rest of the population used Prakrit. The use of Persian in administration during the Moghul period was, however, tied to class (elite) ideologies. In other words, Persian, like Sanskrit, had a restricted use—as the language of administration and court, and high culture. In sum, neither Sanskrit nor Persian ever served beyond the domain of elite discourse and its fellowships.

English, on the other hand, represented an ideology that emphasized the transformation of traditional caste and class elites into colonial elites. This ideological transformation—from Sanskrit and Persian to English— resulted dialectically in, on the one hand, a new social-class apartheid (cf. Ramanathan, 1999), its linguistic reproduction now ensured by the acquisition of Standard English, and, on the other hand, linguistic acts of resistance and transgression through its local uses, as discussed in Bhatt (2002a).

Additionally, we must consider the pragmatics of English language use, that is, English as a tool of verbal expression of native-indigenous histories, ideologies, cultures, and current practices. Vivekananda, the founder of Ramakrishna Mission, used English to "put the ancient truths of Vedanta in it, [and] broadcast them to the world ..." (quoted in Kachru, 2001, p. 12). Gokak (1964) puts this pragmatic function of English in globalizing local practices more forcefully:

> The English language has linked India with the world. It has conducted sparks of inspiration from the world outside to India and from India to the world. We are blessed with the two-way traffic that English has afforded us. We have paid a heavy price in the past for this privilege. But in our indignation over the price that has been paid, let us not throw away the privilege that is already ours. (p. 178)

---

[9]A subtractive orientation perceives the newly learnt second language as eliminating or replacing one's competence in the first language.

The creative writers in India use English "unselfconsciously," as Vikram Seth (1993) notes, because it "doesn't have any colonial associations for them [writers]. They use it as freely as their own language" (p. 20). This local ownership of global English—"as one of our own"—comes out clearly in Raja Rao's (1978) work:

> Truth, said a great Indian sage, is not a monopoly of the Sanskrit language. Truth can use any language, and the more universal, the better it is .... And as long as the English language is universal, it will always remain Indian ... we shall have the English language with us and amongst us, *and not as a guest or a friend, but as one of our own, of our caste, our creed, our sect and of our tradition.* (emphasis added, p. 421)

The symbolic power of English in India is captured even more faithfully in a conversation that takes place between a farmer and the character Mann in Vikram Seth's (1993) novel, *A Suitable Boy:*

> "Do you speak English?" he said after a while in the local dialect of Hindi.
>
> He had noticed Mann's luggage tag.
>
> "Yes," said Mann.
>
> "Without English you can't do anything," said the farmer sagely.
>
> Mann wondered what possible use English could be to the farmer.
>
> "What use is English?" said Mann.
>
> "People love English!" said the farmer with a strange sort of deep voiced giggle. "If you talk in English, you are a king. The more people you can mystify, the more people will respect you." He turned back to his tobacco. (p. 501)

Such widespread acceptance of the need of English is backed by the economic notion of English as capital:[10] the acquisition of English in anticipation of profits. Amy Waldman (2003) of the *New York Times* reports on a study by Forrester Research of Cambridge, MA, which estimated that outsourcing or offshoring "could send 3.3 million American jobs overseas by 2015. India, with its large pool of English-speakers and more than two million college graduates every year, is expected to get 70 percent of them" (p. x). She further reports that American companies are using Indian labor to do research and development, prepare tax returns, evaluate health insurance claims, transcribe doctors' medical notes, analyze financial data, dun for overdue bills, read CAT scans, create presentations for Manhattan investment banks,

---

[10]I am using the metaphor of language as capital from Bourdieu's (1977) model of linguistic exchanges as participating in a market relation. The panoply of terms relating to this model—that is, commodification, linguistic market, symbolic capital, and so forth—are used in the discussion that follows.

handle customer reservations for airlines, and much more. These factors show that the role of English in India is different from the past hegemonies of Sanskrit and Persian. Although some prestige varieties of English are still in the control of elite groups, English enjoys mass appeal and wider currency than the previously hegemonic languages in Indian history.

Let me turn now, very briefly, to the second fallacy—Is English bilingualism in India subtractive or replacive? I use mainly Kashmiri as a case study because Phillipson and Skutnabb–Kangas specifically mention that the cultural resources and heritage of Kashmiri (and countless other languages) are being lost. This example is quite opportune as I have been working on Kashmiri linguistics and sociolinguistics for quite some time (Bhatt, 1983, 1989, 1994, 1997, 1999).

My own work on sociolinguistics of Kashmiri in Kashmir (Bhatt [Mohan], 1983, 1989), and those of Koul and Schmidt (1983) and Kak (2001), show language shift of Kashmiri not to English, but to Urdu, the official language of the State of Jammu and Kashmir. Similar trends of language shift to local dominant languages are found in Pandharipande's (1992) study of language maintenance and shift among Marathi speakers to various local languages, Satyanath's (1982) study of language shift among Kannadigas in Delhi, and Mukherjee's (1980) study of language maintenance and language shift among Bengalis and Punjabis in Delhi (see also Srivastava, 1989).

A careful reading of Indian multilingualism reveals that the phenomenon of language shift to local-regional languages of wider communication (not English) is in fact more widespread in tribal minority languages. Singh (2001, p. 66) notes that "although the total tribal population of India is 7.8 percent, speakers of tribal languages are only 4 percent, suggesting a language shift among the minorities." Breton (1997, pp. 30–31) also argues that most tribes are involved in a general process of linguistic acculturation in favor of the regional language. The process of linguistic acculturation among minority language groups can be seen along a continuum, from those who have kept the tribal language as a second language and have adopted the regional language as their mother tongue to those who have become monolingual in the regional language (Breton, 1997; Ishtiaq, 1999). Abbi (1995) notes the following:

> It is a sad fact that the Kurux and Kharia languages are quickly disappearing from most of the urbanized area of the Ranchi district. This trend indicates that the urban tribals seldom consider it their privilege to speak their mother tongues. On the contrary, ignorance of the tribal languages is regarded as an enhancement of status and prestige. In speaking Hindi they feel superior in comparison to other fellow-tribals who cannot speak it. (p. 177)

The overwhelming evidence of language shift among minority language groups notwithstanding, it must be emphasized that several minority ethno-linguistic groups such as Khasis, Nagas, Santals, and Khonds show fierce language loyalty. In some cases, their language loyalties have found political expression as language movements (Ekka, 1979; Mahapatra, 1979). What we learn from this short discussion of Indian multilingualism is that language maintenance, language shift, and language acculturation are all actively negotiated by the local people to suit their interests. This is characteristic of the dynamic of language contact. Furthermore, it suggests that the view of the new didacts that English is the culprit of all sociolinguistic evil in India is a simplistic and clearly flawed view of the history and current practices of language use in India.[11]

So far, in this section, I have exposed the flaws in the thinking of expert discourses in their various manifestations through history—from the blatantly coercive discourses of colonialism to subtler present-day discourses of condescension. It is important to understand their limitations if we are to construct more egalitarian discourses that acknowledge the validity of local Englishes. I now move on to provide examples of local appropriations of English to illustrate the creativity and vitality of the local linguistic life— which I have only alluded to in this section. It is important to understand the evolving norms and practices of local linguistic usage to construct more democratic discourses in our profession.

## GLOBALITY, LOCALITY, AND HYBRIDITY

A particular form of the colonization-appropriation dialectic in contemporary times is the struggle between globally dominant forms of (linguistic, cultural) practices and those that have only local currency. The discourse of globalization tends to underrepresent the power of the local to appropriate dominant codes and discourses. The dominant ideology misrepresents a bid for global hegemony as a benign, indeed altruistic, attempt toward linguistic empowerment for local communities (see Honey, 1997; Quirk, 1996; for examples of such discourse). Phillipson (1992, 1998), in a series of articles, has successfully argued that English is imposed in postcolonial contexts by agencies of linguistic coercion, such as the British Council (and the TESOL organization). He further argues that the imposition of Standard English has a clear ideological function: to exert the domination of those groups which have both the means of imposing Standard English as "legitimate" and a monopoly on the means of appropriating it. This linguistic imperialism thus results in hegemonic value judgments, material and

---

[11]Notwithstanding the experts' comments, it is worthwhile pointing out that Nehru, the first prime minister of India, discussing the language problem in India (1963), wrote that the contact of English with regional languages had enriched them, in developing new forms of expression.

symbolic investments, and ideologies that represent the interests only of those in power.[12]

Phillipson's argument, however, misses a sociolinguistically significant fact: that the globalization and commodification of English has produced alterations in linguistic markets yielding homegrown, nativized varieties of English that have transformed the hierarchy of power into a network of alliances. The new Englishes now compete with standard Englishes (British and American) for profit sharing in domestic, regional, and international linguistic markets (Bhatt, 2001a, 2001b). The socioeconomic stability of these varieties threatens the hegemony and monopoly of Standard English. The contested space of English linguistic markets invites divergent discourses of dominance and resistance, especially in the postcolonial contexts of English language learning, teaching, and use. The most comprehensive statement of the acts of resistance to linguistic imperialism in English teaching is found in Canagarajah (1999). Although such acts of resistance and appropriation have been going on from colonial times, it is recently that postcolonial scholars have begun describing and theorizing them to contest the biased expert discourses.

The legacy of English linguistic imperialism, I argue, has given birth to a hybrid sociolinguistic reality in postcolonial contexts (Bhatt, 2001b). The colonial idiom gets recontextualized, giving rise to a new, local articulation of the former. This hybridity invites what Ashcroft (1989) calls the following:

> "devices of otherness," the devices which appear specifically utilized to establish the difference and uniqueness of the postcolonial text.... [S]uch devices include syntactic fusion, in which English prose is structured according to the syntactic principles of a first language; neologisms (new lexical forms in English which are informed by the semantic and morphological exigencies of a mother tongue); the direct inclusion of untranslated lexical items in the text; ethno-rhythmic prose which constructs an English discourse according to the rhythm and texture of a first language; and the transcription of dialect and language variants of many different kinds, whether they come from diglossic, polydialectical or monolingual communities. (p. 72)

The power of English, through its hybridity, draws on both global and local resources, allowing language consumers to glide effortlessly among local, national, and international identities. The hybridity manifests itself through a complex of language behaviors that produce and reproduce identity "positionings" (a la Davies and Harré, 1990) that link the global—that is, the transnational English culture—to the local—that is, the urban-

---

[12]The ideologies of colonialism and imperialism have, to some extent, fostered hierarchical perceptions of linguistic merit of postcolonial Englishes that reflect the hegemonic structure of colonial expansion and administration.

ized vernacular Indian English culture. This hybridity—and its linguistic, sociolinguistic, and literary expressions—negates the Standard English ideology which implies that clarity, logic, and loyalty depend on the adoption of a monoglot standard variety in public discourse (Bhatt, 2002a; Labov, 1972; Lippi-Green, 1997; Silverstein, 1996). Indian Englishes, I argue later, allow their consumers to (re)position themselves with regard to new community-practices of speaking and writing, creating counterdiscourses to the ideology of a monoglot standard. There are at least three dimensions of hybridity along which global and local identities are negotiated: hybridity in linguistic forms, hybridity in sociolinguistic forms, and hybridity in literary forms.

## Hybridity in Linguistic Forms

In multilingual, polyglossic sociolinguistic contexts of language use in India, hybridity in linguistic form is inevitable, as demonstrated most notably in seminal studies of Emeneau (1956), Masica (1976), and Gumperz and Wilson (1971). With respect to English in India, the linguistic convergence of its form and functions gives rise to possibilities for new meanings and, at the same time, presents a mechanism to negotiate and navigate between a global identity and local practices. The most striking illustration of the tension, and its resolution, between the global and the local is the use of tag questions in Indian Englishes where clearly English language use seems constrained by the grammar of local culture (cf. Bright, 1968; D'souza, 1988; Hymes, 1974).

In Standard Indian English (SIE), which is the variety of English in India that is closest in its form to Standard British and American English, tag questions are formed by a rule that inserts a pronominal copy of the subject after an appropriate modal auxiliary. A typical example is given in (1).

> (1) John said he'll work today, didn't he?

Tags have also been analyzed as expressing certain attitudes of the speaker toward what is being said in the main clause; and in terms of speech acts or performatives. Functionally, tags in English behave like epistemic adverbials, such as *probably, presumably*, and so forth, as shown in (2).

> (2a) It's still dark outside, isn't it?

> (2b) It's probably dark outside.

Undifferentiated tag questions, such as in (3a) and (3b), serve as one of the paradigm linguistic exponents of the Indianization of English, the Vernacular Indian English (VIE; cf. Bhatt, 2000, for the syntactic behavior of VIE).

> (3a) You are going home soon, isn't it?

(3b)  You have taken my book, isn't it?

The undifferentiated tags play an important pragmatic role in the Indian English speech community. In most cases, the meaning of the tag is not the one appended to the meaning of the main proposition; it is usually the tag that signals important social meaning (Bhatt, 1995). In fact, tags in VIE are a fascinating example of how linguistic form (e.g., of the tag) is constrained by cultural constraints of politeness. The undifferentiated tags in VIE are linguistic devices governed by the politeness principle of nonimposition: they serve positive politeness functions (a la Brown & Levinson, 1987), signaling deference and acquiescence. Notice, for example, the contrast in tag expressions between VIE in (4) and Standard Indian, British, and American English in (5).

Unassertive and mitigated: (VIE):

(4a)  You said you'll do the job, isn't it ?
(4b)  They said they will be here, isn't it ?

Assertive and intensified: (SIE)

(5a)  You said you'll do the job, didn't you?
(5b)  They said they will be here, didn't they?

In contrast to the canonical tag expressions in (5), speakers of Indian Englishes find the undifferentiated tag expressions in (4) as nonimpositional and mitigating, as argued by Bhatt (1995). This claim is more clearly established when an adverb of intensification and assertion is used in conjunction with the undifferentiated tag; the result is, predictably, unacceptable (shown as starred sentences, following) to the speakers of Indian Englishes:

(4a)  *Of course you said you'll do the job, isn't it?
(4b)  *Of course they said they'll be here, isn't it?

In a culture where the verbal behavior is severely constrained, to a large extent, by politeness regulations, where nonimposition is the essence of polite behavior, it is not surprising that VIE has replaced SIE tags with undifferentiated tags. To provide an explanatory account of why Indian Englishes have chosen to add the use of undifferentiated strategy in their repertoire of linguistic constructions, we may adopt the notion of *grammar of culture* (Bright, 1968; D'souza, 1988). Global grammatical norms are modified by local cultural conditions, engendering alternate systems of usage.

Undifferentiated tags are not exclusive instances in the grammar of Indian Englishes where one finds the linguistic form constrained by the grammar of culture. The influence of the grammar of culture on linguistic expressions of Indian Englishes can be seen elsewhere in the use of modal auxiliary *may*. *May* in VIE is used to express obligation politely; see data in (6), which contrasts systematically with Standard British English (7; data taken from Trudgill & Hannah, 1985, p. 109):

(6) Vernacular Indian English:
   (a) This furniture may be removed tomorrow.
   (b) These mistakes may please be corrected.

(7) Standard Indian (British) English:
   (a) This furniture is to be removed tomorrow.
   (b) These mistakes should be corrected.

In sum, the linguistic form of localization appears in the choices offered by the grammar of English language variation in India. The alternation between the undifferentiated tag question (*isn't it*) and the canonical tag question can be explained following the logic of Brown and Levinson's politeness theory (1987): the choice of undifferentiated tag questions is governed by the positive politeness regulations of the culture, expressing solidarity and acquiescence, whereas the choice of the canonical tag, the contextually formal variant of the undifferentiated tag, is governed by the negative politeness regulations of the culture, expressing power. In all informal, intimate, and solidarity domains of English language use in India, the use of undifferentiated tag is the optimal, grammatical choice, based on the cultural grammar of politeness.

**Hybridity in Sociolinguistic Forms**

One key aspect of globalization, according to Chouliaraki and Fairclough (1999), is the unsettling of the boundaries between different domains of social use of language, resulting in a discoursal hybridity—intermixing of discourses and genres. In terms of language use, the distinctive hybridizations emerging from intermixing—code-switching and code-mixing—of English with indigenous languages of India permits cultural articulations of the mutual embeddedness of the local and the global (cf. Dissanayake, 1997, p. 136). The hybridization, accomplished via code-switching and mixing, is able to successfully decolonize and democratize English language use, disrupting colonial claims to its cultural-linguistic authenticity. A new, hybrid code thus develops offering multilingual experiences of cultural difference as well as a sense of the entanglement of different cultural traditions. The most impressive evidence of this linguistic hybridity is presented in (8; taken from *Times of India*, 2001/October 12):

(8) There have been several analyses of this phenomenon. First, there is the "religious angle" which is to do with Indian society. In India

> a man feels guilty when fantasizing about another man's wife, unlike in the west. The *saat pheras* [= seven rounds] around the *agni* [= fire] serves as a *lakshman rekha* [= Lakshman line][13]

The bilingual mode of this news-feature presentation, leaving the Hindi idiom untranslated, is in fact not uncommon in major English newspapers in India. There is nothing in the context to suggest to a monolingual reader the general sense of the Hindi expressions. The Hindi items in (8) are rooted in the most important historical narratives (Vedas) and the great Hindu epic (the *Ramayana*) of India, and a full appreciation of the text therefore demands knowledge of the Sanskrit Vedic traditions and cultural-historical literacy of the indigenous peoples. The switch to Hindi in (8) realizes a significant sociolinguistic function: these words serve as vehicles of cultural memory, insofar as their significations are concerned. The untranslated code-switched data in (9) serves the same function: recalling within the global, the local-cultural practices of the past; that is, the cultural memory.

> (9) Perhaps, the rulers in Ahmedabad could take a lesson in *raj dharma* (= duty of the sovereign, State-craft) from Buriya, says Princess Singh (2002, p. 1).

The bilingual code-switched mode in (8) and (9) serves several other functions as well: (a) it authentically expresses the socio-historical experiences of the English bilingual population, (b) it captures the cultural-semantics of the utterance, and (c) it reflects the hybrid, bicultural nature of identity of the speakers. In the latter case, the medium becomes the message.

In (10), the switch to Hindi is significant only in its historical-cultural interpretations. In the premodern, and even modern-rural, India, the traditional schools, *paThshalas*, were not made of bricks and cement, but were rather structurally unstable dwellings. Multistoried contemporary structures for schools are a relatively recent and mostly urban phenomenon.

---

[13]The contextually appropriate translations of the code-switched items are as follows: (a) *saat pheraas*—The term refers to the ritual in which the bride and the groom walk around the fire together, pledging commitment to each other for seven births; *agni*—the sacred fire in the wedding ritual. Fire is believed to be the messenger (or priest) who operates on behalf of the people who perform the sacrificial ritual. Agni takes the prayers of the people to gods in the heaven, and brings back their blessings to the people; and *lakshmana rekha*—This refers to the line of protection drawn by Lakshmana (in the epic Ramayana) around Sita's hut to protect her from dangers of the external world. Maricha, the demon (in the form of the deer), disguised his voice as Rama's, and called for Lakshmana's help. This was a trick to lure Lakshmana away from Sita and give an opportunity to Ravana to approach Sita who would be left unprotected. Lakshmana, however, draws a line around the hut and tells Sita not to cross it lest she will encounter a danger. Thus the term *Lakshmana rekha* (literally, a line) has become a symbol of protection, and transgressing it has acquired the meaning of allowing undesirable results to occur.

(10) "Bhagavatula Charitable Trust (BCT) started integrated rural development in 40 contiguous villages ... A project has been launched for the construction of 100 schools with pucca [= solid] buildings." (*Vasant Bahaar*, 2002).

The next three pieces of evidence (11–13) show that code-switching between English and Hindi foregrounds the contrast between cultures and ideologies; specifically, the appearance of Hindi enables representation of the local-indigenous social and cultural practices in a global idiom. Significantly, English translations are missing from all these examples (and many more in the data I have collected). The only evidence of code-switching in such cases is that the switched items in each of these instances are italicized. In (11), the switch to *sambandhi* indicates a special place of the in-laws in the hierarchy of kinship relations in India. In (12), the semantics of *layak bahu* is socioculturally grounded, its explication offered in the relative clause that follows the noun *bahu*. The switching to Hindi in (13) serves to highlight a particular ritual-cultural practice that cannot be adequately translated into English without engendering cultural-semantic distortions.

(11) "But on the first evening my *sambandhi* [= relative, in-law], who lives in the US arrived and I had to keep him company" (Das, 2002).

(12) "What's more we should respect her [Sonia Gandhi] for being a *layak* [= competent] Indian *bahu* [= daughter-in-law] who stayed on to do her duty by her husband's family, she reared her children and instilled in them the best Indian values, she took care of her mother-in-law and husband's legacy—the Congress" (*Times of India*, Support for Sonia, 2002).

(13) "The young women—always overdressed—will typically say, '*Mummyjee, aap rahne deejeye, Chai mein bana ke laungi, mujhe apne kartavyon ka ehsas hai.*' [= Mom, you leave it (do not worry). I will make (and bring) tea. I am aware of my responsibilities]" (Support for Sonia, 2002).

Finally, (14) (from Bhatia, 1989) shows that the choice of the Hindi pronoun intensifies the expressive force of the message. The use of *woh* ("her"—i.e., the other woman) expresses strong negative meaning (social-moral indignation)—reflecting contextual appropriateness. A non-code-switched form would not enable a meaning that has its proper codification in the cultural context of use. Code-switching thus expands the possibilities of bilinguals' creativity (Kachru, 1987).

(14) She fell in love with him and played the *woh* (3rd, singular) in the love triangle.

In sum, code-switching between English and Hindi yields a hybridity that makes the semantic possibilities more flexible, the movement between global and local identities more manageable, and the goal of decolonization and democratization of English more feasible. We find recognition and acceptance of this linguistic hybridity in local, popular print-news media. Gurcharan Das (2001), for instance, opines about it in the following manner:

> We are more comfortable and accepting of English today, I think, partly because we are more relaxed and confident. Our minds have become decolonised and "Hinglish" increasingly pervades our lives. For a hundred years the upper middle classes have mixed English words in their everyday talk, but the present media argot is the creature of the new satellite and cable channels. Zee, Sony and Star, supported by their advertisers, have created this uninhibited hybrid of Hindi and English. Avidly embraced by the newly-emerging middle classes, this new popular idiom of the bazaar is rushing down the socio-economic ladder. (Das, 2001)

## Hybridity in Literary Forms

The most visible expressions of hybridity (for those outside India) appear in literary forms, especially in the works of postcolonial writers. The Indian English writers face the following paradox: how does one use an impersonal global medium to represent local and native messages? Their narratives are usually situated in local geographies requiring a linguistic fusion of the alien and the native. This fusion is made possible by subtle inversions of Standard English syntax, code-switching using liberal sprinkling of native terms and expressions, and linguistic and cultural transcreations, all reflecting the complex multilinguistic realities of India. For most of these writers, English is their second or third language and, therefore, it is not uncommon to find a consistent representation in English of an Indian language. Salman Rushdie's literary works are a case in point: they stand out as a linguistic representation of a decolonized imagination. His style resists the homogenization of English language, culture, and practices through its Indianization.

Rushdie resolves the paradox of using the English linguistic medium to represent the indigenous culture by the use of two different strategies: (a) recruiting Indian varieties of English—Bombay English in *Midnight's Children*, Babu English in *The Satanic Verses*, and Cochin English in *The Moor's Last Sigh* (cf. Goonetilleke 1998)—to present indigenous voices; and (2) code-switching (generally unitalicized), using quaint Hindustani expressions of colonial era "as textual reminders of the colonial past and to portray aspects of contemporary Indian life which have continued after the colonial era subsided" (Langeland, 1996, p. 17). The resulting hybridity derides English by flouting its lexico-semantic constraints, and by overwhelming it with a linguistic plurality. The linguistic strategies employed by Rushdie to subvert and to corrupt the purity of English can be categorized in terms of four types of transfer effects (from native language). The first type, see (15) to (18), is the idiomatic transfer characterized by the appearance of certain proverbs and speech functions of the native language in the use of English. The data in (15) show evidence of the nativization of speech functions such as abuses, curses, and so forth. Further, the duplication of items, a pervasive linguistic phenomenon characteristic of Indian languages, results in the intensification of meaning of the item. In (16), the idiomatic transfer from Hindi as in *puffing up with pride* does not carry negative, but rather, positive connotation. In (17), *chamcha*, which refers to a toady, is not translated. Such untranslated words, according to Ashcroft, Griffiths, and Tiffin (1989), "do have an important function in inscribing difference. They signify a certain cultural experience, which they cannot hope to reproduce but whose difference is validated by the new situation. In this sense they are directly metonymic of that cultural difference which is imputed by the linguistic variation" (p. 53).

Idiomatic transfer:

(15) "Go, go, eat air" (SV, p. 312)[11]

(16) "Now there will be pats on the back, sweetmeats, public announcements, may be more photographs; now their chests will puff up with pride" (MC, p. 194).

(17) " 'Bhai, wow. I'm tickled, truly. Tickled pink. So if you are an English *chamcha* these days, let it be. Mr. Sally Spoon. It will be our little joke' " (SV, p. 83).

The second type of transfer is the pragmatic transfer, as shown in (18) and (19). In this type, the semantic formulae characteristic of the speech acts in the native tongue are transferred in the performance of analogous speech acts in English. The data in (18), using nativized syntax and lexical expression ("baba"), show appreciation, whereas the use of the discourse particle "na" in (19) shows intimacy, solidarity, and rapport, forbidden in formal contexts of use.

Pragmatic transfer:

(18) " 'My God, Vallabbhai,' he managed, and embraced the old man. The servant smiled a difficult smile. 'I *grow* so old, *baba, I was thinking* you would not recognize'" (SV, p. 65; emphasis added).

---

[11]The following abbreviations are used in the citation of data from literary texts: MC = *Midnight's Children;* SV = *Satanic Verses.*

(19) "Mishal saw her mother fumbling feebly with a molten lipstick and asked, 'What's bugging you, ma? Relax, *na'* " (SV, p. 486).

The third type of transfer is the syntactic transfer, exemplified in data (20) to (23). The example in (20) exhibits the typical reduplication pattern of Indian languages—that is, "Coke-shoke"—the function of which is to intensify or explicate the meaning. A similar reduplication process appears in (21), albeit with a slight difference: the Hindi switch is accompanied by translative elucidation in English. The data in (22) and (23), on the other hand, show syntactic transfer from Hindi, evidenced by the absence of auxiliary inversion and the absence of the preposition (cf. Bhatt, 2000). Note that in addition to the use of IVE syntax in (23), Grace Kelly is cleverly hybridized with the Hindu goddess Kali (Langeland, 1996, p. 20), creating a lexico-cultural pun and ambiguity.

Syntactic transfer:

(20) "Go and drink your Coke-shoke in your AC vehicle and leave us yatris in peace" (SV, p. 478).

(21) "O God, Saleem, all this tamasha, all this performance, for one of your stupid cracks?" (MC, p. 194).

(22) " 'And where your family members are?' " (SV, p. 185).

(23) " 'What you waiting? Some Goddess from heaven? Greta Garbo, Gracekali, who?' " (SV, p. 25).

Finally, the fourth type of transfer is the attitudinal transfer, as evidenced by the presence of the discourse particle "huh" in (24). The discourse particle "huh" identifies this use with American English, and the local attitude towards it is expounded in the sentence following "huh."

Attitudinal transfer:

(24) " 'I suppose,' she addressed her glass, sitting at the old pine table in the spacious kitchen, 'that what I did was unforgivable, huh?' That little Americanizing *huh* was new: another of her infinite series of blows against her breeding?" (SV, p. 403).

To sum up the discussion so far, hybridity in literary forms validates the local cultural voices in a global norm. The cross-fertilization of English with local indigenous languages thus presents the possibility of choice, plurality, and bilingual creativity. The tension between an "abrogation" of the English language and an "appropriation" of it is resolved in favor of the latter. The ownership of English is secured, as Rushdie does, by intermittently code-switching to Hindi, effecting transient abrogations. Indian English literatures have come of age, as Naik (1992) points out, with their own identities, an amalgam of the East and the West:

In fact, the course of Indian English literature is an absorbing record of the steady march of the Indian writer in English from sheer psittacism to authentic literary expression. Far from remaining merely "bastard bantlings of the British," Indian English writers, struggling valiantly against prejudice, neglect and ridicule, have, at their best, proved themselves to be proud heirs to the two equally rich worlds of the East and the West. (Naik, 1992, p. 290)

## CONCLUSIONS

English remains varied and wonderful, notes Green (1998), and concludes, quoting Anthony Burgess, that English is as follows:

[A] whole language, complete with the colloquialisms of Calcutta and London, Shakespearian archaisms, bazaar whinings, references to the Hindu pantheon, the jargon of Indian litigation and shrill Babu irritability all together. It's not pure English, but ... the language of Shakespeare, Joyce and Kipling—gloriously impure. (p. 111)

It is, as I have argued in this chapter, the "gloriously impure" local Englishes that present the possibility of understanding the limitations of our disciplinary discourse that has so far produced incomplete, and oftentimes misleading, understandings of the phenomena of the spread, functions, and acquisition of Englishes worldwide. To capture the complexity of linguistic hybridities associated with plural identities, as discussed earlier, our disciplinary discourses of the global use and acquisition of English must bring into focus local forms shaped by the local logics of practice. This shift in the disciplinary focus has larger theoretical aims: on the one hand to enable a more nuanced analysis of the globalization and localization dialectic and, on the other, to invert the tyrannical imposition of the universal (cf. Lyotard, 1984). With this shift, we begin to see how local communities have been appropriating global norms, adopting various strategies (such as the linguistic, sociolinguistic, and literary hybridization analyzed earlier), even as the global produces progressively subtler discourses to control the local.

This process of inversion requires, in the context of the observations of hybridity in Indian Englishes, a reevaluation of disciplinary discourses of standard language, native speakers, and intelligibility. In this chapter, I have attempted to expose the different ideological mechanisms through which such disciplinary constructs are produced and imposed as "received wisdom." The evidence of hybridity—linguistic, sociolinguistic, and literary—confronts the limited and entrenched knowledge these constructs offer and demands that they be replaced with a knowledge that is faithful to linguistic difference and to the global realities in which the difference obtains. The evidence presents the urgency with which we need to redefine the disciplinary discourses of abstract and theoretical dichotomies (language–interlanguage, standard–nonstandard, native–nonnative, target–fossilized) to validate and incorporate the local hybridities. As we move toward reconfiguring our disciplinary discourses, we have to consider the following:

- "Standard language" has to be treated as endonormatively evolving from within each community according to its own histories and cultures of usage. Standards can't be imposed exonormatively from outside one community.
- Appropriated forms of local English are not transitory and incomplete "interlanguages." If they manifest a stable system over time with a rule-governed usage in the local community, such varieties have to be treated as legitimate languages. Similarly, "fossilization" should be used (if at all) for individual manifestations or idiolects of speakers who are new to a language. It shouldn't be used to label sociolects, which display collectively accepted stable norms of usage in a community.
- We have to abandon the use of the label "non-native speaker" for multilingual subjects from postcolonial contexts. In the case of communities which have appropriated English and localized its usage, the members should be treated as "native speakers." We have to explore new terms to classify speakers based purely on relative levels of proficiency, without employing markers of ethnicity, nationality, or race, and overtones of ownership over the language.
- We have to encourage a mutual negotiation of dialectal differences by communities in interpersonal linguistic communication, without judging intelligibility purely according to "native" speaker norms. Both parties in a communicative situation have to adopt strategies of speech accommodation and negotiation to achieve intelligibility.

Let me conclude by presenting some theoretical speculations on the design of a socially-realistic linguistic model of description that does justice to local appropriations of English. First and foremost, the model should embrace Ferguson's (1978) insight on multilingualism as an object of linguistic description. This shift will lead us to conceive of a Bilingual Grammar. Such a grammar, for example, will take the syntactic differences between Indian Vernacular English and Indian Standard English, as discussed in (1) to (5), and code them in terms of their functional properties, that is, their diglossic distribution along the dimensions of Power and Solidarity. The model would capture the relations between languages in contact, embedding speaker awareness of issues such as diglossia, linguistic ideology, ethnolinguistic sensitivity, and sociolinguistic power differentials in the grammatical system. Using insights from Politeness, Accommodation, and Identity theories, the model would specify the relations between interactive participants, that is, what interactants do to or for each other through language use.

Furthermore, the model would use the notion of competing grammars, such that any linguistic output—that is, an utterance—is interpreted as a reflex of "optimization" among the competing linguistic options in a particular context of use. Optimization, in the sense of Elster (1986) and Coleman and Fararo (1992), is a mechanism that requires that sociolinguistic costs and benefits of all linguistic choices be specified, and then postulates that the speaker would pick the linguistic option that maximizes the difference between costs and benefits. The best, optimal, candidate—that is, the linguistic utterance produced—will, generally, reflect social accreditation. An illustration of it will help situate the notion. Consider the following instance of English language use (an instance of code-switching or style-shifting) reported by Mesthrie (1992): A young South African Indian English-speaking attendant at the security section of the airport asked him, "You haven' got anything to declare?" There are, surprisingly, several "nonstandard" English features in this use: namely, the lack of (subject-auxiliary verb) inversion, the lack of the application of the English rule of *do*-support, the use of contracted negated auxiliary *have*, and the use of *got* as an auxiliary. In a formal context, such a use of English may appear unacceptable, unless we assume that the use of this variety of English in the context is rational, meaningful, and socially appropriate. A socially-realistic linguistic grammar, as outlined earlier, would provide an explanation of this linguistic behavior. Given the competing choices of English variants available to the South African Indian security guard— from basilect and mesolect to acrolect, along the continuum of relatively more standardized variants of a language (in ascending order)—he chose to use the mesolectal variety with Rajend Mesthrie, himself a South African Indian. He does this to defuse the syntax of acrolectal power—"Do you have anything to declare?"—in favor of mesolectal solidarity—"You haven' got anything to declare?"—(Mesthrie, 1992, p. 219). This is an expression of a bilingual's creativity and requires a different paradigm of explanation such as that described earlier (cf. Kachru, 1987).

The beginnings of such a socially-realistic linguistic framework will find a place in a model of ELT that is based on the assumptions of plurality and multiple standards (à la Canagarajah, 1999; Quirk, 1985). The guiding slogan for ELT should be as follows: local standards for local contexts. The norms for learning and teaching in such a plural model must be endonormative, as argued in Kachru (1986, 1995, 1997), so that the learning content is in communicative and sociolinguistic harmony with the new contexts of use. This pedagogical shift carries the empirical advantage of making the "available" Englishes "accessible" to the potential consumers, enabling expressions of local identities in the use of these norms. The creative use of language variation, representing plural identities, must find a space in the local pedagogical practices, in the English teaching curriculum generally, and more specifically in the construction of instructional materials.

Such a redefinition of disciplinary discourses, incorporating local linguistic practices within the framework of its conceptualization, promises an analytical perspective that is sociolinguistically responsible, empirically relevant, and intellectually honest.

# REFERENCES

Abbi, A. (1995). Small languages and small language communities. *International Journal of the Sociology of Language*, *116*, 175–185.

Agnihotri, R., & Khanna, A. L. (Eds.). (1995). *English language teaching in India*. New Delhi, India: Sage.

Ashcroft, B. (1989). Constitutive graphonomy: A post-colonial theory of literary writing. *Kunapipi*, *11*, 58–73.

Ashcroft, B., Griffiths, G., & Tiffin, H. (1989). *The empire writes back: Theory and practice in post-colonial literatures*. London: Routledge.

Baumgardner, R. (Ed.). (1996). *South Asian English: Structure, use, and users*. Urbana: University of Illinois Press.

Bereiter, C., Engelman, S., Osborn, J., & Reidford, P. (1966). An academically oriented pre-school program for culturally deprived children. In F. Hechinger (Ed.), *Pre-school education today* (pp. 105–137). New York: Doubleday.

Bhatia, T. (1989). Bilingual's creativity and syntactic theory: Evidence for emerging grammar. *World Englishes*, *8*, 265–276.

Bhatt [Mohan], R. (1983). *Language maintenance and language shift: The case of Kashmiri in Kashmir setting*. Unpublished master's thesis, University of Delhi, Delhi, India.

Bhatt [Mohan], R. (1989). Language planning and language conflict: The case of Kashmiri. *International Journal of the Sociology of Language*, *75*, 73–85.

Bhatt, R. M. (1994). *Word order and case in Kashmiri*. Unpublished doctoral dissertation, University of Illinois, Urbana.

Bhatt, R. M. (1995). Prescriptivism, creativity, and world Englishes. *World Englishes*, *14*, 247–260.

Bhatt, R. M. (1997). Constraints, code-switching and optimal grammars. *Lingua*, *102*, 123–151.

Bhatt, R. M. (1999). *Verb movement and the syntax of Kashmiri*. Dordrecht, The Netherlands: Kluwer.

Bhatt, R. M. (2000). Optimal expressions in Indian English. *English Language and Linguistics*, *4*, 69–95.

Bhatt, R. M. (2001a). World Englishes. *Annual Review of Anthropology*, *30*, 227–250.

Bhatt, R. M. (2001b). Language economy, standardization, and world Englishes. In E. Thumboo (Ed.), *The three circles of English* (pp. 401–422). Singapore: UniPress.

Bhatt, R. M. (2002a). Experts, dialects, and discourse. *International Journal of Applied Linguistics*, *12*(1), 74–109.

Bhatt, R. M. (2002b). Review of Suresh Canagarajah's resisting linguistic imperialism in English teaching. *Language in Society*, *31*, 631–634.

Bourdieu, P. (1977). The economics of linguistic exchanges. *Social Science Information* *16*, 645–668.

Breton, R. J.-L. (1997). *Atlas of the languages and ethnic communities of South Asia*. New Delhi, India: Sage.

Bright, W. (1968). Toward a cultural grammar. *Indian Linguistics*, *29*, 20–29.

Brown, P., & Levinson, S. (1987). *Politeness: Some universals in language*. Cambridge, England: Cambridge University Press.

Canagarajah, A. S. (1999). *Resisting linguistic imperialism in English teaching*. Oxford, England: Oxford University Press.

Chomsky, N. (1986). *Knowledge of language*. New York: Praeger.

Chouliaraki, L., & Fairclough, N. (1999). *Discourse in late modernity: Rethinking critical discourse analysis*. Edinburgh, Scotland: Edinburgh University Press.

Coleman, J., & Fararo, T. (Eds.). (1992). *Rational choice theory: Advocacy and critique*. Manoa, HI: Sage.

Cook, V. (1999). Going beyond the native speaker in language teaching. *TESOL Quarterly, 33*, 185–209.

Crystal, D. (1997). *English as a global language*. Cambridge, England: Cambridge University Press.

Das, G. (2001, November 18). Inescapably English. *Times of India*, p. 14.

Das, M. (2002, April 26). Surrender your anger to the divine. *Times of India*, p. 12.

Davies, A. (1989). Is international English an interlanguage? *TESOL Quarterly, 23*, 447–467.

Davies, A. (1991). *The native speaker in applied linguistics*. Edinburgh, Scotland: Edinburgh University Press.

Davies, A. (2001). Review of T. Bex & R. Watts (Eds.), Standard English: The widening debate. *Applied Linguistics, 22*, 273–281.

Davies, B., & Harré, R. (1990). Positioning: The discursive production of selves. *Journal for the Theory of Social Behavior, 20*, 40–63.

De Certeau, M., Julia, D., & Revel, J. (1975). *Une politique de la langu. La révolution Française et les Patois*. Paris: Gallimard.

Dissanayake, W. (1997). Cultural studies and world Englishes: Some topics for further exploration. In L. Smith & M. Forman (Eds.), *World Englishes 2000* (pp. 145–159). Honolulu: University of Hawaii Press.

D'souza, J. (1988). Interactional strategies in South Asian languages: Their implications for teaching English internationally. *World Englishes, 7*, 159–71

Ekka, F. (1979). Language loyalty and maintenance among Kuruxs. In E. Annamalai (Ed.), *Language movements in India* (pp. 99–105). Mysore, India: CIIL Publications.

Elster, J. (Ed.). (1986). *Rational choice*. New York: New York University Press.

Emeneau, M. (1956). India as a linguistic area. *Language, 32*, 3–16.

Ferguson, C. (1978). Multilingualism as object of linguistic description. *Studies in the Linguistic Sciences, 8*, 97–105.

Foucault, M. (1972). *The archaeology of knowledge and the discourse on language*. (A. M. Sheridan Smith, Trans.). New York: Pantheon.

Foucault, M. (1980). *Power/knowledge: Selected interviews and other writings 1972–1977*. (C. Gordon, Ed.; C. Gordon, L. Marshall, J. Mepham, & K. Soper, Trans.). New York: Pantheon.

Giroux, H. (1981). *Ideology, culture, and the process of schooling*. Philadelphia: Temple University Press.

Gokak, V. (1964). *English in India: Its present and future*. Bombay, India: Asia Publishing House.

Goonetilleke , D. C. R. A. (1998). *Modern novelists: Salman Rushdie*. New York: St. Martin's Press.

Green, J. (1998). English in India—The grandmother tongue. *Critical Quarterly, 40*, 107–111.

Gumperz, J., & Wilson, R. (1971). Convergence and creolization: A case from Indo-Aryan/Dravidian border in India. In D. Hymes (Ed.), *Pidginization and Creolization of languages* (pp. 151–167). London: Cambridge University Press.

Honey, J. (1983). *The language trap: Race, class and 'Standard English' in British schools.* Kenton, Middlesex, England: National Centre for Educational Standards.

Honey, J. (1997). *Language is power.* London: Faber & Faber.

Hosali, P., & Aitchison, J. (1986). Butler English: A minimal pidgin? *Journal of Pidgin and Creole Languages, 1,* 51–79.

Hymes, D. (1974). *Foundations of sociolinguistics: An ethnographic approach.* Philadelphia: University of Pennsylvania Press.

Ishtiaq, M. (1999). *Language shifts among the scheduled tribes in India: A geographic study.* Delhi, India: Motilal Banarasidass.

Johnson, H. (1992). Defossilizing. *ELT Journal, 46,* 180–189.

Kachru, B. (Ed.). (1982). *The other tongue: English across cultures.* Urbana: University of Illinois Press.

Kachru, B. (1983). *The Indianization of English: The English language in India.* Delhi, India: Oxford University Press.

Kachru, B. (1986). *The alchemy of English: The spread, functions and models of non-native Englishes.* London: Pergamon.

Kachru, B. (1987). The bilingual's creativity: Discoursal and stylistic strategies in contact literature. In L. Smith (Ed.), *Discourse across cultures: Strategies in world Englishes* (pp. 125–140). Englewood Cliffs, NJ: Prentice Hall.

Kachru, B. (1995). Teaching world Englishes without myths. In S. K. Gill et al. (Eds.), *Intelec'94: International English Language Education Conference, National and International Challenges and Resources* (pp. 1–19). Bangi, Malaysia: Pusat Bahasa Universiti Kebangsaan Malaysia.

Kachru, B. (1997). World Englishes and English-using communities. *Annual Review of Applied Linguistics, 17,* 66–87.

Kachru, B. (2001). *On nativizing mantra: Identity construction in Anglophone Englishes.* Unpublished manuscript, University of Illinois, Urbana.

Kak, A. A. (2001). Language maintenance and language shift in Srinagar. Unpublished doctoral dissertation, University of Delhi, Delhi, India.

Koul, O., & Schmidt, R. L. (1983). *Kashmiri: A sociolinguistic study.* Patiala, India: Indian Institute of Language Studies.

Kramsch, C., & Sullivan, P. (1996). Appropriate pedagogy. *ELT Journal, 50,* 199–212.

Labov, W. (1972). *Sociolinguistic patterns.* Philadelphia: University of Pennsylvania Press.

Langeland, A. (1996). Rushdie's language. *English Today, 45,* 16–22.

Lippi-Green, R. (1997). *English with an accent.* London: Routledge.

Lyotard, F. (1984). *The postmodern condition: A report on knowledge.* Manchester, England: Manchester University Press.

Macaulay, T. B. (1957/1835). Minute of 2 February 1835 on Indian education. In G. M. Young (Ed.), *Macaulay, prose and poetry* (pp. 721–724, 729). Cambridge, MA: Harvard University Press. (Originally published 1835)

Macedo, D. (2000). The colonialism of the English only movement. *Educational Researcher, 29*(3), 15–24.

Mahapatra, B. P. (1979). Santali language movement in the context of many dominant languages. In E. Annamalai (Ed.), *Language movements in India* (pp. 107–117). Mysore, India: CIIL Publications.

Masica, C. (1976). *Defining a linguistic area: South Asia.* Chicago: University of Chicago Press.

Medgyes, P. (1992). Native or non-native: Who's worth more? *ELT Journal, 46,* 340–349.

Medgyes, P. (1994). *The non-native teacher.* London: Macmillan.

Mehrotra, R. R. (1997). Reduplication in Indian Pidgin English. *English Today, 50,* 45–49.

Mehrotra, R. R. (2000). Indian pidgin English: Myth and reality. *English Today, 63,* 49–52.

Mesthrie, R. (1992). *English in language shift.* Cambridge, England: Cambridge University Press.

Mugglestone, L. (1995). *'Talking proper': The rise of accent as social symbol.* Oxford, England: Clarendon.

Mukherjee, A. (1980). *Language maintenance an. l language shift among Punjabis and Bengalis in Delhi.* Unpublished doctoral dissertation, University of Delhi, Delhi, India.

Naik, M. K. (1992). *A history of Indian English literature.* New Delhi, India: Sahitya Aakademi.

Nelson, C. (1992). Bilingual writing for the monolingual reader: Blowing up the canon. *World Englishes, 11,* 271–275.

Phillipson, R. (1992). *Linguistic imperialism.* Oxford, England: Oxford University Press.

Phillipson, R. (1998). Globalizing English: Are linguistic human rights an alternative to linguistic imperialism? *Language Science, 20,* 101–112.

Phillipson, R., & Skutnabb-Kangas, T. (1996). Is India throwing away its language resources? *English Today, 45,* 23–27.

Pyles, T., & Algeo, J. (1982). *The origins and development of the English language.* New York: Harcourt Brace Javonovich.

Quirk, R. (1985). The English language in a global context. In R. Quirk & H. Widdowson (Eds.), *English in the world: Teaching and learning the language and literatures* (pp. 1–6). Cambridge, England: Cambridge University Press.

Quirk, R. (1990). Language varieties and standard language. *English Today, 21,* 3–10.

Quirk, R. (1996). *Grammatical and lexical variance in English.* London: Longman.

Rahman, T. (1999). *Language, education, and culture.* Karachi, Pakistan Rahman: Oxford University Press.

Ramanathan, V. (1999). "English is here to stay": A critical look at institutional and educational practices in India. *TESOL Quarterly, 33,* 211–231.

Rao, R. (1978). The caste of English. In C. D. Narasimhaiah (Ed.), *Awakened conscience: Studies in commonwealth literature* (pp. 420–422). New Delhi, India: Sterling.

Satyanath, T. (1982). *Kannadigas in Delhi: A sociolinguistic study.* Unpublished master's thesis, University of Delhi, Delhi, India.

Seidlhofer, B. (2001). Closing a conceptual gap: The case for a description of English as a lingua franca. *International Journal of Applied Linguistics, 11,* 133–158.

Selinker, L. (1972). Interlanguage. *International Review of Applied Linguistics, 10,* 209–231.

Selinker, L. (1993). *Rediscovering interlanguage.* London: Longman.

Seth, V. (1993). *A suitable boy.* New York: HarperCollins.

Sharp, H. (Ed.). (1920). *Selections from educational records.* Calcutta: Bureau of Education, Government of India.

Silverstein, M. (1996). Monoglot "standard" in America: Standardization and metaphors of linguistic hegemony. In D. Brenneis & R. K. S. Macaulay (Eds.), *The matrix of language: Contemporary linguistic anthropology* (pp. 284–306). Boulder, CO: Westview.

Singh, U. N. (2001). Multiscriptality in South Asia and language development. *International Journal of the Sociology of Language, 150,* 61–74.

Smith, L., & Nelson, C. (1985). International intelligibility of English: Directions and resources. *World Englishes, 4,* 333–342.

Sridhar, S. N. (1994). A reality check for SLA theories. *TESOL Quarterly, 28,* 800–805.

Srivastava, R. N. (1989). Perspectives on language shift in multilingual settings. *International Journal of the Sociology of Language, 75,* 9–26.

*Times of India* news brief. (2001). Retrieved October 12, 2001, from www.timesofindia.com

Trudgill, P., & Hannah, J. (1985). *International English.* London: Arnold.

Vasant, B. (2002, April 21). Asha-UC current projects, p. 5 [pamphlet]. The event was sponsored by Asha-Education, Urbana–Champaign chapter.

Viswanathan, G. (1989). *Masks of conquest: Literary study and British rule in India.* London: Faber & Faber.

Waldman, A. (2003). More can I help you? Jobs migrate from U.S. to India. *New York Times,* May 11, p. 4.

# Chapter 3

# Language Death Studies and Local Knowledge: The Case of Cajun French[1]

Dominique Ryon
*University of Louisiana at Lafayette*

> *We have only to speak of an object to think*
> *that we are being objective. But, because*
> *we chose it in the first place, the object*
> *reveals more about us than we do about it.*
> —*Gaston Bachelard* (1964, p. 1)

This chapter uses Foucault's work on knowledge and power to show that the politics of language and the politics of researching it are closely related. As a discipline, sociolinguistics has barely begun to investigate the relation between academia and issues of power, and the different ways it ultimately may reinforce the interests of a dominant linguistic group. Language loss studies tend to emphasize demographic and economic factors over other social issues. This study about Cajun French, a fast-eroding French dialect still spoken by around 250,000 people in Louisiana, argues that language loss is a social as well as a discursive process and that academic knowledge and discourse both play a significant role in language politics. The study ad-

---

[1]This is a revised and expanded version of an article that appears in the *Journal of Language, Identity, and Education, 1,* pp. 279–293.

vocates the use of local knowledge to enhance our understanding of sociolinguistic realities involving unequal power relations.

## INTRODUCTION

Most linguistic studies on French in Louisiana tend to be descriptive analyses of the language (Conwell & Juilland, 1963; Klingler, 1996; Valdman,
1997) or examine the situation of this linguistic minority within the context
of what has come to be known as "language death studies" (Rottet,1996,
2001). This emerging sub-field of research is increasingly popular among
sociolinguists. Nancy Dorian (1989) stresses "the recent and current growth
of the literature" (p. 6) on the subject and the activities of the researchers at
sharing and disseminating methodologies, data, and ideas.

I have started to investigate the fact that "language death studies" rather
than "language revival studies" tended to be more popular among linguists
working on endangered languages in a book review of *French and Creole in
Louisiana* (Valdman, 1997) published in *Etudes Francophones* (Ryon, 1999,
pp. 244–248). In this article, I have stressed first, the fact that death studies
should not be considered scientifically more relevant than revival studies
and second, that scientific discourse could be biased by broader issues of
power and social control. Michel Foucault's work on discourse and power,
Bourdieu's analysis on social and linguistic representations as well as symbolic power, the "empowering research" model designed by the Lancaster
group of researchers (Cameron, Frazer, Harvey, Rampton, & Richardson,
1992), Catalan and Occitanist sociolinguistic theory of language conflict
(Boyer, 1991; Lafont, 1997), and the recent textual turn in anthropology
which emphasizes the role of discourse in science and the representation of
culture (Mangano, 1990), have provided the main conceptual and critical
tools in this investigation of the relation between academic knowledge,
power, and language loss in Louisiana.

If institutional knowledge tends to ignore the significance of this relation, local knowledge on the contrary offers substantial evidence of the relevance of such a link. In the context of this study, local knowledge refers to
native representations and discourse on linguistic issues, especially linguistic assimilation. The originality of local knowledge, expressed most clearly
in the new Cajun literature and popular songs, is to bring to the fore the
sociopolitical nature of linguistic assimilation and the essentially conflictual
nature of cultural and linguistic contact. By contrast, the acknowledgment
of the political and conflictual nature of the process of language loss is completely absent from theoretical paradigms used in academic knowledge
about language loss and social change in Louisiana. In this manner, local
knowledge challenges the academic representation of such controversial
linguistic realities.

The objective of this study is twofold: (a) first, to highlight the social and discursive nature of academic knowledge, and its implications for sociolinguistic situations involving unequal power relations, especially those of local endangered languages; and (b) second, to promote local knowledge (which is, of course, also socially defined) as a valid, necessary, and complementary resource for academic research. Language loss in Louisiana and its scholarly investigation is used as a case study.

## SELECTION AND CLASSIFICATION: THE POLITICS OF WHAT IS SAID AND WHAT IS NOT SAID

The fact that social and linguistic research is inspired by the need to understand problems but also to contain them has been persuasively demonstrated by Michel Foucault. Foucault (1971a) observes that knowledge is power, that citizens of modern democracies are controlled less by the army, police, economic power, or a centralized, visible state apparatus, than by pronouncements of expert discourse, which he calls "regime of truth." According to Foucault, expert discourse has a powerful impact on society as much through what it says as by what it does not say; as much by what is constructed as an object of investigation as by what is rejected as insignificant and then left beyond representation. Foucault argues that "no power can be exercised without the extraction, appropriation, distribution or retention of knowledge" (1971b, p. 283). In other words, there is no power relation "without the correlative constitution of a field of knowledge, nor any knowledge that does not presuppose and constitute at the same time power relations" (1975, p. 32). He then turns his attention to the development of "disciplines," which he views as a procedure to limit and control discourse. The emergence of disciplines is usually regarded as a positive step as it provides resources for new discourses, but Foucault invites us to also consider their "restrictive" and "constraining function" (1971a, p. 38). In the same way, the development of a subfield such as "language death studies" could be viewed as a restrictive and constraining process in the building of sociolinguistic knowledge. This paradigm does not disqualify the scientific value of knowledge produced within the field of language death study. It simply points out that much can also be learned from the acknowledgment of what is not taken into account by these disciplines, subfields, and their theoretical and conceptual apparatus.

This interplay of power and knowledge poses a special challenge to minorities, who are not only facing linguistic, economic, and social pressures, but also a distorted, unilateral, and fragmented representation of their lived experience through expert discourse. Foucault shows how power is organized and manifested through knowledge and through practices such as surveillance, imprisonment, and classification—especially classification of mad people in his study, *Madness and Civilization* (1972a). Pierre Bourdieu (1982) also stresses the purpose of classification which he sees as "always subordinated to practical means and oriented towards the production of social effects" (p. 135). Could the current trend in academic discourse of classifying linguistic minorities as dying (instead of resisting or struggling, for example) be part of a similar process? One of the social effects of the wide use of such a classification and representation of the Cajun linguistic community is obviously the reluctance of the educational system to provide linguistic instruction in Cajun French. If a language is considered dying and if the process is widely assumed irreversible, then it is logical to consider as a waste of time and money both the production of pedagogical material in that language and the training of teachers to teach it. On the contrary, if the community is widely perceived as resisting linguistic assimilation, then it becomes rational to develop practical means—such as linguistic instruction in the minority language—either to reverse the language shift or to prevent its total extinction.[2]

In the case of the Cajun linguistic community, most experts agree to declare it a dying linguistic community. Jerah Johnson (1976) has even been able to predict the exact time of the disappearance of the language as 2010. Based on data from both the census and the study of Bertrand and Beale (1965), he projected that the decline in the use of French would proceed in a simple arithmetic evolution of 10% per decade. When applied to the number of French-speaking Cajun households existent in 1970, this formula showed that the number of French-speaking native families will be zero by the end of the first decade of the 21st century. We are now much closer to the deadline, and it is already clear that Johnson's assumptions were wrong. They were wrong because Johnson's premises were wrong. His tendency to consider languages as autonomous and natural products (thus usable in arithmetic models), separate from any social change or event, prevented him from foreseeing the development of immersion programs in Acadiana in the early 1980s. In 1999 and 2000, there were around 2,200 students en-

---

[2]The Diwan schools system, which provides full education in Breton (a Celtic language still spoken in Brittany, France) from kindergarten to high school, is also a good illustration of the relation between classification, practical means, and social effects. In 2001 and 2002, 2,613 students were enrolled in one of the 37 Diwan schools (Information retrieved December 12, 2001, from the World Wide Web: http://www.diwanbreizh.org). The existence of such schools is a direct consequence of local activism and political awareness of some members of the Breton community, who unambiguously perceived themselves as engaged in a struggle against cultural and linguistic assimilation. This intellectual stance makes them more circumspect to official forms of discourse and knowledge on their account. In other words, Diwan schools were neither an institutional initiative nor a direct social effect of academic knowledge on the Breton language and its prospects. It is actually interesting to note that Lois Kuter (1989) does not even mention the existence of these schools and this movement in his article on the Breton language published in *Investigating Obsolescence: Studies in Language Contraction and Death*, edited by Nancy Dorian (1989, pp. 75–89).

rolled in 27 schools of the eight Louisiana parishes offering French immersion programs. These programs are not currently reversing language shift in Louisiana, but they are playing a decisive role in maintaining the language in households where it would not otherwise have been maintained. This fact is especially observable in strong Cajun French speaking communities, much less elsewhere, where immersion programs are used less as linguistic preservation programs for the benefit of children from Cajun families than as enrichment programs for children from English-speaking families (Tornquist, 2000). The role played by immersion programs at the community level still needs to be empirically investigated. However, the lack both of data on and interest by researchers in some issues, this one for example, is precisely one of the problems raised in this study.

Recent empirical studies in the field of language attitudes also offer additional examples of how linguistic research seems to be programmed to only document facts of linguistic loss and not of linguistic recovery. Different empirical studies have shown the shift in language attitudes of young people under 30 toward Cajun French (Dubois, 1997; Ryon, 1997). In sharp contrast with the older generation of fluent Cajun French speakers, younger people now express positive feelings toward the French vernacular. Dubois (1997) observes "that it is the youngest members of these communities who seem the most open to learning Cajun French" (p. 61). However, no further attention is given to that fact on the basis that only an increase in the number of Cajun French speakers can be considered as evidence of a linguistic revival (Dubois, 1997, p. 69). The rationale behind this selection of what is valuable as an object of scientific inquiry and what is not is that only facts within the paradigm of language loss are given scientific relevance and carefully examined. As seen in the example earlier, the significance of facts highly depends on the theoretical framework in use. The scientific value of the very same fact changes substantially when the paradigm of language revival is applied rather than the perspective of the dominant language.

Occitanist sociolinguistic theory and Bourdieu's works both investigate the importance of representations in the study of sociolinguistic behavior. Although Boyer (1991, p. 44) stresses the role of representations in the linguistic aspects of intercultural conflicts, all of them emphasize the social power of representation and its repressive as well as liberating potential (Bourdieu, 1982, pp. 140–42; Boyer, 1991, pp. 39–52). Robert Lafont (1997, pp. 90–122) explains how linguistic revitalization starts first at the psycholinguistic level, that is to say at the level of linguistic representations, for both speakers (or semi-speakers, or passive speakers) and of course language experts and educators. In that light, the shift of language attitudes of young Cajuns is highly significant because it indicates that one necessary (but not sufficient) condition is now fulfilled for linguistic revival. What is done with this fact is then the responsibility of the scientific community and of course of the Cajun community itself. However, the role played by experts is quite important because by acknowledging it, by investigating it closely, by making it public, scientific discourse will socially legitimize it. It will raise the level of linguistic awareness of the community as well as its level of confidence in the possibility of a linguistic reversal. As shown in the earlier example, the positive impulse toward language revival is immediately discredited by academic discourse. What if, on the contrary, one decides to study the recent shift of language attitudes? Then a chain reaction is immediately engaged, although in a reverse direction. Pierre Bourdieu (1982, p. 140) states that just the fact of talking about something, of objectifying it through discourse, produces social effects. Knowledge is intimately linked to discursive practices, such as the formation of conceptual apparatus, methods of work, and internal controversies, which in turn provide resources and legitimacy for social action. Such resources are significantly lacking in Louisiana as educators and parents are currently wondering whether the introduction of the teaching of Cajun French is a reasonable initiative as well as a feasible one (Ancelet, 1988). For this reason, what has been called the "Louisianification" movement of the teaching of French in Louisiana, promoted by Cajun and Creole activists, has progressed very slowly since its inception in the 1980s. But the reserved attitude of the community at large is well understandable given the lack of sustained support from "officially qualified speaking subjects" as well as the overall pessimist tone over the future of the language. Why should anyone bother to save a language condemned to die? Why save the language if one can claim being Cajun without speaking French? As I have argued in a previous study, social theories promoting the separation of the linguistic component in cultural identities are on the rise nowadays and may, as an ideological and social effect, play some role in the linguistic resignation of some ethnic minorities (Ryon, 2000b).

Academic discourse is, of course, not the only factor involved in the process of language revival, but what language experts say and do not say seem to have significant consequences and should be as carefully examined as other social and economic factors.

## LINGUISTIC LOSS, TEXTUAL PLAY, AND METAPHORS SOCIOLINGUISTS LIVE BY

Claiming the "death" of a traditional culture or ethnic community was common practice in early anthropological writings and modernist ethnographies. Anthropologists gained professional reputations and added substantial drama to their narratives by claiming to be the last witnesses of vanishing worlds! Today, it would be considered highly inappropriate and ideologically questionable to do so within the context of this discipline. Moreover, postmodern anthropological criticism has shown how rhetoric and its figures, rather than authentic representation of cultural reality, have shaped anthropological written accounts of this period (Clifford & Marcus, 1986; Geertz, 1988). Discursive practices and the relation between oral and written accounts were brought under close scrutiny as the link between "the appropriation of Other and the discursive forms that contain the act of appropriation" (Mangano, 1990, p. 3) was progressively unveiled. Ideologies claiming transparency of representation and of the linguistic medium were seriously discussed, as was the relation between discursive boundaries and ethnocentric representation. Slowly, scholars' attention was displaced from fieldwork to texts, and the whole discipline gained a new awareness of its own global implications.

Sociolinguistic representation is also inseparable from discursive, rhetorical, and narrative processes. First, research not only involves fieldwork but also text-making. Second, our language about language draws widely on what Nietzsche calls an "army of metaphors, metonymies and anthropomorphisms" (quoted by Mangano, 1990, p. 17). Language "erosion," "death," and "loss" are metaphorical concepts which partially structure the understanding of the "object" being studied. As George Lakoff states, "a metaphorical concept can keep us from focusing on other aspects of the concept that are inconsistent with that metaphor" (Lakoff & Johnson, 1980, p. 10). From the vantage points of literariness, textual play, and cultural representations, sociolinguistic writings on Cajuns and their language provide interesting data. Consider the sentence quoted in *French and Creole in Louisiana* (Valdman, 1997), in which the author expresses the hope that linguists now "equipped with the scientific attitudes and rigorous techniques of structuralism, will return to the bayou country to continue the urgent harvest of the vestiges of French speech in that part of the New World" (p. 2). Rhetorical figures abound in this short passage which, on the one hand, clearly shows the textual and rhetorical operations at work in linguistic accounts, and on the other hand, the ideological implications of their use. The use of the figure "bayou country," to refer to the place where Cajun French is spoken, is questionable on two accounts: first, it fails to convey accurate information on where the language is actually spoken in Louisiana (which extends far beyond the region of the bayous); second, it reinforces cultural stereotypes about Cajun speakers who are endlessly portrayed as people living in that kind of exotic environment. The metaphor of the "harvest," on the other hand, offers an interesting new insight on linguistic fieldwork since its reclassification of the collection of linguistic data as an economic rather than as a mere technical procedure, emphasizes as well as it unveils the economic nature of the process involved in the exchange of knowledge between dominant and minority groups. As to the "vestiges" of

French speech, the metaphor indicates the overall aesthetic conception of the language as well as the fact that its "structural architecture" is ruined and beyond all repair. Finally, the fact of using the expression *New World,* a term from the colonial period, to refer to Louisiana does not require further explanation. Geertz's suggestion that ethnographic texts ought to be "looked at as well as through" (1988, p. 138) seems to be a good suggestion for sociolinguistic texts too, because, as we have seen, they are not immune to rhetorical and literary processes.

## LINGUISTIC ASSIMILATION AND ITS REPRESENTATIONS

Robert Lafont, one of the main theorists of occitanist sociolinguistics, also commonly called "sociolinguistique de la périphérie" (sociolinguistics from the periphery), questions the objectivity of the discourse about diglossia coming from dominant groups in dominant languages. He observes that these studies unvariably suggest the end of minorities' linguistic problems through their successful integration to the dominant group (1997, p. 91). Georg Kremnitz (1981, p. 65) stresses "the descriptive and static terminology used in North American sociolinguistics" which largely fails to acknowledge the political dimension involved in the process of language loss. Henry Boyer (1991, p. 10) explains how concepts such as "diglossia," "language contact," or "bilingualism" tend to present a linguistic shift in terms of a "peaceful co-existence" instead of a violent, political, and conflictual process. Language loss in Louisiana has never been studied as the result of cultural and political conflicts (Ryon, 2000a). On the contrary, academic discourse tends to emphasize the voluntary decision of this linguistic community to abandon its language. Kevin Rottet states that "since English is the language of the dominant American society, members of ethnic communities *who* want to advance outside the local community often assimilate, partially or totally, into that society" (1996, p. 119, emphasis added). This account of the assimilation process is misleading on two accounts. First, it problematically gives the active role in the assimilation process to the ethnic community itself and not to the dominant group. Second, it also implies that they have the choice to control the degree of their assimilation. Such accounts definitely promote an idyllic and nonviolent version of linguistic assimilation. Because assimilation is such a natural, ineluctable, and peaceful process, decades of repressive measures, institutional intimidation (especially through schooling), and procedures of humiliation, have left assimilationist mechanisms and strategies largely unaccounted for and undocumented in sociolinguistic knowledge. Once again Foucault's reading is enlightening:

> If power is properly speaking the way in which relations of forces are deployed and given concrete expression, rather than analyzing it in terms of

cession, contract or alienation, or functionally in terms of its maintenance of the relations of production, should we not analyze it primarily in terms of struggle, conflict and war? (1980, p. 90)

To get that version of the story in Louisiana, however, one must turn to local knowledge.

## LOCAL KNOWLEDGE ON LANGUAGE LOSS: A DIFFERENT STORY

Local knowledge constitutes a significant resource for studying fields of human experiences forgotten, censored, or excluded from expert discourse. As a "non-centralized kind of theoretical production whose validity is not dependent on the approval of the established régimes of thought" (Foucault, 1980, p. 81), local knowledge (or "subjugated knowledge") retains memories of struggles and conflicts. It allows us to discover "the ruptural effects of conflict and struggle that the order imposed by functionalist or systematizing thought is designed to mask" (Foucault, 1980, p. 82).

Local knowledge on language loss in Louisiana is accessible primarily through recent creative texts written in Cajun French as well as popular songs. The emergence of a written literature within the context of a traditionally oral culture is in itself a significant sign of resistance and of a struggle to survive. The 1980 publication of *Cris sur le Bayou* (*Cries on the bayou*), with its evocative title, is usually considered as the manifesto of the birth of Cajun literature. It is also one of the first attempts to give a written form to the Louisiana French vernacular. Since its publication, the Cajun literary corpus has grown to include texts such as *C'est p'us Pareil* (1982) by Richard Guidry, the anthology *Acadie Tropicale* (1983), *La Charrue* (1982) by Carol Doucet, *Trois Saisons* (1988) by Antoine Bourque, *Je suis Cadien* (1994) by Jean Arceneaux, *Faire récolte* (1997) by the famous Cajun songwriter and musician Zachary Richard, *Lait à mère* (1997) by David Cheramie, a collection of plays from the company Le Théatre Cadien edited by May Waggoner (1999), and texts regularly published in literary magazines such as *Feux Follets* in Lafayette, Louisiana, and *Éloizes* in New Brunswick, Canada. The birth of Cajun literature offers a new medium of expression for native discourse on a wide range of topics, but especially on the language itself and its loss. These creative texts can still be considered a valid testimony of unregulated and unofficial forms of knowledge and discourse given the general conditions of their production and distribution. Most of them indeed are printed in a limited number of copies (200 copies for *C'est p'us Pareil*) and distributed locally mainly through cultural centers, museums, and small bookstores. It is revealing that none of them are currently available at the local Barnes and Noble. This situation might change quickly, however, and Cajun literature might reach a broader audience and obtain soon some economic value on the publishing market, as Cajun music and Cajun food have in the last two decades. For example, Zachary Richard's (1997) last book, *Faire récolte,* including its CD-ROM, was on display in a major bookstore in Montreal last September while a Cajun poem was included in the last edition of the French language textbook *Chez Nous: Branché sur le monde francophone* edited by Valdman, Pons, Scullen, & Jourdain (2001, p. 70).

This body of texts provides a unique resource and testimony on the reality of linguistic assimilation as it is experienced by native population itself. It constitutes unique "documents" as life takes over theory in the depiction of what is linguistic assimilation. On the contrary to what was suggested elsewhere, language loss is not portrayed as a mellow process, but as a painful, humiliating, confusing experience; one that brings both despair and anger. These texts especially bear witness to the psycholinguistic methods involved in the assimilationist process and the emotional and mental violence involved in the formation of a new "linguistic habitus." In his famous poem *Schizophrénie linguistique* (Linguistic Schizophrenia), Jean Arceneaux (published in *Cris sur le Bayou,* 1980, p. 16) offers an expressive testimony of this undocumented side of linguistic assimilation:

> I will not speak French on the school grounds.
> I will not speak French on the school grounds.
> I will not speak French …
> I will not speak French …
> I will not speak French …
> Hé! ils sont pas bêtes, ces salauds.
> Après mille fois, ça commence à pénétrer
> Dans n'importe quel esprit.
> Ça fait mal; ça fait honte;
> Puis là, ça fait plus mal.
> Ça devient automatique,
> Et on speak pas French on the school grounds
> Et anywhere else non plus.
>
> I will not speak French on the school grounds.
> I will not speak French on the school grounds.
> I will not speak French …
> I will not speak French …
> I will not speak French …
> Well, they are not stupid, those bastards.
> After one hundred times, it begins to penetrate
> In anyone's mind.
> It hurts, it brings shame;
> And suddenly, it does not hurt anymore.
> It is almost natural,
> And we don't speak French on the school grounds
> And anywhere else either.

We are far from the analysis of language shift in terms of social necessity and economic advancement of the ethnic community or in terms of grammatical erosion and statistical speculation. This text, like so many others, tells a different story about linguistic assimilation, one that emphasizes authoritarian methods of linguistic enforcement, through affective and emotional intimidation. Psycholinguistic aspects of linguistic assimilation are still the "dark continent" of sociolinguistic research on linguistic minorities, but their study would certainly provide decisive insights on mechanisms of social and linguistic control as well as social and linguistic emancipation.

David Cheramie, one of the most promising "Néo-Cadien" (New Cajun) poets, also clearly reminds us that intercultural relations in situations characterized by inequality are inherently violent.[3] In the early 1990s, while ethnic cleansing was ravaging former Yugoslavia, Cheramie (published in *Éloizes*, 1994, p. 39) stressed the relation between this devastating civil war in Europe and the apparently peaceful ethnic and linguistic assimilation process in Louisiana:

| | |
|---|---|
| Comme Sarajevo | Like Sarajevo |
| l'Amérique veut pas savoir | America does not want to know |
| qui sont ses bâtards | who its illegitimate children are |

Cheramie's book, *Lait à Mère* (1997),[4] bears in epigraph the following quotations from Herman Hesse and André d'Allemagne, respectively: "true suffering only exists when two civilizations meet" and "colonialism reduces the culture of the dominated people to mere folklore and propaganda." Therefore, Cheramie exposes the deception over Cajun traditional "joie de vivre" widely promoted by commercial propaganda, cultural tourism, and the media (p. 15):

Asteur, les bons temps ne sont plus après te tuer
demain encore
on fera bouillir les crabes
fraîchir la bière
pour tromper ta mémoire, vieux violoneux
pour faire des accroires au monde
qu'un Cadien est toujours heureux.

---

[3]In a previous study (Ryon, 2000b, p. 177), I have defined as "Néo Cadiens" (New Cajuns) the "new generation of French speakers in Louisiana who mainly have been educated in French through schooling." Typically, they have learned French as a second language and are fluent speakers of Standard French rather than Cajun French, but many of them, such as the poet David Cheramie, come from families who still speak Cajun French at home and value the vernacular language which they try to rehabilitate in their creative writing as well as through social and educational activism.

[4]The title "Lait à mère" means "mother's milk" but can also be read as "bitter milk" by homophony with "lait amer."

Right now, good times are not killing you anymore
tomorrow again
crabs will be boiled
beer will be fresh
to fool your memory, old fiddler
to make people believe
that a Cajun is always happy

Charles Larroque, a Louisiana native and currently a teacher of French
in an immersion program, also eloquently expresses the repressive and
threatening context of assimilation through the use of powerful military
and farming metaphorical figures in his poem *Route d'évacuation* (Evacua-
tion Road) published in *Éloizes* in 1994. However, it is in Zachary Richard's
songs and poetry that the most expressive poetic statements of indignation,
anger, and despair about linguistic assimilation can be found. His song
(2000), *Réveille!* (Wake Up!), is well known across the French-speaking
world, whereas his poetry bitterly exposes the state of powerlessness in
which his community is maintained. In his poem (1994, pp. 28–31) *La Vérité
va Peut-Être te Faire du Mal* (The Truth Might Hurt You), he not only blames
materialism introduced by "the Americans" and the Catholic religion with
its "Complex of Sacred Persecution" but, above all, the linguistic resignation of the Cajun community itself. In his in-depth study of Cajun self-representation through Cajun music and dance, Charles Stivale (2003, p. 68)
also stressed the brutal "rejection of self-pity for the Cajuns' linguistic dilemma" expressed in this poem and the blasphemous tone of the final
verses, which he translated as follows:

À l'autel de la Sainte Persécution Complex
Au nom de la merde, du pisse et du petit pipi
Parle franç ou crève maudit

On the altar of the Holy Persecution Complex
In the name of shit, piss and little wee-wee,
Speak French, or die accursed.

These texts on linguistic assimilation definitely offer a different perspective compared to texts coming from academic circles. They eloquently and
unequivocally "document" linguistic assimilation as a cultural struggle and
painful conflict and, more importantly, as a struggle not yet over. The use of
literature and poetry as a valid source of data for sociolinguistic research,
and especially for sociolinguistic criticism, would probably be challenged by
positivist scholars. The purpose of social studies should, however, go beyond stating regularities, predicting outcomes, presenting data in tables,
providing statistics, and describing observable phenomena in law-like general terms. It should also be open to various forms of epistemological criti-

cism and receptive to its results. But important philosophical issues are also at stake in this discussion. As Cameron, Frazer, Harvey, Rampton, and Richardson (1992) state, if these philosophical issues "are not always discussed explicitly, they are fundamental to all empirical research, not just linguistic research. Epistemological assumptions determine the way in which a researcher interacts with the researched: thus they influence methods and indeed research findings" (p. 5). Similarly, epistemological assumptions have also determined the way in which various forms of cultural and material evidence were gathered and used in this study. Even the most positivist scholar should see the potential scientific significance of the identification of this discrepancy between both the academic and the native versions of linguistic assimilation, and should somehow wonder why it was not unveiled or noticed before by "hard" methods for eliciting data.

Scientific discourse, in general, tends to ignore or disqualify local knowledge, particularly when it revolves around sensitive social issues. Foucault (1980) states that the strength of this form of unofficial discourse lies precisely on the "harshness with which it is opposed by everything surrounding it" and he adds that it is precisely through the appearance (or reappearance) of this disqualified knowledge that "criticism performs its work" (p. 82). Robert Lafont (1997, p. 28) offers a sociolinguistic application of this idea when he stresses the necessity to reinterpret the history of diglossia or assimilation by promoting native militant literature, popular songs, and the teaching of the minority language (in his case the Occitan language).

## EXAMINING THE HISTORIOGRAPHY OF CAJUN FRENCH

The control of the future depends on the control of the past; who controls the past controls the future. As Antoine Bourque states "Un peuple sans passé est un peuple sans futur" (a society without a past is a society without a future; Brasseaux, 1992, epigraph). As far as history is concerned, the Cajuns, along with other diaspora communities, have one of the heaviest pasts, so the real issue is (again) what is told about the past and what is not.

Louisiana Acadian and Cajun historiography safely tends to confine itself to the 18th and 19th centuries: the Deportation of Acadians from Nova Scotia in 1755, their installation in Louisiana (1765–1803), and the transformation of their culture and society from Acadian to Cajun through the 19th century (Brasseaux, 1987, 1992). Brasseaux acknowledges that "violence has been an integral part of Louisiana Acadian life since the 1755 dispersal" (1992, p. 112). However, he emphasizes and documents the violence within the community and the violence organized by Cajuns themselves against other social groups, especially through their vigilance committees in the second part of the 19th century (1992, pp. 112–153). The cultural and linguistic assimilation of the Cajuns (which started in the mid-19th century and intensified through all of the first part of the 20th century) is examined in exactly the same terms as elsewhere; only demographic and economic facts are emphasized and given social significance. Brasseaux unsurprisingly affirms a dominant opinion on the subject when he states that, in Canada as well as in Louisiana, "assimilation of these francphones into Anglophone society was largely voluntary and economically motivated" (p. 91). Such assumptions have serious consequences because no further attention is given to the process of assimilation. Therefore the question is left as if everything had already been said about it and as if it had no topicality anymore because the choice has supposedly already been made, for economic reasons, a long time ago, by the Cajuns themselves. Moreover, the use of such paradigm places the responsibility of linguistic assimilation on the Cajuns themselves because *they* have made that choice for economic reasons instead of bringing to the fore more complex and persistent symbolic and social mechanisms of linguistic and cultural control. Even more aggravating in this study on social struggles in Louisiana is the conclusion that the Acadian/Cajun community has "remained a society at war *with itself*" during the 19th and "much of the twentieth century" (1992, p. 153, emphasis added). Obviously, academic historiography is based on a complex and selective reconstruction of facts. Some are used conveniently to blame the victims, some others, more disturbing, are forgotten, and evidence of the sociocultural and linguistic war against the Cajuns themselves is left unreported and undocumented.

Power is an elusive force and its most efficient strategies are not economic or even legal or juridical in nature, but symbolic (Ryon, 2000a, pp. 10–11). Bourdieu stresses that "the distinctiveness of symbolic domination lies precisely in the fact that it assumes, of those who submit to it, an attitude which challenges the usual dichotomy of freedom and constraint" (1999, p. 51). He also argues that it is "the propensity to reduce the search for causes to a search for responsibilities" that "makes it impossible to see that intimidation, a symbolic violence which is not aware of what it is (to the extent that it implies no act of intimidation) can only be exerted on a person predisposed (in his habitus) to feel it, whereas others will ignore it" (p. 51). Symbolic forms of domination and the active part they play in the social and linguistic control of populations can only be seen and investigated if the existence of power relations is first acknowledged. As this study shows, academic historiography and sociolinguistics have largely failed on this account, and as a result, an important part of the history of the Cajuns and of the way they are losing their language is still to be told.

Foucault (1980) pointed out that it is not institutional knowledge such as a semiology of the life of the asylum or even a sociology of delinquency, which produced the most effective tool to the understanding of the asylum and the prison systems, but what people caught up and sub-jugated by such systems had to say or had said about it. Likewise, the whole issue of language loss in Louisiana (and of language loss every-where) will certainly be better understood if what the linguistic commu-nity is saying about it is fully acknowledged by academic discourse and practices, not in a condescending way but in a theoretical way. Foucault's concept of genealogy which he defines as the association be-tween erudite knowledge and local memories "to establish a historical knowledge of struggles and to make use of this knowledge tactically to-day" (1980, p. 83) is particularly valuable and helpful in that regard. He mainly suggested this type of method for historical documents, but it undoubtedly has heuristic value for the study of many other social and linguistic issues as well.

A turn in the direction of including local knowledge in academic prac-tice and discourse has already taken place in some sociolinguistic circles. However, it is still a marginal trend, as shown, for example, by the label used for one of these schools: "sociolinguistics from the periphery." Sim-ilar theoretical and methodological interests can also be found among the Lancaster group of researchers who advocate "empowering re-search" (Cameron et al., 1992). They define this concept as a "research on, for and with" members of the minority communities (p. 22). "Em-powering research" adopts the following principles: first, the use of in-teractive and dialogic research methods; second, the importance of participants' own agendas; and third, the question of the "feedback" and sharing of knowledge (p. 23). Cooperation between experts and commu-nity members should not be understood as the traditional use of commu-nity members as informants or auxiliary consultants but as an active participation at all levels of the research process. William Labov's works brought some attention to power and social issues involved in socio-linguistic methods, but this mainly led him to systematically examine the social conditioning of linguistic variables and not the social conditioning of sociolinguistic research itself and all its implications. This new field of research in sociolinguistics is still at an exploratory stage, but it seems to announce that some long overdue changes and questionings are finally taking place within the discipline. An ongoing research project led by Al-bert Valdman (Indiana University) in Louisiana seems promising in that regard, because a collaborative team of four linguists and two commu-nity members are equally involved in the process of producing a compre-hensive dictionary of Cajun French. This collaborative effort has already generated positive and unusual results as a special edition of the dictio-nary will be released before the scientific version, for the benefit of the community.

## CONCLUSION

This chapter exemplifies the value of sociopolitical, sociohistorical, and discoursive forms of criticism, as mainly applied to sociolinguistic scholarship. It has used indiscriminately, and as a necessity, a wide range of data coming from inside as well as from outside academia. The discrepancy between the two versions of linguistic assimilation—one coming from the victor, or dominant group, and the other from the defeated or linguistic minority—should be given a close examination. The chapter should also raise some questions about the failure of more empirical, positivist, and supposedly more "scientific" methods to see and investigate that fact. But as long as sociolinguistics will be committed to the obviousness and unproblematic status of what it can observe, it will stay blind to facts and issues, most of them of critical importance for linguistic minorities.

## REFERENCES

*Acadie tropicale*. (1983). Lafayette: Éditions de la Nouvelle Acadie.

Ancelet, B. (Ed.). (1980). *Cris sur le bayou* [Cries on the bayou]. Montreal, Canada: Les Éditions Intermède.

Ancelet, B. (1988). A perspective on teaching the "problem" language in Louisiana. *The French Review, 61*, 345–354.

Arceneaux, J. (1980). Schizophrénie linguistique [Linguistic schizophrenia]. In B. Ancelet (Ed.), *Cris sur le bayou* [Cries on the bayou] (pp. 16–17). Montréal, Canada: Les Éditions Intermède.

Arceneaux, J. (1994). *Je suis Cadien* [I am French]. New York: Cross-Cultural Communication.

Bachelard, G. (1964). *The Psychoanalysis of fire* (A. C. M. Ross, Trans.). Boston: Beacon Press. (Original work published 1949)

Bertrand, A., & Beale, C. (1965). The French and Non-French in rural Louisiana. *Agricultural Experiment Station Bulletin, 606*. Baton Rouge: Louisiana State University.

Bourdieu, P. (1982) . *Ce que parler veut dire: L'économie des échanges linguistiques* [What speaking means: The Economy of Linguistic Exchanges]. Paris: Fayard.

Bourque, A. (1988). *Trois saisons* [Three seasons]. Lafayette, LA: Éditions de la Nouvelle Acadie.

Boyer, H. (1991). *Langues en conflit* [Languages in conflict]. Paris: L'Harmattan.

Brasseaux, C. (1987). *The founding of New Acadia: The beginnings of Acadian life in Louisiana, 1765–1803*. Baton Rouge: Louisiana University Press.

Brasseaux, C. (1992). *Acadian to Cajun: Transformation of a People, 1803–1877*. Jackson: University Press of Mississippi.

Cameron, D., Frazer, E., Harvey, P., Rampton, M. B. H., & Richardson, K. (1992). *Researching language: Issues of power and method*. London: Routledge.

Cheramie, D. (1994). La Contre-danse d'un contre-temps. *Éloizes, 22*, 36–39.

Cheramie, D. (1997). *Lait à mère* [Mother's milk]. Moncton, New Brunswick, Canada: Les Éditions d'Acadie.

Clifford, J., & Marcus, G. C. (1986). *Writing culture: The poetics and politics of ethnography*. Berkeley: University of California Press.

Conwell, M., & Juilland, A. (1963). *Louisiana French grammar I: Phonology, morphology, and syntax*. The Hague, The Netherlands: Mouton.

*Cris sur le bayou*. (1980). Montreal: Les Éditions Intermède.

Dorian, N. (Ed.). (1989). *Investigating obsolescence: Studies in language contraction and death*. Cambridge, England: Cambridge University Press.

Doucet, C. (1982). *La charrue* [The plow]. University of Southwestern Louisiana: Éditions de la Nouvelle Acadie, The Center for Louisiana Studies, University of Southwestern Louisiana.

Dubois, S. (1997). Field method in four Cajun communities in Louisiana. In A. Valdman (Ed.), *French and Creole in Louisiana* (pp. 47–70). New York: Plenum.

Foucault, M. (1971a). *L'ordre du discours* [The order of discourse]. Paris: Gallimard.

Foucault, M. (1971b). Théories et institutions pénales. *Annuaire du Collège de France, 1971–72*. Paris (Summary of M. F.'s course for the academic year 1971–1972).

Foucault, M. (1972a). *Madness and civilization*. New York: Pantheon.

Foucault, M. (1972b). *The archeology of knowledge*. New York: Pantheon.

Foucault, M. (1975). *Surveiller et punir* [Discipline and punish]. Paris: Gallimard.

Foucault, M. (1980). *Power/knowledge: Selected interviews and other writings by Michel Foucault 1972–77*. New York: Pantheon.

Geertz, C. (1988). *Works and lives: The anthropologists as author*. Stanford, CA: Stanford University Press.

Guidry, R. (1982). *C'est p'us pareil* [It's not the same anymore]. Lafayette, LA: Éditions de la Nouvelle Acadie.

Johnson, J. (1976). The Louisiana French. *Contemporary French Civilization, 1*, 19–37.

Klingler, T. (Ed.). (1996). *Plurilinguismes 11* [Multilingualisms]. Paris: Centre d'Études et de Recherches en Planification linguistique.

Kremnitz, G. (1981). Du bilinguisme au conflit linguistique. Cheminement de termes et de concepts [From bilingualism to linguistic conflict. Development of terminology and concepts]. *Languages, 61*, 63–73.

Kuter, L. (1989). Breton vs. French: Language and the opposition of political, social, and cultural values. In N. Dorian (Ed.), *Investigating obsolescence: Studies in language contraction and death* (pp. 75–89) . Cambridge, England: Cambridge University Press.

Lafont, R. (1997). *Quarante ans de sociolinguistique périphérique* [Forty years of sociolinguistics from the periphery]. Paris: L'Harmattan.

Lakoff, G., & Johnson, M. (1980). *Metaphors we live by*. Chicago: The University of Chicago Press.

Larroque, C. (1994). La Route d'évacuation. *Éloizes, 22*, 53–55.

Mangano. M. (1990). *Modernist anthropology: From fieldwork to text*. Princeton, NJ: Princeton University Press.

Richard, Z. (1994). La vérité va peut-être faire du mal [The truth may cause you pain]. *Éloizes, 22*, 28–31.

Richard, Z. (1997). *Faire récolte* [Harvest]. Moncton, New Brunswick, Canada: Éditions Perce-Neige.

Richard, Z. (2000). Réveille [Wake up]. On *coeur fidèle* [Faithful heart], CD. LA: Les Éditions du Marais Bouleur. Words available at http://www.zacharyrichard.com/richardfrench/discocoeus.html. Discography available at http://wwwzacharyrichard.com/

Rottet, K. (1996). Language change and language death: Some Changes in the pronominal system of declining Cajun French. *Plurilinguismes, 11*, 117–151.

Rottet, K. (2001). *Language shift in the coastal marshes of Louisiana*. New York: Peter Lang.

Ryon, D. (1997). *Variantes dialectales et enseignement du français en Louisiane* [Dialectal variations and the teaching of French in Louisiana]. Paper presented at the annual meeting of the Conseil International d'Études Francophones, Guadeloupe, France.

Ryon, D. (1999). French and Creole in Louisiana [Review of the book]. *Études Francophones, 14*, 244–248.

Ryon, D. (2000a). Logique d'État et aménagement linguistique du français en Louisiane [Reason of State and linguistic planning of the French language in Louisiana]. *La Revue Française, 9*, 7–20.

Ryon, D. (2000b). Conflit, assimilation et revendication de l'identité ethnolinguistique en Louisiane francophone [Conflict, assimilation and ethnolinguistic identity issues in French-speaking Louisiana]. *Études Francophones, 15*, 171–190.

Stivale, C. (2003). *Disenchanting les bons temps*. Durham, NC: Duke University Press.

Tornquist, L. (2000). *Attitudes linguistiques vis-à-vis du vernaculaire franco-louisianais dans les programmes d'immersion en Louisiane* [Linguistic attitudes toward Louisiana French vernacular in immersion programs in Louisiana]. Unpublished doctoral dissertation, University of Louisiana at Lafayette.

Valdman, A. (Ed.). (1997). *French and Creole in Louisiana*. New York: Plenum.

Valdman, A., Pons, C., Scullen, M. E., & Jourdain, S. (Eds.). (2001). *Chez nous: Branché sur le monde francophone*. Upper Saddle River, NJ: Prentice Hall.

Waggoner, M. (1999). *Une fantaisie collective: Anthologie du drame louisianais cadien* [A collective fantasy: Anthology of Louisiana Cajun plays]. Lafayette, LA: Centre d'Études Louisianaises.

# Chapter 4

# The Ecology of Writing Among the Kashinawá: Indigenous Multimodality in Brazil[1]

Lynn Mario T. Menezes de Souza
*University of São Paulo, Brazil*

## INTRODUCTION

In his *Local Histories/Global Designs*, Mignolo (2000) argues that the economic conditions created by globalization contributed to the rise of a form of thinking he calls "barbarian theorizing" or "border thinking" (pp. 308–309). He uses "barbarian" not in the sense of being in opposition to a purported "civilized" form of thinking, but as a displacement and departure from models considered to be universally valid from an (unselfconsciously or uncritical) Euro-centric or western perspective. In this sense, "barbarian theorizing" is theorizing from the "border," where the "border" means both threshold and liminality, as two sides connected by a bridge, as a geographic and an epistemological location. This means thinking as someone who has both "the formation in 'civilized theorizing' and the experience of someone who lives and experiences, including the training in 'civilized theorizing,' in communities that have been precisely subalternized and placed in the margins by the very concept and expansion of European civilization" (Mignolo, 2000, p. 309).

---

[1]This chapter was adapted from an article which appeared in *JLIE*, Vol. 1, No. 4, 2002.

"Barbarian theorizing" requires addressing the colonial difference present in the process of globalization (seen as the historic transfiguration of the process of colonization), in which the coevalness[2] of cultures, languages, and knowledges is denied. If globalization involves the remapping of a new world order, then, for Mignolo, from the perspective of "barbarian theorizing," this implies remapping cultures of (Euro-centric) scholarship and their loci of enunciation (i.e., the location from where such discourses are articulated). "Border thinking" thus seeks to illustrate this liminality—that is, the bringing together of and erasing of the frontiers between knowing *about* and knowing *from*. This may be seen as a contribution toward imagining a world without rigid frontiers and linear one-sided histories; for, after all, "knowledge ... did not begin with the Greeks but simply with life" (Mignolo, 2000, p. 310).

Hill (1996) proposes the concept of "ethnogenesis" to refer to the process of the historical emergence of peoples who define themselves in relation to a specific sociocultural and linguistic heritage. It considers culture and language as developing from an ongoing process of conflict and struggle between different cultures in contact against the backdrop of a history of domination. This involves a process whereby subalternized or threatened cultures struggle to create enduring identities in contexts of radical change and discontinuity amidst an amalgam of global and local histories. Where Mignolo focuses on ethnogenetic processes of the local–global conflict on a macrointercontinental scale, emphasizing the West and its colonial and global designs on the Americas, similar ethnogenetic conflicts occur on a microscale within nation-states such as Brazil.

In the South American context, as a result of 19th-century movements of independence against Spanish and Portuguese colonial domination, liberal Euramerican states like Brazil were created. The nation-building process that ensued, trapped local precolonial indigenous cultures located in their territories in a suffocating double-bind. Although indigenous peoples were considered as potentially equal, they needed to be educated and brought into direct relations with their fellow citizens of European descent. This was because the Euro-liberal notion of equality was based on the concept of the "citizen" which implied the existence of a culturally, racially, and politically homogeneous nation-state. The double-bind meant that within the liberal nation-state model, at the same time as the existence of indige-

---

[2]Coevalness refers to an equality of rights, values and status between the colonizing culture and its citizens and the colonized culture and its subordinated citizens. As a result of the colonizing process, equality and coevalness were upheld at a philosophical level (all the citizens of the colony were "citizens") but denied at a pragmatic, political, everyday level (the citizens of the metropolis, the colonizing community, were allocated more privileges than those of the colonized community, hence institutionalizing the so-called "colonial difference.") Much of the postcolonial effort on the part of the colonized communities was placed on denying the denial of coevalness. For a discussion of this notion, see Mignolo, 2000.

nous cultures and peoples was officially guaranteed, their difference could not be tolerated. This led, in many cases, to the extermination or assimilation of indigenous cultures (Hill, 1996, pp. 11–12).

In this chapter, an exercise in "barbarian theorizing," considering my locus of enunciation within Brazil, I focus on what I consider to be a specific aspect of this double-bind resulting from ethnogenetic local–global conflicts filtering down to the microlevel of the writing practices among the Kashinawá indigenous community. (The Kashinawá inhabit the Amazonian state of Acre in northwestern Brazil; Aquino & Iglesias, 1994.) I analyze a Kashinawá book of published texts, and an example of a multimodal Kashinawá text, both written in Portuguese. Considering the sociohistoric backdrop of a continuing process of ethnogenetic conflicts in the region, I see Kashinawá multimodal writing as part of a struggle to create an identity in the face of the radical changes and discontinuities that accompany their contact with the policies of the englobing Brazilian nation-state. Although much of the discussion on the local–global relation seems to focus on the level of the "inter-" (i.e., inter-national, inter-linguistic, inter-cultural), this chapter, focusing on a microlevel within a nation, discusses the local–global dynamic in terms of the "intra-" (i.e., intranational, intralinguistic, and intracultural). This analysis is an attempt to demonstrate the inseparability of the "macro" and the "micro," the "inter-" and the "intra-."

## The Context

In indigenous education in Brazil, the traditional focus of attention on literacy and writing has recently shifted to one on the indigenous school. The official recognition of the rights of indigenous communities to establish and run their own schools with their own curricula, containing their own local knowledges came with the new Brazilian federal constitution of 1988. Later, in 1998, the Ministry of Education drew up a proposal for a national curriculum for indigenous schools, and attention has since been concentrated on developing syllabi and teaching materials. This activity has unfortunately deviated attention from the need for more critical consideration of issues of writing in indigenous communities. In the words of Silva

> When debating the indigenous character of the schools, almost always the discussion becomes focussed questions of method, course content and teaching materials (bilingualism, ethnoscience, etc.) and fundamental presuppositions are not discussed, exactly because one uses a general "common sense" which does not question (or rather does not deepen the knowledge of) ones own concepts, on the one hand, what a school is (and its role as an instrument for the production and reproduction off the social), and on the other, what social organizations, beliefs, indigenous traditions etc might be. (1994; quoted in D'ángelis & Veiga, 1997, p. 21)

Monte (1984) quotes a letter received in November 1982 from leaders of the Kashinawá indigenous community, as saying, "We want to learn to do arithmetic, we want to learn to calculate what is owed to us, we no longer want to be exploited by the rubber plantation owners. We want to be able to read the receipts of the purchase of goods to know the value of what we have produced" (p. x).[3] Monte situates this letter as the origin of and reason for the later creation of various literacy and educational programs in Portuguese for this community in the state of Acre. These programs at present feed the now officially recognized indigenous education schools in the region.

Implicit in the use of this letter, as the justification for this and other similar indigenous educational policies and programs in Brazil, is the demand for social and political agency attributed to the voice of the indigenous subject. Such a subject is seen here as a dis-empowered subaltern incapable of self defense—a kind of nonsocial agent, locked within an ahistoric limbo of mythic time-space which does not equip him adequately as a social subject. The consequent result is that literacy and writing tend to be associated with the advent of history and subjecthood, which seem to be accompanied by a promise of the end of subalternity. Literacy and modern education are assumed to empower the indigenous subject. This notion, in turn, reinforces the developmental myth of literacy as technology (Street, 1984), which itself is based on a graphocentric[1] view of preliterate orality as functionally and communicatively deficient (Souza, 2001). In addressing such issues, my analysis risks being interpreted as a facile indictment of indigenous education in Brazil. On the contrary, I hope to contribute toward responding to Silva's plea (quoted earlier) by addressing issues that seek to investigate some of the fundamental presuppositions that are not discussed because one uses a general "common sense" which does not question certain basic concepts. The subject that I specifically address in this chapter is the concept of writing and its inter-relatedness to the concepts of time and history.

## Writing and Indigenous Education

One of the first publications of the Kashinawá indigenous educational project was a collectively-authored 1984 book called *O Jacaré Serviu de Ponte* (i.e., "The Alligator Became a Bridge"), containing texts in Portuguese and written largely by Kashinawá authors during a course to train indigenous

---

[3]Translation mine.

[1]Graphocentrism refers to the notion that Western literate cultures allocate a high value to written texts and documents, whose structures and characteristics are considered to be almost synonymous with knowledge and truth; these cultures tend to adopt the view that oral non-Western cultures, lacking in written texts, are thus necessarily deficient and inferior. From this literate, graphocentric perspective, the complexity and wealth of oral traditions remain invisible and go unperceived.

teachers for local schools. This book, presented in the preface as "a book of stories," was the product of a module of the course whose triple objectives according to Monte (1984) were as follows: (a) to teach writing in Portuguese, (b) to produce teaching materials for the prospective indigenous teachers to use in their local indigenous schools, and (c) to valorize local indigenous cultures by bringing into the written texts as much of indigenous culture as possible.

As a product of quality and persistent human investment, involving good will and a keen political interest in the emancipation of the indigenous peoples of the Brazilian Amazon, the publication of this book is commendable. This book is the result of one of the first well organized and successful attempts to train indigenous teachers and to publish indigenous writing in Brazil with the aim of supplying indigenously produced teaching materials for local indigenous schools. As it stands, however, this book is worth commenting on because, like others of its kind, it is permeated with the "common sense" concepts of the nonindigenous teachers and patrons of indigenous education in Brazil. As Mignolo (2000) warns, the epistemologies of the colonial difference created the illusion of transparency and universality within knowledge systems originating in the West, which tended to universalize both the relevance and the applicability of their concepts. Such commonsense concepts include "education," "school," "agency," "subjecthood," "emancipation," and, of course, "writing."

We are told in the preface of the book that the pioneering course, from which the book originated, (typical of similar courses of indigenous education throughout Brazil) was organized and given by nonindigenous teachers who then "selected the best texts written by the trainees" to be included in the book. We are also told that of the 25 trainees attending the course, "only a few of them were able to write this genre of stories of the past." However, no mention is made of the criteria used for selecting the texts that were to be included in the book, although we are told that "some spelling and punctuation corrections" were necessary. The "stories" of the book are organized in two parts: "Stories of Today" (*Estórias de Hoje*) and "Stories of Long Ago" (*Estórias de Antigamente*). Moreover, we are told in the preface that the "material was also illustrated" by the trainees. Incipiently conscious of indigenous multimodality,[5] Monte (1984) says, "We believe in the force of the image, in the pleasure of drawing and we discovered together the enthusiasm of telling stories through drawing." However, we have no information about the multimodality of the inter-relation between the drawings and texts of the original manuscripts and if this relation was maintained or

---

[5]Kress and van Leeuwen, 1996, define multimodality as the inter-relation of varying modes of representation, including the verbal and the visual; here it refers to the intermixing of writing and drawing.

modified in the publishing process. In other words, although "telling stories through drawing" is indeed mentioned, these stories are not presented as such in the book, and they are not organized in a separate category as are the two sections of "Stories."

The book gives more importance to the written narratives and uses the visual color drawings as illustration of the themes dealt with in the written narratives (for example, rubber extraction, *ayahuasca*,[6] feasting, rituals, and myths), rather than as texts in themselves. The preference for the term *stories* (*estórias*, fictions in Portuguese, as opposed to *História*, History, the Past, Factual events of the Past) to refer to both the narratives of the past and those of the present, emphasizes their apparently fictional and subjective aspect and reduces the legitimacy and interpretive validity of these narratives. The preface tells us that the section "Stories of Today" tells about

> the daily routine of the villages; the work of the rubber extractor, the present day experience of cooperativism, the relationship with nature, planting, hunting and fishing; also technical knowledge about making objects and instruments for working, living and feasting ...; the changes that have been taking place since the contact with urban areas; their way of life, their feelings. (Monte, 1984)

In this commonsense division between the past and the present, several important concepts go unattended. First, the nine narratives of "Stories of Long Ago" clearly follow a traditional Euro-centric concept of myth and legend and its attendant genre markers. All except one begin with expressions such as "long ago" (*antigamente*), "once upon a time" (*era uma vez*), and "at that time" (*naquele tempo*), used in the Western genre of myth to refer to a distant unspecified past, unrelated to the present and with no truth value whatsoever. Also typical of the Euro-centric genre, they are all narrated in the impersonal voice of a third person narrator. Clearly these narratives are to be read as fictions.

In the section "Stories of Today," there is no clear genre common to all the texts. Six of the 44 texts follow a narrative chronological structure, whereas the rest follow a loose descriptive and explanatory structure. Only four are clearly first-person narratives. Five texts make use of the narrative initiatory formula "I am going to tell about ..." (*Eu vou contar sobre ...*) and then lapse into descriptions and or explanations. Recurring expressions in these narratives are the undefined existentials "there is/are" (*tem*), the first-person collective "we" (*nós*) and the impersonal generic term *the Indian* (*o*

---

[6]This refers to the so-called "hallucinogenic" vision-producing drink ritually taken by the Kashinawá, and considered to be a source of knowledge, power, and healing. Note that the term *hallucinogenic* itself is culture-bound. For the Kashinawá, what they see in a vision is sacred and as real as so-called ordinary reality. Following is a discussion of the intermingling of the metaphysical and the everyday in this and other Amazonian cultures.

*índio, os índios*). All the narratives in this section display either a predominant or exclusive use of the present tenses in Portuguese.

The contrast and separation between the exclusive use of the mythical unspecified past time in the "Stories of Long Ago" and the predominant use of the present tenses in the "Stories of Today" unwittingly seem to reinforce the Euro-centric stereotype which portrays indigenous cultures as cultures without history. In this view, the indigenous subject is seen as locked either within an eternal present or a distant past. As such, the indigenous subject is considered to be apolitical, lacking in agency and subjecthood, and consequently, condemned to not learn from, and hence repeat, the past. In other words, the indigenous subject is incapable of initiating change and transformation on his or her own.

This Euro-centric stereotype of indigenous oral cultures accompanies the "autonomous" (Street, 1984) view of literacy and writing as a technology which, permitting the past to be recorded, accumulated, and reflected on, sees written culture as the basis of history and hence writing as the harbinger of modernity, agency, and transformation. This view of writing is often used by developmentalists, missionaries, and activists alike, interested variously in modernizing, converting, or emancipating indigenous cultures.

## HISTORY AND TIME:
## THE UNIVERSALIZED GLOBAL PERSPECTIVE

In part, this deficient view of the indigenous subject is reinforced by Levi Strauss's (1966) famous contrast between the existence of "cold" societies (such as indigenous Amerindian societies) supposedly without history and "hot" societies (like western societies) with history. According to Hayden White (1987), however, any distinction between cultures as supposedly historical and nonhistorical would be as absurd as the distinction between two periods of time: one prehistorical and the other historical; that is, such a distinction could only be based on the curious belief that there could be a point in the development of human culture after which its development could be represented in a discourse different from that in which this evolution in its earlier phase is represented. As White points out, rather than contrasting distinct human societies, it is more a matter of proposing different sociocultural discursive representations of time.

For White (1987), the representation of the development of certain cultures (such as Western cultures) in a specifically historical, linear, and progressive kind of discourse is based on the fact that these cultures produced, preserved, and used written records. In this sense, the use of written records is intrinsically related to and responsible for the western concept of linear progressive time. The lack of written records in cultures which do not make use of them is not therefore sufficient grounds for regarding these cultures as continuing to persist in a putative condition of prehistory. White observes the following:

> "history" of "historical" cultures is by its very nature as a panorama of domination and expansion, at the same time the documentation of the "history" of those supposedly non-historical cultures and peoples who are the victims of this process. Thus, we could conclude, the records that make possible the writing of the history of historical cultures are the very records that make possible the writing of the history of the so-called non historical cultures. (1987, pp. 55–56)

The view of cultures without history is thus a product of cultural contact in asymmetrical power relations, such as those of external or internal colonization, where the local and the global (in this case, the nation-state and the local community) interact conflictingly in what Hill (1996) called the process of ethnogenesis. The stereotype of the ahistorical indigenous culture is also a product of what Chakrabarty (1992) called "de-provincializing," and what Fairclough (1999)[7] refers to as the "natural attitude." Both are phenomena produced in incommensurable encounters which, as Mignolo (2000) shows, transform the local knowledge of the more powerful into "global designs" or universal values through the power and knowledge collusion.

Pursuing the discussion of the putative lack of historicity of indigenous cultures, Overing (1995) shows how the western concept of time is seen as abstract, independent of specific cultural practices, and is hence decontextualized ("globalized" in Mignolo's terms); moreover, it is linear, progressive, and causal. In this view of time, causality pushes the flow of time forward so that causes are seen to precede effects. By contrast, Amazonian indigenous concepts of time, according to Overing, are always contextualized and related to other aspects of their social, political, moral, and daily practices. From this situated and local indigenous perspective of time, the historical process is always seen as incorporating and not separate from mythical events. In this sense, mythical time is not seen as a distant and already occurred past time, but as an omnipresent time which has constant and continuous effects over the present with which it coexists simultaneously; besides, these

---

[7]To quote Fairclough, "A further important point is that language is widely misperceived as transparent, so that the social and ideological 'work' that language does in producing, reproducing or transforming social structures, relations and identities is routinely 'overlooked.' Social analysts not uncommonly share the misperception of language as transparent, not recognizing that social analysis of discourse entails going beyond this natural attitude towards language in order to reveal the precise mechanisms and modalities of the social and ideological work of language" (1999, p. 204).

effects of mythical time on the present may be as unforeseeable as the intentions of the mythical beings that inhabit this plane of mythical time which Sullivan (1988) calls the *primordium*.[8]

Thus, whereas from the Euro-centric perspective the actions of an unchangeable past are seen as the cause and the justification for the consequences of the present, from the indigenous perspective of time, the actions of the present are the visible and palpable evidence of the unforeseeable interferences from and interactions with the ever-present mythical and metaphysical past. For the Kashinawá, for example, it is through the ritual use of *ayahuasca*, or the intercession of the shaman, that one gains access to knowledge from this mythical plane. This knowledge helps in two ways: to understand the causes of present actions and to remedy present effects by taking different courses of action. In this sense, the Kashinawá constantly interact with the metaphysical plane of the so-called mythical past. This means that, like the present, the past also is in a constant state of flux.

Therefore, from the perspectives of White and Overing, indigenous cultures cannot be said to be lacking history. Where the Euro-centric concept of time sees history as a solid basis of linear events, the indigenous Amazonian concept of time will see history as unstable, unforeseeable and in constant flux. Thus, contextualized indigenous Amazonian concepts of time will conflict with abstract decontextualized and stable Euro-centric concepts of time and are, therefore, incommensurable. It is this incommensurability that has to be accounted for in the linguistic and cultural contacts of indigenous education.

For Overing (1995), the linear progressive concept of Euro-centric time produces a cultural logic in which one believes that what comes first acts on what comes next. This, in turn, leads, in such cultures, to the establishment and justification of apparently natural hierarchies in which an individual or group has justifiable power over those that follow, such that elders have power over their juniors and, by implication, leaders have power over their followers. By contrast, in Amazonia, where this linear and progressive concept of time does not hold, there is no institutionalization of the hierarchical principle. These are societies which do not follow the hierarchical models of the state, and their concept of the relation between time and power is radically different from the Euro-centric

---

[8]The *primordium* is shown to exist in Amazonian cultures as a space-time plane existing parallel to the present. It does not have the same value as the Euro-centric *past*, considered distant and static. The *primordium*, on the contrary, is a plane inhabited by spirits and deities at the moment of creation, before the visible and tangible forms of the present were given to living beings. Dialogue and interaction with the beings of this plane is possible and constant, often mediated by the shaman.

concept. For the Kashinawá, for instance, knowledge is not the privilege of a select group within the society, but is accessible to all through the ritual use of *ayahuasca*.[9]

Like White, Overing (1995) also emphasizes the fact that the Euro-centric concept of time is associated to concepts of causality and, consequently, affects its concept of power. As Euro-centric culture sees its concept of time and history as reflecting reality "as it really is," Western culture does not perceive the fact that this leads to value judgements on the concept of time of other cultures and results in the uncritical imposition of Western norms. Thus, both Euro-centric and indigenous concepts of time in their own manners (but with radically different consequences) affect not only the way in which each comprehends history but also the way in which each interprets historical events and, therefore, affect how each sees other cultures with different concepts of time.

The Western concept of linear and progressive time also brings with it the idea that the passage of time has a cumulative effect. This means that those who come later have greater access to and may benefit from the knowledge that results from the progressive accumulation of experience of the past. In this sense, from the Euro-centric perspective, what comes later may be qualitatively better than that which precedes it. This then justifies the fact that modern nation-states may get larger and their civilizations may, as a result, become better than those of smaller communities or cultures which will tend to be seen as primitive and backward in comparison. This above all appears to justify, again from the Euro-centric perspective, an apparent moral obligation of these larger nation-states to protect, lead, and "develop" smaller communities.

At the same time as this "universalized" concept of time and history may be the aspect of Euro-centric culture that motivates and produces well-meaning nonindigenous "caretakers" of indigenous cultures, it is also the force behind the double-bind mentioned by Hill (1996). This double-bind motivates nation-states such as Brazil to protect and consider indigenous cultures as equal on a local level. But simultaneously, it leads them to interpret equality at the nation-state level as cultural and linguistic homogeneity, often threatening the survival of the very same indigenous groups they seek to protect at the local level. In epistemological terms, the double-bind implies that the Euro-centric nation-state, although it seeks to respect and protect indigenous cultures, is unaware of the "locality" of its own epistemologies and knowledge systems and demands a homogeneity of ("universal-

---

[9]Restrictions of access to knowledge do occur, but they are qualitative and not quantitative; thus there are gender divisions which permit women access to some knowledge and practices and men to others. Although all may take "ayahuasca," it is the shaman who can deal with certain inhabitants of the metaphysical plane more efficiently due to his shifting powers.

ization" of) epistemologies at the nation-state level. Contact between the indigenous community and the nation-state ideology does not occur only at the official, governmental level. As we shall see, it also occurs (perhaps less innocuously) through the contacts these communities establish with other informal representatives of this Euro-centric ideology, such as nonindigenous teachers, NGO's, and other disseminators of writing. This double-bind is therefore also visible in much of indigenous education in Brazil and, not unsurprisingly, in the writing practices disseminated as part of these educational policies.

For instance, in the Kashinawá book *O Jacaré Serviu de Ponte*, the separation between "Stories of Today" (containing narratives pertaining to the everyday, to cultural habits and rituals), and "Stories of Long Ago" (containing mythical narratives relating to the metaphysical), would seem to be irrelevant from the indigenous perspective which, as we have seen, considers both the mythical past and the present as coexisting simultaneously. Also, within this indigenous perspective, the mythical past is directly related to the present in which it unforeseeably interferes.

Unlike the Western perspective, daily cultural practices in indigenous Amazonian cultures are directly connected to the metaphysical plane, and often include rituals (see Overing, 1995). Ritual is not necessarily an occasional event, but may be a daily event occupying hours of a community's activities. It is thus difficult to separate indigenous ritual practice from their daily practice (and, hence, from the metaphysical plane) because one is often constitutive of the other. For instance, in the four narratives which deal with the *ayahuasca* (*cipó* in Portuguese) rituals, these practices are inseparable from various metaphysical beliefs and are narrated in the "Stories of Today," such as the belief in the healing power of the anaconda, the visionary capacity of the shaman to "see" all diseases, the ritual use of *ayahuasca* to receive knowledge ("*Cipó* teaches us many things"), and the use of the "master medicine" which can help "us to do anything we want to do" (i.e., from "not catching diseases" and "attracting women" to helping one "to have perfect aim" in hunting). Once again, this knowledge of indigenous culture was not apparently available to the organizers of *O Jacaré Serviu de Ponte*, and led to the separation of narratives of daily and ritual practices from the mythical metaphysical narratives as two distinct categories, reminiscent of the Western separation of the profane and the sacred.

In some of these texts which, from the Euro-centric perspective, one would expect to be narratives as they are included in the section of "Stories of Today," there are, however, no chronological and causal sequences of events. This may be explained in the light of a different Kashinawá logic of time and sequence as we saw earlier. This is the cultural logic which emphasizes simultaneity and juxtaposition rather than chronological and causal order. Consider, for example, the narratives[10] called "There are Days" (*Tem dia*) and "I am Indian" (*Eu sou índio*):

**There Are Days**[11]
There are days when
Indians eat
There are days when
Indians don't eat
There are days when
Indians hunt
And there are days when
Indians don't hunt

There are days when
Indians work
And there are days when
Indians don't work
                                        —*Julio Barbosa Cupi*

**I am Indian**
I am Indian because we speak our language
And also because we dance the mariri
And also because we have our own baptism
And also because we catch fish with arrows
And also because we plant our food
It is manioc and banana and corn and cotton and tingui and peanuts
That's what we plant.
...
*                                      —*Norberto Sales Tener*

As can be seen, the nonindigenous organizers of the book, probably unaccustomed to "narratives" of this type with no explicit chronological or causal connections between the events contained in them, gave these texts the paratactical format of poems, probably taking recourse to the written Euro-centric concept of poetic license to accommodate texts of no recognizable written genre.

   In the second text, in spite of the appearance of the subordinate marker "because" (*porque*), there is no real logical subordination in the information given, permitting an inversion with the same informational result: "I am Indian because we speak our language," or "We speak our language because I am Indian." Similarly, in the first narrative, no explicit causal or chronological connection is given to explain, for instance, why Indians don't work on some days, or if the days on which they don't eat are a result of or the cause

---

[10]The Western concept of narrative necessarily includes a logic of causality and chronological sequence. For the unwary Western reader, this logic makes it difficult to see these texts in Portuguese as narratives.

[11]Both of these poems were originally written in Portuguese. The English translations were done by Lynn Mario T. Menezes de Souza.

*Note: The chapter author made every attempt to obtain permission for "There Are Days" and "I am Indian," despite the extreme difficulty of communicating with the publisher due to its remote location.

for the days on which they don't hunt or don't work. As we shall see later, these narratives also suffer from the lack of accompanying drawings which, besides contextualizing the narratives and juxtaposing them to the meta-physical plane, help to make them more "legible" at least to a Kashinawá reader accustomed to multimodality.

What one may conclude from this analysis of the book *O Jacaré Serviu de Ponte* (Monte, 1984) is that the model or concept of writing used in such courses of indigenous education are only vaguely sensitive to indigenous cultures as far as content is concerned. Content here seems to be mainly un-derstood as theme or topic (ritual, daily activities, myths, customs), rather than as substantial appreciation of local indigenous knowledge (perceiving, for example, the connection between ritual, metaphysics and daily prac-tices), as we saw earlier. Considered from the perspective of the colonial dif-ference and border thinking, there is no awareness that models of writing may in themselves be culture-specific and localized and not universal or transparently and ideologically neutral. This book is merely illustrative of many similar books produced under similar circumstances in programs of indigenous education in Brazil, probably displaying similar distortions.

## REMAPPING WRITING

In relation to the use of models of writing in indigenous education courses, there appears to be at least three problems:

- A lack of awareness of the complexity of writing as a cultural practice and not merely as a technology of representing speech.
- A lack of awareness of the sociocultural specificity of writing models.
- A lack of awareness of multimodality and synaesthesia in oral and writ-ten communication.

In his *The Problem of Writing Knowledge*, Bazerman (1988) describes his dis-covery of the complexity of writing as a multidimensional activity whereby he was forced to "confront the traditional view of the word as a separable, textual fact. If the written word could only be understood within a historical, social moment, that would vex many of our habits of looking at language and texts as fixed structured systems of meaning" (p. 5). In a similar vein, Syverson (1999) pleads for what she calls an "ecology" of writing denouncing composi-tion researchers for still being constrained by commonsensical cultural as-sumptions, such as the idea that writing is a personal cognitive act of individuals seeking merely to represent their thoughts, isolated from the ex-treme complexity of the physical, material and sociocultural conditions of its production and use. She argues the following:

> Composition does not consist in transferring what is inside the head onto pa-per or a computer screen. It is a manifestation of the coordination between

internal and external structures, which are constituted by and expressed through cultural and cognitive dimensions of every human activity. (Syverson, 1999, p. 183)

In relation to the cultural specificity of writing models, Scollon and Scollon (1995), in their analysis of the essayist model of writing, attempt to identify the sociocultural and historical origins of writing, specifically situating the supposedly universalized and globalized essayist model squarely within a rational and positivistic Euro-centric tradition originating in the European 17th century, and producing what they call the "utilitarian" or "C-B-S style of discourse," highlighting the characteristics of *C*larity, *B*revity, and *S*incerity.

Also emphasizing the culturally specific nature of writing, Bazerman (1988) tells us that "as a historically realized, social, epistemological activity, writing is carried on through people. People write. People read. What a text is must take into account how people create it and how people use it" (p. 5). Focusing on the child's acquisition of literacy in his own analyses of writing and orality, Kress (1997) also situates writing within the context of a society's cultural practices. Unlike Bazerman, Syverson, and the Scollons, Kress emphasizes the importance of the symbolic aspect of writing, seeing writing as a means through which a society represents itself to itself. Writing, for Kress, naturalizes certain representational habits and makes these habits available or "at hand" for a particular community. It is through the acquisition of these representational means that they have "at hand" that the members of a community become social beings and agents of writing as a social practice. This seems to echo Freire's (1972) perspective on literacy and education in general which heavily emphasized the importance in the teaching of writing to establish a dialogue with the local context, and with the needs and habits available "at hand" in a particular local culture.

## KASHINAWÁ MULTIMODALITY

In spite of the fact that the written multimodal narrative in Fig. 4.1[12] may not appear as a narrative to the unwary nonindigenous reader, it was written and drawn by a Kashinawá trainee teacher in an indigenous educational course for teachers in the state of Acre in northwestern Brazil. The text was written as part of a writing course in Portuguese for Kashinawá teachers of Portuguese and presented to the nonindigenous teacher of the course as a gift in homage to her participation in the course.

In their discussion of multimodality, Kress and van Leeuwen (1996, p. 39) present the following hypotheses: (a) human societies use a variety of

---

[12]The original is in color.

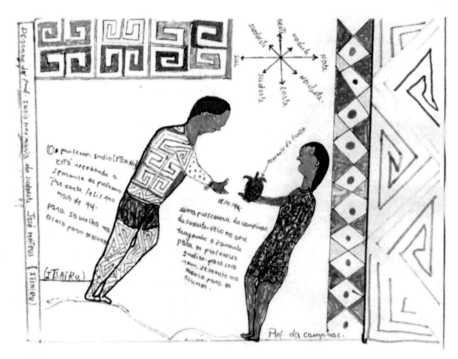

FIG. 4.1.   An example of multimodal (alphabetic and visual) Kashinawá writing.

modes of representation; (b) each mode has a different representational potential for meaning-making; (c) each mode has a specific social valuation in particular social contexts; (d) different potentials for meaning-making imply different potentials for the formation of subjectivities; (e) a range of representational modes may be used, and a range of means of meaning-making are available, each affecting the formation of the users' subjectivity; (f) the different representational modes are not separate but interact; and (g) each representational mode is continually evolving and adapts to new uses and function.

Written and drawn on a sheet of paper, the text is composed of various representational modes, among which are geometric abstract colored drawings, figurative colored drawings and handwritten alphabetic texts. On the upper and right sides of the sheet of paper, there is a frame formed by the abstract colored geometric drawings. In the center of the sheet there is a visual scene composed of figurative drawings representing a masculine indigenous character and a feminine nonindigenous character. The body of the masculine character is covered by the abstract geometric drawings in the form of what appear to be tattoos, identifying him as not only indigenous but also Kashinawá. The feminine character is holding a fruit in her outstretched arms, offering it to the indigenous man who (also with arms outstretched) receives the fruit. Covering the blank spaces of the sheet of paper, between the drawings of the two figures, are two "blocks" of hand-written alphabetic text in Portuguese saying, respectively, the following: (a) "The indigenous teacher (Itsairu) is receiving a seed from the teacher. Gift. Happy New Year 94 to sow in his school with his students," and (b) (date) "A teacher from Campinas in the Southeast came to Acre bringing the seed for the Indian teachers. To take the seed back to their schools for their students." Besides these two sets of alphabetic verbal written text, there also appear on the sheet the names of the teacher and the Kashinawá author of the text; there is also an arrow aimed at the fruit saying "fruit seed."

The two blocks of verbal text appear to form a seemingly banal narrative whose protagonists are the two characters figuratively represented on the page. The figurative drawings appear thus to be redundant, apparently merely repeating, illustrating, or complementing the verbal narratives of the two sets of alphabetic text. However, as we see later, the meaning of this multimodal text for a Kashinawá reader goes beyond this.

## From the Local Perspective: *Kene*, *Dami*, and the Anaconda

The Kashinawá use two basic modes of visual representation on paper. The first is a highly codified set of abstract geometric patterns called *kene* which may appear in reduced size in the form of an "icon" in the corner of a page or as a frame occupying the margins of the page. *Kene* drawings may also appear as tattoos covering a human figure or an object on the page. *Kene* drawings may occur alone on the page or in multimodal combinations with the other kind of drawing (called *dami*), together with alphabetic text. The second visual mode of representation, *dami*, consists of figurative line drawings and may be used to represent animals, objects, or human and supernatural beings. There is no attempt made to preestablish a point of view for an observer of the drawings, so no perspective is imputed to the drawings. The *dami* drawings rarely appear alone and normally occur in sets of figures suggesting a narrative scene or sequence.

For the Kashinawá, the visual mode of *kene* patterns metonymically represents the patterns on the skin of the anaconda (the mythical cultural hero, Yube) who brings culture, wisdom, and knowledge. The anaconda also signifies the origin of *ayahuasca* (Camargo, 1999; Lagrou, 1998), the ritual drink of the Kashinawá. According to the myth, Yube was a man who fell in love with an anaconda who he saw transforming itself into a beautiful woman. He goes to live with her in the underworld where he is introduced to the use of *ayahuasca* as a means of access to knowledge and healing. Yube one day decides to return to his human family and brings with him the secret of how to make and use *ayahuasca*. From that day on, the Kashinawá have used the drink ritualistically to acquire knowledge, healing, and power.

The Yube-anaconda myth, as yet another Kashinawá representational mode, illustrates an important aspect of this indigenous culture that Levi-Strauss (1995) defined as being "open to otherness," a characteristic of the duality permeating Amerindian philosophies. In a similar vein, Lagrou (1996, 1998) describes the Kashinawá concept of identity as constructed on a cline between the opposing poles of the "I" and the "radical Other," passing through the intermediary points of the "non-I" and the "non-Other." These intermediary poles accommodate the social categories of relatives, affines, foreigners, and potential enemies. However, it is the pole of the "radical Other" that is most feared, as it paradoxically represents both total destruction and the possibility of regeneration. It is at this pole that the feared deity Inka is located; as such, Inka is capable of total destruction and regeneration

As in the Yube-anaconda myth, the ethic of "openness to the Other" leads the Kashinawá to see contact with radical alterity as both dangerous and desirable, where one is always transformed when one enters into contact with a "radical Other." In this process of identity-construction, the Kashinawá is encouraged to seek contact with an "Other." Once contacted, on the territory of the "Other," the Kashinawá allows himself to be transformed into the "Other" (his previous state of being having been destroyed in the process); once transformed into the "Other," he then transforms whatever he learns or acquires from the "Other," domesticating and hence reducing the radical alterity of the "Other." Once the alterity of the "Other" has been transformed, the Kashinawá now returns home taking his newly acquired power, strength, or knowledge with him. Such is the Amerindian dialectic of otherness, where the subject transforms into the object or "Other" and back into the subject; the return to subjecthood, however, is the "return" to a newly transformed subject, and not the same subject at the start of the process.

In Kress and van Leeuwen's (1996) terms, the Yube-anaconda myth in itself already signifies many things through various representational modes of meaning-making in Kashinawá culture: at a verbal narrative level, it tells the story of Yube and his love for the anaconda woman; at another verbal narrative level, it tells the story of the origin of *ayahuasca*; at a metaphoric and symbolic level, it represents the ethic of openness to "Otherness," and this is symbolized in Kashinawá culture by the image of the anaconda that regularly transforms itself by a periodic change of skin to survive. Hence through these various modes of representation and meaning-making, the anaconda myth represents in Kashinawá culture the high value given to transformation and change which bring with them survival and well being.

The importance of the Yube-anaconda myth and its reference to the desirable openness to "Otherness" is reflected in the *kene* patterns which may now be seen as a mode of representing the patterns on the skin of the anaconda—a reference to the mythical metaphysical plane of Kashinawá culture and, hence, the beginning of a path of potential transformation and survival. The reverence with which the culture treats the image of the anaconda is reflected in the high degree of codification of the *kene* patterns, each of which has the name of a totemic animal. In contrast, the figurative *dami* drawings are free and uncodified. Whereas the *kene* pattern is seen as indicating the presence of the desirable force and process of transformation, the figurative *dami* drawings are used to represent the products of this process.

With the advent of writing among the Kashinawá, new cultural modes of representation have developed. The preliterate oral–verbal narratives are now transferred to paper. This enterprise, however, is not an innocuous and simple transference from one medium to the other. The previously oral representational modes interact with the new written modes of representation and the new materials available (such as the alphabet, colored pencils, and paper), transforming the previous modes and producing a mew multimodal written discourse. For instance, the high value attributed to the *kene* patterns means that their presence on the written page now functions as a marker of truth-value and legitimacy.

In the Kashinawá language, there are two verbal suffixes which function as markers of modal truth-value, and correspond to the use of *dami* and *kene* drawings in multimodal writing. According to Camargo (1996), the suffix "*-ki*" in a sentence indicates that the speaker is the source of the information in his speech. As this information has not been witnessed or legitimated by the social collectivity, in certain contexts information marked with "*-ki*" acquires the aspect of subjectivity and low truth-value. On the other hand, the suffix "*-kin*" in a sentence indicates that the information has been legitimated by the collectivity and, therefore, has high truth-value. Mythical narratives are narrated with the suffix "*-kin*." In multimodal writing, a parallel may be made between the use of the suffix "*-ki*" and *dami* drawings and the suffix "*-kin*" and *kene* patterns. The advent of writing and the introduction of the new representational modes of meaning-making on paper and with writing means that the previous meaning-making function of the oral suffixes "*-kin*" and "*-ki*" have been transformed into written language on paper with the multimodal use of the *kene* and *dami* drawings.

## MULTIMODALITY AS ETHNOGENESIS

Returning to our analysis of the multimodal Kashinawá text in Fig. 4.1, it now becomes clear that besides the two blocks of verbal alphabetic narrative, the actual narrative value of the text as a whole appears in different nonverbal manners. First, the scarce verbal alphabetic narrative refers, as we have seen, to an event in which a seed is brought by a nonindigenous female teacher from afar and given to the indigenous male teacher. This seed will generate fruits which will benefit not only the indigenous man but future generations as well, represented by his students. The marked presence of the *kene* patterns in the text, both framing the page and in the form of tattoos on the body of the male indigenous teacher (in the event narrated he is the student of the teacher from afar), indicate the presence of the force of transformation in the narrated event.

Moreover, as we have seen, the codified *kene* pattern, like the "-*kin*" suffix, refers to the mythic plane and to legitimated collective information of high truth-value. In this multimodal text, it is at this level of collective cultural knowledge on the mythical and metaphysical plane that the work of intertextuality is set into play, making present to the mind of the Kashinawá reader, through the *kene* pattern, echoes of the myth of the anaconda-Yube. Just as in the verbal (alphabetic) and figurative (*dami*) narrative, the indigenous man receives a gift from the woman from afar which will transform him, in the myth, the male Yube is attracted to, and receives something valuable from the woman from afar that will transform him. At yet another level of collective knowledge, the multimodal narrative also echoes the Amerindian ethic of openness to the "Other." This dynamic intertextuality mingles the present tense of the verbal narrative with the mythical and metaphysical plane and the ethical code of the community, leading the Kashinawá reader to dynamically and simultaneously identify the wisdom or "moral of the story" contained in the apparent banality of the narrated event. As we saw earlier, the already existing plurality of meanings present in the oral myth of Yube and the image of the anaconda itself has, with the advent of writing, now been transferred to the written medium.

However, Kashinawá culture, because of its vision-seeking rituals of *ayahuasca*, and its wealth of mythical oral meaning-making modes, has placed high value on the visual mode of meaning-making. With the introduction of alphabetic writing, the Kashinawá feel[13] that alphabetic writing on paper is insufficient and needs to be complemented by other visual modes of representation. Or rather, as we have seen in our reading of Fig. 4.1, it is the alphabetic mode that is seen as insufficient. The visual modes of *kene* and *dami*, rather than functioning as mere complements of the alphabetic text, are themselves complemented by the alphabetic text.

However, for the uninformed nonindigenous reader, unaware of local indigenous concepts of time, history, and modes of representation, the text

---

[13]This information is based on recorded interviews carried out with Kashinawá adult writers in January 2001 by Terezinha Maher.

in Fig. 4.1 appears as primitive and infantile, marked clearly by a paucity of information and communicative function. Consider the following case: If an unwary nonindigenous reader were to consider including this text within an anthology of indigenous writing, the only information that would probably be considered would be the two scarce blocks of alphabetic narrative, hardly sufficient on their own to constitute an independent written text even if given the paratactical format of poetry:

> "The indigenous teacher
> Is receiving a seed
> From the teacher.
> Gift.
> Happy New Year 94
> To sow in his school with his students."

> "A teacher from Campinas
> in the Southeast
> came to Acre
> bringing the seed
> for the Indian teachers.
> To take the seed back
> to their schools
> for their students."

Devoid of its multimodality, the text in Fig. 4.1 has been transformed into something else, to say the least.

Hence, from the local Kashinawá perspective, one may but imagine the plurality of meaning-making modes and elements that may have been dispensed with in the publication of the narratives of the book *O Jacaré Serviu de Ponte* (Monte, 1984). One can only imagine the meaning-making wealth that texts such as "There are Days" and "I am Indian" may have had in their original manuscript multimodal forms.

## CONCLUSION

The risk, then, for those nonindigenous well-wishers and specialists involved in indigenous education in cultures such as the Kashinawá is to underestimate the complexity and importance of considering writing within a sociocultural perspective and to underestimate the meaning-making potential of nonalphabetic forms of writing. As Mignolo (2000) and Boone and Mignolo (1994) point out, there is also a serious risk of not being aware of the existence in oral cultures of forms of writing and text-making which are other than alphabetic, such as ceramics, textile weaving, tattooing, and so forth, which often erroneously fall into the categories of utilitarian material culture or decorative art.

From this perspective of the unwary and uninformed Euro-centric reader, a multimodal text is more visible in its absences (no text, no story, no organization, no information, no content) than its potential for meaning-making. And this reinforces the stereotypes we saw earlier of indigenous peoples as being ahistoric, primitive, and in need of protection.

From the Kashinawá perspective, however, the persistence of and fascination with multimodal writing represents the efforts at resistance of a supposedly subdued local indigenous culture against the all-englobing national culture. Caught in the process of ethnogenesis, or globalization at the microregional level, through the appropriation of writing, the Kashinawá have sought to not only gain access to the cultural capital that writing accrues in the dominant national culture but also use writing as a means to inscribe their difference from, and thus cope with, the dominant culture on their own local terms. In this sense, the multimodal Kashinawá text may be considered symbolically as a microarena of the ethnogenetic political, social, cultural, and linguistic wars waged in Amazonian Brazil (Boone & Wright, 1988).

Equipped only with their language, their identity and, above all, their ethic and metaphysic of *ayahuasca* rituals and the "openness to the Other," the Kashinawá (like other indigenous communities caught within the double-bind of the homogeneous identity-formation process of the Euramerican nation-state) continue in their efforts to survive. This survival is not unlike the anaconda—through constant changes of skin, they seek to remain themselves by becoming different; not only allowing themselves to be transformed in the process but also transforming whatever they come into contact with, the Kashinawá have learned to write but neither writing nor the Kashinawá have emerged from this conflicting encounter unscathed; and the offspring generated from this encounter is the multimodal text.

"Barbarian theorizing" or "border thinking," as Mignolo (2000) emphasized, involves rejecting the search for totalities and the appreciation of the idea of networks and interdependence. As such, I have sought here to contribute to the de-articulation of the colonial difference, denying the denial of coevalness implicit in indigenous education in Brazil, materialized by its concepts of time, history, and writing. Like Mignolo (2000) and the Kashinawá, we need to recognize that peoples, languages, and cultures "have the right to be different precisely because 'we' are all equals" (p. 311).

## REFERENCES

Aquino, T., & Iglesias, M. (1994). *Kaxinawá do Rio Jordão—História, território, economia e desenvolvimento sustentado* [The Kashinawá of the Jordan River—History, territory, economy and sustained development]. Rio Branco, Brazil: CPI do Acre.

Bazerman, C. (1988). *Shaping written knowledge: The genre and activity of the experimental article in science*. Madison: University of Wisconsin Press.

Boone, E. H., & Mignolo, W. (1994). *Writing without words: Alternative literacies in Mesoamerica and the Andes*. Durham, NC: Duke University Press.

Camargo, E. (1996). Des Marqueurs modaux en Caxinaua. [On modal markers in Kashinawá]. *Amerindia, 21,* 1–20.

Camargo, E. (1999). Yube, o homem-sucurijo: Relato caxinauá [Yube the anaconda man: A Kashinawá narrative]. *Amerindia, 24,* 195–212.

Chakrabarty, D. (1992). Provincializing Europe: Postcoloniality and the critique of history. *Cultural Studies, 6*(3), 337–357.

D'Angelis, W., & Veiga, J. (Eds.). (1997). *Leitura e escrita em escolas indígenas* [Reading and writing in indigenous schools]. Campinas, Brazil: Mercado de Letras.

Fairclough, N. (1999). Linguistic and intertextual analysis within discourse analysis. In A. Jaworski & N. Coupland (Eds.), *The discourse reader* (pp. 183–212). London: Routledge.

Freire, P. (1972). *Pedagogia do oprimido* [Pedagogy of the oppressed]. Oporto, Portugal: Afrontamento.

Hill, J. D. (Ed.). (1996). *History, power and identity: Ethnogenesis in the Americas 1492-1992*. Iowa: University of Iowa Press.

Hill, J. D., & Wright, R. (Eds.). (1988). *Rethinking history and myth. Indigenous South American perspectives on the past*. Urbana: University of Illinois Press.

Kress, G. (1997). *Before writing: Rethinking the paths to literacy*. London: Routledge.

Kress, G., & van Leeuwen, T. (1996). *Reading images: The grammar of visual design*. New York: Routledge.

Lagrou, E. M. (1996). Xamanismo e representação entre os kaxinawá [Shamanism and representation among the Kashinawá]. In E. J. M. Langdon (Ed), *Xamanismo no Brasil: Novas Perspectivas*. Florianópolis, Brazil: Editora da UFSC.

Lagrou, E. M. (1998). *Caminhos, duplos e corpos: Uma abordagem perspectivista da identidade e alteridade entre os kaxinawá* [Paths, doubles, and bodies: A perspectival approach to identity and alternity among the Kashinawá]. Unpublished doctoral dissertation, University of São Paulo, Brazil.

Levi-Strauss, C. (1966). *The savage mind*. Chicago: University of Chicago Press.

Levi-Strauss, C. (1995). *The story of lynx*. Chicago: University of Chicago Press.

Mignolo, W. (2000). *Local histories/global designs: Coloniality, subaltern knowledges and border thinking*. Princeton, NJ: Princeton University Press.

Monte, N. L. (1984). *O Jacaré serviu de Ponte* [The alligator was a bridge]. Rio Branco, Brazil: Comissão Pró Indio do Acre.

Overing, J. (1995). O Mito como história: Um problema de tempo, realidade e outras questões [Myth as history: A problem of time, reality, and other issues]. *Mana, 1*(1), 107–140.

Scollon, R., & Scollon, S. W. (1995). *Intercultural communication*. Oxford, England: Blackwell.

Silva, M. (1994). A conquista da escola: Educação escolar e movimento de professores indígenas no Brasil [The conquest of the school: Schooling and the indigenous teachers movement in Brazil]. In *Em aberto 'educação escolar indígena '63* (pp. 15–18). Brasília: INEP.

Souza, L. M. T. M. (2001). Para una ecologia da escrita indígena: A escrita multimodal Kaxinawá. In I. Signorini (Ed.), *Investiganda a relação orall esrcito e as teorias do letramento* [Toward an ecology of indigenous writing: Kashinawá multimodal writing]. Editora Mercado de Letras, Carpihas.

Street, B. (1984). *Literacy in theory and practice*. Cambridge, England: Cambridge University Press.

Sullivan, L. E. (1988). *Icanchu's drum: An orientation to meaning in South American religions*. New York: Macmillan.

Syverson, M. (1999). *The wealth of reality: An ecology of composition*. Carbondale: Southern Illinois University Press.

White, H. (1987). *The content of the form*. Baltimore: Johns Hopkins University Press.

# Part II

# INTERROGATING
# LANGUAGE POLICIES

# Chapter 5

# The Language Issue in Brazil: When Local Knowledge Clashes With Expert Knowledge

Kanavillil Rajagopalan
*State University at Campinas (UNICAMP), Brazil*

## SETTING THE STAGE

Local knowledge all too frequently finds itself in direct confrontation with knowledge that specialists would like to bring to bear on local issues. Generally speaking, specialist knowledge is knowledge produced and disseminated in the heartland of academia, composed mainly of high-profile universities, prestigious research centers and the like that somehow manage to exist in cozy and self-imposed isolation from the communities that host and maintain them. As it happens, scholars who are actively engaged in the production and dissemination of specialized knowledge are generally persons with plenty of bookish knowledge, but often with little practical or hands-on experience. Small wonder therefore that, in the last two decades or so, these scholars have increasingly become easy target for charges of elitism and social irrelevance, coming from both the left and the right of the political spectrum. According to those who look at the problem from a leftist point of view, many of these intellectuals have opted to quarantine themselves from the community outside the campuses with whose members they used to work in close unison in the past. And even more disappointingly, they have allowed themselves to be co-opted into the power structures rep-

**99**

resented by the university (Jacoby, 1987). Those who criticize them from a rightist perspective would like to see these "public intellectuals" made more and more accountable to the public at large and the results of their research subjected to market forces and quality controls, in such a way that success becomes synonymous with survival in "the public intellectual market" (Posner, 2000).

Specialist or expert knowledge is all-embracing in its ambitions and global in its reach and, in order to maintain it that way, researchers concentrate on what is universally valid, sweeping aside everything that is subjective, occasional, sporadic or ephemeral. The so-called experts typically approach local problems with concepts and categories of analysis that were formulated *a priori* and without taking into account the specificities as well as the diversities of local environments. It is the logic of rationalist thought functioning at its relentless best. According to that logic, individual cases must somehow all be "cribb'd, cabin'd and confin'd" in terms of preconceived conceptual grids before they can be accounted for or explained away—that is to say, brought underneath an overarching explanatory framework even if this means forcing each and every one of those cases, including the ones that reveal themselves to be stubbornly recalcitrant, into the Procrustean bed of readymade definitions valid for all times and climes.

In this chapter, my aim is to turn the spotlight onto one such case of conflict between expert and local knowledge. The expert knowledge that I shall look at is the knowledge accumulated over the years—well-nigh a century to date—by the science of "modern linguistics," where the qualifier "modern" is meant to be a constant reminder of the discipline's self-proclaimed status as the sole custodian of sound, scientific knowledge about language, against all rival claims. To take a typical example, here is what Postman and Weingartner (1966, p. 5) had to say as they sought to explicate the scientific nature of the discipline:

> The facts of linguistic science in 1935 may be different from the facts of linguistic science in 1960, which in turn may be different from the facts of linguistic science in 1980. But what remain essentially unchanged and continually productive are the process of inquiry that we define as *linguistics* or, if you will, the *linguistic enterprise*.

In other words, part of what is meant when its practitioners call linguistics a science is that the kind of knowledge it produces is timeless. Furthermore, it is believed to be equally well applicable to *all* cases, no matter how geographically or culturally diverse they may happen to be from one another. Notice, incidentally, that the authors of the passage just cited make no reference to dates earlier than 1935. This is by no means fortuitous, because the science of modern linguistics is also anxious to deny its own historicity (Ehlich, 1981, p. 154). Just as modern chemistry is anxious to distance itself from alchemy, from which it historically evolved, so too modern linguistics will have no truck with philology, which preceded it. The "linguistic enterprise" consists, so it is claimed, in a certain *attitude* to the very business of inquiry, not in this or that specific finding it may provisionally arrive at at any given moment. Linguistics is a science in that it aims at overarching explanatory frameworks, where all individual cases—past or present or the ones yet to present themselves—can be neatly accommodated.

The local knowledge that I shall be looking at in this chapter is what is often pejoratively referred to as "folk wisdom" about what natural languages are and how they function in real life. All cultures, all societies, have their own "home-grown" theories about language, how individual languages came into being and so forth. Furthermore, in any given culture, ordinary men and women are typically wont to say that they know enough about language to be able to give their own opinions concerning how languages should be taught, cultivated, preserved and protected against forces of deterioration or defilement et cetera. Unfortunately, professional linguists tend to brush aside all those opinions and beliefs which they consider worthy of being studied at best as a matter of anthropological curiosity. In other words, modern linguists, who pride themselves on being the only scholars who approach language in a truly scientific spirit, are loath to listen to the ordinary person in the street, preferring to dismiss all folk wisdom as naïve, pre-scientific, or irremediably muddle-headed.

The specific case that I shall zero in on is a spirited debate over language that is currently under way in Brazil. Brazil stands apart from the twelve other nations that, together with it, make up the continent of South America, in that it is the only country which has Portuguese as its national language (Spanish being the overwhelmingly predominant language on the rest of the continent, spoken alongside a number of indigenous languages spoken by isolated pockets of native Indian populations scattered across the entire continent—most of them on the verge of extinction, and a sprinkling of French, English, and Dutch, mostly confined to the Guianas). In Brazil, as already noted, the language issue is at this moment one of the most passionately disputed ones. On one side of the dispute are those who think that Portuguese is under an imminent threat from English and believe that there is an urgent need to do something about it, such as the enactment of appropriate laws to curb the advance of the world's leading lingua franca, lest its growing presence in the country should negatively impact the local culture and, with it, jeopardize the very survival of the national language, Portuguese. On the other side are those who believe that there is no such threat to begin with and that what the advocates of legislative intervention into the linguistic reality badly need is some familiarity, however modest, with the enormous wealth of scientific knowledge about language, painstakingly accumulated over the years by professional linguists. Linguistics, it is argued, has long tackled the issue of language change and that the predominant view among linguists is that change is neither for the better nor for the worse, but simply takes place in tandem with changing relations of contact and approximation amongst different speech communities. The controversy over whether or not to enact laws to protect Brazil's national language, (Brazilian) Portuguese, reveals a scenario in which the local knowledge of lay persons is at loggerheads with the global knowledge that linguists, persons who claim to be specialists on language, would like to bring to bear on the same issues.

It is reasonable to expect that an examination of the way the dispute has been conducted over the last few years, as well as the arguments used by both sides to advance their claims, and the rhetorical ploys used by each side to dismiss or belittle the opponent's arguments, will shed some light on the kind of stalemate which usually results from such confrontations and which the Brazilian case seems to confirm. Needless to say, it would be ironic, not to say foolhardy, to expect to derive global, universally valid lessons from a study of individual cases of clash between global and local knowledge, although one should not rule out the prospect of there emerging some discernible tendencies. What I do hope to achieve is, more modestly, a clearer appreciation of the reasons for the continuing stand-off between expert and lay knowledge as brought to the fore by the Brazilian example, and the need for attempting, before anything else, to bridge the communication gap observed to exist in this situation, and make some speculative remarks as to what sort of concessions either side may need to make in order that conditions for a fruitful dialogue might be made available.

## AN ORIENTATION TO LINGUISTICS

As the controversy rages and the battle lines are drawn with increasing precision, it has become clear that linguists have suddenly found themselves having to combat not only public opinion at large, but rival "specialists" who claim expertise of their own on language: so-called "traditional grammarians." Now, old-fashioned grammarians have served as the linguists' favorite "sparring partners" ever since the discipline consolidated itself. Professional linguists characteristically see them as the main culprits for the perpetuation and proliferation of so many false ideas about language in the society at large. Students of introductory courses in linguistics are routinely told that it is the grammarian who stands in the way of popular knowledge about language taking the scientific turn. For the grammarian typically dictates how language *should be* used, in sharp contrast with the scientifically oriented linguist who is interested in finding out how language *is* used. The one *prescribes* where the other *describes*. Unlike the grammarian who, according to the linguists, stipulates the *dos* and *don'ts* of usage, and is a "self-appointed gatekeeper" of the community's language and a "pompous meddler" in matters linguistic, the linguist is a "neutral" observer who is careful not to take sides. On their part, the traditional grammarians are no less suspicious of the linguist who is, in their view, an upstart and a latecomer to the field who has no real sensibility for language nor respect for the wealth of literature produced by generations of its speakers.

What is seldom admitted by the linguists is that there are a number of intricate ties between folk wisdom and the traditional grammar. A notable early exception is Bloomfield, who pointed out that the former is frequently invested with a certain air of authority by being incorporated into volumes of reference grammar and learned treatises on language:

> Traditional lore ... is occasionally put into literary form and developed in detail, as in the well known treatise of Richard Grant White, *Words and Their Uses, Past and Present: A Study of the English Language* (New York, 1870). (Bloomfield, 1944, p. 46)

In many societies, the grammarians are looked upon as veritable savants, the true guardians of their languages. Many of the ideas contained in folk wisdom probably had their origin in the compendiums of grammar. In their turn, as pointed out by Bloomfield, grammarians often reproduce deeply ingrained beliefs (including prejudices) about language that are widely disseminated in the societies in which they live and work. Thus the idea that there is a correct way to speak one's own mother tongue whose rules have to be learned as such is just as much part of the folk wisdom in many societies in the world as it is a guiding principle of traditional, prescriptive grammars. In this case, as in several other similar cases, it is difficult to tell where the idea first originated.

Once again, it is important to refrain from making hasty generalizations. There is nothing universal about the felt need to control linguistic usage through normative rules. Among scholars who have contested the idea of language standardization as a universal tendency in all speech communities is Milroy. Milroy (2001) argues that the very idea of there being a "correct" or canonical form of language is the result of what he refers to as "the ideology of the standard language." In his view, "standardization consists of the imposition of uniformity upon a class of objects [namely, in our case, usages]" (Milroy, 2001, p. 531). Milroy goes on to argue that there are many societies where the idea of standardization is still an alien concept and whose languages are considered "primitive" (for, among other things, *precisely* this reason).

It is important to point out that the linguists' distrust of folk wisdom and traditional grammar is due not always to a perception that the latter have *no* theory to back them up. It is rather that they are based on the *wrong* kind of theory, often followed without any awareness of it. Furthermore, the kind of informal theory from which they draw their sustenance has no scientific rigor. Indeed, as a matter of general rule, it is hardly ever the case that a person's reasoned claims are based on no theory at all. Thus ordinary, everyday expressions like "to learn something by heart" or the word "sanguine" meaning "hopeful," which we routinely use in our everyday speech, betray past theories about where the seat of learning was believed to be or what caused emotions to rise, although those who use these expressions regularly may not be conscious of that fact. The fact that we continue to use "to learn by heart" no more commits us to the theory that initially justified it than does the use of "sunrise" and "sunset" which, if literally true, would mean that the solar system still works the way Ptolemy thought it did. What this goes to prove is that, in the present stand-off between the linguist and the lay person, as revealed by the evolving language dispute in Brazil, the expert (the linguist) is not posing as the one who "knows everything one needs to know," locked in an unequal dispute with someone who "knows nothing" but unfortunately is unaware of even that. Linguists know only too well that the lay person is as convinced about the "rationality" of their arguments as is the linguist; the only difference between them has to do with the kind of authority they each invoke and the criteria they employ to justify that rationality.

Modern, scientifically oriented linguists (from now on, simply "linguists") often do concede that the ordinary people have their "informal" theories about language. But they typically either ignore them or treat them as "museum pieces," at best interesting from an anthropological perspective (Niedzielski & Preston, 1999). Contemporary linguistics is, one may say, founded upon the outright rejection of what the ordinary person has to say about language (Hutton, 1996). Ferdinand de Saussure (1916), universally hailed as "the father of modern linguistics," was openly scornful of folk wisdom about language, and Leonard Bloomfield, his North-American counterpart (referred to as the "real founder of American linguistics"— Hall, 1955, p. 41) advised young field linguists to turn a deaf ear whenever their informants would volunteer opinions *about* their language (Bloomfield, 1944). Despite all his revolutionary zeal and desire to turn the tables on his structuralist predecessors, Noam Chomsky declared absolute fidelity to the founding principle of the discipline when he said that a truly scientific grammar "attempts to specify what the speaker actually knows, not what he may report *about* his knowledge" (Chomsky, 1965, p. 8; emphasis added).

In what follows, I first present a bird's-eye view of the controversy between local and specialized knowledge, between folk linguistics and "scientific" linguistics, as it is currently playing itself out in Brazil. In the next two sections, I look at the controversy from the perspective of each of the contending sides. Then, I attempt to draw some lessons from it, offering some explanations as to why I think no genuine dialogue is possible under the existing circumstances. The final section contains some tentative proposals for possible solutions.

## THE PORTUGUESE LANGUAGE IN BRAZIL
## AND THE "THREAT" OF ENGLISH

Over the last few years, Brazil's intelligentsia has been riven by a growing dispute over a supposed threat to the country's national language, Portuguese. At the root of the problem is the speed with which English has been replacing French as the country's favored foreign language and is being welcomed by the upper and middle classes as the language of the globalized world and the road to success in the emerging world order. A clear sign of the insatiable demand for learning English is the amazing number of language schools opening new branches throughout the length and breadth of the country, their enrollment figures swelling by geometric proportions (cf. Rajagopalan & Rajagopalan, in press). An advertisement recently put out in one of the country's leading newspapers by one of these language schools told the reader that 80% of world's income is in the hands of English speakers (native or non-native) and that in many cases a knowledge of English helps double your paycheck. "It is a must," the copy-writer concluded, "in the 21st century." However, alarmed by the increasing presence of English in the country's day-to-day life, more and more people, including many who have acquired a reasonable degree of proficiency in the language, are starting to believe that there is an urgent need to put a damper on the relentless advance of the "alien" language and thereby guarantee—in their view—the survival of their native language.

   Now, it is a well-known fact that national languages often function as extremely powerful flags of allegiance (Rajagopalan, 2002). "Languages," as Dr. Johnson put it, "are the pedigree of nations" (quoted in Snead, 1990, p. 231). A threat to a nation's language is all too often interpreted to be a threat to that nation's very integrity. The crucial connection between the two was pointed out by Buck several decades ago:

> Of all the institutions which mark a common nationality, language is the one of which a people is most conscious and to which it is most fanatically attached. It is the one conspicuous banner of nationality, to be defended against encroachment, as it is the first object of attack on the part of a power aiming to crush out a distinction of nationality among its subject peoples. (Buck, 1916; cited in Greenfield, 1998, p. 635)

Small wonder therefore that the alleged threat to Brazil's national language has become a burning issue and has attracted a considerable amount of

public attention. There have even sprung up local movements such as the
Rio de Janeiro-based "Movement for the Valorisation of the Culture, Language and Riches of Brazil" (MV-Brasil), founded by groups of concerned
citizens with the explicit purpose of bringing the weight of their opinion to
bear on their elected representatives.

Their numbers have been steadily increasing, as can be easily attested by
the media attention the topic has received in recent years. Hardly a day
passes by without an extremely worried member of the public sending a letter to their local newspaper, voicing their apprehension about the presence
of English words in their language. English words have been incorporated
into Portuguese in their thousands, often supplanting already available native equivalents. Called *estrangeirismos* ("foreignisms"), these words have become the lightning rod for public criticism concerning the growing
presence of English in their midst which is typically viewed as the most visible sign of globalization and what many critics see as Brazil's inadvertent
and ill-advised entry into a new world order where the country has, in their
view, more to lose than to gain.

Sometimes their fury is targeted against the very media to which they
turn in order to air their grievances. Some time ago, *Folha de São Paulo*, one
of Brazil's leading national newspapers, published a letter from an enraged
reader condemning what he felt was the completely unwarranted use of
English words even in titles given to the different supplements of the very
newspaper: the supplement devoted to adolescents is called *Folhateen*
(where the suffix *teen* is a straightforward borrowing from English) and the
one on finances and money investments is called *Folhainvest*. "Is it really in-
dispensable to have recourse to foreign languages to name the different
sections of the newspaper?" asked the irate reader who wrapped up his brief
note of protest with the following ironic punch line: "Or could it be the case
that it has somehow escaped my attention that the newspaper is already cir-
culating in the United States?" (Rocha, 2001, p. 3).[1]

Indeed, so sensitive has the whole issue become that some politicians, eager to reap electoral benefits from the whole situation, have come up with
suggestions for legislative measures aimed at curbing the use of English.
One such step is a bill proposed by a Congressman by the name of Aldo
Rebelo, which has already passed muster in the lower house of Brazil's legis-
lature and is waiting for its turn for discussion in the upper house, the Senate. The bill proposes, among other things, tough penalties, including
hefty fines, for the use of foreignisms in all but a handful of situations. A
copy cat bill by a state representative by the name of Jussara Cony is being
debated by the legislative assembly of the southern state of Rio Grande do
Sul. Another bill, presented by Senator Gilvan Borges, aims at forbidding

---

[1]All passages cited from Brazilian sources have been translated into English by the present
writer. For the sake of idiomaticity, I have sometimes sacrificed the letter to reflect the spirit.

universities and other institutions of higher learning in the country from stipulating prior knowledge of foreign languages (generally English, French and German) as a prerequisite for admission to graduate programs for the alleged reason that the vast majority of the country's population do not have a working command of any of them. Encouraged by the huge repercussion of these legislative proposals in the media, many other politicians have actively joined the crusade and others are struggling to come up with ingenious proposals of their own. A municipal councilor in the city of São Carlos (the State of São Paulo) by name Idelso Marques de Souza lost no time in presenting a bill prohibiting the use of English words on all signboards, posters, neon signs, newspaper advertisements, and publicity leaflets within the jurisdiction of the city.

The following remark by Congressman Rebelo, explaining the *raison d'être* for his proposed bill, synthesizes the main political argument for legislative intervention:

> How can one explain this undesirable phenomenon [the transformation of Portuguese by the invasion of foreignisms], a potential threat to one of the most vital elements of our cultural heritage, the mother-tongue, which has been under way with growing intensity in the last 10 to 20 years? How can one explain it except by pointing to the state of ignorance, to the absence of critical and esthetic sense, and even to the lack of self-respect [of segments of our country's population]? (Rebelo, 1999, pp. 184–185)

Politicians are not the only ones who have added fuel to the fire of popular discontent over the way the government has handled language policy in the country. Many academics, including notably traditional grammarians, have joined the fray on behalf of those who urge the government to step in. Pasquale Cipro Neto, a grammarian whose widely read syndicated weekly column is featured in the country's leading newspapers, is among those harsh critics whose number is today legion. Here is an excerpt from one of his recent writeups:

> The other day, in a radio news bulletin I heard something I just couldn't believe. Referring to the selling price of a certain product on the world market, the newsreader said that it cost "8 *dolares*" (Eight U.S. dollars) and "43 cents." I confess I simply go mad every time I hear one of these barbarisms in the mass media. Well, the expression I would personally prefer to use is not exactly "barbarism," it is something else, perhaps unprintable. "Cents" is the plural of "cent" in English. I would very much like to know what led the newsreader, who is presumably a speaker of Brazilian Portuguese, to pronounce the word "cents" [rather than "*centavos*"]. Why "*dolares*" in Portuguese and "cents" in English? There is only one word for it: underdevelopment. Deep-rooted. Cultural. (Cipro Neto, 2001, p. 18)

Such outbursts of anger might lead someone unaccustomed to the politics of language currently playing itself out in Brazil to conclude that they are simply the typical reaction from purists unwilling to accept neologisms or changes of whatever kind in their language.

It so happens, however, that the language issue in Brazil is—as it is possibly elsewhere in the world—deeply implicated in the geopolitics of the whole region. In most of Latin America, the advance of the English language is typically viewed as the most visible sign of the role played by the United States as the post-cold war period's only remaining superpower. There is widespread resentment about the fact that, in the emerging world order, the countries in South America are being reduced to the status of mere satellite nations. "The distrust of foreignisms," wrote Garcez and Zilles, "is the distrust of Anglophone presence in the day-to-day life in Brazil, especially that of the symbolic omnipresence of North-American corporate interests" (2001, p. 22). The following remark by Pennycook is very much to the point: "... a more critical analysis of the global spread of English reveals a broad range of questions about its connection to social and economic power with and between nations, to the global expansion of various forms of culture and knowledge, and various forces that are shaping the modern world" (1994, p. 23).

In order to get a grip on what is really happening in Brazil at this moment, it is absolutely crucial that we understand the reasons for the growing public apprehension at the (real or imagined) prospect of being systematically robbed of their national identity, thanks to the presence of an alien language in their midst. It is important to recognize that the rise of nationalism in many parts of the world today is a perfectly understandable (albeit ultimately indefensible) reaction to what the ordinary people see as the aggressive incursion into their lives of alien values and lifestyles, paraded before them as symbols of the new spirit of globalism and internationalism currently sweeping across the continents. As Giroux (1994) has put it,

> As old borders and zones of cultural difference become more porous or eventually collapse, questions of culture become increasingly interlaced with issues of power, representation and identity. Dominant cultural traditions once self-confidently secure in their modernist discourse of progress, universalism and objectivism are now interrogated as ideological beachheads used to police and contain subordinate groups, oppositional discourses, and dissenting social movements. (p. 29)

Now, it is all too easy (but, as I argue later in this chapter, totally counterproductive) to dismiss the growing popular reaction in Brazil against the unbridled advance of the English language as an irrational outburst of pent-up fury and frustration from a misinformed and frenzied mob, of the kind uncharitably described by Shakespeare as "the blunt monster with uncounted heads, the still discordant wavering multitude." Confronted with mob mentality, experts typically tend to brush it aside as unworthy of attention. However, we ignore at our own peril the fact that, in the absence of a more tangible alternative, these ordinary persons in the street are finding themselves left with no option but to assume an openly defiant stance that is, perhaps unbeknownst to themselves, dangerously chauvinistic (Rajagopalan, 2002). Interestingly enough, the very same persons, when consulted in their more sober moods, are likely to express opinions in favor of greater contacts between peoples and cultures around the world. Opinion polls have repeatedly shown that sizeable segments of the country's population are satisfied with the way Brazil has, over the last decade or so, opened itself to greater contact with the rest of the world. Barring very few exceptions, no one wants to go back to the days of isolationism and the disastrous policy of narcissistic navel-gazing in the name of self-reliance that marked populist governments in the past, not only in Brazil but right across the entire South American continent.

In other words, it is important to point out that local knowledge is often hopelessly riddled with internal contradictions. Folk wisdom seldom comes under critical scrutiny at the hands of people at large themselves. As a result, one should not be surprised to find radical and reactionary elements peacefully cohabiting in these thought patterns. It is here that the need for expert critical intervention arises, aimed at, before everything else, teasing out the contradictions that plague those structures. We shall return to this issue later on. Meanwhile, it might be interesting to take a look at the way professional linguists in the country—the self-styled experts in matters linguistic in Brazil and indeed elsewhere—have reacted to the challenge from the streets. As we shall see, dogmatic and often arrogant postures of experts in their effort to deal with local knowledge only help make things worse than they already are, instead of helping to defuse the standoff.

## THE ROLE OF ACADEMIC LINGUISTS
## IN THE ONGOING DISPUTE

The initial reactions from linguists to the growing demand for legislative measures to curb the advance of English in Brazil were mostly muted, marked by stunned silence and total disorientation. Slowly but steadily, however, they recovered their nerves and, as a first step, closed their ranks. An early reaction came from Carlos Alberto Faraco, an influential linguist, who wrote the following in a widely commented article published in *Folha de São Paulo*:

> It is probably no exaggeration to suggest that for most people the claim that human languages can be the object of science may sound rather strange. Normally, it is believed that the old compendiums of grammar contain everything that needs to be said about a given language. There is even a quasi religious reverence towards works of grammar. At the same time, common

sense saddles the language with a set of categorical (not demonstrated) statements that together constitute a powerfully mystical discourse of great social
penetration. (Faraco, 2001a, p. 37)

These opening words were followed by the self-reassuring remark:

> Be that as it may, since the end of the 18th century, there has been in steady
> process of construction a body of scientific knowledge about human lan-
> guages. This science—linguistics—is already established securely in uni-
> versities all over the world and has steadily been piling up a respectable
> wealth of knowledge, comprising observations and analyses, that corrode
> to its very entrails the quasi religious veneration of old grammar books, in
> its [self-assumed] role as the mythical discourse of common sense. (Faraco,
> 2001a, p. 37)

The passages just cited confirm a number of the characteristic features of
the typical attitude of linguists vis-à-vis all other discourses about language
that compete with their exclusive and exclusionary claims to truth. Here is
the most important amongst them. The choice between linguistics on the
one hand and folk wisdom as encapsulated in traditional grammar on the
other is a choice between modern science and old-fashioned religion (twice
referred to in quick succession). Linguistics is thus a true child of the Enlightenment spirit that is believed to have helped drive away all mystical
and religious superstitions and in Kant's celebrated words, borrowed from
Horace, paved the way for the new role of man as the maker of his own destiny: "*Sapere aude*" (Have the courage to use your own reason).

The Popperian idea of science as a cumulative enterprise is also very
clearly evident in the eagerness with which Faraco delves into history in order to stretch the historicity of the "modern science of language" farther
back in time than most authors of introductory textbooks seem willing to
go. Presumably, the contending Kuhnian view of science as "progressing"
by fits and starts, stumbling along from paradigm to paradigm, would probably have meant having to seriously consider the possibility that the tussle
between modern linguistics and traditional grammar is one between a lat-
ter-day paradigm still struggling for recognition by the public at large and a
fully consolidated one within a long tradition of thinking about language
rather than one between science and superstition, as Faraco is eager to
portray it.

The universality of the kind of knowledge accumulated over the years by
linguists is also highlighted in the reference to "universities all over the
world." The unstated claim here is that linguistic knowledge cuts across language boundaries. Linguistics is universal in that scholars who pursue the
study know no linguistic or cultural barriers. What a Brazilian linguist has to
say is readily understood by their Japanese counterpart, whose views, in
their turn—insofar as they are rigorously scientific—have nothing so exclu-

sively Japanese about them that they cannot be readily comprehended by, say, a Kenyan linguist groomed in the same scientific "culture." The language of science is truly universal. In fact, it is the possession of this wonderful asset that makes a linguist different from the lay person. Whereas the latter is parochial in their worldview as well their aspirations, the former is a true "citizen of the world." In short, the linguist is a scientist, in possession of the metalanguage of science which is fully free from the cultural elements that characterize the language of ordinary people. As Davis (1997) puts it: "The reason linguists are still firmly attached to believing that there is and must remain a major difference between lay and theoretical metadiscursive remarks is that linguists are still tied to believing in the objectivity of linguistic facts" (p. 33). And also, as he might have added, tied to believing the fully transparent nature of the metalanguage at their disposal—"writing degree zero" as Roland Barthes (1975) famously characterized it, making it eminently suitable for representing those objective facts with no distortion whatever. The universal aspirations of the language of modern science were eloquently made clear by Leibniz who, thoroughly impressed by the impeccably universal character of the language of mathematics, is said to have speculated that if God Almighty were someday to vouchsafe a tête-à-tête with ordinary mortals on earth made in His own image, the only language of communication they could possibly have between them would be that of mathematics! (i.e., an all-perfect God must use an all-perfect language to communicate His thoughts).

Other Brazilian linguists have not been slow in voicing their concern over the political fall-out from the ongoing controversy. If Faraco, as we haven seen, vindicates the superiority of the science of language by invoking such of its characteristics as its institutional prestige, its universality and its cumulative nature, Garcez and Zilles (2001) insist on the timelessness of the linguists' claims. By contrast, commonsense is tied to the "here" and "now" of particular historical moments whose interest and validity may or may not outlast the very moment in which they are deemed relevant or topical. In other words, the common person is unwilling and, more importantly, unable to step outside the specificities of the particular historical moment in which they find themselves and, as a result, is prevented from identifying the true universal ensconced in particular events and episodes. At the same time, the person in the street is also given to unwarrantedly universalizing events that are in fact episodic and of passing historical significance, thanks to their refusal or inability to take a transcendental view in respect of their lived experience. All these ideas are there as a backdrop when the authors claim:

> Many of those who discuss the question seem to believe that foreignisms are a phenomenon unique to the contemporary historical moment, symptomatic of an insidious alien invasion by means of language. Upon observing the frequency, no doubt very high indeed, of elements from the English

language in [contemporary] Brazilian Portuguese, a presence that can also
be observed in other languages such as German, there are those who imagine that the agenda of Anglo-American imperialism is being put into practice by undermining the thought processes of Portuguese speakers through
the introduction of words from English. If this were indeed the case, it
would make perfect sense to mobilize all resources to defend the Portuguese language and the Brazilian people from the attack under way.
(Garcez & Zilles, 2001, p. 24)

Another linguist, Marcos Bagno, uses no self-restraint while venting his
fury over the fact that Congressman Rebelo, who is currently spearheading
the national debate on behalf of public opinion and lay wisdom, frequently
invokes the authority of traditional grammarians like Evanido Bechara and
the members of *Brazilian Academy of Letters*. In his own words:

For God's sake, why should a caucus of forty or so people—in their majority,
not even writers, not even philologists—there being amongst their ranks
medical doctors, journalists, jurists, business entrepreneurs, army officers,
clerics, economists etc.—be entrusted with the task of making decisions
about the destiny of a language spoken and written in a country of 170 million inhabitants? What scientific credentials do these vainglorious ladies and
gentlemen have in order to legislate over the issue? Wouldn't it be more reasonable to consult , for example, the nearly two thousand members of the
Brazilian Association of Linguistics which has amongst its ranks scientists, researchers, teachers and other specialists on questions relating to language,
linguistic communication and teaching of languages? After all, who would
dare propose a law on surgical procedures if it were rejected, *in limine*, by the
*Federal Advisory Board on Medical Practices*? Who would go ahead with a legislative bid to discipline the practice of jurisprudence, if it were rejected as pre-
posterous by Brazil's *Order of Advocates*? (Bagno, 2001, p. 52)

The preceding passage is interesting for several reasons. The tone of in-
credulity and impatience regarding public ignorance of the achievements
of modern linguistics and also a blind trust on their part in the authority of
the "immortals" of the (largely ceremonial) Academy of Letters needs no
further comment. What does impress the reader, though, is the author's in-
sistence on indulging in recriminations against all those who fail to see the
rights of professional linguists to be consulted on all linguistic matters and
to be treated on a par with doctors and lawyers, whose opinions are often
taken to be the last word insofar as their respective areas of expertise are
concerned. Thus Bagno continues:

Nonetheless, although we have in Brazil centers of teaching and research
concerned with linguistics and recognized internationally as centers of excellence in the area and from where have come forth negative reactions to
the bill proposed by the congressman, there seems to be a general tendency
among the lay public to listen—when the topic of discussion is language—to
persons who have at most heard the cock crow, but have no idea where, nor

for that matter *when*, given that the vast majority of the superstitions that flourish in the common sense view of language have their origin in a pre-historic period well before the birth of Christ and, hence, well before the era of modern science as we know it. (Bagno, 2001, p. 52)

Another linguist expressed his resentment thus:

Why is it that linguistics does not get attention from the media? Because it is liberatory: what it has to say—namely, that everybody is capable of speaking quite appropriately the language they speak, or that there is no such thing as wrong speech or dialect, from the point of view grammatical organization—will not only deprive the [traditional] grammarians of their livelihood, but more importantly, will make ordinary people think that they can open their mouths and speak out, registering their desires and their grievances, without fear of having to feel ashamed about not knowing their language well enough. (Guedes, 2001, p. 129)

It is clear that for this linguist a "liberatory" attitude goes against the value-judgements of traditional grammarians and the public. But this attitude too limits the contribution linguists can make in debates of this nature. The public is concerned about taking a stand on important social issues. But the non-committal stance of experts fails to answer the concerns and needs of the people who want to adopt a position on the inequality and conflict between languages.

To recapitulate the point developed in this section: if one attempts to capture the general tone of the reaction from linguists to the growing clamor from the streets to legislatively intervene in the linguistic situation in Brazil, one will find that the consensus view among those who have expressed their opinions in this regard is that the linguists have been unfairly set aside in the whole discussion. To make matters worse, they complain, the discussion so far has been practically dominated by traditional grammarians and other self-styled pundits who do not have the necessary scientific training to back up their views.

## THE CONTINUING STALEMATE

The debate over the language issue in Brazil has so far produced more heat than light. And, as far as one can tell, there is no immediate prospect for a negotiated settlement of the issues that divide linguists and the public at large, egged on by traditional grammarians as their self-appointed champions. As we have seen, the only argument that linguists have been able to put forward is that their opponents, mainly traditional grammarians, have no clue as to the real nature of language. So, in their view, the only solution is taking the message of linguistics to the wider public. Here is an example:

Linguistics has not yet succeeded in going beyond the four walls of the centers of research and spreading its message across the society at large so that its discourse could serve as a foil to the other discourses that address the language issue in Brazil ... Insofar as the national language issue is concerned, we seem to be living in a pre-scientific, dogmatic and obscurantist period. (Faraco, 2001a, p. 39)

It is the same Enlightenment message of the darkness of ignorance being dispelled by the refulgent light of genuine science (The actual origins of this powerful metaphor may in fact date back to pre-Socratic Greece; cf. Borzacchini, 2001). As self-styled heirs to that scientific tradition, the linguists are saying that the lay persons are being misled by what Francis Bacon, in his *Novum Organum*, condemned as the four "idols" of the mind: namely, (a) the idols of the tribe (*idola tribus*), (b) the idols of the cave (*idola specus*), (c) the idols of the marketplace (*idola fori*), and (d) the idols of the theater (*idola theatri*). Idols of the first two kinds refer to the typical tendency among ordinary persons to conceive of ordinary things anthropomorphically (in the case of language study, this tendency manifests itself whenever we speak of the birth, growth, and death of individual languages and also when we refer to some of them as sister languages, deriving from a common parent language) and the tendency to accept unconditionally views that have been handed down from generation to generation, respectively. By (c), Bacon meant deception by the very language we speak and by (d) deception by established opinions, whose very antiquity often confers upon them an air of awe-inspiring respectability and unquestionable authority. From the contemporary scientific linguist's point of view, the two are best represented by the distrust of common, everyday speech (whereof the quest for a *metalanguage* as the proper medium of scientific discourse) and the unconcealed disdain for the traditional grammarians (seen as the champions of deeply entrenched prejudices).

The only problem with such a rhetorical strategy is that it has so far failed to produce any satisfactory results. If anything, the general public seems to be growing more and more impatient and unwilling to grant the linguists the last word. Their distrust of the "self-styled experts on language" was exploited in a masterly fashion by Congressman Rebelo in a rebuttal of Faraco's criticism of his proposed bill. In his reply, the Congressman proclaimed:

Language, like the Indian club, the sword, the gunpowder, and modern technology, has been a powerful instrument of conquest. The dominant culture forces its vocabulary on the culture under domination. When the Indonesian troops occupied East Timor in 1974, the first step taken by the invaders was to prohibit the teaching and the use of Portuguese. Banned from the schools, Portuguese was from then on defended by the armed guerrillas of Fretilin, who re-instituted the use of the language, as soon as they

gained autonomy for the ex-Portuguese colony. There is an eloquent example in Brazilian history of the use of the word for the conquest of nations and
territories. When Portugal decided to colonize the land, it also decided to
impose a language so as to be able to communicate with the natives. (Rebelo,
2001a, p. 23)

What makes a passage such as that one different is that there is no sign of
pent-up rancor or apparent ill-feeling (or, if there is, it has been superbly
well concealed) toward those who do not share the same viewpoint. Instead
of appealing to the authority of science or whatever, the argument is based
on facts of history that most ordinary persons in Brazil are already familiar
with. As a seasoned politician, the congressman knows that an argument is
won, not necessarily by dint of logically fool-proof arguments backed up by
solid scientific reasoning, but by means of persuasion and the use of a rhetorical style, at once simple and aimed at striking a favorable chord in the
minds of those to whom the argument is addressed. Besides, no one can disagree with the congressman when he calls attention to the political use of
the language issue and cites concrete examples from history.

Now, as it happens, the typical reaction from linguists to such arguments
of extraordinary persuasive power has been to insist that natural languages
are integral wholes that can, as it were, "take care of themselves" and are
best left to themselves and not tampered with. As Bagno put it,

> The use of language needs no legislation. Language is a self-regulating sys-
> tem, it takes care of its own necessities. On its own, it absorbs what is useful to
> its needs and throws out what it can do without.... A language does not need
> to be "defended," much less defended from its own speakers, who are its le-
> gitimate users and as such ought to have the liberty to do with it what it best
> pleases them to do. (Bagno, 2000, p. 61)

In so putting forward their case, linguists like Bagno are being rigorously
faithful to their structuralist origins. Isn't a structure, by definition, integrated and fully self-sufficient unto itself? Doesn't the much-celebrated
*clôture* of a structure guarantee for it a high degree of resilience from outside pressures?

The only hitch is that, prized off from their historically determinate context, such claims tend to strike the ordinary people, untutored in the kind of
discursive practices linguists are familiar with, as contrary to common
sense. If languages are such self-contained wholes, immune to pressures
from the outside, how come—they ask—they are capable of being planned?
Isn't language planning at all possible precisely because individual languages do react to outside pressures?

The fact of the matter is that they—the non-linguists—are dead right on
this last point. No matter what the linguists might wish languages were like
in an ideal world, in actual reality there are plenty of cases where the desti-

nies of individual languages have been sealed by decisions taken by a handful of persons, mainly politicians and dictators. And history is all too full of
examples of languages being molded to suit political interests. The ban on
the use of Portuguese in East Timore by the Indonesian occupation forces
that the congressman refers to is a case in point. Equally importantly, in any
society the need (real or presumed) to protect the society's language against
foreign influences is a powerful rallying point, behind which politicians
know they can drum up all the popular support they need. Ordinary people
are particularly sensitive to the appeal of what Fishman (1968) called
"nationism," meaning the need to legislatively intervene in the linguistic
reality of a nation-state.

It may well be worth asking at this stage why it is that linguists have systematically turned a blind eye to what has been happening all over the
world? Why are they reluctant to admit that human languages are often subject—whether for the better or the worse—to policy decisions made by governments? The short answer is that they have been prevented from
admitting that national languages are charged with immense political connotations, thanks to one of the axiomatic principles that they have accepted
as part of the design features of their discipline: the idea that a scientific
study of human languages should consider those languages *apart* from the
ideas and attitudes ordinary people entertain about them. Barring very few
exceptions, linguists are still given to thinking of languages as though they
existed quite apart from the social settings in which they are spoken and
hence free from the political connotations with which they are infused.

As we saw in the opening section of this chapter, the very discipline of linguistics is founded on a summary dismissal of what the ordinary folks "out
there" think and believe about language. As scientists, linguists think they
are entitled to such an act of distancing from those who act as their informants and who furnish them with the data on which they work. In this, they
believe they are acting just like, say, physicians. A doctor is not obligated
(except for reasons other than strictly scientific or medical) to listen to the
kind of explanation their patients might have concerning the malady they
suffer from. A doctor's patients typically have no specialist knowledge about
medicine, so their opinions simply should not count when the doctor is engaged in diagnosing their illnesses or in deciding on the right therapy.

However, as linguists in Brazil (and possibly elsewhere in the world) are
slowly beginning to discover to their consternation, it is one thing to admit
that language is a social phenomenon, but a completely different matter to
fully face up to the implications of that admission. Individual languages are
also social *possessions*. Ordinary speakers are as convinced as their more erudite counterparts on campuses that they have an equal stake in the destiny
of their language. And, to be sure, they do. It is not by flaunting their academic and scientific credentials that professional linguists are going to

make any headway in their relations with the community at large. Before anything else, they need to *talk* to them. And in talking to them, it is important that they start with what the ordinary people think and believe about language.

In other words, it is the unavailability as yet of a common language in which to thrash out their differences that is making it extremely difficult to find a solution to the continuing standoff between expert and local knowledge on the issue of language as it is currently playing itself out in Brazil. Neither side is willing to listen, let alone budge from the position each has already assumed. The experts will not listen to the lay public for reasons we have already looked into; it is, as far as they are concerned, a sheer waste of time. The ordinary people do not have the intellectual wherewithal in order to make sense of what they, the self-appointed experts and guardians of the only scientific knowledge on the subject, are talking about. In their turn, the public at large will not listen to the linguists either, because they think that the kind of expertise they have to offer is too otherworldly to be of any practical use or immediate relevance to their concerns. Against the perfectly understandable, down-to-earth concerns voiced by the ordinary persons in the street, all that the professional linguists have to offer is highfalutin' theory (and a dismissive shrug of their shoulders), packaged in an impenetrable jargon that sounds even more alien to their ears than the foreign language, whose growing presence in their midst was what set off the whole public debate to begin with.

To go back to the point about languages as self-contained wholes, often used by linguists to counteract demands for intervention into specific practices involving language, it is interesting to note that the political implications of such a stance actually play into the hands of those who advocate linguistic engineering. In a pungently worded reply to the attacks from linguists, entitled "Neoliberal neo-language," Congressman Rebelo rebuffed his detractors with the following words:

> Is language like the market, in that neither needs the mediation by laws and nation-states? Or could it be that the one just as much as the other ... is urgently in need of rules that will restrain the economic, social, and linguistic Darwinism they have set off? (Rebelo, 2001b, p. 19)

In one swift stroke, the Congressman thus politicizes the whole issue, or rather, shows how decisions taken allegedly on purely theoretical grounds nonetheless have important political implications. Where the linguists see science, the politicians sense politics. In this case, what the astute politician is doing is cashing in on the powerful anti-globalization feelings sweeping across many countries, especially in the developing world, where the local populations have been getting more and more worried about being left behind in the mad rat race to which they think the world economy has been reduced. He is reminding his readers that just as the market has become a free-for-all where the powerful call all the shots precisely in virtue of the state's refusal to interfere in the economy, so too a national language left to its own fortunes can easily play into the hands of powerful interest groups from the outside who have no commitment to local concerns. No wonder that ordinary Brazilians are easily swayed by an argument such as this which highlights the political dimensions of a nation's language.

## CONCLUDING REMARKS

In all fairness, it should be noted that, in the context of the evolving language dispute in Brazil, the country's linguists have also realized that it is a political struggle that they have ahead of them. Faraco expressed this in no uncertain terms:

> Linguists are faced with the challenge of approaching these questions as fundamentally political questions and thinking about ways of making their voices heard, thus contributing to the beginning of an urgently needed cultural war among contending discourses that address the language of Brazil. (Faraco, 2001, p. 31)

But politics here is practically synonymous with lobbying. It is, in other words, all a matter of putting political pressure on those who have the final say on the issue. One step in that direction was taken when, in an open letter signed by the presidents of the *Brazilian Association of Linguistics* (ABRALIN), *Association of Applied Linguistics of Brazil* (ALAB) and National *Association of Graduate Programs in Letters and Linguistics* (ANPOLL), and addressed to the president of the Special Commission on Education of Brazil's Senate, the need for establishing guidelines for a linguistic policy at a federal level was highlighted. Among the key features of the set of guidelines were a systematic effort to combat linguistic prejudices of all kinds and a plain recognition of Brazil's status as a multilingual nation.

Apart from the jitters that talk of Brazil's status as a multilingual state is most likely to cause (especially among the lawmakers in the country who know only too well that such an admission would inevitably entail new demands from minority groups to receive education in their own languages and is therefore completely unhelpful as an argumentative move at this stage), the tone of the letter also betrays a deep-seated conviction on the part of linguists. It is as though they were saying that they know for sure what the exact status of Portuguese in Brazil is. "All we need is your backing to eradicate all the prejudices and erroneous beliefs that proliferate among the lay public." What is not at all being considered is the crucial fact that their credentials as reliable experts to be consulted on issues related to language are precisely what need to be established first, at least as far as the members of the legislative bodies are concerned. After all, these lawmakers themselves represent a cross-section of the very population whose members are, as we have already seen, prone to be swayed by the arguments of the traditional grammarians, whom they have for long held in high esteem and whose authority they have no convincing reason as yet to call into question.

But, perhaps even more importantly, what is egregiously missing in the stance taken by linguists in Brazil vis-à-vis the ongoing dispute involving the country's national language is a willingness to consider the possibility that there may be a need to review some of the postulates of their own science in light of the concrete case that they have decided to address. What the linguists urgently need to recognize is that there is more to language policy than the linguistics of it. As Kaplan put it recently:

> Language policy is, in fact, a manifestation of *human* resource development policy, and many polities have chosen not to engage in such policy development or have done so in an ad hoc manner, often with unfortunate results. By way of contrast, nations have frequently undertaken *natural* resource development planning—the building of the Aswan Dam in Egypt, or of the complex Three Gorges dam project currently being undertaken in the people's Republic of China are examples that come readily to mind. (Kaplan, 2001, p. 81)

So long as those who claim to possess global, specialist knowledge refuse to consider it even as a remote possibility that they may need to make some fundamental readjustments in their mindset to suit local circumstances, it is unlikely that their efforts will bear any fruit. Needless to say, for a genuine dialogue to take place, both sides will need to give in. Together, they will need to negotiate an intermediate position that will steer clear of, on the one hand, the Scylla of passive acquiescence and, on the other, the Charybdis of defiant chauvinism, up until now considered the only viable alternatives. This can only be done if the experts recognize the importance of engaging the lay public in a genuine dialogue and, in their turn, the ordinary persons admit the possibility that their perfectly legitimate grievances over and spontaneous reactions to such an emotive issue as their national language do need to be submitted to close scrutiny with the aid of cool reason before they can be incorporated into a plan of action. If there is any lesson to be learned from the Brazilian case, it is that there is also a need to address the common people in the kind of (meta)language they are most used to, respecting their opinions for what they are worth, and trying to build on from what there is already in place. Insofar as it is a matter of utmost political urgency, the issue of a country's national language must be approached, not in the spirit of cold and dispassionate scientific reason but with the tact and rhetorical skills that all politically sensitive issues call for. Languages have to be contextualized in sociohistorical realities, and their relationships have to be analyzed in terms of differing material and political prospects.

## ACKNOWLEDGMENTS

I am grateful to the CNPq (National Council for Research and Development), a funding agency maintained by Brazil's Ministry of Science and Technology, for financing my research (Process No. 306151/88-0).

## REFERENCES

Bagno, M. (2000). O deputado e a língua [The deputy and his tongue]. *Boletim da ALAB, 4*(4), 55–61.
Bagno, M. (2001). Cassandra, fênix, e outros mitos [Cassandra, Phoenix, and other myths]. In C. A. Faraco (Ed.), *Estrangeirismos: Guerras em Torno da Língua* (pp. 49–84). São Paulo: Editora Parábola.
Barthes, R. (1975). *The pleasure of the text* (R. Miller, Trans.). New York: Hill.
Bloomfield, L. (1944). Secondary and tertiary responses to language. *Language, 20,* 45–55.
Borzacchini, L. (2001). Light as a metaphor of science: A pre-established disharmony. *Semiotica, 136*(1/4), 151–171.
Buck, C. D. (1916). Language and the sentiment of nationality. *American Political Science Review, 10,* 44–69.
Chomsky, N. A. (1965). *Aspects of the theory of syntax.* Cambridge, MA: MIT Press.
Cipro Neto, P. (2001). *Groselha.* Retrieved December 20, 2001, from www.uol.com.br/linguaportuguesa/home.htm
Davis, H. (1997). Ordinary people's philosophy: Comparing lay and professional metalinguistic knowledge. *Language Sciences, 19*(1), 33–46.
Ehlich, K. (1981). Native speaker's heritage: On philology of "dead" languages. In F. Coulmas (Ed.), *A Festschrift for Native Speaker* (pp. 153–168). The Hague: Mouton.
Faraco, C. A. (2001a). Guerras em torno da língua. In C. A. Faraco (Ed.), *Estrangeirismos: Guerras em Torno da Língua* [Foreignisms: Wars over languages](pp. 37–48). São Paulo: Editora Parábola.
Faraco, C. A. (Ed.). (2001b). *Estrangeirismos: Guerras em Torno da Língua* [Foreignisms: Wars over languages]. São Paulo: Editora Parábola.
Fishman, J. (1968). Nationality-nationalism and nation-nationism. In J. Fishman, C. A. Ferguson, & J. Das-Gupta (Eds.), *Language problems of developing nations* (pp. 98–112). New York: Wiley.
Garcez, P. M., & Zilles, A. M. S. (2001). Estrangeirismos: desejos e ameaças [Foreignisms: Hopes and threats]. In C. A. Faraco (Ed.), *Estrangeirismos: Guerras em Torno da Língua* [Foreignisms: Wars over languages] (pp. 15–36). São Paulo: Editora Parábola.
Giroux, H. A. (1994). Living dangerously: Identity politics and the new cultural racism. In H. A. Giroux & P. McLaren (Eds.), *Between borders: Pedagogy and the politics of cultural studies* (pp. 29–55). New York: Routledge.
Greenfield, L. (1998). Nationalism and language. In J. L. Mey (Ed.), *Concise encyclopedia of pragmatics* (pp. 635–641). Oxford: Elsevier.

Guedes, P. C. (2001). E por que não nos defender da língua? In C. A. Faraco (Ed.), *Estrangeirismos: Guerras em Torno da Língua* [Foreignisms: Wars over languages] (pp. 127–142). São Paulo: Editora Parábola.

Hutton, C. (1996). Law lessons for linguists? Accountability and acts of professional classification. *Language and Communication, 16*(3), 205–214.

Jacoby, R. (1987). *The last intellectuals in the age of academe.* New York: Basic Books.

Kaplan, R. B. (2001). Language policy and language teaching. *Applied Language Learning, 12*(1), 81–86.

Milroy, J. (2001). Language ideologies and the consequences of standardization. *Journal of Sociolinguistics, 5*(4), 530–555.

Niedzielski, N., & Preston, D. R. (1999). Folk linguistics. In *Trends in Linguistics: Studies and Monographs, 122.* Berlin: Mouton de Gruyter.

Pennycook, A. (1994). *The cultural politics of English as an international language.* London: Longman.

Posner, R. (2000). *Public intellectuals: A study of decline of critical analysis.* Boston, MA: Harvard University Press.

Postman, N., & Weingartner, C. (1966). *Linguistics: A revolution in teaching.* New York: Dell Publishing Co.

Rajagopalan, K. (2002). National languages as flags of allegiance; or the linguistics that failed us: A close look at emergent linguistic chauvinism in Brazil. *Language & Politics, 1*(1), 115–147

Rajagopalan, K., & Rajagopalan, C. (in press). The English language in Brazil—A boon or a bane? In G. Braine (Ed.), *Teaching English to the world.*

Rebelo, A. (1999). Projeto de Lei nº 1676 de 1999. In C. A. Faraco (Ed.), *Estrangeirismos: Guerras em Torno da Língua* [Foreignisms: Wars over languages] (pp. 177–185). São Paulo: Editora Parábola.

Rebelo, A. (2001a, April 15). A intriga das línguas [The conspiracy of languages]. *Folha de São Paulo. MAIS!*, pp. 22–23

Rebelo, A. (2001b, June 3). A neolíngua neoliberal [Neoliberal neolanguage]. *Folha de São Paulo. MAIS!*, p. 19.

Rocha, B. R. (2001). Língua [Language]. *Folha de São Paulo* (Painel do Leitor). 31/03/2001.

Saussure, F. de (1916). *A course in general linguistics.* New York: Philosophical Library.

Snead, J. (1990). European pedigrees/African contagions: Nationality, narrative, and communality in Tutuola, Achebe, and Reed. In H. K. Bhabha (Ed.), *Nation and narration* (pp. 231–249). London: Routledge.

# Chapter 6

# Negotiating a Language Policy for Malaysia: Local Demand for Affirmative Action Versus Challenges From Globalization

Maya Khemlani David
*University of Malaya*

Subra Govindasamy
*International Islamic University, Kuala Lumpur, Malaysia*

## INTRODUCTION

The outlook most societies in the world are constructing for themselves today is shaped by global interactions, global travel, global job seeking, and global business ventures—in short, by borderless communication and trade. To this list, global education must certainly be added. The compelling reason is that it prepares learners for achieving at least some of the aforementioned goals of contemporary societies. The ancillary reason for global education is the establishment of a global network through the medium called the Internet. The Internet has grown in stature from its humble beginnings and is currently largely responsible for tracking international developments right down to keeping people well informed about local conflicts. More recently, scholarly developments have found their way to many homes via this medium. A pragmatic reason for global education is that employers, especially from multinational firms, are interested in recruiting those who have professional skills and a linguistic ability to connect with the rest of the world. Because the predominant language of the Internet and globalization is English, the language appears to have a disproportionately high economic value compared to other languages used beyond one's borders.

It is not surprising then that many aspiring developing countries in Asia have placed greater value in English language education. The countries that place a high premium on English such as Hong Kong, Singapore, Taiwan, Philippines, Thailand, and Malaysia also boast of very robust economies. Malaysia, a multiracial and multilingual country, which had until recently emphasized the importance of using the national language, Malay, in education and for all official purposes has become embroiled in discussions as to whether English medium education needs to be revived. Its leaders have suggested that if the people elected for an English medium education, the government will support it (English anyone?, 2002). The circumstances surrounding this change in language policy are largely related to the maintenance of a competitive edge in global business as well as the economics of unemployment of graduates from the Malay community. Malay graduates have not acquired the desirable professional skills because of a low English language proficiency. The Malaysian Prime Minister recently revealed that 94% of the unemployed graduates in the country are Malays and that they are unable to procure jobs because industrial jobs called for a high English language competency (Not many jobs, 2002). If thousands of graduates are unemployed or underemployed largely due to their linguistic inability, his call to the nation to institute changes to its language policy is timely.

The responses to this call have been very favorable from those who had historically remained loyal to English language education in the country, especially the members of non-Malay ethnic minority communities (i.e., Indians and Chinese). There appears to be a more cautious attitude among the academics, teachers, and Malay political groups who have shown less enthusiasm toward the proposal. Such an impasse is to be expected given the historical complexity in relation between the various ethnic groups in the country. The Indian and Chinese groups had envisaged a postcolonial Malaysia that is truly modern and industrialized. This vision included not only economic development but also the growth of sociocultural values believed to be foundational in nation-building. These priorities assumed greater significance in response to a political dynamism that enveloped the country during the latter half of the 20th century. The sociocultural values advanced at this crucial juncture included promotion of certain symbols, chief among them was the use of a national language, that is, Malay, to bring about national identity and unity.

To understand this group's hesitance in endorsing the proposal to have English medium schools, we have to view it in historical context. It waged a protracted battle against the government to convert postcolonial English medium schools into Malay schools. The minority ethnic groups initially resisted, but eventually accepted the Malay medium schools. This historical complexity of interracial relation and the turn of events in the last four decades are developed in the first part of this chapter. The effects of the conversion of English schools on the different communities in the country are discussed in the second part. We argue that Malays have largely become monolinguals and have lost the competitive edge, compared to the minority communities who have surprisingly maintained English in their linguistic repertoire (see David, 2001a; David, Naji, & Sheena Kaur, 2003; David & Nambiar, 2002). Communities who maintain English in their linguistic repertoire are poised to benefit from the highly valued global business ventures enveloping most of Far East Asia. The third part of the chapter deals with the uphill task currently facing the country to build up its English language skills in the face of globalization, without antagonizing local nationalistic sentiments.

This chapter culls information from books and research articles in journals that have been published in the last four decades to explore the scholarly contribution to language policy debates in Malaysia. In addition, to understand current thoughts on the replacement of the medium of instruction and other related issues, news and feature articles published during the last 2 years in the three major English language newspapers in the country—*The Star*, *The Sun*, and *The New Straits Times*—are sourced. The researchers also interviewed some informants to understand how they were affected by the language policy decisions.[1]

## LANGUAGE POLICY CHANGES: A HISTORICAL OVERVIEW

Malaysia is a multiethnic, multilingual country with a population of about 22 million people and at least a hundred languages. There are three main ethnic groups in Malaysia, that is, Malays and other indigenous groups (61%), Chinese (28%), and Indians (8%) (Khoo, 1991, p. 40). Although the Malays, who form the majority of the population, are indigenous, the non-Malays (i.e., the Chinese and the Indians) are considered immigrant communities. The bulk of their ancestors were encouraged to come into the country by the British colonial regime. Within each ethnic group there is a variety of languages and dialects. Reflecting the cultural diversity, the country also has a variety of schools. Malaysian schools are divided into national

---

[1]Open-ended interviews were conducted with 67 respondents ranging from educators, parents, professionals, and students of various ages and different ethnic groups who had experienced schooling in different language streams, to determine how individuals coped with the changes which resulted from such language policy decisions. The major interview question was "How did you personally cope with changes in language policy?"

or national-type schools. Malay is the medium of instruction in national schools, which are fully government assisted. In contrast, Chinese and Tamil are used as the medium of instruction in national-type vernacular schools, which are partially government assisted in terms of funding. The Chinese and Tamil media primary schools exist to fulfill a parental choice option in multilingual Malaysia. However, at the secondary level, all Malaysians attend national schools where Malay is used as the medium of instruction. A very small percentage of the students elect to pursue their secondary education in a few privately run English or Chinese schools.

Given this multiracial and multilingual setting, language policy planning must take into account the interests of all communities. Even if one language takes precedence over others, the nation needs to display other equitable measures so that these measures may foster "instrumental attachments out of which sentimental ones can then gradually emerge" (Watson, 1983, p. 152). In other words, allowing for the proper development of all languages in multilingual communities is important in language planning in plural societies. A concern for others as well as benevolent values were manifested in the language planning scenario in Malaysia (then, Malaya) in the years immediately after gaining independence. However, the political dynamism that appeared in the late 1960s went against the cultivated wisdom of the earlier years. The consequences of policy developments of this period have had a reverberating effect on the country till today.

In colonial Malaya, English was the official language and Malay, Chinese, and Tamil languages were considered vernaculars. With the coming of independence in 1957, the leaders of the major communities decided to accept Malay as the national language, a symbol of national unity. According to Asmah (1997), Malay was chosen to fulfill this function because of "its indigeneity, its role as a lingua franca, its position as a major language, its possession of high literature, and the fact that it once had been an important language of administration and diplomacy in the Malay archipelago" (p. 15). Even before independence, political parties like the Malay UMNO (United Malay National Organization) and the Chinese MCA (Malaysian Chinese Association) had agreed that Malay would be the national language, according to a memorandum in August 1953. Thus there was little controversy over the acceptance of Malay as the national language. Article 152 of the Malaysian constitution confirms this. However, the constitutional framers did not phrase Malay as the "official" language, a stamp that allows the language to be used for all official purposes. From 1957 to 1967, English continued to fulfill this official role and would have continued unabated but for the rise in linguistic nationalism among Malay nationalists.

After independence, the leaders of the country chose to progress along a pragmatic path, pacifying minority communities of the continued role for their languages and at the same time assuring Malay nationalists of a greater role for Malay. At this time it was apparent that the nationalists would not accept the notion of a multilingual nation. The Malay nationalist groups, particularly the powerful Federation of Malaya School Teachers' Association and the Malay National Action Front, were unhappy with the provisions of the 1967 National Language Act and criticized it as not enhancing the status of Malay as the primary language of the nation because the Act asked for the continued use of English (Mitchell, 1993). The opposition to continued use of English is understandable. Chai (1971) observes the following: "English came to be regarded not only as the language of colonial education but also, after independence, as an obstacle to the educational, social and economic advance of the majority of Malays" (p. 61). Their suspicion was confirmed by an important fact: there was a steady increase in enrollment in English medium secondary schools (Watson, 1983). Table 6.1 displays this situation.

The student enrollment in English schools appears to have increased steadily from 1957 to 1962. In the years following 1962, when most Chinese secondary schools were discontinued, there was an upsurge in the number of students (including Malays) attending English medium schools. This trend must have irked the Malay nationalists tremendously. To add to this trend, the Malay nationalists felt the resistance to the use of the national language by some non-Malay groups as an act lacking in appreciation for the government that had been quite liberal on the question of citizenship for the immigrant groups. The resistance to using Malay took on more vigor especially before the 1969 general elections. The results of the general election and the subsequent race riots were crucial for hardening the resolve of the Malay nationalists. Mitchell (1993) observes the following: "Although for many years Malay intellectuals had advocated a Malay-based literary culture as the foundation for a national culture, it took the 1969 ri-

TABLE 6.1

Student Enrollment in Government Secondary Schools in West Malaysia
(Adapted From Watson, 1983, p. 138)

| School | Malay Medium | | English Medium | | Chinese Medium | |
|--------|--------|------------|--------|------------|--------|------------|
| Year | Number | Percentage | Number | Percentage | Number | Percentage |
| 1957 | 2,315 | 2.9 | 48,235 | 59.8 | 30,052 | 37.3 |
| 1960 | 4,953 | 4.3 | 72,499 | 62.3 | 38,828 | 33.4 |
| 1962 | 13,224 | 10.0 | 119,219 | 90.0 | * | |
| 1965 | 67,484 | 24.5 | 208,363 | 75.5 | * | |

*Chinese secondary schools ceased to be aided schools and Chinese students enrolled in English schools from 1962 onward.

ots to move the Malay political elite away from the ideology of cultural pluralism towards greater cultural hegemony" (p. 55). The rhetoric that the national language, the nation's main cultural symbol, was central to uniting the various peoples of Malaysia, took center stage. The proposition that English could become the common language was rejected. The issue was put beyond debate when Parliament, the highest legislative body, passed the Constitution (Amendment) Act of 1971. The Act prohibits "the questioning of any provision in Article 152 and makes it seditious, punishable under Sedition Act, 1948, for anyone who questions the Article except in regard to the implementation thereof" (R. Nik, 1981, p. 296). The Article safeguards the special privileges of the Malays—that is, Islam as the state religion and Malay as the national language.

The rhetoric that sought to entrench the status of the Malay language was followed by a theme that Malay-medium education would help Malays regain their sovereignty. Even Malay intellectuals rationalized that English in colonial Malaysia "produced a detrimental effect on the development of the Malay language. Confined as the language of the home and the medium of instruction of a limited number of primary schools, Malay was deprived of the opportunity to develop" (S. Nik, 1981, p. 45). It was therefore considered timely to "release the Malay from the shackles of British colonialism which was best represented in the vestiges of the English language" (Mitchell, 1993, p. 61). Although there may be some truth to what the Malay nationalists and intellectuals felt about the development of Malay language and indigenous rights, the rationalizations remain purely rhetorical because the compelling reason for the accelerated use of Malay, especially in education, was to some extent based on the belief that the non-Malays had done well in English medium schools and at tertiary institutions (Watson, 1983). The English educated urban non-Malays had dominated major commerce and business sectors as well as the professions whereas the largely rural Malay population had been bypassed. There was tremendous resentment at this state of affairs. To redress the imbalance, education was chosen as the primary mode for instituting changes. The language policy changes that came into effect in the country in the 1970s included the following:

- Malay would replace English as the medium of instruction in all English medium primary and secondary schools. This task was completed in 1978.
- All university education would be conducted in Malay. This exercise was to be completed in 1983, but it took longer because of problems in implementation.
- The Higher School Certificate (A-level) and School Certificate (O-level) examinations (which were conducted by Cambridge Univer-

sity), as well as other national examinations, would be offered in Malay. The A-level and O-level examinations were replaced by the STPM and SPM[2] (national examinations that were largely based on the same syllabuses but conducted solely via the Malay language), respectively.

- Most importantly, students would have to obtain a credit in Malay to be awarded the SPM certificate, the prerequisite to obtaining a tertiary education, government jobs, teacher training opportunities, and so forth.

In addition to the aforementioned educational policies, the setting up of other completely Malay-based institutions—such as the MARA[3] Institute of Technology, junior science colleges, and a large number of residential science schools—an almost unlimited funding for Malay scholars, and preferential treatment for them in employment in the public sector can be classified as affirmative action[4] designed to ensure the correction of the ethnic socioeconomic disparity existing in the country. This wide-ranging affirmative action was expected to bring about outcomes that could truly empower the Malays vis-à-vis the other communities.

The use of affirmative action as a strategy in Malaysia came out of a historical consensus on the special position of Malays in the country. This action is a "measure to ensure that a group or groups who had been unfairly discriminated against in the past, would have real chances in life" (Salbiah, 2001, p. 1). In defending this measure (in reference to education in the United States), Sturm and Guinier (2000) opine that the value of scores on

---

[2]STPM stands for *Sijil Tinggi Pelajaran Malaysia* (i.e., Malaysian Certificate of Higher Education); SPM stands for *Sijil Pelajaran Malaysia* (i.e., Malaysian Certificate of Education).

[3]MARA stands for *Majlis Amanah Rakyat*, that is, Council of Trust for the Indigenous People.

[4]The use of the expression *affirmative action* is very recent in Malaysia. It was widely known as special privileges of the indigenous people of the country (also known as Bumiputera). However, more recently, more Malay researchers have used the term affirmative action to refer to the set of special privileges accorded to the larger Malay group of people. Affirmative action as perceived by Malaysians is somewhat more wide-ranging than is understood in the rest of the world. For instance, affirmative action in America refers to offering college admission or work opportunities to marginalized communities. In Malaysia, educational quota for entrance into public universities is just one among the various features of affirmative action instituted here. There are other additional features to this policy as applied here. In the words of Dr. Zainal Aznam Yusof (2001, p. 22), "There are grounds, in my view to re-look at the affirmative action policies and to consider re-basing them on the population shares of each ethnic group. It must be remembered that the explicit employment quota under the New Economic Policy (NEP) was for employment at all levels to reflect the racial composition of the country's population. There is an embedded sense of fairness in sharing wealth and resources on the basis of proportional representation in the nation's population. There is, even under the NEP, an asymmetry in affirmative action policies: while employment was to reflect the racial composition of the population, the ownership of capital and wealth was based on the 30:40:30 principle, i.e., 30 per cent Bumiputera, 40 per cent non-Bumiputera and 30 percent foreign interests." All is not well with the use of this policy and this must have prompted the Prime Minister to recently say, "Malaysia's affirmative action policy to achieve equality among the races has resulted in some people becoming too laid back …" (Negative aspect, 2001).

paper-and-pencil tests is overrated. According to them such a system is "fundamentally unfair." They believe, in American education, that test results restrict "opportunities for many poor and working-class Americans of all colors and genders who could otherwise obtain a better education" (p. 1). Affirmative action as a measure is also supported by its successful implementation in South Africa and India (Salbiah, 2001). The question that is being raised here is not about the moral rationale of affirmative action but about its actual effects—that is, whether such an action is a disservice rather than a long-term benefit to the community it is intended to help, and, in the process, whether it adversely affects other communities. In the words of Usher and Edwards (1994), "To optimize the performance of a system requires that all the variables affecting the system can be known and calculated and therefore predicted" (p. 181). The question is whether the planners were aware and had some measure of control over all the variables that would eventually unfold. The chapter carefully examines these variables. First, we deal with the features that affected the Malays, and next the non-Malays.

## LANGUAGE POLICY CONSEQUENCES: DISEMPOWERMENT OF MALAYS

The replacement of English from its preeminent position in the Malaysian schools and tertiary institutions beginning from the 1970s was regarded as the main means of empowering the Malays. Although many Malay intellectuals welcomed this move, they appeared to have some reservations about the implementation process (R. Nik, 1981; Soepadmo, 1981; Suhaimi, 1981; Tunku, 1981; Voon, Zaharah, & Khoo, 1981). The distress signals they emitted show the hastiness with which the replacement was taking place. The issues that emerged included some easily noticeable ones such as the following:

- The suitability of the Malay language for academic purposes, given its development at that point in time.
- Malay students' academic performance.
- Malay students' proficiency in the Malay language.
- Malay students' proficiency in English.

Speaking about the suitability of the Malay language (or Bahasa Malaysia) for academic purposes, Asmah (1981) mentions that the direct transfer of English syntactic patterns into Malay was one of the strategies employed to cope with the situation. In fact, this anglicized construction was initially described as "pollution" by grammarians and Malay language teachers. Asmah describes the genesis of this style:

> ... the native speakers of Bahasa Malaysia have become well-acquainted with the sciences only via the English medium, such that when the time came for the implementation of the national language as a medium of teaching the sciences, these very people, not having previously used Bahasa Malaysia to convey scientific ideas, found it difficult to do so. Hence, there arose at one stage a negative attitude among certain Malaysians towards the capacity and ability of their own language in expressing scientific thoughts and ideas. Those who tried using the language in their scientific discourse are much influenced by the English construction that have been habitualized into a direct transfer of the English sentence into Bahasa Malaysia using Malay words and assimilated loan words, and maintaining the positional relationship of the words both in phrasal and clausal contexts. (Asmah, 1981, p. 76)

The inference from the aforementioned description is that there was little time for natural growth of expression to accomplish the demanding task imposed on the teachers.

Similar concerns have been echoed in other academic disciplines. Voon et al. (1981) mention that "even translations of geographical works into Bahasa Malaysia were not undertaken until, of course, the current exigencies arose" (p. 258). Expressions such as *paucity of terminology* and *a serious handicap* find their way into their research study. They further surmise that "Total efforts in book translation in the country must be vastly increased in order to cope up with the increasing demand for geographical literature by students whose proficiency in English is expected to be lower than before" (p. 268). The task of such translators must be insurmountable considering that the number of geographical journals increases every year and the total number of journals published in 1971 was 2,415.

Suhaimi (1981) opines that there is little difficulty in borrowing strictly scientific terminology such as *atom*, *electron*, and *nucleus*. However, he foresees difficulties regarding "common terms that have acquired specific meanings or functions in scientific expression such as evolution, assimilation, typical succession and productivity" (p. 273). He further explains that the local equivalent words for such terms appear to have certain cultural constraints such that "when these words are used for scientific expressions, in non-human conception of the universe, they appear out of place" (p. 273). Again, given a longer period of language development, such problems could have been solved.

The readiness of the national language for academic use was just one of the problems that affected students, the ultimate consumers of education. There were other problems, including their ability to handle academic subjects. Sargunan and Nambiar (1994) mention that Law undergraduates who have undergone many years of Malay medium education chose to complete their assignments in English "since most text-books and reference materials are in English" (p. 106). The reason for this surprising finding is that the students "find it easier to transfer the contents from one to the

other, i.e. from the books to their assignments" (p. 106). Those who were
not proficient enough in English used Malay especially during tutorials and
examinations because in these situations they cannot "borrow" expressions.
In the same study, the Law lecturers mentioned that almost 90% of their
students do not read beyond their lecture notes and their basic reference
material. This may not be surprising given the fact that most reference materials are in English. It is this lack of competence in English that must have
prompted a Law lecturer to comment as follows:

> It is not an exaggeration to say that during the past five years, the standard of
> English has deteriorated. If the situation is left unchecked, there is a danger
> that the quality of education will go down as well, as the years go by, because
> most of the literature for purposes of university education are still in the Eng-
> lish Language. (R. Nik, 1981, p. 297)

Rashid Nik further comments that "the standard of Malay among the non-
Malay English medium students is much higher than the standard of English among the Malay medium students. Where does the fault lie?" (1981, p.
301). Other research conducted in the 1980s and early 1990s also appears
to indicate the disempowerment of the Malay students. Habibah and Wan
Rafaei (1994) point out that the Chinese students in their study showed
more positive study habits compared to Malay students. The study also revealed that Chinese students performed much better than Malay students
in quantitative and creative courses. Other studies (as reported in Habibah
& Wan Rafaei, 1994) point to higher motivation and performance of the
Chinese.

Finally, the lack of proficiency in English was, and is, more apparent
among the rural students. Ee's (2001) study reveals that students and teachers in Trengganu—a Malaysian state where Malays predominate—perceive
English as a threat to the Malay language. Malaysian leaders are aware of
this prevalent attitude toward English among the rural people. The Prime
Minister, discussing the attitude of Malay students toward English, says that
Malay students themselves think that if they learn English they are not being nationalistic, that is, they are not supporting the Bahasa (Build vision
schools, 2000). The English divide between the urban and rural student is
wide and getting wider by the year. Unfortunately, this rural–urban English
divide is also, by and large, a divide between Malays and non-Malays (see
also David, 2000). In a survey among Malay medium pupils in selected
schools in Selangor, it was noted that pupils who are not competent in English come from a non-English-speaking environment. This finding
strengthens the assumption that Malay medium learners of English are in-
sufficiently exposed to English, explaining their poor performance. An earlier study by Chandrasegaran (1979) also showed that urban Malay medium
learners of English do better than rural students in English. She rationalizes

that living in an environment where there is opportunity for speaking and using English helps in the acquisition of the language. Many rural Malay respondents explained that they had not been interested in learning the English language while in school because those in their larger environment, which included both friends and family, did not use English. "Malays seldom speak English in their homes, compared with other races in the country," says Malek (2000, p. 4). In this way, the rural Malays have, in effect, disempowered themselves, notwithstanding an affirmative policy which aims to empower them. Explaining the linguistic plight of the Malays, Musa, an ex-deputy Prime Minister, says, "In language, Malays generally are monolingual whereas non-Malays are at least bilingual or trilingual" (Musa, 2001, p. 6). This passion for Malay and relative noninterest in English has "led to the shutting of children's minds from the world, as well as keeping global developments out of the reach of most adults" (Pathmanabhan, 2001, p. 22). It is not surprising, then, to be informed that Malay students are performing disappointingly in institutions of higher learning (Mahadzir, 2001). This is also reflected in the lack of reading culture. Mitchell (1993) states that the increase in Malay literacy did not bring about corresponding increases in consumption of literary texts. The Noor Azam report characterized the nation as a "society which lacked an interest and proficiency in reading and whose students did not enjoy reading" (Mitchell, 1993, p. 234).

These studies certainly point to a lack of empowerment of Malay learners over the two decades following the implementation of the national language policy. The studies also indicate that these performance-related findings are symptoms of a larger issue at stake here for the development of Malay learners' cognitive and academic ability. We are of the opinion that greater effort should have been expended to making Malay students competent bilinguals. This competency in two languages—Malay and English—may have been useful in overcoming some of the shortcomings mentioned by Rashid Nik (1981), Habibah and Wan Rafaei (1994), and Sargunan and Nambiar (1994). Other research by Tunku (1981), Soepadmo (1981), Suhaimi (1981), and Voon et al. (1981) highlight the need for a slower implementation of the language replacement policy. These researchers give credence to the notion that an expanded exposure to English medium education may have extended the legacy with print literacy and consequently effected a transition that was less damaging to the psyche of Malay students. In early 2002, it was reported in the major newspapers that there were 24,000 unemployed graduates from the Malay community (Be resourceful, 2002). It was also reported that many were unable to procure jobs because of their limited English language skills. Such a bleak scenario could have been averted if the nationalists had understood the cognitive and social advantages of bilingualism. Their failure has resulted in depriving Malay graduates of their rightful place in the global economy and employment market.

## LANGUAGE POLICY CONSEQUENCES: DISEMPOWERMENT OF NON-MALAYS?

Until 1967, the established language of administration and the language of education for urban children was largely English. The conversion of the English medium schools to Malay medium began in 1968. By 1976, all English medium primary schools were completely converted into schools where Malay was used as the medium of instruction. By 1982, all the former English medium secondary schools were converted to National Schools in Peninsular Malaysia (Solomon, 1988). With the conversion, non-Malays felt disenfranchised to some extent. This lack of power by the non-Malay communities has to be examined from the macrolevels and microlevels. At the macrolevel, the Chinese and Indians perceived a threat to the maintenance of their cultural identity. In hindsight, this feeling of disempowerment was misplaced, although to many it appeared real. However, this perception resulted in decisions that made it harder for the children as they had to undergo various mediums of instruction. At the personal level, the learners from these communities had to face almost insurmountable difficulties during the early years of the replacement. Interviews conducted with several respondents who were personally affected by the move disclosed the personal hardships they experienced as a result of failure in major exams due to poor performance in the Malay language.

At the macrolevel, the non-Malays were unprepared for the change in medium. They had held English education in high esteem. This reputation for English grew out of a historical necessity to communicate with the colonial masters. Being beneficiaries of the urban-based mission schools, they realized that English education opened doors to a better life. They willingly accepted the schooling system in English in place of an education via their mother tongue, Mandarin or Tamil, although such schools were popular in rural areas where English education was not available. The non-Malays were not coerced into the schooling system. Their association with the language brought with it a knowledge about Western ideas on democracy, human rights, and, most importantly, literature. They had become very familiar with the works of those such as Shakespeare, Mark Twain, and Robert Frost. The urbanites had also used English in their daily communication. This had to change in postindependent Malaysia. Although the non-Malays had accepted Malay as the national language and had always recognized it as the lingua franca of the country and the region, they had not developed any sentimental attachments for the language as they had for English. This made it harder for them to accept the replacement of English in the national schools.

Sentimentality apart, they perceived the move by the Malay nationalists as forced assimilation (Mitchell, 1993; Watson, 1983). Although they did openly exhibit some measure of resistance to the implementation of the language policy (R. Nik, 1981), the Constitution (Amendment) Act of 1971 prohibited anyone from questioning the policy. Feeling trapped, the non-Malays adopted a strategy: promoting the importance of mother-tongue education in the formative years. This strategy was in response to the earlier one displayed by the Malay nationalists that only Malay can unite the various ethnic groups into one nation. In light of this development, the non-Malay communities saw mother-tongue education as a strategy for maintaining Mandarin and Tamil. It was also for this reason that the Chinese appear to reject the concept of "vision schools" (i.e. national schools and vernacular schools sharing the same premises) promoted by the Education Ministry which believed (and continues to believe) that the vision schools would help to foster greater unity among the various ethnic groups. The Chinese, perceiving this move as encroaching on the identity and characteristics of the Chinese schools, have not supported the concept (Build vision schools, 2000).

In 1994, the non-Malay communities were pleasantly surprised by the government's proposal to allow the teaching of science in English (Schiffman, 1997). The heavy criticism that the proposal garnered from the association of Malay teachers was enough to kill the idea. This was particularly disappointing to the non-Malay communities because they anticipated all Malaysians to respond to the government's initiative to promote Malaysia's ability to become an industrialized nation by developing science and technology through the English medium. When the proposal fell through, the chance for greater national unity was further delayed (Schiffman, 1997).

At the personal level, when the changeover of medium was instituted, many problems were encountered. The first issue that immediately affected the non-Malays was the short exposure to English in the vernacular primary school. English is taught as a subject from the first year of schooling in government (i.e., national) schools. In contrast, in vernacular schools, Malay is introduced in the first year of schooling and English in the third year of school entry (this oversight is to be corrected in the near future). Many felt that a reduced input in English could affect students' mastery of English and result in an unfair advantage to students in the national schools. Such a variation could disempower minorities and cause differences in proficiencies in the respective target languages. In response, vernacular schools have employed a strategy to overcome this disparity. Some teachers disclosed that they do not always comply with the prescribed schedule— many vernacular schools start both the Malay and English classes from the very first year of school. A respondent to our survey, a Tamil school teacher in an urban Tamil school, reported that the school started English classes from Standard 1 onward, and although the official school hours ended at 12:30 p.m., the students were given an extra half hour daily of English classes from 12:30 to 1 p.m. Another respondent, a Chinese parent, said that her son had Saturday classes that were mainly language (both Malay and English) classes. Yet, another parent said that although her child was in the morning school session, he returned home only in the evenings as the school conducted extra language classes in the afternoon. Such classes are not official and are not reflected in official timetables. It appears that longer school hours and extra classes in Malay and English have enabled the non-Malay minority student to master three languages (i.e., Malay, English, and the mother tongue).

The next problem was the one that affected the primary school graduates. The transfer from a vernacular school to a Malay medium secondary school (because there were hardly any secondary non-Malay medium schools) necessitated a rite of passage through what is known as the "remove class" to enable a shift to a Malay-speaking environment. Students from Mandarin and Tamil primary schools were emplaced in these transitory classes for a year to enable them to acquire a higher competency in the Malay language. Many respondents reminisced that they lacked confidence and were very embarrassed when forced to use Malay in such classes. A Tamil respondent in her mid-30s, who is now teaching Malay in a Tamil school, when recalling her experience in the remove class, said, "We had no confidence in using Malay. We felt we didn't want to study. We wanted to leave the school." Another Indian respondent said the same thing, although a little differently: "so shy, seldom talk."

Other respondents said that the remove class did not provide them with opportunities to use the target languages, that is, English or Malay, as the other students in the class also came from the same ethnic group. However, most respondents who experienced remove classes said that after some problems of adaptation, they did settle down to a new language as the medium of instruction. The coping strategies they reported using to learn Malay included learning from friends, going for tuition classes, memorizing, learning from dictionaries, listening carefully to the pronunciation of Malay when watching Malay programs, listening to songs in Malay, singing songs, and talking to their friends in Malay.

Today, the remove classes, which were initiated in the 1960s, are a dying institution and are found only in some schools. In fact, the transition rate of Standard 6 students from Chinese and Tamil schools to remove classes has dropped considerably from 86.07% in 1987 to 47.5% in 1997. The fact that it is no longer necessary to attend remove classes before moving on to the Malay medium in the secondary school shows that students are obtaining satisfactory grades for the test on Malay language in the UPSR examination (one that is taken at the end of the first 6 years of schooling). The earlier battle over the lack of competency in Malay seems to have been won. It appears that the non-Malays have negotiated the local needs quite adequately.

There is no doubt that vernacular students who are successful in learning three languages have to walk that extra mile. In fact, some Chinese independent secondary schools that are outside the national system conduct two sessions. The session in the morning uses Mandarin as the medium of instruction and this leads to examinations conducted by the Association of Chinese Schools. The session in the afternoon has Malay as the medium of instruction and the same students sit for the national examinations, which are in Malay. The ability to speak and write in Mandarin, besides being fluent in Malay and English, is regarded as a hallmark of the Malaysian Chinese community, says Fong, the Minister of Human Resources (cited in Much to Reap freom Chinese Education, 2001).

Third, the greatest uncertainty that non-Malay students suffered was at the exit point of school. When a pass in the Malay language in the Malaysian Certificate of Education (MCE), which is the school-leaving certificate, was first made compulsory, the percentage of passes for this examination in the former English medium schools fell drastically, mainly because of failure in Malay language proficiency. Pillai (1973) reports that in 1972, more than 50% of the English medium pupils who performed well in other subjects failed to obtain the MCE because they did not pass Malay. Many of these students were non-Malays. Thus initially, many non-Malay students were disenfranchised by the change in the language policy which made the passing of the test on Malay language compulsory to gain a school-leaving certificate and to move on to pre-university classes. If one passed all other subjects with distinction but did not obtain a credit in the Malay paper, the door to local universities was permanently closed.

One affected respondent, who is now a professional, reminisced as follows: "My whole world collapsed when I could not do Form Six (pre-university class). I did not get a credit in Bahasa Malaysia (Malay Language). I passed with good grades in all my other papers. I had to re-sit the whole exam the following year." Another respondent, who is presently a lecturer in a teacher-training college, said the following: "I tried three times before I got a credit in Bahasa Malaysia. Only then I was admitted into a college." Another respondent did not wait to get a credit in Malay to get into the pre-university program in Malaysia. He quipped, "Instead, I went to India to pursue a medical degree. When I came back to work in Malaysia, I had to pass Bahasa Malaysia to be confirmed in service." This respondent tried three times before he passed the test on language at the SPM level.

A change in the language policy can empower or disenfranchise individuals, but ultimately it is the responses of individuals to such policy changes that determine the outcome (David, 2001b). Many of them were able to overcome the turmoil largely due to a flexible attitude displayed by teachers and lecturers at the forefront of the implementation of the policy. The teachers facilitated the transition of many students, irrespective of ethnicity, from an English medium of instruction to Malay. Many respondents gratefully remember those lecturers who allowed them to write class test papers in English, although the medium of instruction had been changed to Malay.

It is generally agreed that positive attitudes to learning a language influence proficiency and help overcome resistance (English ills and cures, 2001). An Indian male respondent in his late 30s, who was affected by the changing language policy while in college, recalled that his problem was "a great deal of resistance to Malay—only after some time your mind accepts it" (i.e., the change to Malay). This is when he realized that passing the paper meant passing the examination (SPM), which in turn had future career implications. When a language has instrumental value as Malay has (a credit in Malay at the SPM level is a requirement for civil service jobs), learners are willing to make mind-set changes. In the subsequent years, the resistance to Malay did decline as more and more non-Malays accepted the language as it is widely used in the larger environment. Many non-Malay respondents in the civil service stated that their initial resistance to Malay as the medium of instruction was eroded on postings to parts of Malaysia where the majority population comprised ethnic Malays. In such settings, to not feel disadvantaged and remain outsiders, they had no option but to use Malay.

## THE TASK AHEAD: ENGLISH EDUCATION
## AND GLOBALIZATION

In the face of the harmful social and educational consequences resulting to all communities from the narrowly conceived imposition of the dominant vernacular, some pragmatic moves have been made in the last decade or so to develop learners' proficiency in English. National leaders and language planners, despite criticisms from Malay nationalists, appear to share one platform. They realize that a high proficiency in English is essential. Gomez (1999), a language planner in the country, affirms it as follows: "Given the aspiration of this country to become a fully developed nation, the proficiency we want our young citizens to acquire is more than a minimum competency" (p. 20). The leaders also acknowledge that the 11 years in school is certainly not sufficient for the students to reach this level of competency.

In trying to arrest the deterioration in English language competency, national leaders have constantly stressed the importance of English to the nation. This has, in turn, caused a reemphasis on the learning of English, especially for the rural students. In the past few years, there has been a great deal of debate and discussion on measures to improve their proficiency in

English. These include programs to upgrade the professionalism of teachers and the bringing in of foreign teachers. And, in 2000, after a gap of about 20 years, English was reintroduced as a subject in pre-university classes and students who wish to enter local universities are compelled to sit for the Malaysian University English Test. The most important decision promoting English in the educational system has been the liberalization of education in Malaysia which resulted in the opening of private institutions of higher learning where English is the medium of instruction. This change in policy in 1996 brought about a surge in the number of private colleges: from 50 colleges before this period to 650 colleges and almost 200,000 students enrolled in 2001. Many of these institutions have twinning programs with foreign universities, hence English medium instruction is the obvious choice. Malaysians of all ethnic groups now have more options and they can choose this medium for tertiary education.

The year 2002 has been a year of great awakening for the country as a whole because time and again the Prime Minister, concerned about Malaysia's ability to compete globally in offering goods and services, suggested the setting up of English medium schools in the country that can produce graduates highly proficient in English. Heeding this call, there was an unprecedented move by a vice-chancellor of a Malaysian public university to use English as the medium of instruction in 50% of its courses by 2004. A week later, the Education Minister reported the setting up of an institution (Malaysian English Language Teaching Centre) to retrain 30,000 English language teachers in the country (Refresher courses, 2002). The editor of a major newspaper, Abdullah Ahmad, lauds the moves, saying "English has become even more important than before. Development in knowledge is articulated in English, and not mastering it is to deny ourselves a bigger canvas, education, encounter with humanity and life of inquiry and questioning" (Ahmad, 2002, p. 10).

The leaders of the country have generally spoken up for the reintroduction of English medium schools. In a democratic country, it is essential that the people's voices are heard regarding the issue as education of a future generation and the identity of a nation is in the balance. When the leaders first proposed the idea of reviving English medium schools, over 500 readers sent e-mails to a national newspaper generally applauding the move (Respondents back proposal, 2002). A leading English language national newspaper conducted a poll to study Malaysians' reaction to the proposal. A great majority of the respondents (4,142 or 97%) favored reviving the English medium schools. And if such schools did not materialize, a big majority urged that the instruction of some subjects be carried out in English minimally (Support from Chinese, 2002). The enthusiastic respondents could be from non-Malay ethnic groups who have supported English education from the beginning.

Meanwhile, hesitance shown by others and the cautious statements that have come from Malay intellectuals and politicians show some wariness that English would replace Malay in the country. One academic stated the following: "I laud any move to improve the command of English but the implications of the proposal are far-reaching and need to be analyzed from all aspects" (*The Star*, 2002e, p. 4). His concerns could be the future status of Malay as well as the ability of teachers and students to cope with the pressure of teaching and learning in a foreign language. Another Malay academic has written forthrightly in a newspaper article that it is perfectly healthy to maintain Bahasa Malaysia as a medium of instruction (Sharmini, 2002). An English lecturer herself, her suggestion to improve students' proficiency in English is to place greater emphasis on speaking and listening skills. The Communicative Syllabus that was implemented in the early 1980s was specially designed to improve students' speaking and listening skills. It appears that this emphasis has not appreciably improved the subskills of Malaysian learners.

Meanwhile, political groups and newspapers have been extremely guarded in showing support for the proposal. Malay-based opposition parties have been particularly cautious in their statements. They point out that reintroducing English schools will go against the National Education Policy. Their concern is explicable in terms of losing electoral support in the Malay heartland from which they operate. The same concern has prevented UMNO (United Malayan National Organization), the backbone of the National Front coalition party ruling the country, from firmly espousing the proposal. It has suggested that science and mathematics be taught in English for all. The Malay newspapers have also suggested that greater discussion be carried out before taking this action (the teaching of mathematics and science in English has been implemented in the first year of schooling in the academic year 2003).

It is apparent that Malay interest groups as well as academics are wary of promoting English at the expense of Malay. These groups are well aware that those who elect for a college education in English, either within the country or overseas, need not possess a high proficiency in Malay. Only those who aspire for employment in teaching or civil service need to be proficient in the national language. Most other jobs in the private sector place a premium on English. The Malay groups must realize that those who choose English education tend to benefit more than those who opt for other media of education. In the long run, Malay students should not be influenced by the attitude of the nationalistic groups toward the English language. As the Malaysian Employers Federation executive director Shamsuddin Bardan highlighted, "employers were reluctant to hire local graduates because they were not able to communicate well in English ... This is one of the reasons there are so many unemployed bumiputra graduates whereas the percentage of non-bumiputras who are unemployed is very low" (Employers and union, 2002).

The authors believe that although reviving English medium schools may show an improvement in English language proficiency and academic competence among Malaysian students, there might be a decline in proficiency in other languages, particularly Malay. This situation may not be in the best interests of Malaysians as all learners ought to be at least minimally bilingual as part of a language maintenance strategy. The avowed goal of the nation is not to create more Anglophiles in the country who will eventually turn out to be monolinguals. The goal is to have citizens who are adequately equipped with skills and who are able to compete globally. And, to acquire all the skills that can empower them, English has become a necessity. This skills acquisition process, however, must not be at the expense of learning one's own language, literature, and way of life. It is therefore important that each community strategize to maintain its own as well as the national culture and language. The continued use of Malaysian languages in the national scene along with a good command of conversational and academic English for international communication and transactions appear to be a desirable goal.

## CONCLUSION

Given the circumstances of the postindependent period in Malaysia, there were compelling reasons for instituting changes to the existing language policy in the country. Malaysia "inherited" a multiethnic and multilingual society, a result of colonial policies in the early 1900s. In trying to give the indigenous population a headstart to compete with the immigrant Chinese and Indian communities, a wide-ranging set of affirmative policies that included economic and educational policies were effected. There was relatively less resistance to economic policies than to the replacement of English in the educational system. This resistance made the nationalists more resolved, and with great hastiness the new policy was implemented. The reports from various researchers from Malaysian universities have shown that there was an unassailable constituent underlying the replacement: a state of unpreparedness. The change in the medium of instruction has affected the proficiency in English and, consequently, hindered the performance of the Malays at the tertiary level. Unfortunately, it continues to disempower them even today (Govindasamy, 2001), as most reading and reference materials are in English. It also initially brought great hardship to non-Malays. They had to overcome this difficulty with great determination. The latter's performance has not deteriorated as they have maintained some measure of competency in English, whereas their proficiency in Malay has improved tremendously.

Furthermore, the Malay nationalists have inadvertently contributed to the disempowerment and dismal performance of the Malay students, especially at the tertiary level. Their action has limited a large number of Malays from becoming bilinguals and benefiting from greater exposure to the print legacy of the Western world. This group of Malaysians has to feel confident that the Malay language cannot be replaced by English or any other language in the country. Such confidence may pave the way for a gradual reintroduction of English for the teaching of science. Nadkarni (1983) offered the following suggestion: "If the English of science is what the science student needs, what better way is there to impart this than using English itself to teach science" (p. 155). Another educationist, Daun (2002), conjectured that a globalized economy requires its students to become "creative, innovative, and flexible to find new solutions to new problems" (p. 20). For Malaysian students, to be able to function optimally (and taking into consideration Daun's suggestion), they need to have a high academic language proficiency in English to be globally competitive. Malaysian educationists and intellectuals have to boldly advocate the use of English as an additional medium of education in the primary and secondary national schools to help students develop academic language proficiency in English.

There are lessons from the Malaysian experience for other postcolonial communities. In multilingual nations, empowering the vernacular is a controversial activity. First of all, there are diverse vernaculars belonging to other minority ethnic groups that need to be accommodated by the majority. In this sense, what is really the "local" interest in language policy planning becomes questionable. (Tamil and Chinese are certainly local, given the long history of these communities in Malaysia; prioritizing Malay at the expense of these vernaculars generates conflicts among local communities.) Furthermore, thinking in terms of "national" policies goes against the trend of transnationalism in contemporary social life. Postcolonial communities have to negotiate global and local interests with imagination and wisdom in their language policy. Thankfully, there is a "local knowledge" that is developing among Malaysian people from their shared history of conflicts and losses deriving from the extreme forms of affirmative action practiced in their country. Ironically, this local knowledge emphasizes more engagement with translocal interests and values. This local knowledge develops a healthy skepticism toward the dominant ideology of "affirmative action" that is increasingly being questioned in other parts of the world.

## REFERENCES

Ahmad, A. (2002, April 17). Realism at last on English. *The New Straits Times*, p. 10.

Asmah, H. O. (1981). The Malaysian national language in academic discourse. In O. Asmah & M. N. Noor Ein (Eds.), *National language as medium of instruction* (pp. 73–92). Kuala Lumpur, Malaysia: Dewan Bahasa dan Pustaka.

Asmah, H. O. (1997). A discussion of the path taken by English towards becoming a Malaysian language. In M. S. Halimah & K. S. Ng (Eds.), *English is an Asian language: The Malaysian context* (pp. 12–21). Kuala Lumpur, Malaysia: Persatuan Bahasa Modern Malaysia & The Macquarie Library Pty. Ltd.

Be resourceful, jobless grads told. (2002, May 6). *The Star*, p. 6.

Build vision schools with clear guidelines. (2000, August 14). *The Star*, p. 24.

Chai, H. C. (1971). *Planning education for a plural society*. Paris: United Nations Educational, Scientific, and Cultural Organization, International Institute for Educational Planning.

Chandrasegaran, X. (1979). Problems of learning English in national schools in Johore, Malaysia: An investigation of attitudinal and motivational variables, learning strategies and exposure to English. Singapore: Regional English Language Center.

Daun, H. (2002). Globalization and national education. In H. Daun (Ed.), *Educational restructuring in the context of globalization and national policy* (pp. 1–31). New York: Routledge Falmer.

David, M. K. (2000). Status and role of English in Malaysia: Ramifications for English language teaching. *English Australia, 18*, 41–50.

David, M. K. (2001a). *The Sindhis of Malaysia: A sociolinguistic account*. London: Asean.

David, M. K. (2001b, February). *Language policy and results: Focus on Malaysia*. Paper presented at the conference on English Language and Education in the 21st Century, Aga Khan University, Karachi, Pakistan.

David, M. K., Naji, I., & Sheena Kaur, X. (2003). The Punjabi community in the Klang Valley, Malaysia—Language maintenance or language shift? *International Journal of the Sociology of Language, 161*, 1–24.

David, M. K., & Nambiar, M. (2002). Exogamous marriages and out-migration: Language shift of the Malyalees in Malaysia. In M. K. David (Ed.), *Methodological issues in language maintenance and language shift studies* (pp. 136–145). Frankfurt, Germany: Peter Lang.

Ee, C. L. (2001). *Rural/cultural factors in the learning of English*. Unpublished master's thesis, University of Malaya, Kuala Lumpur, Malaysia.

Employers and union laud English schools move. (2002, May 8). *The Star*, p. 4.

English anyone? Government seeks your views on reintroducing English medium schools. (2002, May 7). *The Star*, p. 1.

English ills and cures: Why is English proficiency 'declining' and what can be done about it? (2001, January 14). *The Star*, pp. 2–5.

Gomez, X. A. (1999). TESL in Malaysia: Coping with the realities. In M. S. Azlina & M. Mutiara (Eds.), *English language teaching and learning: Traditions, changes and innovations* (pp. 13–21). Sintok, Malaysia: UUM Publications.

Govindasamy, S. (2001, April). *Learning style preferences of IIUM Engineering and Law undergraduates*. Paper presented at the Department of English Language and Literature's Colloquium, International Islamic University, Kuala Lumpur, Malaysia.

Habibah, E., & Wan, R. R. (1994). Achievement motivation training module for university students. *Journal of Educational Research, 16*, 87–98

Khoo, S. G. (1991). *Population Census Volume 1*. Kuala Lumpur, Malaysia: General Report of the Department of Statistics.

Mahadzir, K. (2001, May). Opening Speech, "Bumis still lagging behind in varsities," Colloquium on the Performance of Malay Students at Institutions of Higher Learning. Genting Highlands, Pahang, Malaysia.

Malek, H. B. (2000, December 30). English imperative for progress: Exco man. *The Sun,* p. 4.

Mitchell, C. L. (1993). *Language as an instrument of national policy: The Dewan Bahasa dan Pustaka of Malaysia.* Unpublished doctoral dissertation, University of Wisconsin–Madison.

Much to reap from Chinese education. (2001, May 20). *The Star,* p. 30.

Musa, H. (2001, May 11). Memorial lecture on education and excellence: Challenges of the 21st century. *The Sunday Star,* p. E6.

Nadkarni, M. V. (1983). Cultural pluralism as a national resource: Strategies for language education. In C. Kennedy (Ed.), *Language planning and language education* (pp. 151–159). London: Allen & Unwin.

Negative aspect of affirmative action. (2001, August 31). *New Straits Times,* p. 7.

Nik, R. (1981). The teaching of law in the Malay language: An assessment. In O. Asmah & M. N. Noor Ein (Eds.), *National language as medium of instruction* (pp. 295–305). Kuala Lumpur, Malaysia: Dewan Bahasa dan Pustaka.

Nik, S. K. (1981). Bahasa Malaysia as a medium of instruction in a modern, plural society. In O. Asmah & M. N. Noor Ein (Eds.), *National language as medium of instruction* (pp. 44–57). Kuala Lumpur, Malaysia: Dewan Bahasa dan Pustaka.

PM: Not many jobs for arts or religion grads. (2002, May 5). *The Star,* p. 2.

Pathmanabhan, K. (2001, May 13). Who will speak for English? *The Sun,* p. 22.

Pillai, J. (1973, July 12). Loyalty has nothing to do with learning the language. *New Straits Times,* p. 4.

Refresher courses for teachers. (2002, April 6). *The Star,* p. 3.

Respondents back proposal. (2002, May 8). *The Star,* p. 4.

Salbiah, A. (2001). *Achieving equality.* Retrieved March 20, 2002, from http://www.equality.htm

Sargunan, R. A., & Nambiar, M. K. (1994). Language needs of students at the Faculty of Law, University of Malaya. *Journal of Educational Research, 16,* 99–117.

Schiffman, H. F. (1997). *Malaysian Tamils and Tamil linguistic culture.* Nikos Drakos, Computer based Learning Unit, University of Leeds, England.

Sharmini, P. (2002, May 8). Cautious 'aye' to re-introducing English medium school system. *New Straits Times,* p. 1.

Soepadmo, E. (1981). Malay as medium of instruction in teaching biological subjects—problems and prospects. In O. Asmah & M. N. Noor Ein (Eds.), *National language as medium of instruction* (pp. 278–286). Kuala Lumpur, Malaysia: Dewan Bahasa dan Pustaka.

Solomon, J. (1988). *Bilingual education.* Kuala Lumpur, Malaysia. Pelanduk.

Sturm, S., & Guinier, L. (2000). *The future of affirmative action.* Retrieved March 20, 2002, from http://www. Affirm~1.htm

Suhaimi, A. (1981). National language in the teaching of natural sciences. In O. Asmah & M. N. Noor Ein (Eds.), *National language as medium of instruction* (pp. 272–277). Kuala Lumpur, Malaysia: Dewan Bahasa dan Pustaka.

Support from Chinese education group. (2002, May 11). *The Star,* p. 19.

Tunku, S. B. (1981). Bahasa Malaysia: Its policy and implementation in the Faculty of Arts and Social Sciences, University of Malaya. In O. Asmah & M. N. Noor Ein (Eds.), *National language as medium of instruction* (pp. 163–177). Kuala Lumpur, Malaysia: Dewan Bahasa dan Pustaka.

Usher, R., & Edwards, R. (1994). *Postmodernism and education.* London: Routledge.

Voon, P. K., Zaharah, M., & Khoo, S. H. (1981). Formula for dynamism in the teaching of geography in Bahasa Malaysia. In O. Asmah & M. N. Noor Ein (Eds.), *National language as medium of instruction* (pp. 255–271). Kuala Lumpur, Malaysia: Dewan Bahasa dan Pustaka.

Watson, J. K. P. (1983). Cultural pluralism, nation-building and educational policies in Peninsular Malaysia. In C. Kennedy (Ed.), *Language planning and language education* (pp. 132–150). London: Allen & Unwin.

Yusof, Z. A. (2001, May 22). Educating ourselves on affirmative action. *New Straits Times*, p. 22.

# An Educational Policy for Negotiating Transnationalism: The Dominican Community in New York City[1]

Sharon Utakis
Marianne D. Pita
*Bronx Community College*

## INTRODUCTION

Global economic and technological developments have resulted in changes in migration patterns in recent years. Some migrants travel back and forth between the United States and their country of origin, creating communities that transcend national boundaries (Glick Schiller, 1999; Glick Schiller, Basch, & Blanc-Szanton, 1992). The Dominican[2] community in New York City is a paradigm case of this kind of transnational community, in which migrants move between the Dominican Republic and the United States, maintaining strong ties with both places. Transnational Dominicans ex-

---

[1]Although all faults remain our own, we would like to thank Angus Grieve-Smith, Michael Newman, and Suresh Canagarajah for helpful comments on this chapter. We would also like to thank the students and school staff who participated enthusiastically in the interviews. Finally, we would like to acknowledge a President's Grant from Bronx Community College and a PSC/CUNY Research Grant which helped to fund the research mentioned in this chapter.

[2]We have generally used the term *Dominican*, rather than *Dominican-American*. Because of the transnational nature of this community, many migrants prefer the unhyphenated term.

ploit global transportation and communication networks to create a community that spans political and geographical space.

We argue that language education in the United States does not serve the needs of transnational migrants. Education for immigrants has historically been designed to teach them to become American, to learn English, and to assimilate into the new culture. Most bilingual education programs use a transitional model, in which instruction is given in the children's first language only until they are considered sufficiently proficient in English. However, to effectively serve the needs of a particular community, language education should be responsive to local context, to the lives, histories, and goals of the population. In the case of a transnational community, local knowledge must include an understanding of both native and host contexts and how the transnational community experiences the connection between the two places.

As English teachers at Bronx Community College (BCC), we have observed a disconnect between language education practices in New York City and the needs of our transnational students and their children. Most of our ESL students are Dominican, and many go back and forth between the Dominican Republic and New York. Yet the official goal of most language education programs in New York City is to teach immigrants English without regard for the development of their native language. We discuss the problems with language education in this community based on our own experience and interviews we conducted with 10 Dominican students from Bronx Community College as part of ongoing qualitative research on language and identity in this transnational community. All of our informants have spent significant amounts of time in both countries and have gone to school in both places. In addition to a language survey, we conducted 1-hr to 2-hr open-ended interviews in Spanish or English, depending on the language preferred by the students. A list of guiding questions used for the open-ended interviews is given in the Appendix. In addition to at least one of the principal investigators, a Dominican research assistant was present at all sessions to help with any idiomatic language or cultural questions. Interviews were conducted on the BCC campus, and all interviews were recorded and transcribed. Unless otherwise stated, all quotations from the interview are in English. We include their voices in this discussion.

We argue that the increasingly transnational character of the Dominican community in New York City necessitates changes in classroom practice. These students need to learn two languages and be able to live in two cultures. Educators should help students develop and maintain fluency and literacy in both languages and help students negotiate the global reality of a life lived in two places. In this chapter, we begin with an overview of the transnational Dominican community. We discuss transnational identity, review current educational policy in New York City, and describe the problems faced by Dominican students in two school systems. Finally, we suggest a shift in perspective that would allow teachers to take into account the transnational educational needs of this community.

## THE TRANSNATIONAL NATURE
## OF THE DOMINICAN COMMUNITY IN NEW YORK CITY

The Dominicans are the largest immigrant group in Manhattan (Ayala, 2002). Jennifer Chait of the New York Department of City Planning estimates that there are 600,000 people of Dominican origin in the city (Kugel, 2001). In spite of these large and growing numbers, there was no category for Dominicans in the 2000 U.S. Census, the way there was for Cubans, Mexicans, and Puerto Ricans. As a result, Dominicans had to choose "Other Hispanic," which appears to have resulted in an undercount of Dominicans (Ayala, 2002). Although Cuban, Mexican, and Puerto Rican immigrant communities in the United States have been the subject of extensive linguistic and sociological studies, Dominican immigrants, who have come to the United States more recently, have been the subject of significantly less research (Sagás, 1998).

Dominicans maintain close ties to their native country through global networks that facilitate language and cultural maintenance. These migrants can go back for vacations or extended visits because of inexpensive air fares, and they stay in regular contact with family, friends, and institutions through phone calls, faxes, and the Internet. A 1997 poll published in the Dominican Republic reports that half of all Dominicans have family in the United States, and over 65% would move here if they had the opportunity (Rohter, 1997). In a monograph on the Dominican community in Washington Heights, Jorge Duany (1994) describes transnational communities as "characterized by a constant flow of people in both directions, a dual sense of identity, ambivalent attachment to two nations and a far-flung network of kinship and friendship ties across state frontiers" (p. 2). The transnationalism of the Dominican community can be seen in the economic, political, social, cultural, linguistic, and educational ties between the two countries.

Evidence of the economic links between New York City and the Dominican Republic can be seen in the businesses that proliferate in the Dominican neighborhoods of New York: *agentes de dinero extranjero* (foreign money brokers), *mudanzas* (movers), *envios* (shipping), and *agencias de turismo* (travel agencies). Peddlers, operating between the Dominican Republic and the United States, form part of the economic infrastructure which is the basis of transnational exchange (Itzigsohn, Dore Cabral, Hernández Medina, & Vazquez, 1999). As noticeable as the economic impact of this transnational community is on New York City, the impact on the Dominican economy is even more substantial. The remittances sent home by Dominicans are the second largest source of hard currency for the Dominican Republic (Itzigsohn, 1995).

Transnational political ties attest to the importance of transmigrants and the money they send home. In recognition of the dual identity of many Dominican migrants, the Dominican Republic changed its constitution in 1994 to allow citizens living abroad to hold dual citizenship and vote in national elections. Two of the major political parties in the Dominican Republic have branches in New York, and presidential candidates conduct campaigns and raise funds in the city (Itzigsohn et al., 1999) while New York politicians visit the Dominican Republic to garner support among Dominicans.

Dominicans place a strong value on *familismo*, commitment to extended family (Castillo, 1996; Pita, 2000). In this transnational community, many families have relatives in both countries, and strong kinship ties are maintained by regular travel. Lacking adequate day-care facilities in New York, parents often send their young children back to be cared for by grandparents. With family in both countries, parents can send teenagers to the Dominican Republic to shelter them from gangs, drugs, and early sex (Georges, 1990). Our students at BCC at times have to leave in the middle of the semester to go back to care for sick relatives or attend funerals. Many Dominicans save money so they can buy a house or a business in their native country and retire there, rejoining family left behind. In 1996, more than 50% of the Dominicans who died in New York City were returned to the Dominican Republic for burial (Sontag & Dugger, 1998).

Clubs in New York City associated with particular towns in the Dominican Republic funnel money back to support community development projects (Graham, 1998) and reinforce ties to migrants' hometowns. In the Dominican Republic, there are several organizations of transmigrants that assist returning migrants and work to improve the image of Dominicans who have lived abroad (Itzigsohn et al., 1999).

Dominican migrants maintain their ties to their native land on a daily basis. *El Nacional*, a leading newspaper in the Dominican Republic, has a New York edition with a daily circulation of 25,000 copies. In addition, five more dailies from the Dominican Republic are sold in New York (Smith, 1997). Dominicans in New York also access Dominican newspapers online and watch Dominican television programs on cable (Itzigsohn et al., 1999).

In an extensive survey of language use in the Dominican community in Washington Heights, Sue Dicker and Hafiz Mahmoud (2001) found that these migrants are moving toward acquisition of English and greater participation in the larger society while maintaining their native language and involvement and interest in Spanish cultural activities. Whether this transnational community can maintain their native language over the long term is a question for further research. The final item in the language survey asked participants whether they plan to stay in the United States or return to the Dominican Republic. Among those planning to stay in this country, a significant number also indicated plans to return to the Dominican Republic. Staying in this country and returning to their native country were not seen as mutually exclusive.

Although there are few links between educational institutions in the Dominican Republic and the United States, one transnational initiative is a graduate program in bilingual education of the Universidad Autónoma de Santo Domingo. Dominican teachers, among others, take coursework in New York City and the Dominican Republic, graduating with a master's degree that is recognized in the United States (Itzigsohn et al., 1999).

We have demonstrated the transnational character of the Dominican community in New York. Now we turn to the complex process of identity formation in the context of this geopolitical reality.

## TRANSNATIONAL IDENTITY

Identity has usually been connected to national origin. For immigrants, a hyphenated identity is associated with a past in one country and a present and future in another. In contrast, transnational migrants are forging an identity that spans two countries. Many Dominican migrants view their identity positively. In a survey of Dominican high school students in New York City, Castillo (1996) found that 95% considered themselves "Dominicans and proud of it, regardless of where they were born" (p. 51).

However, many Dominican migrants face conflicts trying to create a transnational identity. In the Dominican Republic, although lower nonmigrant classes look up to the migrants as role models and "a sort of revenge against the traditional elites" (Guarnizo, 1997a, p. 305), the upper classes call them *Dominicanyorks*, a term used pejoratively for transnationals stereotyped as drug traffickers (Castillo, 1996; Duany, 1994; Smith, 1997). In addition, transmigrants face discrimination in business associations, private social clubs, schools, and housing in the Dominican Republic (Guarnizo, 1997b).

Nevertheless, some younger Dominican migrants in New York are reclaiming the term "*Dominicanyork*." As one 25-year-old informant said, "We identify *Dominicanyork* with the double life, of being here and being there. It's not really easy to be a *Dominicanyork* because you have feelings here and feelings there ... I identify myself as a *Dominicanyork*, working here, empowering the name that I carry, by being from a particular place in the world."

The process of forging a transnational identity is made more difficult by the discrimination against Dominican migrants in the United States based on race, social class, and language. One of our informants argues that the underlying cause of transnationalism for Dominicans is discrimination: "That is why the Hispanic, as well as the Dominican, comes here with the goal of finishing his studies, working, having a certain amount of money or capital to return to his country and to be in a better position. The reason that ... the Dominican [does that] is because of the discrimination, not for any other reason."[3]

Racial identity is particularly problematic for these transmigrants. Most Dominicans in New York are subject to racial categories that classify them as non-White, which differs from the social construction of race in the Dominican Republic (Duany, 1998). Although 90% of the population of the Dominican Republic is of African descent, Dominicans in the United States resist categorization as Black, preferring to identify themselves as "Spanish" because they speak Spanish (Bailey, 2000). Racial categorization as Black tends to isolate the Dominican population. Duany (1998) attributes the segregation of Washington Heights, where Dominicans live apart from native Whites, African Americans, and other Latinos, to "a long history of institutionalized housing discrimination against black immigrants in North American urban centers" (p. 161). Segregated neighborhoods discourage assimilation and strengthen Dominican identity.

Another reason transnational Dominicans do not assimilate quickly is because of their poverty. Dominicans are the poorest group in New York City, with a poverty rate of 46% (compared with 24% for the entire city and 37% for all Latinos; Sanchez, 2001). Low educational attainment is largely responsible for this poverty. In 1996, 54% of Dominicans over age 25 had less than a high school diploma, compared to 24.1% of New Yorkers (Hernández & Rivera-Batiz, 1997). Low levels of English literacy prevent even those who come to New York with a higher level of education from finding good jobs (Hernández, 2002). Both racism and poverty contribute to the isolation of the community. On the other hand, "Transnational practices allow some individuals to compensate for these limits to their economic advancement. They choose to remain transnational to overcome the blocked opportunities they face in the United States" (Levitt, 2001, p. 205).

Another challenge that Dominicans face in attempting to forge a transnational identity is the relatively low prestige of Dominican Spanish. In the United States, Spanish, especially the Spanish of poor and working class immigrants, has low prestige relative to English (Dicker, 2000–2001). The low prestige of Spanish makes it difficult for Dominican migrants, like other Latinos, to develop academic Spanish while learning English.

---

[3]This is a quotation from the following Spanish original: "Por eso es que el hispano, tanto como el dominicano, viene aqui a una meta a terminar de hacer esos estudios, de trabajar, tener una cierta cantidad de dinero o un capital para volver a su pais y estar en una mejor posision. El problema de que el dominicano [haga eso] es por la descriminasion, no es por otra cosa."

Furthermore, different varieties of Spanish have different levels of prestige within the Spanish-speaking community. Among Spanish speakers in New York, both Dominican and Puerto Rican Spanish have low prestige. Ana Celia Zentella (1997) argues the following: "The negative impact of U.S. language policies on Puerto Rico and of decades of dictatorial repression in the Dominican Republic, as well as the lower incomes and darker skins of Dominicans and Puerto Ricans in NYC, place them at the bottom of the language status ladder" (1997, p. 175). Even among Dominicans themselves, Zentella found that 35% expressed negative opinions about Dominican Spanish, and 80% said that Dominican Spanish should not be taught in schools (1990).

In the United States, many Dominicans feel that they are compelled to choose between Spanish and English, between being Dominican or being "American."[1] Some Dominicans, particularly adolescents and children, feel that to be accepted in this country, they need to abandon their native language and culture. The forced choice pushes others to cling tightly to their native language variety and culture, making it difficult for them to learn English. Because Dominicans live in segregated neighborhoods, they have little need or opportunity to speak English. As a result, Dominicans are disparaged for not learning English and not becoming "American" quickly or completely enough, hence the need for a relevant and effective bilingual education program.

## EDUCATIONAL POLICY IN NEW YORK CITY

The language programs available in New York City public schools perpetuate this forced choice, between learning English and maintaining Spanish. According to the Chancellor's Report on the Education of English Language Learners (New York City Board of Education, 2000), in New York City three currently existing programs are recommended: free-standing ESL, transitional bilingual, and dual language.

Free-standing ESL programs aim to develop the English language proficiency of the students independently from instruction in other courses. Although such programs provide a clear focus on the language needs of immigrant students, they shortchange transnational Dominican students. Although there is evidence that students acquire conversational proficiency in English-speaking classrooms (Cummins, 1992), academic competence in their native language (and in all academic subjects other than English) is sacrificed to expedient and cost-effective English learning (Cummins, 1995).

---

[1]Clearly "American" could refer to anyone from North, Central, or South America; as one informant said, "*Todos somos americanos.*" [We are all Americans.] However, we use the term in quotation marks in reference to people associated with the United States.

Transitional (short-term) bilingual programs are the most common forms of bilingual education in New York City. In Community School District 6, which has the highest concentration of Dominican students, 79% of English language learners are in transitional bilingual programs.[5] Such programs are an improvement over English immersion, but their goal is still monolingualism in English—that is, "to transition students to regular English only classes as quickly as possible" (New York City Board of Education, 2000, p. 17). However, students in transitional bilingual programs are penalized for learning English quickly: as soon as they have reached minimal competence in English, their studies in Spanish are terminated. In New York City, students are expected to exit from bilingual and ESL programs after 3 years (New York City Board of Education, 2000).

Dual language programs, which have the goal of mastering both English and Spanish (New York City Board of Education, 2000), are currently the best alternative available to transnational Dominican students in New York City, but these programs are small in scope and limited in number, usually serving only elementary school students. Evelyn Linares, principal of a dual language program in Community School District 6, notes that her school suffers from high attrition as transnational students go back to the Dominican Republic, and it is difficult to integrate new students beyond the second grade and maintain a balance between English- and Spanish-dominant students.[6]

The educational systems in both New York and the Dominican Republic are beginning to recognize the challenges that these school systems face in trying to meet the needs of transnational students. The State Education Department of New York and the Dominican Department of Education organized an Education Summit in April 2001. A Memorandum of Understanding between the two education departments was signed and included the following statement:

> Each year, large numbers of elementary and secondary school students of Dominican Republic heritage and their families migrate between the Dominican Republic and the State of New York, sometimes more than once in a school year; ... such two-way migration impacts on the continuity and effectiveness of the education of such students ... increased communication, collaboration and sharing between DR [Dominican Republic] and SED [State Education Department] ... is in the best interests of such students of Dominican Republic heritage and of such educational systems. (New York State Education Department, 2001, p. 1)

---

[5]John Acompore, Deputy Director of the New York City Board of Education Office of English Language Learners, reported in spring of 2001 that out of 9,937 general education English Language Learners in District 6 entitled to bilingual or ESL services, 7,850 were in bilingual education, 1,874 were in ESL, and 214 were in neither.

[6]Evelyn Linares was interviewed by the authors on November 30, 2001.

Both the New York State Education Department and the Dominican Department of Education recognize the educational impact of this two-way migration on students. The Memorandum calls for information sharing, instructional material exchange, and school staff exchange programs. However, the Memorandum does not directly address pedagogical alternatives.

## TRANSNATIONAL STUDENTS IN TWO SCHOOL SYSTEMS

The assumptions behind current educational language policy in New York conflict with the lived reality of transnational Dominican students. In the United States, English language teaching is primarily thought of as a tool to help immigrants integrate into American society by replacing the native language with English, and loss of the native language is thought to be a desirable and necessary part of the process of Americanization. Cultural assimilation is also considered an important goal of the curriculum.

Current educational policy presents an unacceptable choice for transnational students. If Dominican students focus on learning English, permitting the loss of their language and culture, they are likely to fail when they return to the Dominican Republic. If, on the other hand, they resist learning English, they are likely to fail in the New York City school system. Because children from the Dominican community move between two school systems, they suffer academically in both countries. Neglecting the needs of these transnational children can lead to devastating academic and social outcomes. We are interested in developing a literacy that doesn't dichotomize the needs and proficiencies of transnational students (i.e., Spanish and English, the home community and host community, or local and global).

According to Luis Guarnizo (1997b), many Dominicans in New York, concerned about the influence of gangs, drugs, and early sex on their school-age children, send the children back to the Dominican Republic to continue their schooling, often against the children's wishes. Some of these children were born in the United States or migrated here at a very young age. Guarnizo (1997b, p. 42) states that "many return children had undergone their primary socialization in the United States and did not even speak Spanish—or if they did, theirs was a limited, domestic Spanish inadequate for schoolwork or 'proper' social communication" (p. 42). At best, these children suffer from a difficult adjustment period with poor academic performance. At worst, they resist their new environment in socially unacceptable ways. Guarnizo (1997b) notes that the challenges posed by these children go beyond the domestic sphere to create "a widespread and neglected social problem" in the Dominican Republic (p. 42).

Many Dominican students also do poorly when they are in New York. Community School District 6 in Washington Heights has one of the state's worst records with extremely low math and reading scores. George Washington High School, with a majority of Dominican students, has one of the highest dropout rates in the United States (Torres-Saillant & Hernández, 1998). Although the causes of this failure are complex, transnational students face extraordinary challenges in this country, including interrupted and sometimes intermittent schooling.

Students may also resist the imperative to move into the English-speaking world. We have seen evidence of such resistance, particularly among students who have been forbidden to speak Spanish in class. Some of our students report that in classes where they are not allowed to speak Spanish, they do not speak at all, refusing to speak in English even in small groups. Other students report that they do speak in Spanish with their classmates as long as the teacher is out of earshot. As one informant put it, "There are times when I have to say something in Spanish, and I do it, but if, for example, I am in front of the teacher or several students that speak English I don't speak Spanish ..." When Spanish is prohibited, some students shut down; finding it difficult to follow the class, they resist in the only way they can, by not learning. Resistance may be seen when students refuse to participate or speak English, or when they behave disruptively. Students who know they will return to the Dominican Republic or want to return do not place the same importance on learning English or studying American history as those who intend to settle in this country.

## A PEDAGOGY FOR THE TRANSNATIONAL COMMUNITY

Educational policy that better serves the transnational community would require cooperation from many educational and governmental organizations. However, on a more local level, educators working in the Dominican community (or in other transnational communities) can adapt their practices to better serve these students with a global perspective. Parents from minority communities can play a big role in lobbying for changes in their schools. Hornberger (1997) brings together studies from diverse communities in the Americas to show that the pedagogical initiatives undertaken in local contexts, often by parents and teachers of disempowered communities, can go a long way in providing meaningful educational alternatives and changing unfair macrolevel policies. She refers to this as "language planning from the bottom up" (in the subtitle of her book). In the most radical example of such local involvement, Freeman (1996) shows how a local Hispanic community in the United States reinterprets the Bilingual Educational Act in creative ways to develop a more effective acquisition policy. Under the influence of the minority community, the school develops an enrichment program that provides equal status for Spanish and English. Both English-speaking and Spanish-speaking students follow classes in both languages. This pedagogy provides scope not only for maintaining Spanish while acquiring English (for Spanish students) but, by asking dominant community students to also learn Spanish, it provides dignity and affirmation for this minority language and equalizes the relation between both groups. Freeman shows that the secret of the program's success is that local parents and teachers take an active role in planning this pedagogy. For Freeman, this is another example of language planning from the ground up. The local community members take over a federal policy and interpret it in their favor to give it radical new ramifications.

Historically, English language teachers have been held responsible for helping students to assimilate by teaching English and those aspects of middle-class Anglo culture that will help them to survive and thrive in the United States. Critical educators argue that this approach to language education is a way of maintaining social control of subordinate groups such as Latinos, by devaluing their language, culture, and history (Darder, 1995; Walsh, 1991). For a transnational community, losing the native language, culture, and history is not an option. Transnational students must be prepared for an educational future in two places. In the Dominican community in New York, teachers should develop bicultural curricula, value Spanish, and incorporate critical language awareness into their classroom practice.

The curriculum should integrate materials that are relevant to students' lives from their home country as well as the United States. Students in a transnational community need a bicultural as well as a bilingual curriculum. Josh DeWind (1997) describes the goals of such programs as follows: "Bilingual/bicultural programs are intended not only to help students develop dual language skills but also to help them become comfortable in both their native and American cultural contexts" (p. 141). Other researchers have pointed out that the reason some of the bilingual education programs fail is because they teach the language while leaving out the local knowledge, community-based texts, and vernacular resources of the minority students (see Aikman, 1999; King, 2001).

As it stands, students in this country study U.S. history, and students in the Dominican Republic study Dominican history. A survey of Dominican high school students in New York City showed that they had very little knowledge of Dominican literature, art, folk culture, and history (Castillo, 1996). However, some teachers in this community have begun to integrate Dominican history into the curriculum. For example, at one elementary school, a Dominican-born teacher led her first-grade class in a play on Taino, Spanish and African influences on Dominican culture (Mandell, 1994). If students have the opportunity to study in a bicultural program in New York, they would return to school in the Dominican Republic with a foundation in Dominican history and literature.

In addition to studying the individual history of each country, students would study the relation between the two nations. The history of U.S. political and economic intervention in the Dominican Republic and the resulting migration patterns are an integral part of students' own histories. Some students are already aware of this history; as one informant put it, "Before I came here, Americans were in my country … I just got here, but you guys been there for years, controlling the government. People don't know that." Examining this intertwined history will help students to deal with the racism and anti-immigrant bias in this country. The program described by Freeman (1996) is successful because the Spanish-speaking students are able to develop a positive conception of their language and themselves as their language is actively integrated into many other areas of instructional and interactive domains in their school.

Besides knowledge of both cultures, it is essential for transnational students to maintain and develop their native language. However, Dominican students are often discouraged from speaking Spanish. In many ESL classes, students are forbidden to use their native language. Although sometimes well-intentioned, when teachers forbid the use of the mother tongue, students may believe their language and culture are being devalued. As one informant put it, "There is something wrong about the American mentality … They expect people to forget about their home language. That is totally wrong."

Because Dominicans in New York City speak a low prestige variety of a low prestige language, it is especially important for teachers, even English language teachers, to help students value their own language. Dominicans in the United States want to maintain their Spanish and want their children to develop fluent Spanish (Castillo, 1996) in spite of some negative feelings about their language variety. Zentella (1990) found that 94% of Dominicans surveyed wanted their children to be bilingual. As one of our informants proclaimed, "My kids, they gonna learn both languages, especially Spanish."

The goal for transnational students is a balanced bilingualism. Maintaining and developing their skills in Spanish is a high priority. Educators should support students in this effort. One way that educators can show that they value students' mother tongue is through critical language awareness. Educators in the Dominican transnational community should help students become aware of the historic, social, and economic reasons why some language varieties are more valued than others. Students need to see the possibility of challenging the status quo that positions Spanish as lower than English and Dominican Spanish as lower than other varieties of Spanish. According to John Willinsky (1998)

> To have students see opportunities to challenge language norms and history has the potential to affect both who speaks and what is spoken, a point that seems all the more promising in an era marked by global change.… I am ad-

vising that as an intellectual right and responsibility of the curriculum we assist students in learning more about how language forms an integral part of a
history that is still unfolding. (p. 211)

Critical language awareness gives students the tools to understand the relation between language and power.

Teachers can create a space where explicitly sociopolitical and linguistic
discussions can occur. For example, readings on bilingual education, the
English-only movement, and assimilation have provoked heated discussion
in our classrooms. Another approach to critical language awareness is described by Catherine Walsh (1991), who used sociodrama to help bilingual
students "to be conscious of the sociocultural, political and ideological context in which the languages (and therefore the speakers) are positioned"
(pp. 126–127).

Hornberger's (2003a, 2003b) notion of "continua of biliteracy" provides
us with a framework to articulate the policy and pedagogical changes that
would do justice to the educational needs of Dominican students. The
framework constitutes a multidimensional continua of relations between
such polarities as oral and literate, vernacular and literary, micro and
macro, and contextualized and decontextualized, with the second construct
in each pair bordering the domain of the traditionally more powerful. Yet,
Hornberger argues the following: "[T]he implications of the model of
biliteracy outlined here are that the more the contexts of their learning allow [bilingual students] to draw on all points of the continua, the greater are
the chances for their full biliterate development" (2003a, p. 26). This
framework enables us to go beyond thinking of literacy or language acquisition of bilinguals as constituting separate or fractured competence in two
languages. It enables us to think of biliterate competence as intercon-
nected, shared, and integrated (see also Bhatt in chapter 2 for a similar
argument).

In terms of pedagogy, this framework enables Hornberger (2003b) to argue that teachers serve students better by accommodating a range of pedagogical strategies and language and literacy input. The low-stakes oral,
vernacular, community-based resources of minority students should not be
ignored in such a pedagogy. The argument we have been making for the inclusion of knowledge relating to Dominican life and the low-prestige Spanish dialect of this community is for the same reason of empowering the
identity of the students and drawing from familiar contexts for developing
proficiency in dominant literacies. Although she is concerned that the dominant educational ideologies and policies in the United States favor monolingualism and monoliteracy (despite the pressures against the autonomy
of the nation-state from above and below—that is, transnational economic
relations and the rise of minorities and immigrants), Hornberger is also of

the opinion that the ideological spaces we open up in the local contexts of classrooms can contribute to changes in the community and society.

Language educators in a transnational community cannot define success solely as proficiency in English and assimilation into mainstream American culture. As teachers, we need to try to enter into the transnational community that our students inhabit. Our students and their families need the opportunity to master both languages and maintain both identities, American and Dominican. Finally, as a society, we need to stop forcing people to choose one language over another, one identity over another.

## CONCLUSION

We have taken the Dominican community in New York as a case study, but we do not believe that this situation is unique. Increasingly, immigrant communities are becoming more mobile and staying more connected to their native countries. For many diasporic and migrant communities, their locality extends beyond national borders. Their sense of community is translocal. These communities are thus constructing "virtual" (or "imagined") localities that are of increasing cultural and political significance. We have to take their aspirations for a hybrid identity and translocal community seriously as we construct suitable educational policies. Needless to say, their linguistic and educational needs are more complex than those of previous generations of immigrants who were forced to adapt to a largely assimilationist educational policy in the United States. In fact, Hornberger's framework shows us that such pedagogies of biliteracy (or multiliteracy—see Cope & Kalantzis, 2000) should be promoted not only because they satisfy the special needs of migrant students, but also because such literacy better serves all of us in a globalized society.

There are, of course, logistical questions about how schools can cater to each and every immigrant community in classrooms that are often mixed. There are other material concerns about finding the resources (textbooks, material, teachers, funds) to cater to every cultural group in a school. But we can always ask teachers to be sensitive to the needs of migrant students. Furthermore, in a student-centered and collaborative learning environment, there are greater opportunities in classrooms to draw from students' local knowledge to facilitate their biliterate development more actively.

## REFERENCES

Aikman, S. (1999). *Intercultural education and literacy: An ethnographic study of indigenous knowledge and learning in the Peruvian Amazon.* Amsterdam: Benjamins.
Ayala, C. (2002). New York City Latino Population Census 2000. Retrieved May 28, 2002, from http://www.lehman.cuny.edu/depts/latinampuertorican/latinoweb/census2000/NYC/main.htm

Bailey, B. (2000). Language and negotiation of ethnic/racial identity among Dominican Americans. *Language in Society, 29,* 555–582.

Castillo, J. (1996). *Young Dominicans in New York City.* Unpublished master's thesis, Teachers College, Columbia University, New York.

Cope, B., & Kalantzis, M. (Eds.). (2000). *Multiliteracies: Literacy learning and the design of social futures.* New York: Routledge.

Cummins, J. (1992). Language proficiency, bilingualism, and academic achievement. In P. A. Richard-Amato & M. A. Snow (Eds.), *The multicultural classroom* (pp. 16–25). Reading, MA: Addison-Wesley.

Cummins, J. (1995). Bilingual education and anti-racist education. In O. García & C. Baker (Eds.), *Policy and practice in bilingual education* (pp. 63–67). Clevedon, England: Multilingual Matters.

Darder, A. (1995). Buscando America: The contribution of critical Latino educators to the academic development and empowerment of Latino students in the U.S. In C. E. Sleeter & P. L. McLaren (Eds.), *Multicultural education, critical pedagogy, and the politics of difference* (pp. 319–347). Albany: State University of New York Press.

DeWind, J. (1997). Educating the children of immigrants in New York's restructured economy. In M. E. Crahan & A. Vourvoulias-Bush (Eds.), *The city and the world: New York's global future* (pp. 133–146). New York: Council on Foreign Relations.

Dicker, S. J. (2000–2001, Winter). Hispanics and the Spanish language: Is their status rising? *NYS TESOL Idiom, 30,* 18–19.

Dicker, S. J., & Mahmoud, H. (2001, February). *Survey of a bilingual community: Dominicans in Washington Heights.* Paper presented at the 23rd Annual NYS-TESOL Applied Linguistics Conference, New York.

Duany, J. (1994). *Quisqueya on the Hudson: The transnational identity of Dominicans in Washington Heights,* New York: The CUNY Dominican Studies Institute.

Duany, J. (1998). Reconstructing racial identity: Ethnicity, color, and class among Dominicans in the United States and Puerto Rico. *Latin American Perspectives, 25,* 147–172.

Freeman, R. (1996). Dual-language planning at Oyster bilingual school: "It's much more than language." *TESOL Quarterly, 30,* 557–581.

Georges, E. (1990). *The making of a transnational community: Migration, development, and cultural change in the Dominican Republic.* New York: Columbia University Press.

Glick Schiller, N. (1999). Who are these guys?: A transnational reading of the U.S. immigrant experience. In L. R. Goldin (Ed.), *Identities on the move: Transnational processes in North America and the Caribbean Basin* (pp. 15–43). Austin: University of Texas Press.

Glick Schiller, N., Basch, L., & Blanc-Szanton, C. (1992). Transnationalism: A new analytic framework for understanding migration. In N. Glick Schiller, L. Basch, & C. Blanc-Szanton (Eds.), *Towards a transnational perspective on migration: Race, class, ethnicity, and nationalism reconsidered: Vol. 645. Annals of the New York Academy of Sciences* (pp. 1–24). New York: New York Academy of Sciences.

Graham, P. M. (1998). The politics of incorporation: Dominicans in New York City. *Latino Studies Journal, 9,* 39–64.

Guarnizo, L. E. (1997a). The emergence of a transnational social formation and the mirage of return migration among Dominican transmigrants. *Identities, 4,* 281–322.

Guarnizo, L. E. (1997b). "Going home": Class, gender and household transformation among Dominican return migrants. In P. R. Pessar (Ed.), *Caribbean circuits:*

*New directions in the study of Caribbean migration* (pp. 13–60). New York: Center for Migration Studies.

Hernández, R. (2002). *The mobility of workers under advanced capitalism: Dominican migration to the United States.* New York: Columbia University Press.

Hernández, R., & Rivera-Batiz, F. (1997). *Dominican New Yorkers: A socioeconomic profile.* New York: The CUNY Dominican Studies Institute.

Hornberger, N. (Ed.). (1997). *Indigenous literacies in the Americas: Language planning from the bottom up.* Berlin, Germany: Mouton.

Hornberger, N. (2003a). Continua of biliteracy. In N. Hornberger (Ed.), *Continua of biliteracy* (pp. 3–34). Clevedon, England: Multilingual Matters.

Hornberger, N. (2003b). Multilingual language policies and the continua of biliteracy: An ecological approach. In N. Hornberger (Ed.), *Continua of biliteracy* (pp. 315–339). Clevedon, England: Multilingual Matters.

Itzigsohn, J. (1995). Migrant remittances, labor markets, and household strategies: A comparative analysis of low-income household strategies in the Caribbean Basin. *Social Forces, 74,* 633–657.

Itzigsohn, J., Dore Cabral, C., Hernandez Medina, E., & Vazquez, O. (1999). Mapping Dominican transnationalism: Narrow and broad transnational practices. *Ethnic & Racial Studies, 22,* 316–340.

King, K. A. (2001). *Language revitalization processes and practices: Quichua in the Ecuadorian Andes.* Clevedon, England: Multilingual Matters.

Kugel, S. (2001, May 20). Dominicans march for voting rights (on the island). *The New York Times,* p. B4.

Levitt, P. (2001). *The transnational villagers.* Berkeley: The University of California Press.

Mandell, J. (1994, March 7). Winning spirit: New teacher used to taking on challenges. *New York Newsday,* p. 15.

New York City Board of Education. (2000). *Chancellor's report on the education of English language learners.* New York: Author.

New York State Education Department. (2001). *Memorandum of understanding between the Department of Education of the Dominican Republic and the New York State Education Department.* New York: Author.

Pita, M. (2000). *Reading Dominican girls: The experiences of four participants in Herstory, a literature discussion group.* Unpublished doctoral dissertation, New York University, New York.

Rohter, L. (1997, February 19). Flood of Dominicans lets some enter U.S. by fraud. *The New York Times,* p. A4.

Sagás, E. (1998). Recently "discovered": Dominicans in the United States. *Latino Studies Journal, 9,* 4–10.

Sanchez, R. (2001, November 19). In the subways: NY Dominicans face sad reality. *Newsday, Queens Edition,* p. A02.

Smith, R. C. (1997). Transnational migration, assimilation, and political community. In M. E. Crahan & A. Vourvoulias-Bush (Eds.), *The city and the world: New York's global future* (pp. 110–132). New York: Council on Foreign Relations.

Sontag, D., & Dugger, C. W. (1998, July 19). The new immigrant tide: A shuttle between worlds. *The New York Times,* pp. A1, A28–A30.

Torres-Saillant, S., & Hernández, R. (1998). *The Dominican Americans.* Westport, CT: Greenwood.

Walsh, C. E. (1991). *Pedagogy and the struggle for voice: Issues of language, power, and schooling for Puerto Ricans.* New York: Bergin & Garvey.

Willinsky, J. (1998). *Learning to divide the world: Education at empire's end.* Minneapolis: University of Minnesota Press.

Zentella, A. C. (1990). Lexical leveling in four New York City Spanish dialects: Linguistic and social factors. *Hispania, 73,* 1094–1105.

Zentella, A. C. (1997). Spanish in New York. In O. García & J. A. Fishman (Eds.), *The multilingual apple: Languages in New York City* (pp. 167–201). New York: Mouton de Gruyter.

## APPENDIX 1

### Questions for Open-Ended Interview

#### *Demographics*

1. Where were you born?
2. When were you born?
3. When you were living in the Dominican Republic, was your family considered rich, poor, or in the middle? What did your father and mother do for a living?
4. How many people were there in your family when you were growing up?
5. Who did you live with?
6. Who do you live with now? Do you have children?
7. Do you consider yourself rich, poor, or in the middle?
8. Do you work? What do you do?

#### *Educational History*

9. Did you do well in school? How do you know that you did or didn't do well in school?
10. Did you study English in the Dominican Republic? Where? How old were you when you started to study English? How successful were you learning English? Why?
11. (If student was in K–12 here) Were you in bilingual education or English only? How successful were you learning English? Why? How successful were you in other subjects? Why? Do you think you would have been more successful in (bilingual education or English only)?
12. How do you think going back and forth between the Dominican Republic and this country affected you? How do you think it affected your schoolwork? How do you think it affected your ability to read and write in Spanish? How do you think it affected your English?
13. How do you think you are doing here at Bronx Community College? What makes you think that? What do you think accounts for your successes? Failures?

### Language Use and Attitudes

14. Where do you usually speak Spanish? At home? With friends? At church? At work? At school? When you are shopping? Why?
15. Where do you usually speak English? At home? With friends? At church? At work? At school? When you are shopping? Why?
16. How do you feel when you are speaking Spanish?
17. How do you feel when you are speaking English?
18. Tell me about a time when you felt you were supposed to speak one language instead of another. How did that make you feel?
19. Tell me about a time when you felt you were supposed to speak (Spanish or English) instead of the other language? How did that make you feel?
20. Do you ever feel like you are supposed to speak only one language at Bronx Community College? How do you feel about that?
21. Do you ever speak Spanish when you feel like you are not supposed to? Why?
22. (If you have children) What language do you speak with your children? What language do your children speak when they talk to you? How do you feel about that? (If not) When you have children, what language do you want your children to use with you?

### Identity

23. I'm going to read you a list of terms and I want to know which ones you identify with and how you feel about each one.
    Dominican
    Dominican-American
    American
    Dominican-York
    New Yorker
    Immigrant
24. Are there any other terms that you identify with? Which do you prefer? Why?

# REFRAMING
# PROFESSIONAL LIVES

# Chapter 8

# Convergence and Resistance in the Construction of Personal and Professional Identities: Four French Modern Language Teachers in London

David Block
*University of London*

> *Accepting this educational system, I will never accept it. It's too bad....*
> *It's too much child-centred and there's a ... I think the big problem,*
> *compared to France, is that there is no way they "double." You know like*
> *we "double" a year in France and it is so important. How many of the*
> *kids in here should have doubled before? Maybe they'd be better now.*
> *The thing is they carry on moving on to the next year, next year, with*
> *big big weaknesses that they will never ... and also they don't care about*
> *the end of the year, really. In France, you have another thing.... If I*
> *don't do it well, I'm going to do it again. And we were the youngest*
> *children, so you want to pass ... While in here, in year nine, where's the*
> *motivation? They don't care.... They're not doing any examination,*
> *school isn't new anymore, it's a ... terrible thing ... and how to motivate*
> *them ... when on top of that, you've got a horrible National Curriculum*
> *... always the same thing....*
> —AL (11/12/00)

## INTRODUCTION

In this chapter, I discuss the discursive construction of national identity, that is, the expression and formation of "a complex of common or similar *beliefs or opinions* internalised in the course of socialisation ... and of common or similar *emotional attitudes* as well as common or similar *behavioural dispositions* ..." (Wodak, DeCillia, Reisigl, & Liebhart, 1999, p. 28; emphasis in original). Following authors such as Hall (1996), Bhabha (1994), Hannerz (1996), and Papastergiadis (2000), I focus on how, via their talk about their lives, four French nationals participating in the study construct nationality-influenced (although not determined) hybrid professional and personal identities, lying in a metaphorical third place between home and London.

The exchange I quoted earlier is taken from an interview I conducted in December 2000 with AL, a French national in her mid-20s, who at the time was about to finish her first term as a newly qualified teacher (NQT) of French in a secondary school in greater London. AL is responding to a question I posed about what she likes and dislikes about her job. She produces a healthy list of negative aspects of her job, such as the educational system in general, the fact that children pass from one year to the next automatically, the lack of motivation which this system engenders and, finally, the "horrible" National Curriculum.[1] Just a few months prior to this conversation, AL, like a growing number of French nationals, had just completed her PGCE (Post Graduate Certificate of Education) course.[2] Interested in living in London and improving her English language skills, AL had begun the PGCE in 1999 thinking that she might work as a secondary school French teacher for "two or three years," making it clear to me that she would leave London and go back to France sooner rather than later.

The kind of life stories I can piece together by talking to AL and other French nationals in her situation have their own intrinsic interest, no doubt; however, they also should be of interest to educational authorities in Britain. I say this because despite the fact that these authorities have been facing an increasing shortage of French teachers over the past several years, they have done very little to recruit teachers from France and other Francophone countries (and, I might add, nothing at all to assure that they will stay long enough to actually act as a solution to the shortage problem). Instead, it seems that these authorities are simply thankful that a constellation of factors have momentarily come together to guarantee a fairly constant influx of prospective French teachers from France. These factors include the fol-

---

[1] Throughout this chapter, all references to the "National Curriculum" refer to the English version of the National Curriculum for the teaching of Modern Foreign Languages.

[2] The Postgraduate Certificate of Education is the essential qualification for anyone who wishes to seek employment as a teacher in Britain.

lowing: (a) free movement inside the European Union (EU) for all citizens of EU member states, as laid down by the 1991 Mastricht agreement, (b) the allure of Britain as an English-speaking country to prospective English teachers who wish to improve their English, and (c) the relative flexibility of the British educational system, which allows transparent and relatively straightforward access from first degree to teacher qualifications to first teaching post and does not require aspiring teachers to pass a rigorous (and by many estimations, unnecessarily difficult) test like the *Certificat Pédagogique pour l'Enseignement Secondaire* (CAPES). This text has for decades acted as an effective and even brutal gatekeeping mechanism for the teaching profession in France.

One question, of course, is how long there will be this heavy flow of French nationals to Britain, which has meant that on many PGCE courses in the London area, as many as 40% or even 50% of the candidates are French nationals.[3] Although I do not intend to answer that question here, I can imagine that as long as the factors listed above apply, the flow will continue. More interesting to me (and, I assume, the reader of this collection) is the question of how the case of French nationals, living and working in Britain, is an example of language teaching practices and identities being negotiated across national borders. Specifically, I am interested in who these French nationals are and how long they are likely to stay. Are they ex-pats, living as French people in London for a limited period of time? Or do they qualify as immigrants, that is, individuals who will settle permanently in Britain and therefore be more likely to alleviate the French teacher shortage in the long term? Whether they ultimately stay or go, what kind of problems do these foreign nationals experience as they adapt to language teaching in Britain? After all, they are products of the French educational system and therefore will have been socialized in a national educational culture, one which is different from that which reigns in Britain. And this socialization surely will make some features of education in Britain puzzling, difficult, and even unacceptable.

Evidence that this is indeed the case can be gleaned from two studies which have explored such issues. First, there is the work of Barry Jones

---

[3] In her report on the recruitment and retention of modern foreign language teachers in London, Julie Adams (2000) cites a survey by Whitehead and Taylor (1998) which shows that in 1997 and 1998 a third of the PGCE candidates across Britain were foreign nationals and that some 75% of these were Francophones (the vast majority of these being French nationals). She goes on to state that "[o]n some PGCE MFL courses, well over half of all students are foreign nationals, with this figure reaching 80% in both UNL's [University of North London's] 1999 and 2000 cohorts" (Adams, 2000, p. 4). The figure for 1999 to 2000 at Institute of Education, University of London, was 45% and I have been informed by colleagues that at present over half of the candidates for 2000 to 2001 and 2001 to 2002 have been foreign nationals. In the cases of both UNL and the Institute of Education, some 70% of these foreign nationals are French nationals.

(2000) who has monitored the progress of "non-English native student teachers" attending a combination PGCE/Maîtrise Français Langue Etrangère organized by Cambridge University in combination with eight French universities. Via interviews with French nationals and diaries they have kept, Jones has compiled an impressive database which documents the trials and tribulations of adapting to British education. He organizes the problems cited by his participants into six general categories (see Jones, 2000). With a little editing on my part, these categories look as follows:

1. Language related problems—This includes English as a part of the PGCE course (understanding acronyms and terminology and using English to write assignments), English on the job (following meetings and understanding fellow teachers and students when all of these contacts with the English language are provided with no concession to the non-English native student teachers); and use of English in the modern foreign language (MFL) classroom (whether appropriacy is a problem)

2. Pedagogic problems—This includes how to give clear instructions (in both English and the target language), how to address student questions, and how and when to use the target language.

3. Teacher–pupil relationships—This is primarily about understanding what students are saying to each other and to the teacher, knowing when students are serious or trying to take advantage, understanding humor and sarcasm, and being made to feel "foreign" by students.

4. Procedure related problems—This includes understanding hierarchies (both in the International Teacher Training institution and in schools), understanding disciplinary procedures for students, knowing what to expect from the mentor, knowing how to deal appropriately with extracurricular activities (how much a teacher is expected to be involved), and knowing about day-to-day activities such as making photocopies, buying coffee and using equipment.

5. Cultural problems—This relates to feeling "foreign" to both students and school staff, dealing with differences between the home educational system and the British system, and constantly having to negotiate individual cultural identity.[1]

6. General living problems—This has to do with accommodation, travel, and medical care.

Elsewhere, Kim Brown (2001) discusses her long-term monitoring of "foreign native speakers" who have attended the Modern Foreign Languages PGCE course at the University of East Anglia (Cambridge) . Brown reports

---

[1] I might add here that, as Adams (2000) and Brown (2001) point out, attrition rates for British nationals are very similar to those for foreign nationals and that the reasons cited do not differ greatly.

that it is primarily discipline problems and the workload (far more than it would be in their home countries, including as it does responsibilities such as form tutoring, and organizing extracurricular activities) that drive foreign national teachers out of teaching. Brown makes the point that leaving the profession is more prevalent among younger individuals with few ties in Britain: the members of her sample who were already settled in Britain (normally married to British nationals and with children) have tended to stay in teaching. In addition, those foreign nationals who do leave the profession, in some cases just after completing the PGCE and before actually taking up a teaching post in Britain, generally go back to their countries of origin. This means that they are lost forever to the profession in Britain.

Interested in how the kinds of adaptation problems identified by Jones and Brown might affect the long-term professional prospects and adjustment to life in Britain of foreign nationals from three EU countries—France, Germany, and Spain—in autumn 1999 I began a study in which I conducted periodic (roughly every 2½ or 3 months) face-to-face interviews with eight French, three German, and three Spanish nationals on the PGCE modern languages course run by the Institute of Education, University of London. I ended the first year of this study with four French nationals, three German nationals, and two Spanish nationals and eventually wrote a report about them, a version of which was published as an article (see Block, 2001). In this article, I charted the ambivalence of these individuals as they moved among subject positions of national identity ranging from integrationist, where they manifested a preference for not being positioned as foreigners, to nationalistic, where they clearly invoked their national educational culture as a template when talking about British practices. In these interviews, the teaching of grammar became a metaphor for academic rigor and to varying degrees all of the teachers decried the lack of language awareness among British students. At the end of the article, I reproduced the following comments from an interview with two German participants, which seemed to capture the feelings of all participants:

HA:    … I don't agree with the school system in England. I think if I don't agree with it now, I either have to get on with it—compromise—or I can't do it, and I have to. I mean that's what I'm doing.

AA:    I'm also compromising…. Sometimes I think, are they really mad here? Because I just don't understand it. But then I think … it's a compromise …. When you compromise, you actually think it's OK. (6/6/00)

I then went on to conclude the article with the following observation:

… perhaps the most salient issue to arise in interviews carried out during this period was the tension between compromise and

resistance, a tension related directly to each individual's long
term plans to either stay in Britain as a modern languages
teacher or to return "home." The jury is obviously still out on
this issue; however, if I am to judge by the general tone of
comments made by the different informants over the academic
year 2000–01, I would say that there is the very real prospect that
only one or two of these teachers will stay in teaching in Britain
for longer than three years. To my mind, this is not a good sign
for the de facto policy of importing modern languages teachers
from continental Europe; however, it is food for thought for
anyone involved in teacher education in Britain, particularly at
the policy-making level. (Block, 2001, p. 309)

My goal in this chapter is to explore in more depth item number 5 in
Jones's (2000) list and to explain the latter part of this statement cited earlier, namely how it is that so few of the original participants have expressed
the clear intention to stay in Britain indefinitely. I shall do so by focusing on
a select subgroup of the nine participants in the study, namely the four
French nationals. I have chosen to focus on these participants and not the
others for several reasons. First, space does not allow fair coverage of the
NQT year of all nine participants. Second, they teach the language that is
studied by about roughly 85% of all secondary school students in British
schools. Third, these participants are perfectly representative of the larger
group, with three (including AL, cited earlier) expressing the fairly firm intention to leave (although, as we observe later, in the cases of AL and another participant, there is some hesitation) and one expressing the firm
intention to stay. Fourth and finally, by focusing on one nationality, I am
able to make more direct and fruitful comparisons between French and
British educational cultures.

In the sections that follow, I explore how, during their year as NQTs, the
four French nationals in this study felt "foreign" in their dealings with students and school staff and the differences between French education and
British education. I do this by focusing on their talk about two aspects of
their teaching experiences: (a) the way that the National Curriculum, as
symbol of an approach to language and language teaching, lacks rigor or
quality (indeed, the National Curriculum is seen to symbolize poor educational practice, most particularly in the case of grammar teaching); and (b)
the supposed greater student-centeredness of British education when compared to French education. Having examined participant comments about
these aspects of their experiences, I relate what they have to say to theoretical frameworks borrowed from recent studies comparing French and British education. I then go on to explore the questions cited earlier: first,
whether we would call these teachers ex-pats, living as French people in

London for a limited period of time, or immigrants, intending to stay perhaps for the rest of their lives; and second, why they have taken the stances they have taken vis-à-vis teaching and living in London. I conclude with some comments about the relevance of this study to British educational authorities and individuals responsible for PGCE courses, before moving to a discussion of how the data and analysis presented in this chapter are particularly relevant to anyone interested in the themes of negotiated pedagogies and identities across borders.

## THE PARTICIPANTS

The teachers I focus on in this chapter are four French women, FN, GL, AL, and DC, who ranged in age from 24 to 32 when the study began in autumn 1999. During the PGCE course, I met with these teachers on several occasions, first individually and later in two separate groups. I initially met with FN and GL as part of a larger group which included a third French national who dropped out of the course after just over one term; I initially met with AL and DC as part of a larger group which included two other French nationals, who also dropped out of the course after just over one term. Thus, by the time the first year of the study had finished, FN and GL formed one "group" and AL and DC formed another. In year 2 of the study, the focus of this article, I met with these participants individually at their schools. I conducted three interviews ranging in length from 40 to 100 min. All interviews were carried out in English, which all four participants spoke very well. These interviews provide the database for this chapter.

FN, GL, AL, and DC came from different parts of France: FN was from Marseilles; GL was from Annecy, a small city near the French–Swiss border; AL was from Paris; and DC was from Bordeaux. However, they shared several key characteristics. First, they were all from middle-class backgrounds and had first degrees from French universities. Second, they shared a love for languages—both French and English—as well as teaching as a profession. AL best sums up this dual love in an interview carried out just as she was beginning the PGCE course in autumn 1999:

AL:      This is what I want to do; I don't want to do anything else than
         teaching French. When I was at school, I was twelve and I had
         this Canadian English teacher and I think maybe she is part of
         the reason why I'm here today. I really admired her.
DB:      Why is that?
AL:      Because I loved English as soon as I started studying and
         learning English. I loved it. She was a great teacher.... Since I

had this teacher—I was twelve—and you know at the beginning
of every year, the teacher always asks you "What do you want to
do when you grow up?" And I used to write "Professeur de
Français a l'Etranger." (AL 10/9/99)

Despite being from different parts of France, FN, GL, AL, and DC had
been educated in very similar ways. This can be gleaned both from the similarity of the comments they make about education (more on this in a moment) as well as explicit comments to this effect. FN, for example explains
matters as follows:

[Educational authorities] … want that everybody in France has to be
    educated in the same way, so that's probably the idea. Because
    it's true for the programme, it's true for even the timetable.
    Some schools might change, just finish at 4:30, because the
    coach is outside or … but it's true that on the whole, everybody
    … I mean this girl (referring to a teacher who had just
    interrupted our conversational to tell FN something), JJ, is
    French as well and … I mean, if we talk about our pupil's career,
    we have exactly the same: the same programmes, the same type
    of teachers and … It's true that …. (FN, 27/3/01)

On another occasion, GL expressed similar views: "… I was talking with
AL and we realised that we did exactly the same programme in Geography
in year 7, so I suppose it was the case for every student in France in year 7
…" (GL, 2/4/01).

GL's reference to having spoken to AL is connected with another shared
characteristic of the four, namely that they often met socially and spoke to
one another on the telephone. Their friendship was such that they often
made passing references to one another during interviews: DC made reference to "the girls" and GL, on one occasion, concluded that they were "like a
little family."

Nevertheless, there is a noteworthy point around which the four have dif-
fered, or in any case, taken distinct and differentiated positions, and that is
whether to stay in London. FN, GL, and AL have repeatedly made it clear
that they would definitely leave London sooner rather than later; FN and
GL said on several occasions that this would happen at the end of the academic year 2000 –01. This did not prove to be the case, although I have repeatedly been assured since this time that they will leave eventually. DC, by
contrast, has always maintained that she will stay in London indefinitely.
Later, I explore why this difference of intentions has arisen. First, however,
I look at what these teachers have had to say about the National Curriculum
and child-centered education, two aspects of their teaching lives about
which they all agree.

## THE NATIONAL CURRICULUM, COMMUNICATIVE LANGUAGE TEACHING, AND GRAMMAR

The National Curriculum for Modern Languages is based on a particular version of communicative language teaching (hereafter CLT) which includes guiding principles such as the extensive preference and use of pair and group work over individual work; the extensive use of information gap exercises (as a means of getting students to use the target language); a preoccupation with making activities similar to "real-world" activities (i.e., simulated "real-world" activities such as buying a train ticket or ordering a meal at a restaurant); the use of authentic materials (where "authenticity" is understood to reside in the origin of the materials and not the use to which they are put or, more importantly, the student's personal investment in them); the exclusive use of the target language by teachers (and the accompanying proscription of English); and an aversion to explicit grammar teaching (considered counterproductive). This version of CLT is partial to say the least, seeming to draw on a rather selective interpretation of pedagogical proposals first put forward in the mid-1970s and the late 1970s (see Morrow & Johnson, 1981). In many ways, it embodies what Thompson (1996) terms "misconceptions" about CLT, such as an overemphasis on speaking and the proscription of grammar teaching.

This rather simplified and dated version of CLT has not escaped the critical eye of modern languages scholars in Britain. For example, Klapper (1997) sees CLT, as practiced in the UK, as "a vague mixture of direct method, use of visuals, games and other oral activities, with a nod in the direction of inductive approaches to grammar learning, but little mention of systematic reinforcement or practice" (Klapper, 1997, p. 27). Elsewhere, Grenfell (2000) laments that the National Curriculum has sent out vague messages about important issues such as the role of grammar: on the one hand there have been recommendations that students should be explicitly taught formal aspects of the target language; on the other hand, recommendations have been in the direction of "supply[ing] lots of comprehensible input from which pupils may induce grammar" (Grenfell, 2000, p. 25). For Grenfell this has meant that "[t]he message has often been interpreted to be that target language is good, English is bad; induction is best, deduction is limited" (2000, p. 25). Finally, Pachler (2000) criticizes how CLT in the UK "has tended to neglect the generative potential of language by downplaying awareness of and knowledge about language by focussing too narrowly on transactional, situationalised language in narrowly defined contexts and idealised discourse patterns" (Pachler, 2000, p. 34).

Perhaps the most interesting aspect of these comments is how much they are in line with what FN, GL, AL, and DC repeatedly have told me about the NC since they first began their PGCE course in autumn 1999. Elsewhere, I discuss some of their comments made during the year they did the PGCE (see Block, 2001) and over the 3-year period of 1999 to 2002 (Block, 2002); here, as noted earlier, we focus on their first year as NQTs. In the following excerpts, FN expresses the frustration she feels at being constrained by a highly prescriptive and tight program; GL laments the lack of grammar instruction and the fact that exams are made too easy for students; AL also focuses on the lack of an explicit focus on form; and DC focuses on how students are taught phrasebook-like language in unanalyzed chunks, a methodology she vividly qualifies as "thick" and "crap":

> We've got coursework to do and because of that we've got to follow a certain programme, so we're not really free. So that's the reason why, I find I am frustrated in a way because ... because of that, we don't have enough time to organise, I mean to do internet sessions or things like that, which would be more motivating for the kids. (FN, 4/12/00)

> In England I think that the National Curriculum should be changed. But I don't think it's going to be the case.... There is an evolution because we are supposed to teach more grammar now. But really, for the GCSE,[5] for example, you know that they have to have write courseworks ... and there's a proper exam, it is a coursework as well, but we give ... them a dictionary, the revision guide, a vocabulary list ... we have practised it before, so it's no more an exam. And even for the mock exams, the questions we are going to ask are given beforehand for them to practise ... So, it's a joke. (GL, 2/4/01)

> The fact that you cannot teach the way you want, really, because the National Curriculum imposes a certain way of teaching, "topic teaching," which is useless, I believe, or non-effective, at least. This communicative approach. What is frustrating is the lack of, the huge lack of knowledge about their own language that people have. I mean a lack of grammar, really. People are not aware that their own language works with ... verb, subject and complement, and then things that are added to that.... And this is very frustrating because ... you wish you could ... once you know that, once you realise how language works, it is so easy to learn it a bit better and there's a lot of waste of time spent from language teachers on trying to teach what is a pronoun ... all that kind of things that I believe are not our jobs, but would be English teachers' jobs. (AL, 15/9/00)

> I just find it hard ... that is a struggle to actually think, "Right, these are these ready made expressions"—even in year 7, which is mad—"Go and learn them" and that's it. They don't have any opportunity to actually play with the language, you know. They are just, the way it's taught here is ... you know with this communicative approach, as long as we understand you, it's fine. It's not about, as you know, the structure ... No, that is really frustrating. I find it really frustrating because it's a thick way of teaching. It's crap. What's the point? ... (DC, 8/12/00)

---

[5]This refers to the General Certificate of Secondary Education exams, taken by students at the age of 16.

A common theme in these and other comments by FN, GL, AL, and DC is the lack of grammar in CLT in the UK. But what do they mean by "grammar"? GL explains as follows: "For example, when I teach grammar I take a sentence, a very simple sentence ... for example, I can say in English 'Peter has a book' ... And I would say, 'Tell me where is the subject. Tell me where is the verb. Tell me where is the complement.... Do you know what is a direct object? ..." (GL, 8/12/00).

However, all four teachers at different times have made the point that they can only do such activities with students who are at more advanced levels and in higher sets. Otherwise, the experience is "frustrating," as AL explains: "It's frustrating. You can't teach grammar because they don't know their own language. When you say, 'What is a verb?' they know 'It's a doing word,' but then you write a sentence on the board, they don't know where the verb is ..." (AL, 11/12/00).

For DC, the problem is that students do not learn about their own language in English classes:

> I don't find that they are that linguistic. They're just more about thinking about an extract of literature and developing that into your own ideas. It's not structured in a grammar way. And I find that the kids would actually find languages easier if they were given the opportunity to deal with its structure base, you know, as soon as they are year 7, instead of learning all these things by heart, you know, like parrots. (DC, 26/3/01)

On one occasion, I asked GL what she thought British students learned in primary school about language. She provided the following rather depressing assessment:

> I imagine that they have never learnt anything about grammar, even for English, with the English language.... Because they don't know what is a verb table ... even a sentence or verbs. They don't know what is a verb. They don't know what is a noun.... in the best case, they will know what is a "doing word" ... They have not been used to learn things off by heart ... They have not been used to care about the spellings and things like that.... What have they learned? I don't know. (GL, 2/4/01)

In these comments, we see the four teachers in general agreement as they frame the National Curriculum and the British version of CLT as limiting and constraining. For these teachers, the National Curriculum means a lack of focus on grammar and this has meant that students have no idea how languages in general work in addition to having no metalanguage to talk about such matters. If the methodology they attribute to the National Curriculum is one source of their problems, another is the child-centered philosophy which also permeates British education.

## CHILD-CENTERED TEACHING AS "SPOON-FEEDING"

One of the basic tenets of the National Curriculum, as laid out by the Department of Education and Skills, is that all teaching should be child-centered. This approach is presented in detail under the heading of "Inclusion." The following excerpt is from this section of the National Curriculum. It manifests the fundamental principle that teachers should adapt their teaching and National Curriculum guidelines to students, and not vice versa:

> Teachers should aim to give every pupil the opportunity to experience success in learning and to achieve as high a standard as possible. The National Curriculum programmes of study set out with most pupils should be taught at each key stage—but teachers should teach the knowledge, skills and understanding in ways that suit their pupils' abilities. This may mean choosing knowledge, skills and understanding from earlier or later key stages so that individual pupils can make progress and show what they can achieve. (Department of Education and Skills, 2002, p. 1)

In their discussion of research comparing French and English primary education, Broadfoot and Osborn (1993) make the following statement about the child-centered approach described earlier, implemented in English schools but relatively absent in French schools:

> In this summary, it may be said that a number of the factors which research suggests to be positive features in teaching, such as teacher warmth, sensitivity to pupils, an emphasis on pupils' positive achievements, working towards pupils' achievement of self-control and autonomy, were all more observed in England than in France. In England also there were a greater number of activities going on in the classroom, more variation of treatment according to pupil needs, more emphasis on teaching for understanding and more concurrent feedback to pupils. (p. 72)

As presented in the National Curriculum and by Broadfoot and Osborne (1993), child-centeredness seems a most humane approach to teaching, which puts individual achievement at a premium. However, for the four French teachers participating in this study, child-centeredness carries a very different meaning. For FN, GL, AL, and DC, "sensitivity to students," the "emphasis on positive achievements," and the "variation of treatment according to pupil needs" have come to mean "spoon feeding," which in turn has the opposite effect intended by the National Curriculum, the nonachievement of "self-control and autonomy." GL expresses the basic problem as follows: "I think that [the National Curriculum] does not teach the students to be independent learners because they are spoon-fed ... because they are ... in fact, they expect the teachers to do everything for them...." (GL, 2/4/01).

What being "spoon-fed" actually consists of is fairly consistent across the four teachers, although at different times they have focused on different areas. Thus, in the excerpts which follow, DC focuses on discipline and "patronizing" attitudes toward students, AL focuses on students having to be hounded to do their homework, GL focuses on the lack of student self-correction and not meeting deadlines, and FN focuses on students coming to lessons unprepared:

> But I do find that patronising because, you know, it's so normal to behave properly in lessons ... but of course they are kids, but I think you should ... you know, the idea of, like, you know, patting them in the back. It's sad, you know.... I think that most kids respond to tougher education, you know, and ... I think sanctions are better, in a way, because they help them growing up a bit more. Whereas (putting on a condescending voice) "Oh, well done...." and that's so patronising. (DC, 26/3/01)

> When I was at school, homework was not for the teacher, it was for the pupils. If you don't do it, you don't do it. It's your problem. That's what I would like to say to them. "I'm saying you should do that because it will help you. If you don't want to do it ..." (AL, 11/12/00)

> We will correct the books, we will correct the mistakes ... in fact, if they don't know, and it doesn't matter. It doesn't really matter, they will redo it. They can always redo it.... And, for example, deadlines. It does not exist here. In France, I can tell you that a deadline is a deadline. In fact, what's the point in setting deadlines because we never expect them.... It's always, "OK, it was a deadline, but I will still accept your coursework ..." So it is part of the spoon-feeding process, in fact.... And in fact, students expect you to check their work all the time. In France, you just check your work yourself. The teacher will not check your work ... (GL, 2/4/01)

> But they are so used to have, I mean to be guided for anything. And it's not even for just using the brain. They don't have their exercise books, for example, and they're like that (plays the part of a student looking distracted). So then you just explode: "What on earth are you doing" ... (adopting a student voice) "Well, I'm waiting. You didn't give me a sheet of paper" ... Or if they were away, they don't make up lessons. They don't have the homework done and the excuse was: (adopting student voice) "I was away" ... (adopting teacher voice) "And?" ... So you know, it's really annoying ... (FN, 4/12/00)

For AL, the child-centered approach simply does not work, as it means that the teachers end up doing all of the work: "I don't think it works at all. I don't think it benefits them. It helps them but it's spoon-feeding. It's more work on the teacher to adapt to their level and helping them, rather than to establish the year and ask them to go to reach the standard" (AL, 20/3/01).

For FN, such an approach to students is a shame because it denies them the possibility to better themselves. As she puts it, "They are really spoon-fed and I think it's a real shame, because if we pushed some of them they could be very brilliant...." (FN, 4/12/00).

In similar terms, GL laments that more is not demanded of students: "In fact the problem is that students are not used to be stretched. Even in my dual linguist group [students doing French and German], when I ask them to revise for a test, they ask me if the spellings are counted" (GL, 2/4/01).

She goes on to compare this behavior with how matters would be in France:

> You will never ever ask this sort of questions in France because when you start school, you know you have to learn the spellings ... you know you have to remember a lot of things off by heart.... So in France, the system is more demanding, so I try to be very demanding with them, to present good habits, so there are plenty of things to learn off by heart ... and the spellings count, of course. (GL, 2/4/01)

The end result of child-centered education for these four teachers is expressed well by FN, who makes reference to the popular television game show, "The Weakest Link":[6]

> I'm convinced that if they don't change something in the education in this country, they're going to be illiterate very soon, particularly now that there is Europe, compared to Germany, compared to Spain, compared to Portugal, compared to France, ... They're going to be the weakest, the weakest link ... (FN, 26/6/01)

Thus, in terms not lacking in force, these four teachers express a dislike for the National Curriculum and, above all, its approach to language and the principle of child-centered teaching. But where did this reaction to the National Curriculum and the resulting critique come from? To answer this question, it is useful to look at recent studies comparing French and British education.

## COMPARING AND CONTRASTING FRENCH AND BRITISH EDUCATIONAL SYSTEMS

There have in recent years been several key publications comparing English and French education. McLean (1995) is an oft-cited discussion of different school curricula in Europe, North America, and East Asia, whereas Alexander (1996, 1999), Broadfoot, and Osborn (1993), and Broadfoot, Osborn,

---

[6]"The Weakest Link" is a television game show in Britain where contestants answer general knowledge questions. Contestants are in competition with one another and there can only be one winner. The program has become very popular in Britain since it first aired in 1999, and the format has been franchised to the other countries, most notably the United States, which has also contracted the host, Anne Robinson. Robinson has become famous on both sides of the Atlantic for her icy style and her trademark line, addressed to losers: "You are the weakest link. Goodbye."

Planel, and Sharpe (2000) are reports of in-depth studies comparing French and English primary school cultures.[7] An examination of these publications allows us to glean two general educational cultures in these two contexts, which are essential if we are to understand the discourse produced during my contacts with the four French nationals participating in my study. McLean (1995), for example, contrasts humanism, the dominant philosophy traditionally underlying English education, and rationalism, the dominant philosophy traditionally underlying French education, as follows:

> Humanism views start from the human ch aracter and its potential rather than the structure of the physical universe. The central aim is to develop qualities among the young, that will serve them in later life, through acquaintance with great achievements of individuals of past generations. The subject matter has focused upon history, literature and the philosophy with which to systematize this understanding. The human-moral motif has been central through Plato and the Renaissance in Europe and in much Christian thought. (p. 22)

> The rationalist view of content, learning and teaching is associated with a systematic view of the physical world. Capacities for logic, deduction and abstraction together with systematization and synthesis should be developed to make sense of this universe and ultimately to change it. The medium is that group of subjects known as languages, mathematics and science through which these qualities can best be trained. But worthwhile knowledge is also external and standardized and the student should cover the encyclopaedic kaleidoscope of all legitimate areas for as long as possible. The private and irrational are rigorously excluded. (p. 30)

In two ambitious studies carried out in the mid-80s and mid-90s, discussed in detail in Broadfoot and Osborn (1993) and Broadfoot, Osborn et al. (2000), respectively, researchers put some empirical meat on these philosophical orientations. Carrying out detailed research in primary schools in urban and rural communities in different parts of England and France, Broadfoot, Osborne, and associates conclude, among other things, that there are "well-established differences in pedagogical approaches between the two countries" (Broadfoot et al., 2000, p. 202). Elaborating on this point, they write the following:

> In France, the underlying educational philosophy is one of "induction" of pupils into established bodies of knowledge, a process that we refer to ... as "catechistic." French teachers are often "drillers," their model of the goals of education largely a convergent one.... By contrast, the established pedagogic tradition in English primary schools has been one that emphasizes discovery and the search on the part of each pupil for a solution to a given problem. Pupils have been encouraged to think for themselves, and their ef-

---

[7]It should be noted that Alexander's work (1996, 1999) involves comparisons with India, Russia, and the United States as well.

forts have been valued in these terms.... In language ..., French pupils were typically "technicians" applying skills they had been taught, often in a decontextualized way, whereas English pupils were more likely to be "explorers" coping well with tasks where the route was not clearly laid out. (Broadfoot et al., 2000, pp. 202–203)

In this quote, and indeed in all of the publications I have examined related to Broadfoot et al.'s studies, I detect a certain bias in favor of English approaches to education. Terms such as *induction, catechistic, driller,* and *technician* certainly have negative connotations when discussing education, particularly when compared to terms such as *emphasize discovery, encouraged to think for themselves,* and *explorers,* which are associated with English education. However, despite their somewhat Anglo-centric contrast of the more student-centered, open-ended English practices and (presumably) less student-centered, more controlled French practices, the authors make the following point:

> Although ... English teachers typically made much more effort than we observed in France to motivate children through arousing their interest, protecting their self-esteem, and avoiding negative feedback, it was French children who were significantly more positive about school. Despite experiencing a typically more formal and authoritarian classroom, they were more likely to see teaching as helpful and useful to them and appeared to be more highly motivated toward educational success and academic goals.... [T]he personality and personal characteristics of the teacher were of less concern to French pupils than to their English counterparts. Most important was that he or she should make them work hard! (Broadfoot et al., 2000, p. 196)

Elsewhere, Alexander (1996, 1999) comes to similar conclusions when discussing a large-scale study he and his colleagues conducted in the early 90's, comparing five educational cultures: England, France, India, Russia, and the United States. Based on numerous interviews and observations carried out in the five countries, focusing on pupils, ages 6 and 9, and their teachers, Alexander was able to identify two contrasted prototypical models of primary school pedagogy. Focusing on direct comparisons between English and French education, Alexander found the general contrasts outlined in Table 8.1.

The upshot of McLean's (1995) discussion and the research carried out by Broadfoot et al. (2000) and Alexander (1996, 1999) is that all of these scholars have found fairly clear differences between English and French educational cultures, that these differences have been shaped both by particular philosophical traditions and historical events (and are continually reshaped by ongoing events in the present), and that these differences manifest themselves in a variety of contexts such as official documentation (e.g., national curricula), observed behavior and the public discourse of education. In broad

**TABLE 8.1**

Comparing English and French Primary Education
(Based on Alexander, 1999, pp. 160–165)

| Pedagogical Practice | England | France |
|---|---|---|
| Use of wall-mounted teaching materials | Teachers tend to post examples of pupils' work in progress or showcase work completed. | Teachers tend to post rules and reminders and work in progress. |
| Lesson length | Lessons vary broadly from 30 min to 85 min in length. | Lessons vary less broadly from 30 to 60 min in length. |
| Structure of lessons | Lessons tend to be more developmental and flexible than formulaic and fixed. | Lessons tend to be formulaic and fixed. |
| Length of episodes | Lessons tend to be made up of irregular, mixed length episodes. | Lessons vary more broadly, with more balance between short, regular episodes, and irregular, mixed length episodes. |
| Balance of oral and written work in lessons | Lessons tend toward a greater emphasis on reading and writing. | Lessons are slightly more balanced as regards oral, reading, and writing. |
| Pedagogical language | Language tends to be more conversational than technical. | Language tends to be more technical than conversational. |
| Teachers' questions | Questions tend to be mixtures of closed and open. | Questions tend to be more closed than open. |
| Breadth and diffusiveness of focus of tasks | Tasks tend to be more broadly focused. | Tasks tend to be more narrowly focused. |
| Balance of emphasis on subjective matter and affective and behavioral issues | There is a balance between focusing on subject matter and behavior. | There is primarily a focus on subject matter. |
| Manner of conveying teaching messages | There is a balance between linear and cumulative presentation and multiple, complex, and simultaneous presentation. | Presentation is primarily linear and cumulative. |
| View of knowledge informing lessons | Knowledge is viewed to be more uncodified, negotiable, and reflective than codified, rule-bound, and received. | Knowledge is viewed to be codified, rule-bound, and received. |

terms, French education is presented as the outgrowth of the universal principles of liberty, equality, and fraternity associated with the French revolution. Education is deemed to be the inalienable right of all French citizens
and the state is seen as a guarantor of these principles and the educational
system itself. The state is able to carry out this role via the maintenance of a
well-defined bureaucracy of civil servants which works hierarchically from
the national to the regional to the local, down to the school and teacher level.
Vinuesa (1996, cited in Broadfoot et al., 2000) makes the point that French
education is based on the institutional values of universalism and collectiv-
ism. In the former case, this means the same education for all citizens; in the
latter case, it means the formation of good citizens who contribute to the per-
manence and cohesiveness of French society. As McLean (1995) points out,
there is a strong emphasis on the "concept of *culture générale* of rational, humane, and scientific knowledge, the possession of which by as many citizens
as possible would both liberate the individual from the narrowness of working life and create a fraternity among the whole population" (p. 66). There is
an apparent sociohistorical refusal to abandon a one-size-fits-all philosophy
as the system continues to work along the universalistic and collectivist political philosophies which form its foundation.

By contrast, English education is founded on the principles of privatism
and individualism associated with the philosophical writings of Adam
Smith and John Stuart Mill. As in the case of France, education is deemed to
be an inalienable right of all citizens; however, until recently in England
there had never been a direct and close relation between the central government and local schools and the system, as such, was guaranteed for almost a
century by schools and teachers operating with very little central control.
This situation changed in the 1980s, when a high degree of centralism was
introduced via the new National Curriculum along with far-reaching accountability and inspection systems. However, in recent years, it has become obvious that despite such centralizing tendencies, education in
England is actually becoming progressively more fragmented with specialist schools, religious schools, selective independent (private) schools, selective state-run schools, and most recently, schools run by private companies,
taking on the uniformity imposed from above in very different ways. The
classical humanist tradition described by McLean (1995) continues to dominate and the emphasis in schools is on developing freethinking individuals
who will make a positive contribution to society, not universalist, rational
thinkers who have been molded into perfect English citizens.

Although it would be absurd to accept the findings of Broadfoot et al.
(2000), Broadfoot and Osborn (1993), or any other study based on a selected sample as the be all and end all of what French and English education
are like at the primary level, I think that such studies, when combined with
other analyses of English education published by British authors (e.g., Pol-

lard, 1996), as well as other works published in French by French authors (e.g., Joutard & Thélot, 1999; La Borderie, 1994; van Zanten, 2001), do provide us with a template or even official story of how English and French education cultures are conceived of and work. Despite the fact that they came from four different parts of France, these four French teachers all invoked in their conversations with me a similar template or official story of French education. However, this template should not be seen to be, in effect, how French education actually works. Indeed, just one of the teachers, FN, actually had any experience as a teacher in France and this was as a supply teacher. Rather, we should see it as an "imagined" French model of teaching and learning or a "symbolic reserve."

The concept of "imagined" models comes from the work of Benedict Anderson (1991, p. 91), who discusses the "imagined" nature of nationalism, and Eric Hobsbawm (1990), who has discussed the "invented" histories of nations. Anderson calls nations and nationalities "imagined communities," describing them as "cultural artefacts of a particular kind," the understanding of which will depend on our ability "to consider carefully how they came into historical being, in what ways their meanings have changed over time, and why, today, they command such profound emotional legitimacy" (p. 4). "Imagined" should not be taken to mean that they are "imaginary," that is, that they have no foundation in anything real in the past, present, or future; rather, nations and nationalities are said to be "imagined" because they are not the only possible way for individuals to affiliate with a collective identity. Elsewhere, Reichler (1992; cited in Reicher & Hopkins, 2001, p. 24) discusses what he calls *la réserve du symbolique*, that is, the bank of symbolic resources available to members of communities, which enable them to make sense of their worlds. The idea of symbolic reserve is an attractive one and articulates well with Stuart Hall's discussion of the nation as a "system of cultural representations ... producing meanings about 'the nation' with which we can *identify* ... [which] are contained in the stories which are told about it ..." (Hall, 1996, pp. 612–613). From this point of view, individuals may be seen to have at their disposal a template, a worldview or a framework to think, act, and understand people and events around them. It is a structure within which they must make their way as individuals living a particular time in a particular place; but it is elastic and movable that their individual agency alters it while drawing on it. It is, in short, constitutive of their way of being in the world while being constituted by how they (and their fellow community members) enact their being in the world.

In the data cited earlier, we see how the four teachers discursively invoke an imagined French way of teaching and learning which in turn acts as a symbolic reserve. For these teachers, French education as imagined symbolic reserve is not based in general on the experience of having taught in France (as I stated earlier, only one of these teachers, FN, has actually taught in France);

rather, it is a model enacted in a particular discourse of education which is "out there" and available as a resource when these individuals are asked to talk about teaching. This is not to say that it is not real—it certainly is real to those who use it as a resource. It also is not to say it is a momentary invention. Like Bourdieu's (1977) concept of *habitus*, the imagined discourses of French teaching and learning have been a given structure for these individuals, born and raised as they were in France. However, at the same time, it has been one which they and many others, through their individual agency, constantly re-shape via their talk about teaching and learning.

One issue which is linked to this discussion of the invoked French national educational culture is what the four teachers are actually doing when they say the things they say. Are they, on the one hand, preparing the ground for an early exit from London and Britain altogether? Or are they working through frustrations as a first step toward a professional stability that will make more likely the prospect of their staying in London in the long term? In either case, they are developing what a variety of authors in recent years (e.g., Bhabha, 1994; Hall, 1996; Hannerz, 1996; Papastergiadis, 2000) have called *hybrid identities* or *third places*. Nikos Papastergiadis (2000) explains as follows what is meant by these terms:

> ... hybridity ... invariably acknowledges that identity is constructed through negotiation of difference, and that the presence of fissures, gaps and contra-dictions is not necessarily a sign of failure. In its most radical form, the con-cept also stresses that identity is not the combination, accumulation, fusion or synthesis of various components, but an energy field of different forces. Hybridity is not confined to a cataloguing of difference. Its "unity" is not found in the sum of its parts, but emerges from the process of opening up what Homi Bhabha has called a "third space," within which other elements encounter and transform each other. Hybridity is both the assemblage that occurs whenever two or more elements meet, and the initiation of a process of change. (p. 170)

Thus far we have examined statements made by FN, GL, AL, and DC in which they all expressed similar ideas about education. These ideas have been consistent with a kind of official story of French education and have appeared to be relatively fixed. Nevertheless, if we move beyond these statements and examine the entirety of what these four teachers have told me about their teaching and their lives in London, we find a high degree of ambivalence. In my view, this ambivalence goes hand in hand with the find-ing of a third place identity, which is more than the sum of the parts and be-yond what might be predicted or expected from the mix of French and British educational cultures and lifestyles. It has tended to manifest itself most when I have actually posed direct questions about how FN, GL, AL, and DC see their futures.

## FUTURE PLANS: COMPROMISING AND RESISTING

One question which I have asked periodically when interviewing FN, GL, AL, and DC is how long they will stay in London teaching French. Of course, it would be possible to leave teaching and still stay in London, either studying or working. Indeed, AL on one occasion mentioned this very possibility after telling me that she was bored with teaching after just 6 months on the job:

> That's the thing, you know, I have reached a stage where I'm getting a bit bored. It's like in the last year, I've learnt so much. It's really hard and really challenging and now it's like when I teach, I'm a teacher now.... I want to do something else. In the last two months I've been thinking of so many things. I've been thinking of going back to study ... changing [schools] or quitting at the end of this year and getting a job in London. Every week I change my mind. (AL, 20/3/01)

Despite this momentary suggestion that there might be life in London beyond teaching, AL (along with FN and GL) has generally expressed the view that leaving teaching will mean leaving London and going back to France or possibly another European country, such as Spain. More importantly, all three have maintained that they will leave London and Britain (because they are also unified in the belief that there is no life in Britain outside London!) sooner rather than later. The general view has been that they must teach for 2 years, but that at that point (the end of the academic year 2001–2002), they would have accumulated enough experience to obtain a teaching post elsewhere.

In the case of FN, an early exit seems highly likely as she has been the most adamant about wanting to return to her home in France. For GL and AL, however, matters are not so clear as both have on occasion indicated that they might be willing to stay in London, if they could find employment in a school with high standards, where they would not have to deal with discipline problems and they would be able to "teach grammar" and not follow so closely the National Curriculum. In Britain, schools offering these conditions are most likely to be independent (private) or state schools which have a selective intake. The issue which seems to weigh on GL and AL when thinking about opting for a more elitist school, which they see as allowing them to realize themselves as teachers, is an ideological one. In the earlier discussion of French education, we observed how there is the principle in France of education of the state guaranteeing a good education for all of its citizens. GL and AL have given voice to this ideal on occasion. For example, GL has stated very clearly that she does not think that people should have to pay for an education:

GL:     Because I have been educated a certain way and it was really
        strict. And, I don't think I can be just cool.
DB:     And you don't see the solution as finding a school with very
        high standards?
GL:     No, because I don't think you have to pay to be educated.
DB:     But even a school that's not paying, but it's selective. A grammar
        school, for example? (GL, 8/12/00)

GL goes on to say that she would not like to work in a selective school. For
her, what is necessary is a change to the entire system in Britain. However,
there is some evidence that both GL and AL have ambivalent feelings on
this matter, allowing for the possibility that private education might be ac-
ceptable as the only way for them to teach in a way which is more consistent
with their principles. The following excerpt from an interview with AL is interesting in this regard:

AL:     If I stay in England, a private school, probably, or nothing almost.
DB:     When you say private, that could also be a selective school.
AL:     Selective school, grammar, grammar school, selective school
        good school.... A school where I be ... or a sixth form college,
        something where I could be teaching more, I want to teach more
        ... to challenge a bit more people. I don't challenge them ...
DB:     Do you have any political problems with that, or not? Or it
        doesn't matter.
AL:     Oh, yes.... Well, I used to have ... and that's what annoys me
        because I've never had an idea of education as being selective
        ... and I remember a conversation with my boyfriend, actually,
        probably a year and a half ago, just before we [DB and AL] met,
        talking about that. And he was saying ... applying only to
        private schools and I was saying, "I think it's disgusting ..." But
        now I'm thinking, the system is the way it is and at the end of
        the day, I'd better think of me ...
DB:     You can't change it.
AL:     So, yes I do have a little political problem, but never mind ...
        (AL, 19/6/01)

    Thus, in parallel to their portrayal of teaching in London as a highly frus-
trating enterprise, GL and AL have, at the same time, elaborated a more
hopeful discourse of staying, even if this means going into selective or private education. In this sense, they have negotiated their way to a third place
professional identity, neither British nor French, but beyond Britain and
France. This is confirmed by GL and AL in the following excerpts:

AL:      I started the year with a big influence from France. I was decided
         that I would do like I wanted. But then the system … it's not the
         same, you just cannot do … you have to do what PGCE says, what
         the National Curriculum says … Their level is really low and they
         lack any type of grammar and of memory. I have the feeling that in
         school in England they're not required to work on their memory
         and … so you can't, you can't, work like we work in France … You
         do a lot of games.

DB:      So you've sort of found a style.

AL:      Uh, yeah. I'm still moaning about that (laughing), but I realise that's
         the way it is and uhm … with year 8 top set, though, that's where
         I'm having the best time. I'm doing a bit of grammar and pushing
         them. I really like it, I really enjoy it, really enjoy it.   (AL, 19/6/01)

> I think I have learnt a lot. And even if I don't agree with a lot of aspects
> of the system, I think it is excellent to go and teach somewhere
> else because there is always something positive to take. And I also
> think that after a few years, maybe you are not, no more really
> French. In fact, there is something that has changed in you and
> maybe you are not aware of it, but I'm sure that something has
> changed deeply and maybe I cannot tell you what has changed
> deeply because I'm not aware of it.   (GL, 2/4/01)

However, despite this hybrid, third place professional identity, a positive
phenomenon which might be seen as an integrationist orientation toward
life in Britain, GL and AL continue to struggle with staying or leaving. As AL
indicated in a previous excerpt, "every day I change my mind." This statement might be seen to apply to GL when she reflects on leaving London to
go back to her home village in France:

> I've still got my friends and I'm very happy to see them when I go back….
> But, in fact, I was not sure, in fact, if I could live in [my village] again, in a
> small town…. I really don't know. Sometimes, I really would like to go back
> … buy a flat, to have the life I had before … And sometimes, I'm just walking
> on the streets of London and I'm saying to myself that I would like to stay be-
> cause … there are so many things to do…. But at the same time, it's really dif-
> ficult to buy something here…. So, in fact, I have the feeling to sit between
> two chairs. I don't know, I don't know what to do. (GL, 28/6/01)

Thus, AL and GL seem caught in the throes of overwhelming ambivalence. This ambivalence flows naturally from the condition of migration in
which they find themselves immersed. They are French nationals in London with no intention of settling down, effectively ex-pats in a city that
makes no demands on conformity or loyalty. They list their friends and ac-
quaintances as almost exclusively members of the huge and mobile foreign

community in London, GL even going so far as to insist on several occasions that she never socializes with English people. However, it is not whether London makes demands on these teachers that is ultimately of importance; rather, it is how they see themselves, how they find their third place identity. GL and AL seem torn between what is becoming increasingly familiar (i.e., a London third place) and what was completely familiar in the past (i.e., home in France and the life they had in London when they first arrived in the city). When they are close to emitting a clear desire to leave London, they interject problems which make bringing their London lives to an end seem precipitated and even unwise. In the following two excerpts, GL and AL cite what they would miss and how disruptive a move back to France would be, respectively:

> I feel it's time to go back and I can't tell you why I feel it exactly…. But yes, last week I was walking in the street and I said to myself, I think I would be sad not to be, not to see that everyday. I think I would feel sad but … at the same time I need to go back. (GL, 8/12/00)

> Already here I feel like in here I've got a home, friends, job … Now it's going to be another step to go back to France, it won't be easy … We'll have to start a new life again, find new jobs, a new place to live … and the more I wait, the more difficult it will be to go back to my own country … (AL, 19/6/01)

By contrast, DC is altogether more decided as regards such matters. She makes her position clear in the following excerpt:

> I never thought of leaving, I never ever thought of leaving, honestly … (putting on a dopey voice) "I mean right, that's it, I'm going back to Bordeaux." Never ever thought of that…. cause I knew how my life was there. I was bored, I was living with my parents, I didn't have a car, I didn't have any money, was completely dependent on everyone. So when I left, it was just like free as a bird, and on my own … (DC, 11/6/01)

DC sees herself as carving out a new identity that involves both her sense of personal self and her sense of professional self:

> … but I don't feel different. I think I'm just taking shape in a sort of English mode. I will always be French and I will always be a pain in terms of like being quite hands expressive and you know, wanting everything to be right … and you know, taking everything seriously … but I … think I'm going into the mode of adapting myself here and how it works. (DC,11/6/01)

As we observed earlier, DC is just as critical of British education as FN, GL, and AL. And, as regards her expressed views on who she is, professionally speaking, she shares with these three teachers a recognition that she is finding a third place professional identity. However, DC has given voice to a clear intention to stay in London, whereas FN, GL, and AL have made clear their intentions to leave, although GL and AL sometimes seem unsure about ending their London experience. The key factor which accounts for these differences seems to be that DC has constructed an immigrant discourse, which means that she not only works for third place professional identity, but also for a third place personal identify. FN, GL, and AL, by contrast, have adopted a discourse of complaint whereby there is too much that they do not like about life in London and too much that they miss about France. The result is that although they have invoked to some degree a convergence or compromise strategy in their teaching, they have invoked a resistance strategy when it comes to taking on a more "British" identity. However, having said this, I might add that given the ambivalence that comes with the experience of migration, there is really no telling at this time if FN, GL, and AL will change their minds. As Papastergiadis (2000) points out, the concepts of hybridity and third places are not only assemblages of the various elements of past and present experiences, they are also part of the process of change, one that's ongoing as long as migration endures as part of the individual's life.

## CONCLUSION

At the beginning of this chapter, I said that educational authorities in Britain have until now made very little effort to recruit teachers of French from France and that they certainly have not taken an interest in whether these teachers actually stay in Britain and thus offer a long-term solution to the shortage problem. In the end, the actual socialization of these teachers to British education and ways of teaching has been left to individual PGCE courses. The PGCE course described in Jones (2000) is an example of a program that has confronted educational culture differences head-on and dealt with them in an in-depth manner. However, it should be noted that his course is a joint British–French program, and therefore not typical of PGCE courses in Britain. Whether more typical PGCE courses contain a strand of what amounts to comparative education for foreign national teachers, these teachers (and here I refer not only to the ongoing conversations with my cohort but informal contact with other teachers classifiable as foreign nationals as well) express the view that they have to make their way as regards this vital part of their learning curve. It seems, then, that PGCE courses need to move away from primarily (or even exclusively) providing these candidates with the technical teaching skills they need, and move in the direction of also exploring educational cultural differences as a starting point to the development of these skills. Such a move would mean an adjustment to official programs and a likely cutback on microlevel technique in favor of a more macrolevel orientation to the task of teaching; the payoff, however, might be a lower attrition rate among foreign nationals who are at present so vital to keeping the teaching of Modern Languages going.

Nevertheless, as we observed earlier, it is not just the world of teaching that is important to decisions to stay in Britain. As Brown (2001) observes, and FN, GL, AL, and DC confirm, it is how they construct their personal identity—if they adopt the status of ex-pat or the status of immigrant—that ultimately will be vital when the time comes to decide whether to stay. FN, GL, and AL seem to have enough resistance to London and sufficient pull toward their environments of origin to make it difficult for them to stay in London for too much longer. DC, by contrast, seems to have decided long ago that she is where she wants to be and that she does not miss enough of her previous life (and what she imagines would be her present life) in France to make her want to go back there. Obviously, educational authorities and PGCE course heads cannot do anything about the personal lives and preferences of foreign nationals on their courses. However, educational authorities in particular need to be aware that the ex-pat status adopted by so many French nationals means that they are not a reliable solution to the shortage problem and that even measures such as "golden hellos," introduced in 2000 to attract more applicants—British and foreign— to PGCE courses, will not guarantee that these teachers stay very long after they have completed the PGCE.

On a broader level, and in the context of this volume, this study has resonance value with regard to several themes. First, there are the possible and interesting comparisons and contrasts to be made between this study, involving movement across the borders of two EU countries, and the global phenomenon of itinerant "native speaker" English teachers who carry and spread their teaching practices around the world. The French teachers in this study were all too aware, from the beginning of their experience as French teachers in Britain, that there were serious educational culture differences to be confronted. As a result, they found themselves continuously engaged in a conscious process of confronting these differences as they worked dialectically toward a third place pedagogical identity. In addition, in the interview excerpts reproduced throughout this chapter, they manifested a sense that they were relatively disempowered and were not able to achieve as much as they might as teachers due to the control exerted on them by the educational system and the National Curriculum. Their awareness of conflict and their efforts to deal with it contrast markedly with what often happens with native-speaker English teachers, who often do not even consider the possibility of conflicts with local educational cultures. As authors such as Pennycook (1994) have pointed out (and as I can corroborate, based on informal contacts with a variety of EFL contexts over the years), these teachers often assume that the default or unmarked way of teaching is some form of communicative language teaching of the type propagated by British Councils and Internal Houses around the world. Of course, the transfer of methodologies across borders is fraught with difficulties and this has been documented by a handful of authors such as Holliday (1994), Duff (1996), and Canagarajah (1999); however, the relative power of these teachers to impose their methodology seems to have greater scope than that of the French teachers. Thus, the question of negotiating identities varies markedly across native-speaker teachers of different languages. This being the case, an interesting niche to explore in future research is the nature of the relative sense of power over their pedagogy held by English speaking ex-pats around the world and teachers of other languages, working away from home

Another theme arising from this chapter concerns the long-term effects of so many French nationals coming into the British educational system. As I ask elsewhere (Block, 2002), in sufficient numbers and proportions in a secondary school French department, might these teachers' local knowledge be a catalyst for the critique and reform of the official language teaching theory, as embodied in the National Curriculum? I do not have information about the number of French nationals currently teaching in British secondary schools, but as far as I can tell from conversations with participants in my study as well as informal contexts with other teachers, it is becoming increasingly common in language departments employing four or five French specialists, for two or more of these to be French nationals. Although heads of department vary in the extent to which they use their position to transform departments, I can easily imagine that if the four teachers discussed here were ever to be heads of department, they would lead from the front and possibly even impose on their colleagues their third place takes on communicative language teaching and child-centered education. They would, in other words, become catalysts for change in the extremely local contexts of particular schools.

Finally, there is a teacher development issue arising from my research. One thing I have wondered about, during the time I have been in contact with these teachers, is the extent to which the very act of meeting with me has helped them get through the educational cultural conflicts they reported to me in our conversations. During the round of interviews carried out in June 2001, as these teachers came to the end of their first years as NQTs, I asked them why they agreed to meet with me and talk to me about their professional and personal experiences living and working in London. The following response, provided by FN, is interesting because of the issues it brings out:

> ... in fact, I found the idea interesting and ... I afterwards I saw you and I mean we get on well together so I'm quite happy to see you (laughing) ... like

a friend. You are like a therapist last year so we really liked to see you, just to ... (laughing and gesturing as if she is pulling problems out from inside her) ... I like this idea of following people just to see the way they change. I mean if we compare the conversations I had last year, they are different, I probably changed my point of view. And I would be interested to know how things evolve. (FN, 26/6/01)

In FN's comments, we see reference to two general purposes served by her contacts with me, one phatic in nature and the other more relevant to professional development. As regards the phatic aspect of interviews, I may be seen by teachers as a sympathetic and friendly interlocutor who is outside their professional context and therefore of no threat to them. I am, in other words, someone with whom they can "unload" the frustrations of their day-to-day lives. On the other hand, the very fact of talking things through with me helps teachers reflect on their teaching practice and overall professional development. As FN puts it, "... if we compare the conversations I had last year, they are different, I probably changed my point of view." In this sense, I am someone with whom they can talk through their teaching experiences, which ultimately leads to greater reflection and an enhanced understanding of their professional lives. To summarize, the favorable response I have had from these teachers, as regards the effect that the interviews have had on them, suggests to me that in effect, merely talking to me has made them feel more empowered. This empowerment comes to these teachers from first being able to offload negative feelings (or let off steam) with an outsider and, second, engaging in a discussion of teaching practice. The lesson for other contexts, where different pedagogical identities come into conflict and are being negotiated, should be obvious.

## REFERENCES

Adams, J. (2000). *The teaching force and the recruitment and retention of modern languages teachers*. London: University of North London, Institute for Policy Studies in Education.

Alexander, R. (1996). *Other primary schools and ours: Hazards of international comparison*. Coventry, England: University of Warwick, Centre for Research in Elementary and Primary Education.

Alexander, R. (1999). Culture in pedagogy; pedagogy across cultures. In R. Alexander, P. Broadfoot, & D. Phillips (Eds.), *Learning from comparing, vol 1: Contexts, classrooms and outcomes* (pp. 149–80). Wallingford, England: Symposium Books.

Anderson, B. (1991). *Imagined communities: Reflections on the origins and spread of nationalism*. London: Verso.

Bhabha, H. (1994). *The location of culture*. London: Routledge.

Block, D. (2001). Foreign nationals on a PGCE modern languages course: Questions of national identity. *European Journal of Teacher Education, 24*, 291–311.

Block, D. (2002). Communicative language teaching revisited: Discourses in conflict and foreign national teachers. *Language Learning Journal, 26*, 19–26.

Broadfoot, P., & Osborn, M. (1993). *Perceptions of teaching: Primary school teachers in England and France*. London: Cassell.

Broadfoot, P., Osborn, M., Planel, C., & Sharpe, K. (2000). *Promoting quality in learning: Does England have the answer?* London: Cassell.

Brown, K. (2001). What happens to the foreign native speakers we train? *Links, 24,* 5–7.

Bourdieu, P. (1977). *Outline of a theory of practice*. Cambridge, England: Cambridge University Press.

Canagarajah, S. (1999). *Resisting linguistic imperialism in English teaching*. Oxford, England: Oxford University Press.

Department of Education and Skills. (2002). *National curriculum: Inclusion*. Retrieved June 1, 2002, from http://www.nc.uk.net/inclusion.html

Duff, P. (1996). Different languages, different practices: Socialization of discourse competence in dual-language school classrooms in Hungary. In K. Bailey, & D. Nunan (Eds.), *Voices from the classroom* (pp. 407–33). Cambridge, England: Cambridge University Press.

Grenfell, M. (2000). Modern languages: Beyond Nuffield and into the 21st century. *Language Learning Journal, 22,* 23–29.

Hall, S. (1996). The question of cultural identity. In S. Hall, D. Held, D. Hubert, & K. Thompson (Eds.), *Modernity: An introduction to modern societies* (pp. 595–634). Oxford, England: Oxford University Press.

Hannerz, U. (1996). *Transnational connections*. London: Routledge.

Hobsbawm, E. (1990). *Nations and nationalism since 1780: Programme, myth, reality*. Cambridge, England: Cambridge University Press.

Holliday, A. (1994). *Appropriate methodology and social context*. Cambridge, England: Cambridge University Press.

Jin, L., & Cortazzi, M. (1998). The culture the learner brings: A bridge or a barrier. In M. Byram & M. Fleming (Eds.), *Language learning in intercultural perspectives* (pp. 98–118). Cambridge, England: Cambridge University Press.

Jones, B. (2000, September). The Post Graduate Certificate in Education (PGCE) and the Maîtrise Français Langue Etrangère (FLE): An account of student teachers' experience. Paper presented at the National Conference for Teacher Trainers in MFL, Trinity and All Saints Comenius Centre, Leeds, England.

Joutard, P., & Thélot, C. (1999). *Reussir l'école: pour une politique educative* [Making a success of the school—For an educational policy]. Paris: Seuil.

Klapper, J. (1997). Language learning at school and university: The great grammar debate continues (II). *Language Learning Journal, 16,* 22–27

La Borderie, R. (1994). *20 facettes du système éducatif* [20 facets of the education system]. Paris: Nathan.

McLean, M. (1995). *Educational traditions compared*. London: David Fulton.

Morrow, K., & Johnson, K. (Eds.). (1981). *Communication in the classroom*. London: Longman.

Pachler, N. (2000). Re-examining communicative language teaching. In K. Field (Ed.), *Issues in modern foreign languages teaching* (pp. 22–37). London: Routledge.

Papastergiadis, N. (2000). *The turbulence of migration*. Cambridge, England: Polity.

Pennycook, A. (1994). *The cultural politics of English as an international language*. London: Longman.

Pollard, A. (1996). *The social world of children's learning*. London: Cassell.

Reicher, S., & Hopkins, N. (2001). *Self and nation*. London: Sage.

Reichler, C. (1992). La réserve du symbolique [Symbolic reserve]. *Les Temps Modernes, 550,* 85–93.

Thompson, G. (1996). Some misconceptions about commutative language teaching. *ELT Journal, 50,* 9–15.

Van Zanten, A. (2001). *L'école peripherique. Scolarité et ségrégation en banlieue* [The school of the periphery. Schooling and segregation in the suburbs]. Paris: Presses Universitaires de France.

Vinuesa, M. (1996). Transmission culturelle par le curriculum cache—La socialisation des enfants de 5 à 7 ans à l'école publique en Franc et en Anglaterre [Cultural transmission through the hidden curriculum—The socialization of infants of 5 to 7 years of age in public schools in France and England]. Unpublished doctoral dissertation, Université de Paris.

Whitehead, J., & Taylor, A. (1998). *Teachers of modern foreign languages: Foreign native speakers on initial teacher training courses in England.* Bristol, England: Faculty of Education, UWE, Bristol.

Wodak, R., DeCillia, R., Reisigl, M., & Liebhart, K. (1999). *The discursive construction of national identity.* Edinburgh, Scotland: Edinburgh University Press.

# Chapter 9

# International TESOL Professionals and Teaching English for Glocalized Communication (TEGCOM)[1]

Angel Lin
*City University of Hong Kong*

Wendy Wang
*Eastern Michigan University*

Nobuhiko Akamatsu
*Doshisha University, Japan*

Mehdi Riazi
*Shiraz University, Iran*

> *How should we write our research? ... the question reflects a central postmodernist realization: all knowledge is socially constructed. Writing is not a "true" representation of an objective "reality"; instead, language creates a particular view of reality.... All social scientific writing depends upon narrative structure and narrative devices, although that structure and those devices are frequently masked by a "scientific" frame, which is, itself, a metanarrative (c.f. Leotard, 1979).... Can we construct a sociology in which narrated lives replace the narrative of unseen, atemporal, abstract "social forces"?*
> —Richardson (1997, pp. 26–27)

---

[1] This chapter was adapted from an article which appeared in *JLIE*, Vol. 1, No. 4, 2002.

## INTRODUCTION

Richardson (1985) intertwines narrative writing with sociological analytic writing in a research-reporting genre which she called "the collective story." The collective story "gives voice to those who are silenced or marginalized" and "displays an individual's story by narrativizing the experiences of the social category to which the individual belongs" (Richardson, 1997, p. 22). To Richardson, the collective story is not just about the protagonists' past but also about their future. Although Richardson (1997) emphasizes the similarity of experiences of "members" of a certain "social category" (identified according to certain similar conditions or experiences; e.g., cancer survivors, battered women), we want to emphasize the fluidity and non-essentialized nature of such social categories and how the rhetorical decisions made in the writing of the collective story contribute to the foregrounding of similarities of experiences, while de-emphasizing dissimilarities. On the one hand, we want to show in our collective story our uniqueness as individuals each having a "unique trajectory that each person carves out in space and time" (Harre, 1998, p. 8). On the other hand, we want to show in our collective story how the "narrated experiences" of each of us are not isolated, idiosyncratic events, but "are linked to larger social structures, linking the personal to the public" and the biographical to the political (Richardson, 1997, p. 30).

Those similarities of experiences and social conditions that each of us found ourselves in constituted the reason for our joining together to embark on the writing of this chapter. Resonating with Richardson's notion of using the collective story as a form of social action with transformative possibilities, we want to use our autobiographic narratives not only to report and interpret action, but also to shape future action, stressing "the prospective aspect of autobiographies" (Harre, 1998, p. 143). Recent works in applied linguistics that drew on narrative analysis and autobiographical data (e.g., Kramsch & Lam, 1999; Lantolf & Pavlenko, 2001; Pavlenko, 1998, 2001; Young, 1999), as well as the endorsement of narrative and autobiographic research as legitimate approaches in recent research methodology discourses (e.g., Casey, 1995; Ellis & Bochner, 2000), have created in applied linguistics a much welcomed niche, a legitimate discursive space for us to explore ways of presenting our experiences as "EFL learners" in different Asian contexts. In presenting these narrated experiences, we are also paving the way to create subject positions more complex than and alternative to those traditionally created for us in EFL learning and teaching discourses (e.g., the Asian classroom learner of English, who is good at reading and writing in English but not as fluent in speaking and listening, and speaks with a characteristic "accent" marking the student out as a "non-native speaker").

We are four TESOL professionals (Wendy Wang, Angel Lin, Nobuhiko Akamatsu, & Mehdi Riazi) who have learned and used English since childhood in different parts of Asia—Mainland China, colonial and postcolonial Hong Kong, Japan, and Iran, respectively. We crossed one another's pathways when we went to Canada to do our doctoral studies in English language education in the early 1990s. We parted on graduation and each went into different career paths under different sociocultural and institutional structures. We decided to present our voices as language learners from different parts of the world to the "mainstream" audience by forming a panel, writing up our autobiographies of our experiences with English, and presenting them at the TESOL convention in 2001 (Lin, Wang, Akamatsu, & Riazi, 2001). Now we want to make deeper sense of what we have written by reflexively analyzing them, linking our autobiographies to current discourses of language learning and identity, and local production of disciplinary knowledge in applied linguistics (e.g., Canagarajah, 2000; Leung, Harris, & Rampton, 1997; Norton, 1997, 2000; Toohey, 2000). As we do not have space in this chapter to present our autobiographies in their entirety, we shall adopt the format of Richardson's (1997) collective story. We shall analyze the story lines of our autobiographies and present excerpts from them to illustrate the story lines. We use the collective story as a format to tell our stories of learning and teaching English in different sociocultural contexts. We discuss how this local, socioculturally situated knowledge can contribute to the knowledge of the discipline and a revisioning of the field.

This chapter is divided into three main parts. In Part I, we critically and reflexively analyze our own autobiographic narratives of learning and teaching English in different sociocultural contexts. In Part II, we engage in discussions which aim at contributing to the disciplinary knowledge and discourse of TESOL and applied linguistics, by illustrating both how English is perceived, learned, appropriated, and used in different sociocultural contexts, and how this local, socioculturally situated knowledge can contribute to the knowledge of the discipline. In Part III, we problematize the discursive and institutional practices of "Othering" by deconstructing and destabilizing the dichotic categories of "native" and "non-native" speakers of English. We propose a paradigm shift from doing TESOL to doing TEGCOM (Teaching English for Glocalized[2] Communication), with suggestions for an alternative theoretical orientation and research program.

---

[2]The term *glocal* and the process verb *glocalize* are formed by blending *global* and *local*. The idea has been modeled on Japanese *dochakuka* (deriving from *dochaku* "living on one's own land"), originally the agricultural principle of adapting one's farming techniques to local conditions, but also appropriated in Japanese business discourse to mean *global localization*, a global outlook adapted to local conditions (Robertson, 1995).

## OUR COLLECTIVE STORY

"Writing exists in the context of an implicit guiding metaphor that shapes the narrative" (Richardson, 1997, p. 17). Examples of these guiding metaphors, cultural narratives, or story lines (Harre & van Langenhove, 1998) can be found in the popular culture in a society (e.g., in movies, novels, or biographies of successful people). For instance, the successful immigrant story line is found in many immigrants' autobiographies (e.g., the immigrant has achieved success and acceptance in the host society through his or her hard work and resolution of conflicts between the indigenous cultural identity and the assimilating identity of the host country, usually by settling down with the possession of middle-class, professional identities; e.g., Lvovich, 1997). Another example is the resistance story line that is often found in the critical cultural studies literature (e.g., the working-class students who engage in oppositional practices that negate the norms and values imposed on them by middle-class adults, with the paradoxical effect of reproducing their working-class habitus and future work paths; e.g., Willis, 1977). Story lines represent how groups of people tend to see the world and interpret and relate events to themselves and their own actions. Instead of talking about story lines as "right" or "wrong," or "accurate" or "inaccurate," one talks about story lines in terms of the meanings people give to events in the world and the visions that people have for themselves in relation to others and the world.

When we reflexively analyze our own autobiographies, we find a comparable story line underlying our different stories. In this section we shall illustrate the story line with excerpts from our autobiographic stories. We shall then critically analyze our own narratives to answer the following questions: Can we reposition ourselves by reimagining the story lines, and in what ways can our stories contribute to the knowledge and discourse of the discipline?

### Learning English in Sociocultural Contexts
### Where English Is Not a Daily Life Language

First of all, all the four learners are situated in a similar set of sociolinguistic conditions with respect to learning English. In their sociocultural contexts, English, not being a language for daily communication within their families or communities, is mainly encountered as an academic subject in school:

> How did I get interested in the English language in a non-English speaking country like China? My parents didn't speak a word of English. My first encounter with English was when I was in the 3rd grade and English was a school subject. In the isolated China in the early 70s, many Chinese kids considered English to be too foreign and irrelevant to their lives; so there was lack of interest in the English subject. (excerpt from Wendy's story)

I grew up in a small town in Fars province, where English was not popular and was taught as a school subject only from grade seven. There weren't any private institutions to teach English either. Moreover, the socio-economic condition of families did not allow for a full-fledged schooling of their children, let alone for extra curricula subjects such as English. Therefore, chances for learning English in families or formal education were very low for us. (excerpt from Mehdi's story)

My parents do not speak any English. People we know all speak Cantonese, which is our daily language. I grew up in a home and community where few had the linguistic resources to use English at all, and even if anyone had, he/she would find it socially inappropriate (e.g., sounding pompous, putting on airs) to speak English. My chances for learning and using English hinged entirely on the school. However, I lived in a poor government-subsidized apartment-building complex (called "public housing estate") in the rural area (the New Territories) in Hong Kong, where schools were mostly put up in the 1960s and they had neither adequate English resources (e.g., staff well-versed in spoken English) nor a well-established English-speaking and English-teaching-and-learning tradition or school culture. (excerpt from Angel's story)

I was good at math and science, and English was also my favorite subject. I felt that English was the easiest subject of all, in terms of getting good marks. Somehow, I could always get good marks on English without studying too hard. In my third year in junior high school (Grade 9), I decided to try to enter the most prestigious high school in my city. (My brother, who was two years older, was studying at that school; it was kind of natural that I was going to take an entrance exam for that school.) In spite of all my efforts, however, I failed the entrance examination for the high school and had to go to another school. I thought that my life was over. In Japan, people tend to believe that a good school makes a good life, and I was, of course, one of them…. When I started my high school life, I was just miserable. The school was not the one I wanted to go to, and I was unhappy about everything around me. I said to myself, "No matter how hard you try, you can't get what you want. This is life." Although I went to school everyday, I didn't study at all; I was just killing my time for nothing. It was one of those days when I met Mr. Okuhara. (excerpt from Nobu's story)

## Meeting with Teachers Who Facilitated Our Appropriation of English to Expand Our Horizons and Identities

Given the situation that English is mainly learned as a school subject for academic grades, one will normally not expect the learner to have developed a high level of communicative competence in English. However, our stories illustrate the important role that our teachers played in helping us appropriate English and in enabling us to engage in practices that expanded our horizons and identities. These moments are experienced as self-transforming, culturally enriching, and also at times psychologically liberating (resonating with the emphasis of recent works on the intimate relations between identity and language learning; e.g., Norton, 1997, 2000; Toohey, 2000).

For instance, the hierarchical schooling system in Japan imposed a failure identity on Nobu when he failed to enter a prestigious high school; his meeting with a very special English tutor, Mr. Okuhara, created a new, expanding identity for Nobu and turned his life around—he wanted to become an English teacher, like Mr. Okuhara:

> Mr. Okuhara was a former English teacher of my mother's friend. Because my mother was worried about me, she asked her friend for some advice. She suggested that she introduce Mr. Okuhara to me.... Although I knew that he had taught English at high school for many years and he was offering private English lessons, my first impression of him was not so great. I was fifteen years old, and he was about seventy-five; we had almost sixty years in age difference, and I was kind of skeptical about his ability as an English teacher.

> The first meeting was very brief; he just read through the textbook and reference books (i.e., grammar books) I was using in my high school and made a few comments on them. He then handed me another book, saying, "Why don't you read this book, as much as you want, and tell me what it says about? How about starting next Wednesday?" So, I went home with the book and started reading it. Boy, it was so difficult! There were a lot of words I didn't know, and some sentence structures were also complex. I could read only three pages or so in a week. This was not just disappointing but also shocking for me because I was very proud of my English at that time. English was one of the very few things I was good at. After a few lessons with Mr. Okuhara, I realized that my English was not good enough to read the book he gave me. I still remember that my "English" world before I met him was like a small pond about which I knew everything. After having studied with him, I felt like I were thrown out into the sea, where I had no idea which way to swim or whether I could swim without drowning. (I found out later that the book I was given was used as a textbook for university students!)

> Mr. Okuhara's study room was small and simple. Basically, there were only a desk and two chairs. We sat at the desk, face to face. The lesson usually began with my reading aloud. I read aloud the text and translated it into Japanese, sentence by sentence. When I was reading aloud, I often stumbled or mispronounced unfamiliar words. My translation was also so poor that sometimes I myself didn't understand what I meant. Mr. Okuhara, however, never showed any negative expressions on his face or in his words. He simply provided the correct pronunciation or explained what made my translation poor. His teaching style, though it was rather old fashioned, surprised me in a sense. Because I was used to the teachers' complaints about the students' poor performance or disgusting expressions towards the students' mistakes, Mr. Okuhara's sincere attitude towards teaching deeply impressed me.

> I studied English with Mr. Okuhara for four years (ages 15 to 19). In those four years, I read a variety of English books with him, such as autobiography, mystery, adventure, and philosophy. My reading ability in English improved so much and I learned many things from the English books I read; however, it is the time I spent with him after each English lesson that I appreciated more. The English lesson with Mr. Okuhara began around 6 p.m. and it usu-

ally continued until around 9 p.m. After the lesson was over, his wife always brought us two cups of tea, fruits, and some sweets. Then, we, Mr. Okuhara and I, talked about many different things over the goodies. He used to tell me about his youth and his teaching experiences. He sometimes showed me his old pictures, explaining each picture, one by one. His talks were always so interesting that I never felt our age difference, and I found myself looking forward to the conversation with him after each lesson. (Mr. Okuhara died in March 1991. It may sound strange, but I still talk to him in my mind once in a while. He was a very special person who influenced me most in my teenage, and he is still my mentor.) ... I realized that I would like to be an English teacher like Mr. Okuhara. (excerpts from Nobu's story)

Learning English in China in the 1970s should have also proved to be a lonely enterprise. However, there were two significant events in Wendy's early learning experience: Wendy's parents desired their daughter to take up the future identity of an interpreter, who would serve as a bridge between the Western world and their own world, and Wendy's meeting with a special teacher, Mr. Qi, who opened up a bilingual discursive space for her to feel secure enough to explore a new world and a new identity in English:

> ... *My parents passed on to me their beliefs and interest in the Western world. They strongly believed that the future of China was to be open to the Western world and English is the key for communication.* As a third grader, I developed an interest in the English language simply because of my curiosity. For me, *English was a mysterious language, representing an unknown world. It fascinated me because it was so different.* I often wondered: Who were the English-speaking people? What did they look like? What would English sound like in real life? My curiosity allowed me to dream of one day meeting these people. *It was exciting to imagine that I could understand them, but I wondered if they could understand me....* My parents believed that I had language talent and could become an interpreter one day. So they seized the opportunity for me by signing me up for a language aptitude test when the Tianjin Foreign Languages School reopened the year after President Nixon's visit to China in 1972. I passed the language aptitude test and was admitted into an intensive English program in 1973. I was 13 years old. Getting into the English program changed the path of my life forever....
>
> ... I enjoyed more when I practiced speaking English with peers and teachers. *All the teachers were fluent speakers of English, though not native speakers.* The classes were small, with no more than 12 students in each class. I enjoyed going to English classes, particularly the English conversation class. Our teacher, Mr. Qi, was fabulous with students. He often carried out conversations with us on topics of our interest and our conversations often went on beyond the class hours. *A unique feature of Mr. Qi was that he liked to code-switch between English and Chinese.* This shaped the way we communicated with each other both in and out of class. We often started a topic in Chinese and ended up in English or vice versa. Everyone was free to join in the conversations in either language. *In switching between the two languages, we learned to relate to each other and communicate in the world we created. The use of both languages signified a sense of belonging to that*

*world.* However, even in the intimate use of the two languages, it was clear to everyone that they played totally different roles in our communication. *Chinese was the language to represent ourselves and English was the language we used to expand who we were and who we wanted to be.* To this end, *English became a language of dreams and a language of freedom.* For this reason, I didn't really feel embarrassed when I made mistakes in English. I truly enjoyed talking to my classmates and sharing ideas in the language we were learning. In fact, it was in the company of the group that I became a *confident* speaker of English....

... The issues we didn't feel comfortable talking about in class often became the topics for discussion in our dormitory. I shared a room with five other female students from the same class and we ended up being good friends. I enjoyed every minute of our discussions in the dorm room. What made our discussions a unique experience was that we exchanged our thoughts in English. *Speaking English gave us a sense of freedom and liberation from being silent on all the social, cultural, and political issues in our first language.* The relaxed atmosphere in the dorm made it possible for us to be open and feel free to question the social, cultural, and political practices in China. *The fact that we chose to experience English as the medium to express our reactions, concerns, frustrations, worries, expectations, and hopes signified our expansion and growth in a new dimension.* (excerpts from Wendy's story; italics added)

Likewise, the arrival of two energetic teachers who taught Angel self-learning strategies with which she could gain access to English set her onto a different path. English later became much more than a school subject to her; it became a tool for her to enrich and expand her sociocultural horizons, and a space for her to negotiate her "innermost self":

At Primary 4 (Grade 4), there came a fresh graduate from the College of Education to our school, and he became our English teacher. His teaching methods were very different from our former teachers. He was friendly and approachable and talked to us explicitly about our need to increase our English vocabulary. He asked us to keep a "rough work book" where we put down all new words or new sentences exemplifying a new grammatical point. He gave us ample practice with word pronunciations and meanings. He explained everything clearly. He also taught us how to use an English dictionary. I started to pick up some confidence and interest in learning English since then....

... At Primary 6 (Grade 6), another recent College of Education graduate, Miss Law, came to our school and took up our English classes. She taught us those funny symbols used in the dictionaries to indicate pronunciation. I learnt that these funny symbols were called "international phonetic symbols," and I took a strong interest in them.... I started to go to the public library to borrow English storybooks and I conscientiously looked up all the new words and practiced pronouncing them. I kept a vocabulary book where I wrote down the meanings, pronunciation (recorded in phonetic symbols) and example sentences of the words (copied from the dictionary) and I read it whenever I had time....

... I had pen-pals from all over the world: England, Canada, U.S.A., Austria and Germany. In my circle of girl-friends, having pen-pals was a topic and practice of common interest and we would talk about our pen-pals and shared our excitement about trading letters, postcards, photos, and small gifts with our pen-pals; we'd also show one another pictures of our pen-pals.... It was a spontaneous "community of practice" (Lave & Wenger, 1991) that had emerged from our own activities and interests.... I also started to write my own private diary in English every day about that time.... Although I had started off this habit mainly to improve my English, later on I found that I could write my diary faster and *more comfortably* in English than in Chinese ... I felt that I could write my feelings *more freely* when I wrote in English—less inhibition and reservation—I seemed to have found a tool that gave me more freedom to express my innermost fears, worries, anger, conflicts or excitement, hopes, expectations, likes and dislikes (e.g., anger with parents or teachers, or a troubling quarrel with a friend at times) without constraint or inhibition—as if this foreign language had opened up a new, personal space (a "third space," Bhabha, 1994), for me to more freely express all those difficult emotions and experiences (typical?) of an adolescent growing up, without feeling the sanctions of the adult world. (excerpts from Angel's story)

Mehdi's location in a tourist spot and his identity as one of the few tourist guides in the community gave him an impetus to learn English. He also met two teachers in the school who put English within a comfortable zone for him. Later, English came to be an important tool for him to acquire a socially upward, professional identity:

My first encounter with the English language was in the form of facing foreign tourists coming to our historical town to visit the historical traces of the past dynasties. This created in me an impetus to learn English. In summer, when schools were closed, one of my hobbies was to find and read simplified English books using a very basic bilingual dictionary. Afterwards, in grade seven, I had my first formal exposure to the English language as a school subject. Though teachers' status and behavior in classes usually imposed a psychological barrier to students' learning, I was one of those rare lucky students who did not have such a problem. That was because my first English teacher in school turned out to be my cousin, and this took away from me any stress....

... In my second year of high school (grade 8), I noticed that my English teacher was a native American, Mr. Rooney (if I am right). That created a chance for me to use English to communicate with him. The chances increased when I noticed that we both had to pave the same route on foot to school every morning. He was friendly and tolerant and I took the opportunity to converse with him all the way to school which lead to a high motivation and desire to learn and improve my English all through high school and afterward....

... Having finished high school, I entered a two-year college program in electronics. Students in this college were required to spend their first quarter totally learning English as all the textbooks were in English and even the language of instruction in some courses was also English. We had ample chances in classes and language labs to improve all the four skills. We had to use English to perform our tasks and assignments. We wrote research papers for English courses and we wrote our technical projects in English. This college program helped me a lot in changing my subject and field of study (from electronics to English) both in entering the field (English program) and later on in fulfilling the requirements of different levels of the English language program. (excerpts from Mehdi's story)

## Anticlimax: Experiences of Being Positioned as an Inferior Copy of "the Master's Voice"

Our story line has so far been one of a successful journey of learning and mastering English for our own purposes. Two of the stories (Wendy's and Angel's), however, have an anticlimax, a difficult situation that destroyed most of their previously built-up confidence about themselves and their English.[3] Positioned as an inferior (or "accented and not-competent" English speaker) by her Anglo classmates, Wendy was made to live with an *imposed Otherness*, and she both missed and had to hide her bilingual, code-switching, confident, hybrid self (cf. Trinh, 1998) that she once had before going to Canada:

> When I went to Canada in the late 80s, I was a relatively fluent speaker of English. However, it didn't take me long to realize that my English was marked. All of a sudden my relationship with English changed. In China, being able to speak English was a plus; therefore I was "I + English." As a *non-native speaker* of English in Canada, the capitalized "I" automatically became a lower case "i" and English became my problem ... Soon after I started the MA program in English at York University, I felt numerous tensions building up around the language I thought I knew well. While I was proficient enough to function in the English-speaking environment as a graduate student, *I had the feeling that the person people saw and communicated with was not the person inside. The "me" shown through the English language was not the same "me" shown when I spoke Chinese or when I "messed up English with Chinese."* I

---

[3]Regarding the possible gender differences in this issue, consider Nobu's interpretation:
Let me make a small contribution to the discussion on the difference between Angel and Wendy, and Mehdi and myself. I am not sure about Mehdi's case, but at least in my case, when I started my MA program in USA, I had low expectations towards life in USA (my first study abroad). I don't recall any specific incidents where I felt discriminated, but even if I had been discriminated, I would have taken it for granted because at that time I felt that I was not fully communicatively competent in English. (I should say that I did have good grammatical competence and academic thinking skills.) Maybe I had encountered such discriminatory occasions, with which Angel or Wendy would have felt annoyed, and I just didn't notice them. When I think back on my life in USA, I was just hoping to acquire more knowledge of TESL, to get an MA, and to come back to Japan. I didn't expect much. I fully accepted my identity as a foreign student from Japan, and therefore, maybe, I didn't care much about and paid little attention to my accent and the discrimination which my accent might have caused.

started to experience a persona split. *I missed the old "me" with two languages in one person.* Now I felt like two people. The English *Me* was definitely much quieter, more reserved, and less confident to the point that my voice became so low that people couldn't hear what I was saying. I was constantly frustrated when people asked me "I am sorry, what did you say?" or "Pardon?" Each time I heard these, I became so self-conscious that I couldn't hear my own voice. It made me feel worse when I heard people say "Never mind!" I felt like an idiot, unable to comprehend what other people had said. All these instances made me wonder what was wrong with my English. Was my English that bad? (excerpt from Wendy's story; italics added)

Likewise, Angel was made to feel ashamed of her English:

English in my secondary school days was something I felt I mastered and owned. I felt competent and comfortable in it. It was not until my first year as an undergraduate English major in the University of Hong Kong that I was induced to feel ashamed about my own English—or made to feel that I hadn't really mastered it or owned it. Many of my fellow students at the university had studied English literature in their secondary schools while I had only the slightest idea of what it was! (English Literature is not offered in the curriculum of most secondary schools, but it is offered in a small number of well-established prestigious schools in the urban area in HK). When I opened my mouth in tutorial sessions, I noticed the difference between my Cantonese-accented English and the native-like fluent English that my classmates and the tutor spoke. It was, however, too late for me to pick up the native-like accent then. (excerpt from Angel's story)

## Searching for Resolution: Reclaiming and Reexercising Ownership of English

Both Wendy and Angel constructed in the latter parts of their narratives a self which has reclaimed ownership of English through continuous education—gaining more linguistic as well as symbolic capital (Bourdieu, 1986):

Continuing education was my remedy for making up *what comes naturally to native speakers, the confidence to speak....* it was not until I started teaching English as a second language with the Toronto Board of Education did I feel comfortable with English and myself. I no longer considered English as their language. It was mine. *It had to be mine before I could teach it to my students.* (excerpt from Wendy's story; italics added)

My life and career took a turn after my Master's degree and my residential years in the Robert Black College. I have acquired both the paper credentials and the linguistic and cultural resources to get and do the job of an English teacher. I had not (and have not) acquired a native-like English accent, but relatively speaking, my spoken English was more fluent and idiomatic than before the Robert Black College years. I no longer felt that I was an "impostor" (Bourdieu, 1991), or an "incompetent" teacher, an object of mockery by my middle-class students and colleagues. I seemed to have somehow managed to enter the elite group of English-conversant Chinese in Hong Kong. (excerpt from Angel's story)

It has to be pointed out that the resolution, which seemed to have come easily, was, in fact, just a temporary resolution. The feeling of having to prove oneself (and one's competence in English) is a recurrent one and the struggle is one that continues, as both Wendy and Angel are reflecting on it now.

## Helping Our Students

In the final part of the story line, all four authors are engaged in the positioning of self as a helping teacher, as someone who wants to help learners like themselves to achieve what they have achieved in relation to English and to life in general:

> I strongly believe that helping learners relate to each other in the target language and develop the confidence to use the language as their own should be the primary objectives at the early stages of second language teaching and learning. (excerpt from Wendy's story)

> ... when I think of all that had happened, I realize that my own chances for socioeconomic advancement seem to have hinged largely on a certain exceptional re-patterning of social and institutional arrangements.... whenever I hear my students express worries about their English proficiency, I also notice that they have had a very different relationship than that I have developed with English over the years. I am still trying to find ways to help them stop seeing English as only a subject, a barrier, a difficult task in their life, but as a friend who would open up new spaces, new challenges and new lands for them, both socioculturally and intellectually.... How do I help my students to turn English from an enemy to a friend, to make use of this medium to express, expand and, possibly, enrich their lives, to transform or hybridize their current identities, to enter into a new world of possibilities as well as relationships with other cultures and peoples in the world? To me, this is a life-long research and practice question to embark on. (excerpt from Angel's story)

> I am not sure how much or if my students are satisfied with my classes, but I've been learning a lot from teaching here. For example, since I came here, I've been more able to put myself in my student place and to improve my way of teaching. I've been not only teaching action research but also using it for my classes. I carrying out action research not for my research interest or publications, but simply for my students; I want to improve my teaching so that the students will benefit from my classes more than they do now.... I'm beginning to feel that I can share what I've learned from my studies with my students and that I can learn from them. (excerpt from Nobu's story)

> Ever since I started my job as a university professor, I have tried to help my students in all aspects to be good learners. I try very hard to create a sense of self-confidence in them and develop their potentials. This, I understand, originates from my own experience as a learner. My students have come to

know me as a caring teacher, an attribute that has occasionally received some criticisms on the part of my colleagues. I do my best to emancipate my students. I believe that human beings, of which students are the best representatives, are capable individuals with complicated and marvelous minds in need of help to flourish, and language plays a very important role in this process. My classes follow a collaborative mode in which we not only improve our learning of English as an academic subject, but also try to discover and construct our "selves" in relation to ourselves and people around us. (excerpt from Mehdi's story)

## Critical Reflexive Analysis of Our Collective Story— Identities Without Guarantees

In writing our autobiographies to present at the 2001 TESOL Conference (Lin et al., 2001), we have at times reproduced the dominant story lines of Self and Other and at other times attempted to put forward alternative subject positions for ourselves. Echoing Hall's (1996) notion of "Marxism without guarantees," we realize the limitations in trying to carve out new subject positions and identities using old discourses. For instance, while attempting to resist being positioned as an inferior copy of the "master's voice," we reproduced at times the dominant story line and the essentialized categories of "native speakers" and "non-native speakers" (e.g., *"All the teachers were fluent speakers of English, though not native speakers"*—excerpt from Wendy's story). Can the subaltern really speak (Spivak, 1988)? Can we speak only through the "master's voice" or speak only as a "domesticated Other" (Spivak, 1988)? Is there any way of finding our voice, remaking our identities, reimagining our story lines, reworking the dominant discourses, and revisioning the field?

The story line of our collective story is a familiar one: "EFL learners" who have worked extremely hard to fulfill their aspiration of mastering the English language have been helped by some special teachers and schools, gained a considerable degree of success, climbed up the socioeconomic ladder partially using this success with English, and found a bilingual self both culturally enriching and psychologically liberating, as if finding a "third space" (Hall, 1996). Then the story line of two of us (Angel as a colonial subject in pre-1997 British Hong Kong, and Wendy as a Chinese immigrant in Canada) gets an anticlimax, which is still a very familiar one. For instance, such an anticlimax is found in the story lines in the biographies of former colonial subjects like Ghandi, who encountered experiences of being "Othered" as "coloured people" in South Africa despite his British education and fluent English (Ghandi, 1982).

Yet, in producing our stories, it is as if we subconsciously wanted to reposition ourselves in a reimagined story line found in idealized stories of cross-cultural encounters, that is, an encounter between equals, a peaceful friendship-building and mutually enriching meeting of different peoples and cultures on egalitarian footings of mutual curiosity and respect (e.g., as found in movies such as *ET*, versus movies or TV dramas such as *Aliens* or *The X-Files*).

Our reimagined story line also says something else: we wanted to gain ownership of the cultural tool of English, to find our place and identity, to define who we are and what we shall become, in a quest for expanded selves. Again, this is a familiar story line—the quest for wider significance and expanded identities, socialness and human mutuality, a quest which Willis (1993) feels to be part of the experiences of being human.

Can our idealized, reimagined story line be realized? Can we overcome those binary, essentialized, and hierarchical categories that saturate our language (e.g., native vs. non-native speakers)? Can we appropriate those "first world" theories to understand and analyze "third world" experiences (Spivak, 1990) while trying to rework and destabilize those categories? In what ways can our local stories and lived experiences contribute to the knowledge and discourse of the discipline? It is to a discussion of these issues that we turn in the next section.

## CONTRIBUTION OF LOCAL KNOWLEDGE TO THE DISCIPLINE: SOCIOCULTURAL SITUATEDNESS OF ENGLISH LANGUAGE LEARNING, TEACHING, AND USE

> Any episode of human action must occur in a specific cultural, historical, and institutional context, and this influences how such action is carried out. (Wertsch, 2000, p. 18)

Although many sociocultural and critical researchers have pointed to the sociocultural situatedness of language learning, teaching, and use (Canagarajah 1999a, 2000; Pennycook, 2000a, 2000b; Wertsch, 2000), mainstream TESOL methodologies are still mainly informed by studies and experiences situated in Anglo-societies such as the United States, Canada, Australia, or Britain. This Anglo-centric knowledge base constitutes the canons of the discipline and often gets exported to periphery countries as pedagogical expertise to be followed by local education workers. Drawing on our own lived experiences in different sociocultural contexts, we shall discuss the value of local knowledge to the discipline with reference to the questions of (a) what counts as "good pedagogy" and (b) the relationship between investment and language learning.

### What Counts as "Good Pedagogy"?

Our local stories and lived experiences tell us that such a question should be rephrased as follows: What counts as good pedagogy *in specific sociocultural contexts*? For instance, consider Mr. Qi's bilingual teaching strategy and

Wendy and her peers' code-mixing and code-switching practices which have helped them gain both confidence and fluency in using English for meaningful communication (see Wendy's story excerpts, discussed earlier). These bilingual teaching and communicative practices are likely to be devalued or frowned on under current Anglo-based orthodox pedagogies of the discipline. Reflecting on these locally viable learning and communicative practices, Wendy writes the following:

> One of the tenets of the communicative approach is to use authentic materials, which are often mis-defined as those written by and about native-English speakers. In the early 70s, when I was learning English in an intensive English program, the only "authentic" material that was available for use was Linguaphone. A challenge of learning to speak English back then was to practice speaking English for meaningful communication. To speak means to speak to someone about something that is relevant to our lives. The Linguaphone materials we used in class, though authentic perhaps for overseas English speakers, were not usable for oral communication in the local context. China was experiencing a social and political turmoil then that affected our lives in one way or another. Our conversation practice often started with friendly exchanges and quickly moved to current issues, and yet few of us were equipped with the language needed to carry out our conversation. We were in desperate need of vocabulary to express our feelings and thoughts that were of our immediate concern, yet the much-needed vocabulary was nowhere to be found in the "authentic" materials. The gap between the language we found in the materials and the language needed for relevant and meaningful communication turned every opportunity to speak English "a creative process of transforming the sign system of English to represent a discourse alien to it" (Canagarajah, 2000, p. 125). We often laughed at each other as we created new words to express ourselves. We were clearly aware that we were speaking Chinese–English, yet in our local context, nothing could be more authentic than that.

Consider also Nobu's encounter with his mentor, Mr. Okuhara. The text reading and translation method of Mr. Okuhara will hardly receive any commendation from current methodologies of the discipline. However, it was precisely Mr. Okuhara's teaching that had turned a little boy around and aroused in him great interest and motivation to learn English, and more importantly, to enter into a new world and learn about that world through English (more on this in the next section).

We believe that the discipline needs to be informed and reshaped by more such local stories as told by different learners, teachers, and researchers situated in different sociocultural contexts. Often found in the discipline are implicit claims to context-free knowledge about ELT methodologies. However, any relevant pedagogical knowledge has to be locally produced and negotiated in different sociocultural contexts (Canagarajah, 1999a, 2000; Holliday, 1994; Lin, 1999; Pennycook, 2000a, 2000b).

## Investment and Language Learning: Agency, Identity, and Ownership

From Wendy's reflection in the earlier section and her autobiographic excerpts, we can see that the question of pedagogy is closely related to the question of what fuels language learning—to the learner's agency and identity-making in appropriating English in his or her learning process (Norton, 1997, 2000). For instance, the bilingual discursive space that was creatively opened up by Mr. Qi helped Wendy and her peers experiment with and expand their identities—they felt liberated to comment on sensitive social and political issues in this bilingual space that they temporarily created and occupied for themselves. In Wendy's words, *English became a language of dreams and a language of freedom.* Furthermore, Wendy's aspired identity (as an interpreter) has fueled her language learning efforts. Reflecting on the question of what fuels her language learning, Wendy writes the following:

> In analyzing my earlier experience as an English language learner, I have come to realize that imagination was an important source of my motivation. With a dream of becoming an interpreter that I inherited from my parents and took it as my own, learning the English language took on a personal meaning. English was no longer a simple school subject; it was a tool for me to realize my dream, to become who I wanted to be. The prospect of becoming an interpreter, a highly desired position in China, continued to fuel my motivation and got me through all the difficult times.

In all of our stories, it appears that issues of agency, ownership, and identity are closely related to the learner's investment in English. For instance, in Mehdi's story, his dissatisfaction with the position and social identity as a "low-level electronic technician" led to his decision to invest in studying English in order to become an English specialist. The decision to shift from the identity of a technician to the identity of a university English major and later an English expert has kept his investment strong despite severe hardships; for example, having to work to provide for his family and at the same time to continue with his university English studies.

In Nobu's story, the examination system constructed a "failure identity" for him when he failed to enter a prestigious high school which his elder brother was attending. He lost interest in learning and studying. His subsequent important encounter with the English teacher, Mr. Okuhara, has turned things totally around for him. Nobu recalls the following:

> Mr. Okuhara's teaching style was quite old-fashioned, mainly grammar-translation based. We sat at a desk, face to face, and I translated sentence by sentence. With this traditional teaching method, which is often criticized

for its ineffectiveness and inappropriateness for second/foreign language learning, Mr. Okuhara opened up a new world for me. I read a variety of English books with him, such as the biography of Dr. Schweitzer, the adventure story of *Arabian Nights*, Sir Arthur Conan Doyle's mysteries, George Gissing's *The Private Papers of Henry Ryecroft*, Bertrand Russell's *The Conquest of Happiness*, and so on and so forth.

Mr. Okuhara validated in Nobu a sense of a worthwhile young man with great potentials to learn different kinds of knowledge in the world: philosophy, biography, adventure, and history. These readings were made available to him through the supportive interactions with Mr. Okuhara, who provided a scaffolding (the L2–L1 annotation format) for Nobu to see his own potential and to develop a new sense of self: He was no longer that failure student, an identity constructed by the examination results; he was a young man being treated with respect and trust by a supportive teacher who lead him into a whole new world of learning, mediated by Mr. Okuhara's text-reading-translating teaching method. Nobu began to know who he was, and who he wanted to become: an English teacher like Mr. Okuhara himself—a new identity totally different from that failure identity imposed on him by the examination system. This lead to his investment in English learning.

In Angel's story, her investment in learning English was initially fueled by her desire to pass examinations, to achieve good results, and to please her parents. However, when she entered into a community of practice in her circle of girlfriends, where it was trendy to write to overseas pen pals, her investment in English was fueled by her desire to enter into a new world with a new self in English; she felt that she could express her feelings more freely, as if in a third space, free from sanctions of the Chinese adult world. Her adolescent bonding with her pen pal, Gretchen, and her opening up of herself in English to her overseas pen pals, has led to a new sense of self for her—that English is not just a tool for getting rewards from adults; it's a tool for her to get into different sociocultural groups, forming new friendships on an entirely different plane from her ordinary friendships.

All these stories witness the complex, intimate relations among agency, ownership, identity, and investment in L2 learning. We can see how learning a language both shapes and is shaped by one's way of knowing, being, and behaving in a specific sociocultural context. This seems to touch on the same point suggested by Canagarajah (2000) when he discusses local agents' appropriation of English in specific contexts. In this regard, stories of language learners situated in different sociocultural contexts can make valuable contribution to the knowledge and discourse of the discipline. Much of conventional SLA research has been written by those who tend to simplify the worlds of their subjects, consciously or unconsciously. Personal stories (which are simultaneously sociological and political) told by the agents themselves unfold the complex and multidimen- sional nature of mastering and appropriating English in different sociocultural contexts. We believe it is time to revision the field and propose an alternative story line and research program for the discipline.

## REVISIONING THE FIELD: FROM TESOL TO TEACHING ENGLISH FOR GLOCALIZED COMMUNICATION

> Rather than a coercive monologue by the industrialized world, contemporary international cultural relations appear more like a dialogue, albeit unbalanced in favor of industrialized countries, but a dialogue still.... "Glocalization," by accounting for both global and local factors, is a more appropriate conceptual framework to capture and accommodate international communication processes ... the concept originated in Japanese agricultural and business practices of "global localization, a global outlook adapted to local conditions." (Kraidy, 2001, pp. 32–33)

In the preceding part, we see that just as Wendy and Angel were beginning to feel that English had become part of their identities, they were confronted with processes of "Othering" which made them feel like "imposters" (Bourdieu, 1991), illegitimate speakers of English, mainly because of their local "accent"—their voices not being heard as "authentic English voices." It seems to be no accident that only Wendy and Angel's stories told of experiences of being "Othered." Unlike Iran and Japan, Hong Kong was a British colony. As for Wendy's experiences in Canada, it is likely that the immigrant speaker is subject to processes of subordination and Othering, a bit like subjects in colonies.

The discourses in the applied linguistics and TESOL literature tend to classify people into native English speakers and non-native English speakers. These categories also frequently appear in job advertisements for English teachers in Asian countries (e.g., "native English speakers preferred," "native English speakers only," found in the classified ads for English teachers in *The Korean Times*, February 10, 2001), and "native" and "non-native" categories of teachers receive different kinds of treatment and status in institutional structures (Canagarajah, 1999b; Lai, 1999; Oda, 1994, 1996; cf. Leung et al., 1997). These dichotic, essentialized categories are so pervasive in our consciousness that we even reproduce them in our own stories. Many learners of English in Asia subscribe to the story line that native English speakers are better English teachers than non-native English speakers. However, the world is increasingly witnessing "the decline of the native speaker," as Graddol (1999) puts it,

First, ... the proportion of the world's population speaking English as a first language is declining, and will continue to do so in the foreseeable future. Second, the international status of English is changing in profound ways: in future it will be a language used mainly in multilingual contexts as a second language and for communication between non-native speakers. Third, the decline of the native speaker will be explored in terms of a changing ideological discourse about languages, linguistic competence, and identity. (p. 57)

Following in the footsteps of researchers doing important work in this area (e.g., Braine, 1999; Canagarajah, 1999a, 1999b; Graddol, 1999; Kubota, 2001), we continue with their work by attempting to further destabilize the native speaker vs. non-native speaker categories and proposing to erase the boundaries. The approach we take is to problematize the colonial *Self-Other* and *Master-Friday* story line underlying these categories.

If altering the discourse can lead to doing things differently (Erni, 1998), what difference will it make when we develop new ways of talking about English speakers and English voices by acknowledging the various, nohierarchicalized ways of being an English speaker? As a step toward such reimagination and recreation of a new discourse, we propose a paradigm shift from doing TESOL to doing TEGCOM. One rationale behind this proposal comes from the recognition that the name TESOL already assigns dichotic *Self–Other* subject positions to teacher and learner: it implicitly positions the Anglo-teacher as *Self* and the learner in a life trajectory of forever being the *Other*, and thus continuing the colonial story line of Friday—the "slave boy" resigned to the destiny of forever trying to approximate the "master's language" but never legitimately recognized as having achieved it (de Certeau, 1984, p. 155). Such a story line precludes an alternative one as proposed above.

If one is willing to shift his or her attention from the differential status of speakers (e.g., "native—non-native," "mainstream—minority," "first world—third world," etc.) to the mutual practice of communication itself (e.g., adopting an alternative story line proposed above), then we see in the postmodern, glocalized world today that there are increasing, legitimate demands for cross-cultural communication to be construed and conducted as an endeavor of mutual efforts on egalitarian footings. The "communicative burden" in cross-cultural, cross-ethnic interaction is increasingly conceived as something that should be shouldered more or less equally by all participants in communication, and not just the "non-native English speaker" (Goldstein, 2003; Lippi-Green, 1997). Both the name and discourses of TESOL assume that it is the "Other-language" speakers who need to be subjected to "pedagogical treatment" (de Certeau, 1984, p. 155)—to enable them to make themselves intelligible to "native English speakers." This lopsided story line has its historical roots in the colonial era. However, in today's multipolar world, we can imagine a TEGCOM class in which all learners are monolingual "native English speakers" who need to be instructed in the ways of using English for cross-cultural communication (e.g., cross-cultural pragmatic skills and awareness) in specific sociocultural contexts (e.g., for conducting business in Japan, China, or Iran). If we can start to reimagine the story lines underlying TESOL and its discourses, we can perhaps rework and destabilize the hegemonic relations in different settings in the world.

Our lived experiences testify to the claim that when English learners have a sense of ownership of the language and are treated as legitimate English speakers, writers, and users, they will continue to invest in learning English and appropriating it for their own purposes in their specific contexts (see earlier discussion). The answer to the question of whether an English speaker will serve as a good teacher or model is largely socioculturally situated (e.g., depending on the interactional practices that the teacher and his or her students co-create in the sociocultural context in which they are situated) and cannot be determined (or even predicted) a priori based on the person's plus- or minus- "native speaker" status. We, therefore, see these dichotic categories more as interested social constructions serving existing power structures (Foucault, 1980) in the TESOL field than as innocuous academic terms with much theoretical or practical value. Yet, our proposal is more than just renaming the field to erase the aforementioned dichotic boundaries. We are proposing a rethinking and revisioning of the field from the perspective of sociocultural situatedness. This involves proposing an alternative theoretical orientation and an alternative research program for the field. We attempt these two tasks in the following two sections.

## Proposing a Theoretical Orientation for TEGCOM: Sociocultural Situatedness, Postcolonial Performativity, and Glocalization

TESOL as a discipline and industry has traditionally seen its mission as that of developing the most effective technologies and pedagogies for the teaching and learning of English around the world (see the mission statement of the organization). Under this view, English is seen as a neutral tool for mediating science and technology and international, cross-cultural communication. Yet, the global spread of English has immense and complex sociopolitical implications that need to be addressed, and those who claim that they are not going to deal politically, and ideologically, with the spread of English are in fact doing what they claim they are not: they are taking a specific ideological position on the global spread of English (Pennycook, 2000b). Our collective stories resonate with Pennycook's notion of postcolonial performativity, which means:

... first, viewing the global dominance of English not ultimately as an apriori imperialism but rather as a product of the local hegemonies of English. As Foucault (1980:94) puts it in the context of arguing for a notion of power not as something owned by some and not by others but as something that operates on and through all points of society, "major dominations are the hegemonic effects that are sustained by all these confrontations." Any concept of the global hegemony of English must therefore be understood in terms of the complex sum of contextualized understandings of social hegemonies ... but such hegemonies are also filled with complex local contradictions, with the resistance and appropriations that are a crucial part of the postcolonial context. (p. 117)

English as appropriated by local agents serves diverse sets of intentions and purposes in their respective local contexts, whether it be the acquisition of a socially upward identity, or the creation of a bilingual space for critical explorations of self and the society. Learning English in the new information age is increasingly oriented toward global, cross-cultural communication in multilingual contexts, and yet there also exist side-by-side local forces and structures which shape a learner's investment and understanding of what it means to learn English in the specific context in which he or she is situated (e.g., for making the grades, passing the exams to enter the university, or for enjoying hip-hop music and raps, doing ICQ or playing games on the Internet). The authors appropriate the term *glocalization* to refer to the interaction of both global and local forces in specific sociocultural contexts where local social actors are confronted with (often, albeit not always, imposed) the task of learning and using English, and where local social actors engage in different creative practices, exercising their creative discursive agency (Lin, 1999) and strategies of appropriation (Canagarajah, 1995, 2000). Although no sweeping generalizations can be made about such strategies and agency, the discipline as we understand it has, so far, not considered it among its central tasks to research on the sociocultural situatedness of TESOL practices, and on how the spread of English has impacted on the lives of local people in different parts of the world, for better or worse. TESOL as a field, guided by its instrumental rationality of finding the most effective technology for teaching and learning English around the world has not concerned itself with the meta-analytical project of reflexively understanding its own implication in shaping the life chances, identities, and life trajectories of local people in different parts of the world. In its single-minded pursuit of the most effective technology of teaching English, it has, however, missed the point: the "good" pedagogy and "effective" methods of learning cannot be found without taking a socioculturally situated perspective, and without addressing issues of agency, identity, creative appropriation, and resistance of local social actors when they are confronted with the task of learning English in their specific local contexts (see earlier discussion). The authors proposal of changing the name of the field is to provoke a rethinking and revisioning of the field, taking into consideration the perspectives of sociocultural situatedness and the processes of postcolonial performativity and glocalization.

## Proposing a Research Program for TEGCOM

To shift the research focus from the pursuit of universal, context-free knowledge about the most effective technology to teach English (which we believe has long misguided the TESOL discipline), the authors propose the following alternative set of central research goals for TEGCOM: (a) a deeper understanding of diverse local pedagogical practices and beliefs in their sociocultural situatedness; (b) a deeper understanding of issues of agency, identity, ownership, appropriation, resistance, and English language learning, teaching, and use in diverse sociocultural contexts; and (c) a deeper understanding of various cross-cultural encounters in diverse sociocultural settings. To achieve these goals, we propose the following preliminary outline of directions for the development of a research program:

*(a) Toward socially, culturally, historically, and institutionally situated perspectives in doing research on English language learning, curriculum development, and teacher education in a variety of contexts; foregrounding the social, cultural, and historical situatedness of human communication and activities.* It is important not to reduce sociocultural situatedness to merely "interpersonal" or "social interactional" (Wertsch, 2000). Many conventional TESOL studies have focused on social interactions in both instructional and noninstructional settings in an attempt to identify optimal linguistic input or expert–novice interactional features for language acquisition to take place. However, few studies have examined these social interactions in their sociocultural situatedness. Nevertheless, it is exciting to find a few recent studies in this direction, for instance, Ouyang (2000)'s anthropological study of a Chinese teacher who tried to apply the communicative language teaching pedagogy in her rural hometown in Mainland China.

*(b) Decentering the production of the discipline's knowledge and discourse from Anglo-speaking countries to a diversity of sociocultural contexts in the world.* It is when the discipline has a focus on the sociocultural situatedness of human activities that it will provide a space for the voices of local teachers, learners, parents, and communities situated in diverse sociocultural contexts of the world to be heard in the discipline's journals and knowledge validating arenas, and will give legitimacy to and value the local knowledge and discourses produced by studies situated in contexts outside of the traditional "English-speaking" countries. To

date, such studies are still in the minority (e.g., Canagarajah, 1993; Lin, 1999; Norton, 1989).

*(c) Drawing on anthropological research methods and interpretive sociological methods, including narrative analysis, discourse analysis, school, cultural, and critical ethnography, cultural studies, and autobiographic studies.* To study the issues of agency, identity, ownership, appropriation, resistance, and English language learning, teaching and use in diverse sociocultural contexts, and various cross-cultural encounters in diverse sociocultural settings, we need to draw on the wide range of anthropological and interpretive sociological research methodologies. For instance, research studies in the literacy field have drawn heavily on anthropological and sociological methods (e.g., Street, 1995, 2001). The feminist methods of narrative analysis and autobiographic studies (e.g., Pavlenko, 1998, 2001; Richardson, 1985, 1997) and methods of cultural and postcolonial studies (e.g., Hallam & Street, 2000) will also be needed, especially in research that engages with issues of agency, identity, appro- priation, and cross-cultural encounters. A recent study in this direction is Lam's (2000) interesting study of a Cantonese-speaking immigrant boy's design of self and English literacy development through creating a virtual community of Japanese pop star fans on the Internet.

By proposing an alternative name, an alternative story line, an alternative theoretical orientation, and an alternative research program for the field, the authors are not "flirting" with interesting ideas or rhetorical moves, but attempting to create alternative discourses and practices, to give legitimacy to local knowledge, to destabilize and rework ideologies that underlie current disciplinary discourses and knowledge production practices. A paradigm shift does not start with a single chapter; there is certainly much, much more work to do. It is, however, with the modest hope that it can initiate some critical discussion and rethinking of the field, that this chapter has been written. Although the aforementioned outline of a research program is still preliminary, we can see that there have already been some exciting studies happening in these directions. We believe that as more and more studies situated in different societies of the world are given a space to contribute to knowledge production of the discipline, the discipline as a whole can be revisioned and regenerated in the postmodern, multipolar, glocalized world.

## ACKNOWLEDGMENTS

We would like to thank the editor, Suresh Canagarajah, for his unfailing support and his many helpful comments and suggestions. Special thanks also go to John Erni, Tara Goldstein, and Allan Luke for reading and commenting on earlier drafts of this chapter.

# REFERENCES

Bhabha, H. (1994). *The location of culture*. London: Routledge.

Bourdieu, P. (1986). The forms of capital. In J. G. Richardson (Ed.), *Handbook of theory and research for the sociology of education* (pp. 241–258). New York: Greenwood Press.

Bourdieu, P. (1991). *Language and symbolic power*. Cambridge, England: Cambridge University Press.

Braine, G. (Ed.). (1999). *Non-native educators in English language teaching*. Mahwah, NJ: Lawrence Erlbaum Associates.

Canagarajah, A. S. (1993). Critical ethnography of a Sri Lankan classroom: Ambiguities in student opposition to reproduction through ESOL. *TESOL Quarterly, 27,* 601–626.

Canagarajah, A. S. (1995). From critical research practice to critical research reporting. *TESOL Quarterly, 29,* 321–331.

Canagarajah, A. S. (1999a). *Resisting linguistic imperialism in English teaching*. Oxford, England: Oxford University Press.

Canagarajah, A. S. (1999b). Interrogating the native speaker fallacy Non-linguistic roots, non-pedagogical results. In G. Braine (Ed.), *Non-native educators in English language teaching* (pp. 77–92). Mahwah, NJ: Lawrence Erlbaum Associates.

Canagarajah, A. S. (2000). Negotiating ideologies through English: Strategies from the periphery. In T. Ricento (Ed.), *Ideology, politics and language policies: Focus on English* (pp. 121–132). Amsterdam: Benjamins.

Casey, K. (1995). The new research in education. In M. W. Apple (Ed.), *Review of research in education* (p. 21). Washington, DC: American Educational Research Association.

de Certeau, M. (1984). *The practice of everyday life*. Berkeley, CA: University of California Press.

Ellis, C., & Bochner, A. (2000). Autoethnography, personal narrative, reflexivity: Researcher as subject. In N. K. Dennzin & Y. S. Lincoln (Eds.), *Handbook of qualitative research* (pp. 733–768). Thousand Oaks, CA: Sage.

Erni, J. N. (1998). Ambiguous elements: Rethinking the gender/sexuality matrix in an epidemic. In N. Roth & K. Hogan (Eds.), *Gendered epidemic: Representations of women in the age of AIDS* (pp. 3–29). New York: Routledge.

Foucault, M. (1980). Truth and power. In C. Gordon (Ed.), *Power/knowledge: Selected interviews and other writings, 1972–1977* (pp. 109–133). New York: Pantheon.

Ghandi, M. K. (1982). *An autobiography or the story of my experiments with truth* (translated from the Gujarati by Mahadev Desai). Ahmedabad, India: Navajivan Publishing House.

Goldstein, T. (2003). *Teaching and learning in a multilingual school: Academic and linguistic dilemmas*. Mahwah, NJ: Lawrence Erlbaum Associates.

Graddol, D. (1999). The decline of the native speaker. In D. Graddol & U. H. Meinhof (Eds.), *English in a changing world* (pp. 57–68). *AILA Review, 13,* International Association of Applied Linguistics.

Hall, S. (1996). The problem of ideology: Marxism without guarantees. In D. Moley & K.-H. Chen (Eds.), *Stuart Hall: Critical dialogues in cultural studies* (pp. 25–46). London: Routledge.

Hallam, E., & Street, B. V. (Eds.). (2000). *Cultural encounters: Representing 'otherness.'* London: Routledge.

Harré, R. (1998). *The singular self: An introduction to the psychology of personhood*. London: Sage.

Harre, R., & van Langenhove, L. (1998). *Positioning theory: Moral contexts of intentional action.* Oxford, England: Blackwell.

Holliday, A. (1994). *Appropriate methodology and social context.* New York: Cambridge University Press.

Kraidy, M. M. (2001). From imperialism to glocalization: A theoretical framework for the information age. In B. Ebo (Ed.), *Cyberimperialism? Global relations in the new electronic frontier* (pp. 27–42). Westport, CT: Praeger.

Kramsch, C., & Lam, W. S. E. (1999). Textual identities: The importance of being non-native. In G. Braine (Ed.), *Non-native educators in English language teaching* (pp. 57–72). Mahwah, NJ: Lawrence Erlbaum Associates.

Kubota, R. (2001). Discursive construction of the images of U.S. classrooms. *TESOL Quarterly, 35,* 9–38.

Lai, M.-L. (1999). JET and NET: A comparison of native-speaking English teachers schemes in Japan and Hong Kong. *Language, Culture and Curriculum, 12,* 215–228.

Lam, W. S. E. (2000). L2 literacy and the design of the self: A case study of a teenager writing on the Internet. *TESOL Quarterly, 34,* 457–482.

Lantolf, J., & Pavlenko, A. (2001). (S)econd (L)anguage (A)ctivity Theory: Understanding second language learners as people. In M. Breen (Ed.), *Learner contributions to language learning: New directions in research* (pp. 141–158). Harlow, England: Pearson Education Limited.

Lave, J., & Wenger, E. (1991). *Situated learning: Legitimate peripheral participation.* Cambridge, England: Cambridge University Press.

Leung, C., Harris, R., & Rampton, B. (1997). The idealized native speaker, reified ethnicities, and classroom realities. *TESOL Quarterly, 31,* 543–560.

Lin, A. M. Y. (1999). Doing-English-lessons in the reproduction or transformation of social worlds? *TESOL Quarterly, 33,* 393–412.

Lin, A. M. Y., Wang, W., Akamatsu, N., & Riazi, M. (2001, February). *Asian voices: Language learning, identity, and sociocultural positioning.* Paper presented at the TESOL Annual Convention, St. Louis, MO.

Lippi-Green, R. (1997). *English with an accent: Language, ideology, and discrimination in the United States.* London: Routledge.

Lvovich, N. (1997). *The multilingual self: An inquiry into language learning.* Mahwah, NJ: Lawrence Erlbaum Associates.

Lyotard, J. P. (1979). *The postmodern condition: A report on knowledge.* Minneapolis: University of Minnesota Press.

Norton, B. (1989). Towards a pedagogy of possibility in the teaching of English internationally: People's English in South Africa. *TESOL Quarterly, 23,* 401–420.

Norton, B. (1997). Language, identity, and the ownership of English. *TESOL Quarterly, 31,* 409–429.

Norton, B. (2000). *Identity and language learning: Gender, ethnicity and educational change.* Harlow, England: Longman.

Oda, M. (1994). Against linguicism: A reply to Richard Marshall. *The Language Teacher, 18,* 39–40.

Oda, M. (1996, June). *Applied linguistics in Japan: The dominance of English in the discourse community.* Paper presented at the International Conference on Language Rights, Hong Kong Polytechnic University.

Ouyang, H. (2000). One way ticket: A story of an innovative teacher in Mainland China. *Anthropology and Education Quarterly, 31,* 397–425.

Pavlenko, A. (1998). Second language learning by adults: Testimonies of bilingual writers. *Issues in Applied Linguistics, 9,* 3–19.

Pavlenko, A. (2001). In the world of the tradition, I was unimagined: Negotiation of identities in cross-cultural autobiographies. *International Journal of Bilingualism, 5,* 317–344.

Pennycook, A. (2000a). Language, ideology and hindsight: Lessons from colonial language policies. In T. Ricento (Ed.), *Ideology, politics and language policies: Focus on English* (pp. 49–65). Amsterdam: Benjamins.

Pennycook, A. (2000b). English, politics, ideology: From colonial celebration to postcolonial performativity. In T. Ricento (Ed.), *Ideology, politics and language policies: Focus on English* (pp. 107–119). Amsterdam: Benjamins.

Richardson, L. (1985). *The new other woman.* New York: Free Press.

Richardson, L. (1997). *Fields of play (constructing an academic life).* New Brunswick, NJ: Rutgers University Press.

Robertson, R. (1995). Glocalization: Time—space and homogeneity—heterogeneity. In M. Featherstone, S. Lash, & R. Robertson (Eds.), *Global modernities* (pp. 25–44). London: Sage.

Spivak, G. C. (1988). Can the subaltern speak? In C. Nelson & L. Grossberg (Eds.), *Marxism and the interpretation of culture* (pp. 280–316). Urbana: University of Illinois Press.

Spivak, G. C. (1990). *The post-colonial critic.* New York: Routledge.

Street, B. V. (1995). *Social literacies: Critical approaches to literacy in development, ethnography and education.* London: Longman.

Street, B. V. (Ed.). (2001). *Literacy and development: Ethnographic perspectives.* London: Routledge.

Toohey, K. (2000). *Learning English at school: Identity, social relations and classroom practice.* Clevedon, England: Multilingual Matters.

Trinh, T. M.-H. (1988). Not you/like you: Post-colonial women and the interlocking questions of identity and difference. *Inscriptions, 3,* 71–77.

Wertsch, J. V. (2000). Intersubjectivity and alterity in human communication. In N. Budwig, I. C. Uzgiris, & J. V. Wertsch (Eds.), *Communication: An arena for development* (pp. 17–31). Stamford, CT: Ablex.

Willis, P. E. (1977). *Learning to labour: How working class kids get working class jobs.* Farnborough, England: Saxon House.

Willis, P. E. (1993). Symbolic creativity. In A. Gray & J. McGuigan (Eds.), *Studying culture: An introductory reader* (pp. 206–216). London: Edward Arnold.

Young, R. (1999). Sociolinguistic approaches to SLA. *Annual Review of Applied Linguistics, 19,* 105–132.

# Part IV

# IMAGINING CLASSROOM POSSIBILITIES

# Chapter 10

# Talking Knowledge Into Being in an Upriver Primary School in Brunei

Peter Martin
*University of Leicester*

## INTRODUCTION

The purpose of this chapter is to look at how knowledge, and what sort of knowledge, is talked into being in one small primary school in Brunei, in an upriver interior community where three minority groups exist side by side. Following a period of ethnographic fieldwork in the community, subsequent visits focused on the school, and on one classroom, in particular. This study provides a microanalysis of the language practices in one lesson. Interaction around text in this classroom plays a key role in shaping what is considered as knowledge and competence for the pupils. Emerging from the discussion, I focus on how such knowledge is talked into being in educational encounters around text. The discussion is framed within the context of the ideologies and tensions of the bilingual education system in Brunei. Following this brief introduction, I provide some background for the study, both the general context of Brunei, and the specific local context in which the study took place. The major part of the chapter is a discussion of one lesson and the way the participants in the lesson attempt to coconstruct the meaning of the text that is the focus of the lesson. In the final part of the chapter, I discuss the ways the participants use local knowledge and a range of linguistic resources to contest the knowledge in the textbook and the curriculum.

## THE BRUNEI CONTEXT

Brunei is an independent Malay Islamic Monarchy on the northern coast of Borneo, sandwiched between the Malaysian states of Sabah and Sarawak. Although the country is small in size (5,765 sq km), and has a population of only 300,000, there is nevertheless a considerable heterogeneity of peoples within its borders.

At its zenith in the early part of the 16th century, Brunei was a powerful maritime empire with influence over a large area. By the mid-19th century, the history of Brunei had become inextricably linked to the ambitions of James Brooke, the so-called first "White Rajah" of Sarawak. Between 1841 and 1905, as Sarawak expanded eastward, Brunei lost approximately 95% of its territory to the Brooke dynasty. By the beginning of the 20th century, Brunei was a "dying kingdom" (Horton, 1988, p. 5) that "teetered on the brink of oblivion" (Saunders, 1994, p. 97) having lost all but 5% of its territory. The reason that Brunei did not disappear from the map altogether was in part due to the fact that, in 1888, Britain had signed a Protectorate Agreement with Brunei that guaranteed the continued existence of the country. This agreement was to last until 1984 when Brunei became independent. Another factor that has had a major impact on modern-day Brunei was the discovery of oil in 1929. This discovery dramatically transformed the economy and fortunes of Brunei. From a country deep in debt at the beginning of the 20th century, by the end of the century it was one of the wealthiest countries (per capita) in the world, and second only to Japan in Asia.

In providing the background for this study, there are a number of central issues to which reference needs to be made. Of fundamental importance is the historical, numerical, and political dominance of the "Malay" center, specifically, the "Brunei Malay" center in the country. The cornerstones of Brunei's desire to assert an identity for Bruneians and to "define the nation in exclusively Malay terms" (Gunn, 1997, p. 214) are the concepts of *bangsa* ("race"), *negara* ("nation" or "state"), and *bahasa* ("language"). The slogan "*Berbahasa Satu, Berbangsa Satu, Bernegara Satu*" ("One Language, One Race, One Nation") is prominently displayed on a mural in the capital city, under the patronage of the red emblem from the national flag. Since independence, the state ideology of *Melayu Islam Beraja* ("Malay Islamic Monarchy") has been reaffirmed. This has been defined by Hussainmiya (1994, p. 31) as "an amalgam of Islamic values grafted onto a Brunei Malay culture." It has become one of the subjects in the school curriculum, with its own set of textbooks, and is a compulsory course in Brunei's only university.

The "Malay" population accounts for 66.9% of the total population in the country. The remainder of the population consists of "other indigenous" (6%), Chinese (15.6%), and expatriate workers (11.5%). Included in the category of "indigenous groups of the Malay race" (Government of Brunei, 1961, pp. 118–120) are two Malay-speaking groups (the dominant *Brunei*, and the *Kedayan*), and five other groups each with their own language (the *Tutong, Belait, Dusun, Bisaya*, and *Murut*). Of the seven groups, the Brunei, Kedayan, and Tutong are all Muslim, and the Belait predominantly so. The three remaining groups are traditionally animist, although increasing numbers of the Dusun and Bisaya groups are becoming Muslim, whereas the majority of the Murut are Christian. The status of non-Muslim "Malays" (which in itself appears to be a contradiction in terms, given the value usually ascribed to "Malay") in Brunei has been a source of some debate. Hashim (1984, p. 4), for example, has suggested that those indigenous people who are non-Muslims, although nevertheless categorized as "Malay," cannot be regarded as full members of the national community.

The official language of the country is *Bahasa Melayu*, but the variety of Malay spoken by the dominant group, Brunei Malay, is the *de facto* national dialect. In most areas of Brunei, although not the area in this study, Brunei Malay, or a form of Brunei Malay, is the language of daily communication. *Bahasa Melayu*, on the other hand, has little currency in everyday interaction. The languages of the other groups (Tutong, Belait, Dusun, Bisaya, and Murut) are used for intraethnic communication in the districts where these groups live, although increasingly a form of Brunei Malay (or a mixture of Brunei Malay and local language) is encroaching on the domains formerly held by the local language (Kershaw, 1994a; Martin, 1996a, 1996b).

I have already made reference to the historical ties between Brunei and Britain. One corollary of this link is the position of the English language in the country. English education first became available in 1951 but only boys considered to have a high academic potential were given the opportunity to go to the one English school. Many of the early graduates of English medium education are now in senior government positions (Ożóg, 1996). Up until independence, there were separate streams of education, with the highest achieving children going to English medium schools and the less academically-gifted children having their education in Malay. In 1985, in the year following independence, a bilingual system of education, referred to locally as *dwibahasa* ("two languages") was implemented. This system, in use today, ensures the "sovereignty of the Malay language," and at the same time recognizes the importance of the English language (Government of Brunei Darussalam, 1985, p. 2). Within this bilingual system of education there is, on the one hand, the emphasis on Islamic and traditional values and, on the other, the stress on technological change and English as the international language of communication. In this system, the first 3 years of primary school, in all areas of the country, are in Malay. From the fourth year of primary school onward, mathematics, geography, and science are all taught in English. From the fourth year of primary school and beyond into secondary and tertiary education, the system actually privileges English.

The emphasis on education in English, despite government rhetoric about the importance of Malay, continues to privilege sections of Brunei society, most notably the elite, and continues to act as an avenue of social mobility (Gunn, 1997; Ożóg, 1996). One stated reason for recognizing the importance of English was based on "its importance for academic study" and its ability to facilitate entry of students to institutions of higher education overseas (Government of Brunei Darussalam, 1985, p. 2). An additional note stated that should Brunei be able to provide its own facilities for higher education in the future, the bilingual policy would be subject to review. Less than a year later, Brunei did establish a university but there has been no change in the policy and, paradoxically, this university actually privileges English at the expense of Malay.

I return to some of the points referred to earlier and a discussion of the paradoxes and tensions inherent in the bilingual education system in Brunei following an analysis of the classroom lesson.

## The Local Context

Having provided some introduction to the wider context of Brunei, I now focus on the local context. The study is situated in the interior of the largest district in the country, at a small upriver community well away from the Malay center. The settlement is one of the most sparsely populated areas of the country, with a total population of 319 (Government of Brunei Darussalam, 1993, p. 4). According to the headman of the community, the population in the 1980s was over 600, but there has been much out-migration to other areas within Brunei, as people seek salaried labor nearer the coast. The main settlement in the area is the village where the school is situated. The community consists of three separate ethnic groups: the *Iban, Penan,* and *Dusun*. The Dusun, it is recalled, are constitutionally one of the "indigenous groups of the Malay race," and it is this group from which the headman is chosen. The other two groups are the Iban and Penan. The Iban are classified as "other indigenous" and are in a majority in the area, and also live in other interior areas of Brunei. The Penan are only to be found in this locality.

Within the major settlement in the community, the Penan, formerly a nomadic group, have settled in a longhouse on one side of the river. The Dusun live in a four-door longhouse, on the opposite side of the river to the Penan house. The Iban live in a number of scattered houses and in a separate settlement about half an hour's walk away from the main village.

I noted earlier that the community has become smaller over the last two decades due to out-migration. There are also changes within the community with increasing numbers of all three groups converting to Islam. Within Borneo as a whole, but especially in Brunei, there has been "a steady flow of individuals out of the non-Islamic ethnic groups … into the Malay ethnic category" (Maxwell, 1980, p. 170). Indeed, it is clear that the policies of the dominant group, the Brunei, have actually promoted the merging of the ethnic groups under the "Malay" umbrella by converting leaders of these groups to Islam (Brown, 1969). Rousseau (1990, p. 283) has noted the "profound effect on social identity" brought about by conversion to Islam. According to Kershaw (1994b, p. xi), for example, the Dusun community "is on the point of disappearance through linguistic and cultural assimilation." With regard to the Penan, Sercombe (1996, 2000) has built up a picture of how this small community is being assimilated and acculturated into Iban cultural practices at the community level and Malay cultural practices at the national level.

Within the community, the language of intergroup communication is Iban (Martin & Sercombe, 1994; Nothofer, 1991), although both Penan and Dusun are used for intragroup communication. Malay (in any form) does not have a wide currency outside the classroom, although as the majority of the teachers in the school are from other areas of Brunei where a form of Brunei Malay is used, communication among these teachers and between the teachers and the villagers is often in Malay. However, in community gatherings, both formal and informal, Iban is the usual means of communication.

The actual focus of this study is one Primary Four classroom of seven pupils out of a total school enrolment of 43. It is recalled that in the bilingual system of education in Brunei, Primary Four is the first year in which some subjects are taught through the medium of English. The class consisted of six girls and one boy. Three of the pupils were Penan, two were Iban (one Muslim and one non-Muslim), and two were Dusun (one Muslim, one non-Muslim). The pupils were, on the whole, very quiet, and little spontaneous talk occurred in the classroom. At break time, however, when the children went out to play on the field adjacent to the school, they became very vocal. Iban is the language of the school playground.

The teacher in the classroom in the study was one of eight teachers in the school. He taught science, mathematics, and geography to this particular class. He had 10 years of teaching experience since the completion of his teacher training certificate at the former Sultan Hassanal Bolkiah Teacher Training College (now part of the Faculty of Education at the University of Brunei Darussalam). He was of Dusun descent, originating from a village in another district. His first language was Dusun and he also spoke Malay (both Brunei Malay and *Bahasa Melayu*), Iban, and English.

## TEXTBOOKS AND KNOWLEDGE

In Brunei, the Ministry of Education provides textbooks for all schools for all subjects. The Curriculum Development Department (CDD) of the Ministry of Education overseas the planning, development, and writing of these textbooks, following closely the syllabus for each subject, which is also devised by the CDD. In line with the aims of the *Dwibahasa* system of education, through its involvement in joint publishing ventures with international publishers, the CDD aims to "provide textbooks which will reflect the culture and aspirations of Brunei Darussalam" (Curriculum Development Department 1990b, Introduction). As the published textbooks follow closely the syllabus devised by the CDD (Curriculum Development Department, 1990a), they have, to a large extent, taken the place of the school syllabi, which have become superfluous for teachers.

Textbooks, according to Barton (1994, p. 180), are used "to learn particular discourses which have been compartmentalized as distinct subjects." His statement that the taking out and putting away of textbooks is one of "the rhythms of school life" (Barton, 1994, p. 181) resonates very clearly with my own observations in this classroom. Textbooks do indeed have a pivotal position in the classroom in this study and in other classrooms that I have observed in Brunei. The teacher usually sticks closely to the textbook, and the content of the textbook in lessons. Much of the lesson is spent talking around specific texts in the textbook, annotating key items in Malay, and only departing from the text to point out differences between the text and the local context.

According to Apple, the major function of the textbook is defining what is taught in schools, that is, "what is granted the status of knowledge" (Apple, 1986, p. 85). A similar claim that the school text embodies "the authorized version of society's valid knowledge" is made by Olson (1989, p. 238). Apple (1993, pp. 55–56) emphasizes the "ideological process" involved in selecting and organizing knowledge for schools, and how this process serves the interests of particular social groups. As we have seen, in the Brunei context, the selection and organization of knowledge in textbooks reflect the "culture and aspirations of Brunei Darussalam." As I noted earlier, the cultural identity of Brunei is positioned as unproblematic by the Malay center in that it is defined exclusively in "Malay" terms. The actual input into the choice of texts and knowledge comes from agencies within this Malay center. In addition, the history of curriculum development, including the organization of textbooks, has been molded by the effects of colonialism in the last two centuries (Heller & Martin-Jones, 2001). Curricular organization and innovation had their roots in Britain, and ideas were transplanted wholesale, into a variety of contexts, such as Brunei.

With regard to textbooks, and the knowledge in texts, the struggle between different interests—those of the Malay center against those of minority groups—can be seen in the lesson which is the focus of this chapter. There are also tensions apparent in the choice of appropriate linguistic resources to talk around the prescribed texts. The interface between spoken language and written text, as noted by Mercer (1995), is clearly important in the construction of knowledge. Heath (1982) has suggested that the social interactional rules of talking around text "define ways in which oral language reinforces, denies, extends, or sets aside the written material" (cited in Heath, 1983, p. 386). This clearly includes the choice of languages. Within the classroom, the role of the participants in the reinforcement, extension, or contestation of what counts as knowledge in the textbook is clearly central to the discussion in this chapter. The central position is taken by the teacher who acts as the mediator of text or, to quote Luke (1988, p. 156), the "custodian and principal interpreter" of the text. Luke's terms not only point to the authoritative nature of the text, and the position of the teacher as the "custodian" of the knowledge enshrined within, but also the teacher's role in the interpretation and, by extension, translation, of the text. The pupils, on the other hand, are positioned as the recipients of teacher-mediated text.

The next section provides the actual analysis of the talk around one particular text in the textbook.

## TALKING KNOWLEDGE INTO BEING IN ONE GEOGRAPHY LESSON

This section looks at how the participants in one classroom unpack the meaning of the textbook, that is, how the knowledge from written text is unpacked or "talked into being" (Green & Dixon, 1993). The aim is to consider how instructional texts are embedded or woven into the interactional practices of the classroom participants, to bridge the gap between the pupils' existing local knowledge and what counts for knowledge in the textbook. For the sake of overall coherence, in the discussion that follows, I focus on one lesson in detail, rather than looking at excerpts from a number of lessons.

The focus of this discussion is a 50-min Geography lesson on the topic, "A Farmer." The lesson centered around the textbook and, in particular, on two texts in English depicting the life of a farmer. One text was a series of nine sketches, with captions underneath, showing the stages of the farming cycle. The other text describes the work of a farmer, named Zainal, during the nine stages of the farming cycle. The reproduced text, provided by the Curriculum Development Department (1990b, pp. 18–19), follows. The terms in bold are as in the original text. The numbers in the text refer to the sketches, which are not reproduced here.

> Zainal bin Ahmad is a farmer. He is self-employed and works on his farm growing vegetables. He must work many hours every day. Zainal **ploughs** his fields ready for the vegetable seeds and seedlings (1). Ploughing is hard work, so he uses a machine to plough the fields. He puts **fertiliser** in the soil to help vegetables grow bigger (2). He grows tomatoes, lettuce, spinach, cucumber and long beans. When he has fertilised the fields, Zainal plants vegetable **seeds** and **seedlings** in neat rows (3). He has to water his growing vegetables every day (4). Every few days, Zainal uses his **hoe** to loosen the soil and to pull out any weeds growing among the young plants (5). Then there are insects who [*sic*] like to eat the vegetables, so Zainal sprays **chemicals** to kill the insects (6). Birds like to eat the vegetables too, so Zainal covers the growing plants with **nets** to keep the birds off (7). After a few weeks, the vegetables are ready to eat. Zainal collects the vegetables. This is called **harvesting** (8). At last the vegetables are ready to be taken to **market** and sold (9). You can see that Zainal must work very hard, but he likes being a farmer.

I first give a brief summary of the 50-min lesson before focusing on particular parts of the lesson in which local knowledge contests textbook knowledge. The lesson started with a brief revision of the topic of the previous lesson, "different kinds of work." Prior to any reference to the textbook, the teacher introduced the "farmer" topic, and placed the topic within the local context. The teacher then told pupils to open their books at page 18, and, for the remainder of the lesson, they mainly focused on, and talked around, the sketches and the written text.

Pupil participation in this lesson was minimal. From the transcripts and my field notes, I counted 35 one-word responses from the pupils, 4 two-word responses, 3 nods of the head, 1 shake of the head, 1 inaudible response, and 1 attempted response where the pupil could not pronounce a word, within the 50-min lesson. There were long stretches of teacher exposition, with no pupil participation. Following the lesson, the teacher suggested that such lack of participation was common in his classroom, and he admitted to being frustrated by this situation. As the excerpts from the transcripts show, Malay was used in an attempt to unlock the meaning of the text, and the teacher encouraged the pupils to use Malay and, on one occasion, Iban.

Clearly, in a chapter of this length, it is not possible to discuss the whole lesson in detail. What I have tried to do is to pick out particular instances where the teacher and pupils negotiate the content of the text. In attempting to provide specific extracts from the lesson there is, of course, the problem that the flow of the lesson is lost. It is, however, not feasible to provide the whole lesson transcript due to space constraints. The actual process of providing an accurate and useful transcript for the lesson is not without problems, too (cf. Alexander, 2000, pp. 438–441). Transcription conventions are provided at the end of the chapter. All names in the transcripts are pseudonyms.

### The "Local Farmer" and the "Textbook Farmer"

Prior to any interaction around the texts, the teacher introduces the topic, "the farmer" (Extract 1, lines 35–38), and contextualizes it within the local situation, attempting to draw on the pupils' existing knowledge. In line 39, there is a shift away from the content of the text. Whereas the text describes (and shows, in the case of the series of sketches) a farmer who grows vegetables and fruit, the teacher introduces the question "how many of your father growing **padi** ('rice')?" (line 39). There is no mention in the text of growing rice. There is thus a distinction between a "vegetable and fruit farmer" (textbook) and a "rice farmer" (local context). The people in this village, and in many other interior communities where there is no easy access to markets, would not necessarily regard those who grow fruit and vegetables for their own consumption as "farmers." The interaction in lines 39 to 54 draws on the pupils' local knowledge of the situation in the village where the school is located.

```
35   (T) OK . but today we are going to learn farmer .. and imam and penghulu
36   <area chief> if you want to know what is a farmer . what does a farmer do
37   every day . ah . where . ah a farmer .. ah . the place where the farmer work .
38   ah . belajar mengenai dengan petani . <learn about farmers> farmer
39   petani <farmer> ah .. how many of your father growing padi? <rice> ah .
40   yang batanam padi berapa orang di sini? . <those of you who grow rice .
41   how many of you here?> Nani . what about your father? .. ada tanam padi?
42   .. <does he grow rice?> what about you Kedong? .. [P NODS HEAD]
43   T: ah . cakap . jangan malu cakap .. <speak . don't be shy to talk> ada tanam
44   padi? ah . <does he grow rice?> Cikgu tahu hal ini . <I know all about
45   this> Cikgu tahu siapa yang tanam padi . siapa yang inda .. <I know who
46   grows rice . who doesn't> what about your father? . tanam padi tak? <does
47   he grow rice or not?>
48   P: [P NODS HEAD]
49   T: ah Mohammad I know . your father growing padi .. <rice> next . tanam
50   padi adalah satu daripada pekerjaan farmer . <growing rice is one of the
51   jobs of a farmer> ah . now . what is a farmer? . what is a farmer? . apa yang
52   farmer itu buat? .. <what is it that a farmer does?>
53   P: menanam padi <grows rice>
54   T: menanam padi . <grows rice> not only padi . <rice> a farmer growing ..
```

A number of observations can be made about this part of the lesson. Despite the teacher's exhortations, and his reference to the local context, the pupils remain, for the most part, reticent. In attempting to draw on the pupils' existing knowledge of the local context, this part of the lesson is accomplished bilingually, in both English and Malay. The teacher annotates much of his exposition in two languages, often following a question or statement in English with the equivalent in Malay (for example, in lines 35–38 and 39–40). A second major point about this extract is the way the teacher contests or extends the textbook knowledge. In the textbook, the "farmer" is positioned as someone who plants vegetables and fruit. This, however, is a normal activity for the majority of folks who live in regions where there is little or no access to markets. Here, in this village, a farmer is someone who plants rice. At the end of this extract, the teacher begins to move back to the knowledge in the textbook with his statement, "not only **padi** ('rice')" (line 54).

In this initial part of the lesson, then, the teacher and pupils establish differences between the local practices of a "farmer" and those suggested by the text. In the next part of the lesson, which I do not discuss in any detail, the teacher directs the pupils to the textbook and, in particular, to the series of nine sketches which show the nine stages of the farming cycle, beginning with "ploughing" (1) and ending with "taking the vegetables to market to be sold" (9). The teacher uses both English and Malay to unpack the meaning of the text in this part of the lesson. The teacher signals the end of this part of the lesson by switching from the pictorial text toward the written text, and he begins to read from the textbook. In the interaction with this text, the teacher and pupils negotiate and contest specific knowledge from the text, and place it within the pupils' own sphere of understanding. The focus, then, is how specific knowledge is talked into being, and what resources, including linguistic resources, the participants draw on, to accomplish this.

### "Mohammed's Father Is Self-Employed"

The teacher begins to read through the "farmer" text to the class (shown later). As he starts the text, he recognizes the potentially difficult item, "self-employed" (line 133), and he annotates his oral rendering of the text with a close Malay equivalent ("bekerja sendiri," literally, "works [by] himself"), and then uses a "completion chorus" strategy to involve the pupils (lines 134–138). The teacher then moves away from the text to exemplify the concept of "self-employed." He refers to the father of one of the pupils who is self-employed. He then asks other pupils in the class and establishes that their fathers work as government employees. The teacher establishes the difference between being "self-employed" and working for an employer such as the Council or Government. In the village, a number of parents work as laborers for the Council, either in the village or in the town on the coast.

132  T: now . what is a farmer? .. [TEACHER READS FROM TEXTBOOK] a farmer "is
133  self-employed and work on his farm growing vegetables" . **jadi petani ini** . *<so*
134  *this farmer>* farmer . **ia bekerja sendiri** . *<he works by himself>* **bekerja** ^
135  *<works* ^ *>*
136  P: **sendiri** *<by himself>*
137  T: self-employed . **kerja** ^  *<works* ^ *>*
138  Ps: **sendiri** *<by himself>*
139  T: **sendiri** .*<by himself>* ah . now . ah .. like . Mohammad . now Mohammad's .
140  Mohammad's father is a self-employed . **dia nada bekerja dengan kerajaan** ..
141  *<he doesn't work with the Government>* like **ah bapa mu kerja sama** ..
142  **Bandaran** . *<your fathers work for .. the Council>* **mereka bekerja dengan** .
143  **kerajaan** . *<they work for the . Government>* employed by the ^ .. Government
144  ah . how about your father?
145  P: **Bandaran** *<the Council>*
146  T: **sama . lagi?** *<the same . any others?>*
147  P: **buruh daerah** *<district labourer>*
148  T: **sama** . *<also the same>* sit down . **bapa kamu semua bekerja dengan kerajaan**
149  *<your fathers all work for the Government>* . **bukan kerja sendiri** . *<they don't*
150  *work for themselves>* . **jadi** *<so>* in this class only one pupil **dia punya** *<whose>*
151  father is self-employed . Mohammad . **yang lain . semua** *<the rest are all>*
152  emmployed by the Government ... **tahu?** *<do you know?>* government .
153  ah government **tahu?** .. *<do you know?>* Inoi . what is a government? . **tahu**
154  **kerajaan**'? *<do you know 'kerajaan'?>* . **tahu kerajaan?** *<do you know*
155  'kerajaan'?>* . ah . ah ... so the farmer "must work many hours every day" .

The teacher's response to the item in the text, "he is self-employed," is to focus on the pupils' existing knowledge of where their own fathers work. To do this, the teacher successfully elicits this information from two pupils, and he is able to use this information in his attempt to make the text meaningful to the pupils. What is clear is that the teacher's and the pupils' transactions around the text are accomplished bilingually. And although the pupils' responses are simple oral completion slots following a cue from the teacher, it is clear that there is some construction of knowledge taking place here.

## "Fertilizing"

The second example demonstrates the confusion between a pupil's own local knowledge and what counts for knowledge in the textbook. The teacher is trying to elicit the term "fertilizing," which appears in the book, both in the caption under sketch number two, and in the written text. The nominated pupil, Siti, has difficulty in pronouncing the term (lines 194–196), and the teacher tries to coax the word out of her, using both English and

Malay. Siti then responds with a Malay label for what she perceives to be happening in the sketch, "scattering." Following the teacher's response, Siti states that "padi" ("rice") is being scattered (line 201). It is clear then, that the meaning of "fertilizing" has not been successfully negotiated at this stage. Following the pupil's incorrect response, the teacher introduces the term *fertilizer* for the first time and then checks whether the pupils understand the term with a question using both English and Malay (lines 202–203). Such a Wh-question is invariably a request for a Malay label, and one pupil duly provides the correct label, "baja" (line 204). After providing positive feedback by repeating the Malay label, the teacher focuses on the pupil's existing knowledge, by asking about names of fertilizers, to which many of the pupils respond (lines 205–207). The final comment from the teacher in this particular sequence emphasizes, in Malay, that rice is planted only after fertilizer has been put down (lines 208–209). The teacher then resumes the oral reading of the text.

193  T: **empat** <*four*> tyre . **dibajak dahulu** . <*it is ploughed first*> what picture is
194  number two? . ah . ah . Siti?
195  P: [ATTEMPTS TO PRONOUNCE 'FERTILISING']
196  T: **boleh sebut** . <*you can pronouce it*> .. number two . picture number two
197  **nombor dua ini** . <*number two*> what picture is number two? . **apa yang dia**
198  **buat**? <*what is he doing?*>
199  P: **bertabur** <*scattering*>
200  T: **apa yang dia bertabur**? <*what is he scattering?*>
201  P: **padi** <*rice seeds*>
202  T: no . not **padi** . not **sayur** <*vegetable*> . no . fertilizer . fertilizer . **tahu** what is
203  fertiliser? <*do you know?*>
204  P: **baja** <*fertiliser*>
205  T: aah . **baja** ah . **apa nama baja**? <*fertiliser . do you know the name of any*
206  *fertiliser?*>
207  Ps: [INAUDIBLE—NAME OF A BRAND OF FERTILISER]
208  T: **kalau baja ditabur baru menanam padi** .. <*once fertiliser has been put down*
209  *only then are the rice seeds planted*> the farmer "plough his field ready for the
210  vegetable seeds and seedlings" . seedlings . seedlings . do you know what is a

The teacher later returns to the subject of "fertilizer," but this time the focus is why fertilizer is used. There is very little pupil response despite much probing in Malay by the teacher (lines 216–223).

216  why the farmer put fertlizer on his land? . **kenapa petani mesti menyimpan**
217  **baja**? . **siapa tahu** . **kenapa** . <*why does the farmer put down fertiliser?*
218  *who knows?. why?*> why? . Kedong . why? . **kenapa dia mesti baja tanah**

219  **dahulu sebelum menanam**? . *<why must he put fertiliser on the land before he*
220  *plants?>* ah . Mohammad . **kenapa**? *<why?>* Nani . **kenapa dia mesti**
221  **simpan baja**? . *<why do they need to put down fertiliser?* **sama dengan kami** .
222  **kami mesti makan** . **untuk apa kami makan**? . *<it's the same as us . we need to*
223  *eat . why do we eat?>*
224  P: **untuk membesar** *<to grow>*
225  T: **untuk mem** ^ *<in order to mem ^ [VERBAL PREFIX]>*
226  Ps: **besar** *<big>* ( **membesar** *<to grow>* )
227  T: ah .. we must eat . ah .ah **kalau** we **mahu besar** . **membesar** . *<if we want to*
228  *get big . to grow>* **begitu juga dengan tanaman tadi** . *<it's the same for plants>*
229  **jadi simpan baja untuk apa**? .. **supaya ia** ^ .. *<so why do we put down*
230  *fertiliser? .. so that ^ >*
231  P: **segar** *<fresh (healthy)>*
232  T: yes **segar** . yes very good **segar** . **sihat** . *<healthy>* ah .. now . "When he has
233  fertilized the fields" . the farmer "plants the vegetable seeds and seedlings in

It is only when the teacher relates to the pupils' own experience that a response is forthcoming (line 224). The teacher's follow-up reinforces the answer with the whole group of pupils (lines 225–226).

## "Have You Ever Heard of Insecticide?"

In the following example, the teacher is reading from the textbook. After reading the first part of the text, the teacher translates it into Malay (lines 268–270), and he also uses translation for the second part of the text. Again, in this sequence, the teacher appeals to the pupils' existing knowledge, whether they have heard of insecticide, whether they have seen it (lines 272–273), and whether they have seen a spray pump (lines 275–276). Despite this appeal to the pupils' own experience, the teacher does not provide much opportunity for the pupils to interact, or for them to display elements of their knowledge.

268  T: *which are>* ah .. **tau** . *<you know>* "There are insects who like to eat vegetables"
269  . **banyak serangga-serangga yang mahu** . **yang kacau** . **makan sayur-sayuran**
270  **tadi** . **macam makan daun** *<there are many insects that want to . that eat the*
271  *vegetables>* ah . ah . and then the farmer "sprays chemicals to kill the insects" .
272  Kedong . **pernah kamu mendengar racun serangga**? . **pernah mu melihat**? ..
272  *<have you ever heard of insecticide . have you ever seen it?>* **pagi- pagi ada yang**
273  **menyembur** . **buang racun** . **ini untuk membunuh serangga** . *<in the early*
274  *morning people spray insecticide . to kill insects>* ah . **dengan menggunakan**
275  **pemancit** . **tau pemancit**? . **macam** pump … *<using a spray . do you know spray*
276  *. like a pump>* spray .

## "Harvesting Fruit and Vegetable or Harvesting Padi"

In this part of the lesson, when the topic of "harvesting" appears in the text, the teacher returns to the differences in the farming cycle in the village and as represented by the textbook. The following example shows the teacher reading from the textbook on the subject of "gathering the vegetables," the process called "harvesting," and annotating the content in Malay. The sketch that accompanies the written text clearly shows the farmer picking fruit or vegetables. The teacher, however, chooses to focus on harvesting rice, referring to the pupils' existing knowledge of this process, a process which is of fundamental importance to the life of the village where the school is located. The rice harvesting season had recently come to an end, and the teacher was able to make reference to this (lines 293–298).

283  T: now . ah . "After a few weeks the vegetables are ready to eat" . after a few weeks
284  . **lebih kurang satu bulan** . <*about one month*> after a few weeks **atau pun**
285  **selepas beberapa minggu** . <*or after a few weeks*> the vegetables are ready to
286  eat . **jadi sayur-sayuran itu tadi sudah boleh dimakan** . <*so these vegetables*
287  *can now be eaten*> now . this is the time when the farmer collects the vegetables .
288  ah . this is the time when the farmer collects vegetables. ah . **ini masanya petani**
289  **tadi** . <*this is the time for the farmer*> ah . **mengumpul hasilnya** . <*collect his*
290  *produce*> now this is called harvesting . harvesting . now . harvesting …
291  harvesting **ialah menuai** . <*harvesting means cutting the rice stalks*> **macam**
292  **menuai padi** .. <*such as cutting the rice stalks*> **baru beberapa bulan yang**
292  **lepas kamu habis menuai** .. <*it's only a few months since you finished harvesting*
293  *the rice here*> **kalau Cikgu nada salah** . Kedong **baru habis baru-baru ini** . ah
294  <*if I'm not mistaken* . Kedong *has only recently finished (harvesting)*>
295  P: [P NODS IN AGREEMENT]
298  T: **baru habis ini menuai** ah . <*just finished harvesting the rice*> now **menuai** is
299  harvesting . **mengumpul hasilnya** . <*collecting the produce*> harvesting ah .
300  harvesting [T WRITES 'HARVESTING' ON THE CB] … now . "At last the
301  vegetables

Throughout the lesson in which the "farmer" text is the focus, the teacher makes reference to the pupils' existing knowledge and, in particular, the way the farming cycle shown in the book differs from the rice cycle in the village. In lines 290 to 291, it is quite noticeable where the teacher adjusts from talking about textbook knowledge to talking about local knowledge. From lines 283 to 289, he is mediating the text. Having introduced the term *mengumpul hasilnya* ("collecting his produce"; line 289), he relates this to the English term *harvesting*, which he repeats three times (line 290). The teacher then switches to a definition of "harvesting," which is more appropriate for the village, that is, the "harvesting of rice." There is a specific

lexical item in Malay for the cutting or harvesting of rice, *menuai*, and this is
the term he uses. At the end of this sequence, there is an attempt to bring
the local knowledge and the textbook knowledge together (lines 298–299).

### "Here It's Not Done Like That"

Talk around the final two sentences of the written text and the last sketch in
the series, labelled *selling*, are the focus of the following analysis.
   After reading the sentence from the textbook (lines 301–302), the
teacher immediately points out the difference, first in English and then in
Malay, between the text and what happens in the village where the school is
located (lines 301–307). He points out that the villagers only grow enough
vegetables for their own use, and that the only crop that is ever sold in the
village is rice. The teacher tries to involve the pupils by asking if their parents have rice to sell, but the only response is a shake of the head (lines
305–308).

300  T: harvesting [T WRITES 'HARVESTING' ON THE CB] ... now . "At last the
301  vegetables are ready to be taken to the market and sold" . but we here . we in
302  Kampung Kesang we do not sell vegetable . now . **di sini kami inda manjual**
303  **sayur-sayuran** . <*here we don't sell vegetables*> **ini cuma tanam untuk makan**
304  **sendiri sahaja** . <*we only grow for our own food*> **kecuali padi sahaja .menjual**
305  **padi** .. <*except for rice . we sell rice*> **siapa yang banyak padi padi dijual di**
306  **sini**? . <*who has got lots of rice to sell here?*> what about you? .. your father?
307  **ada padi dijual**? . **ada**? <*has he got rice for sale? . has he?*>
308  [P SHAKES HEAD]
309  T: **inda tau** . **ada** . **nada tau juga** . <*you don't know . you may have . but you're*
310  *not really sure*> Nani . **nada tahu**? . <*don't you know*>? si-Kedong **sahaja**
311  **yang tau** . <*only our Kedong knows*> **tapi** <*but*> in the town we sell the
312  vegetables . **barang-barang yang banyak** . **kumpulkan hasilnya dan hantar** to
313  market . <*if we have a lot . we collect the produce together and send it to*
314  *market*> we send this to market . and sell vegetable ah . **macam kerja**
315 **pemborong** . <*like the work of a wholesaler*>

The whole thrust of the teacher's talk here is that the villagers do not sell
vegetables (unlike the farmer in the text) but only grow their own food.
   In the final example shown from this lesson, it is clear just how far the
teacher diverges from the text to make useful connections to the local context. Given the way the textbook has been positioned up to this stage in the
lesson, with the teacher sticking closely to the "farmer" text and the series of
sketches, the switch at line 161, "first he must clear all the jungle," and the
subsequent order to the pupils not to look at the book, is quite marked. This
is followed with a statement in Malay that "some of [what is in the book] is

similar to here but there are also things which are not the same as in this village" (lines 163–166). The teacher then begins to provide a brief explanation of the rice cycle ("clearing the jungle," "leaving the vegetation to dry,"
"burning off," "planting"), a totally different farming cycle to that provided
in the textbook. Here the teacher is talking about local knowledge, not the
knowledge as portrayed in the textbook. Interestingly, as part of the sequence here, one of the pupils is able to respond to the teacher's request for
factual knowledge, with a correct response (in Malay): "fire" (line 172).

158  T: —— now since a farmer is self-employed he must work very hard every day .
159  now . if he did not work very hard . now . what happen to his . plants . **kalau**
160  **inda kerja keras . mesti rajin . kerja keras** .. <*if he doesn't work hard . he must*
161  *be hard-working . hard work*> ah .. **mula-mula** . <*first*> first he must clear all
162  the jungle . clear the jungle . ah . cutting down all the trees . **jangan tengok sini**
163  <*don't look here*> [REFERRING TO THE SKETCHES IN THE BOOK] . **ada**
164  **juga yang sama tapi ada yang tak sama dengan yang dibuat di kampung sini**
165  <*some of it is similar to here but there are also things which are not the same*
166  *as in this village*> first we must clearing all the jungle . **menebas dahulu** .. <*cut*
167  *down the trees first*> **hutan-hutan itu** . <*the jungle*> and then . after clearing .
168  ah . and cutting down all the trees . ah . we leave the leave the area . **ladang**
169  **ditinggalkan dalam dua tiga minggu** . <*the area is left for about two or three*
170  *weeks*> about two or three weeks . and then we . **apa yang dibuat selapas atu?** .
171  <*what is done after that?*> **siapa tahu?** . <*who knows?*>
172  P: **api** <*fire*>
173  T: **buat api** . **apa lagi buat?** . <*make fires . what else is done?*> ah . **bikin apa?** .
174  <*what is done?*> ah . **cakap** . <*speak*> Siti . **apa?** . **selepas kawasan sudah**
175  **kering?** . <*what is done? . after the area is dry?*> **rangkai** in Iban . **tahu**
176  **rangkai?** . <*the word in Iban is '**rangkai**' . do you what '**rangkai**' is?*>
177  P: **kering** <*dry*>
178  T: aah . **cukup** . **cukup karing sudah** . <*after it's dry enough*> ah . **kamu boleh**
179  **cakap Iban kalau inda tahu bahasa Melayu boleh** . <*you can speak Iban if you*
180  *don't know Malay*> **dibakar** . <*it is burnt*> ah we must ah . aah .. **kawasan itu** .
181  **selepas tinggalkan dua tiga minggu mesti dibakar** . <*after leaving the area for*
182  *two or three weeks it must be burnt*> **sudah ia hangus** . **baru ia bersedia untuk**
183  **menanam** . <*after it's burnt, only then is it ready for planting*> **apa buat masa**
184  **ini?** . <*what's done during this period?*> **memajak** the land . <*the land is*
185  *ploughed*> **tahu majak?** . **dimajakkan dahulu** . <*do you know what ploughed*
186  *means? . it must be ploughed first*> **tetapi di sini nada buat macam itu** . <*but*
187  *here it's not done like that*> **siapa tahu kabuta?** . **siapa pernah melihat kabuta?**
188  **yang ada gambar di sana** <*who knows what a tractor is? . who has seen a*
189  *tractor? . there's a picture there*> [TEACHER POINTS TO THE SKETCH OF
190  A TRACTOR IN THE BOOK] . yes Nani . **dia macam apa?** . **ada** tyre? . **berapa**
191  tyre? <*what's it like? . does it have tyres? . how many tyres?*>

192 P: **empat** <*four*>
193 T: **empat** tyre <*four*> . **dibajak dahulu** . <*it is ploughed first*> what picture is

Also of interest here is the way the teacher switches to Iban (lines 175–176), one of the few occasions this teacher was observed to use Iban, the language of interethnic communication in the village. At this stage of the lesson, very little English is being used to coconstruct knowledge. Malay has become the major language of the discourse at this stage, and the switch to Iban is to check that the pupils understand the meaning of the Malay term *kering* ("dry"; lines 170–173). Furthermore, the teacher's statement, made in Malay, that "you can speak Iban if you don't know Malay" (lines 178–180), is a telling statement about the positions of these two languages and the views the teacher has about the pupils' competences in the two languages.

Also in this example, at line 184, there is a switch back to a discussion of what counts as knowledge in the textbook. The link made by the teacher between local knowledge ("the burning of the felled trees and shrubs") and the knowledge of the textbook ("ploughing") is potentially confusing for the pupils. The teacher seems to recognize this as he follows up his introduction of the Malay term for "ploughed" with a statement, again in Malay, "but here it's not done like that" (lines 184–187). In the last part of this example, the teacher tries to elicit whether the pupils have ever seen a tractor (lines 187–193). He refers pupils to the sketch of a tractor in the book and asks them to observe how many tires it has.

The examples above show how the teacher in this classroom, although basing the lesson on the textbook, does contest the textbook knowledge to use the pupils' knowledge of the local context. The teacher and pupils, in their talk around the text, also contest the language of the textbook. In the discussion that follows, I relate the practices observed in this classroom to the wider sociocultural and educational context.

## DISCUSSION

What, then, do the practices around text in this classroom tell us about what knowledge is constructed, how knowledge is constructed, and the linguistic resources which are used to construct this knowledge. Two points are immediately clear from an examination of the talk around the text in this lesson. First, the teacher attempts to intertwine what counts as knowledge in the textbook with the pupils' local knowledge. Second, the classroom participants use a variety of linguistic and pedagogic tools to accomplish this.

One particular feature of the teacher's engagement with the text in the lesson about the "farmer" was how he attempted to relate the information in the textbook to the situation in the village where the school was located.

He accomplished this by switching between Malay and English, although he used more Malay than English. The type of generic farming cycle which appeared in the textbook as a series of sketches with captions, and in the written text, had little real meaning for the pupils. The major farming cycle in the village is the rice cycle. On two occasions, the teacher specifically directed the pupils' attention away from the book to explain how farming was different in their village. This is most clearly shown in lines 300 to 315 and 158 to 193. In both of these examples, he made a comment in Malay to the effect that "we don't do it like that in this village." However, even when the teacher touched on aspects of farming which were very real to the students, and used Iban, the intergroup language of the area, there was, nevertheless, a limited response.

Clearly, the interactional practices around text in this lesson provide some indication of the several struggles and tensions inherent in the educational system in Brunei. On the one hand, there is the tension between the "dominance" of the Malay language in line with the state ideology and the definition of Brunei as a "Malay" state (cf. Gunn, 1997, p. 214), and, on the other hand, the way the education system clearly legitimizes English as the dominant language. It has been determined by the Malay center that these pupils should have their education at this level in the English language, although they have little access to the language. English in the bilingual system, it is remembered, was chosen due to its status as an international language.

A further tension is the school textbook. Textbooks for the core subjects (mathematics, science, and geography) at the level of Primary Four and above, are in English. They are designed by a Malay center agency (the Curriculum Development Department), in a joint venture with international publishers, to provide the "culture and aspirations" of Brunei, more precisely, the Malay center of Brunei. In trying to address these tensions, the teacher struggles to juggle the textbook knowledge on the one hand, and the local knowledge on the other. In attempting to do so, he is able to provide some opportunity for introducing the cultural norms of pupils, by diverging from the content of the textbook. The teacher, then, is trying to make sure that curriculum ideas which have their roots in international or Malay center contexts resonate with the pupils in ways that are both culturally and contextually relevant (cf. Samuel, 1997; Warschauer, 2000).

Focusing on the use of language in this classroom, it is clear that, as in many classrooms at the upper primary level in Brunei, the teacher uses a form of Malay to annotate the text, despite the fact that the bilingual system of education requires the use of English at this stage. In their use of Malay, the classroom participants contest the official curriculum which legitimizes English at this stage. Of course, the participants' response is a pragmatic one. In the community where the study took place, and in many other, especially rural, areas in the country, there is little access to English. What is not recognized, however, is that there is also little access to Malay.

The earlier discussion has mainly been concerned with the differences between the local "periphery" and the Malay "center" within Brunei itself. However, the debate can and should be expanded to the wider international context. Within Brunei there are ongoing struggles and tensions between the sovereignty of the state as represented by the Malay language, and the wider international context and the access English gives within this context. As Heller and Martin-Jones (2001, p. 2) point out, there are "new global forms of cultural, economic and social domination" which are shaping contemporary societies. There has been much recent debate about the increasing power of global networks and how this influences the struggle for local identities. For example, with the increasing role of English in the world, Phillipson and Skutnabb-Kangas (1996, p. 429) have shown how most contexts where English is taught as a second language reflect the "diffusion of English paradigm" rather than a situation which promotes diversity, what they refer to as an "ecology of language paradigm." In addition, Warschauer (2000, p. 515) has noted the need to create "opportunities for communication based on the values, cultural norms, and needs of learners rather than on the syllabi and texts developed in England and the United States" (see also Block & Cameron, 2001). An emerging theme from this recent literature, in the wake of new technologies and increasing globalization, is the need to recognize and defend cultural identity and diversity. Nettle and Romaine (2000, pp. 196–197), for example, suggest it is necessary to get rid of the "traditional equation between language, nation, and state." They go on to emphasize the need to "think locally but act globally," making reference to the "clash of values inherent in today's struggle between the global and the local, between uniformity and diversity" (2000, p. 197).

It is not possible to delve further into this literature due to space constraints, but it is, nevertheless, important to locate this study of a small community, not only within the context of the nation, but also within a rapidly changing world, and a world in which the new technologies bring with them their own cultural baggage.

## CONCLUSION

This chapter is an attempt to tell a local story, a story of a classroom where the pupils are members of a small community in a rural area of Brunei. The story is told within the wider context of the power and sovereignty of the Malay center, and with reference to overarching and increasing power of internationalization and globalization. The study has focused on the multilingual literacy pedagogies observed in one classroom, specifically the way the participants talk around text, and how the practices help the participants to negotiate and contest the educational agenda controlled by the Malay center. It shows how the classroom participants incorporate both local and textbook knowledge into their talk. Above all, the study demonstrates a struggle for survival in the quest for knowledge.

**Transcription Conventions**

Conventional punctuation is not used. Full stops indicate pauses.

| | |
|---|---|
| T | Teacher |
| P(s) | Pupil(s) |
| Plain font | English |
| **Bold font** | **Malay** |
| underlining | Iban |
| <*Italics*> | <*Translations into English*> |
| [UPPER CASE] | [CONTEXTUAL DETAIL] |
| CB | Chalkboard |
| "Abu is ..." | Indicates reading from the textbook |
| ^ | Indicates raised intonation from the teacher where teacher expects pupil to orally 'fill in the blank' |

**REFERENCES**

Alexander, R. (2000). *Culture and pedagogy: International comparisons in primary education*. Oxford, England: Blackwell.
Apple, M. W. (1986). *Teachers and tests: A political economy of class and gender relations in education*. New York: Routledge & Kegan Paul.
Apple, M. W. (1993). *Official knowledge: Democratic education in a conservative age*. New York: Routledge & Kegan Paul.
Barton, D. (1994). *Literacy. An introduction to the ecology of written language*. Oxford, England: Blackwell.
Block, C., & Cameron, D. (Eds.). (2001). *Globalization and language teaching*. London: Routledge & Kegan Paul.
Brown, D. E. (1969). *Socio-political history of Brunei, a Bornean Sultanate*. Unpublished doctoral dissertation, Cornell University, Ithaca, NY.
Curriculum Development Department. (1990a). *Geography syllabus for upper primary schools* (Darjah IV–VI). Brunei Darussalam, Bandar Seri Begawan: Ministry of Education.
Curriculum Development Department. (1990b). *Primary geography for Brunei Darussalam. Course Book* (Darjah IV). London: Macmillan.
Government of Brunei. (1961). Undang-undang Taraf Kebangsaan Brunei. Undang-undang No. 4 [nationality enactment laws]. In *Surat-surat perlembagaan Negeri Brunei* (pp. 115–135). Kuala Belait, Brunei: Brunei Press.
Government of Brunei Darussalam. (1985). *Education System of Negara Brunei Darussalam*. Bandar Seri Begawan, Brunei Darussalam: Curriculum Development Department, Education Department.

Government of Brunei Darussalam. (1993). *Summary tables of the population census. 1991.* Bandar Seri Begawan, Brunei Darussalam: Economic Planning Unit, Ministry of Finance.

Green, J., & Dixon, C. (1993). Introduction: Talking knowledge into being: Discursive and social practices in classrooms. *Linguistics and Education, 5,* 231–239.

Gunn, G. (1997). *Language, ideology, and power in Brunei Darussalam* (Southeast Asia Series No. 99). Athens: Ohio University Press

Hashim, A. H. (1984). Tinjauan singkat mengenai identiti Orang Brunei. [A brief view on the identity of Bruneians]. *Beriga, 2,* 6–10.

Heath, S. B. (1982). Protean shapes in literacy events: Ever-shifting oral and literate traditions. In D. Tannen (Ed.), *Spoken and written language: Exploring orality and literacy* (pp. 91–117). Norwood, NJ: Ablex.

Heath, S. B. (1983). *Ways with words: Language, life and work in communities and classrooms.* Cambridge, England: Cambridge University Press.

Heller, M., & Martin-Jones, M. (2001). Introduction: Symbolic domination, education and linguistic difference. In M. Heller & M. Martin-Jones (Eds.), *Voices of authority: Education and linguistic difference* (pp. 1–28). Westport, CT: Ablex.

Horton, A. V. M. (1988). M. S. H. McArthur and Brunei 1904–1908 or a 'Dying Kingdom' reprieved. *Brunei Museum Journal, 6,* 1–32.

Hussainmiya, B. A. (1994). Philosophy for a rich, small state. *Far Eastern Economic Review, 10,* 31.

Kershaw, E. M. (1994a). Final shifts: Some why's and how's of Brunei–Dusun convergence on Malay. In P. W. Martin (Ed.), *Shifting patterns of communication in Borneo* (pp. 247–255). Williamsburg, VA: Borneo Research Council.

Kershaw, E. M. (1994b). *Dusun folktales. 88 folktales in the Dusun language of Brunei with English translations* (Southeast Asian Paper No. 39). Honolulu, HI: Center for S.E. Asian Studies, School of Hawaiian, Asian and Pacific Studies.

Luke, C., de Castell, S., & Luke, A. (1989). Beyond criticism: The authority of the school textbook. In S. de Castell, A. Luke, & C. Luke (Eds.), *Language, authority and criticism: Readings on the school textbook* (pp. 245–260). London: Falmer.

Martin, P. W. (1996a). Social change and language shift among the Belait. In P. W. Martin, A. C. K. Ożóg, & G. Poedjosoedarmo (Eds.), *Language use and language change in Brunei Darussalam* (pp. 253–267). Athens: Ohio University Press.

Martin, P. W. (1996b). A comparative ethnolinguistic survey of the Murut (Lun Bawang) with special reference to Brunei. In P. W. Martin, A. C. K. Ożóg, & G. Poedjosoedarmo (Eds.), *Language use and language change in Brunei Darussalam* (pp. 268–279). Athens: Ohio University Press.

Martin, P. W., Ożóg, A. C. K., & Poedjosoedarmo, G. (Eds.). (1996). *Language use and language change in Brunei Darussalam.* Athens: Ohio University Press.

Martin, P. W., & Sercombe, P. G. (1994). The Penan of Brunei: Patterns of linguistic interaction. In P. W. Martin (Ed.), *Shifting patterns of language use in Borneo* (pp. 165–178). Williamsburg, VA: Borneo Research Council.

Maxwell, A. (1980). *Urang Darat. An ethnographic study of the Kedayan of Labu Valley Brunei.* Unpublished doctoral dissertation, Yale University, New Haven, CT.

Mercer, N. (1995). *The guided construction of knowledge.* Clevedon, England: Multilingual Matters.

Nettle, D., & Romaine, S. (2000). *The extinction of the world's languages.* Oxford, England: Oxford University Press.

Nothofer, B. (1991). The languages of Brunei Darussalam. In H. Steinhauer (Ed.), *Papers in Austronesian linguistics, No. 1. Pacific Linguistics A–81* (pp. 151–176). Canberra: Australian National University.

Olson, D. R. (1989). On the language and authority of textbooks. In S. de Castell (Ed.), *Language, authority and criticism: Readings on the school textbook* (pp. 233–244). London: Falmer.

Ożóg, A. C. K. (1996). The unplanned use of English: The case of Brunei Darussalam. In P. W. Martin, A. C. K. Ożóg, G. Poedjosoedarmo (Eds.), *Language use and language change in Brunei Darussalam* (pp. 156–172). Athens: Ohio University Press.

Phillipson, R., & Skutnabb-Kangas, X. (1996). English only or worldwide language ecology? *TESOL Quarterly, 29*, 429–452.

Rousseau, J. (1990). *Central Borneo. Ethnic identity and social life in a stratified society.* Oxford, England: Clarendon.

Samuel, M. (1997). The challenge of diversity: Culture and recontextualization of pedagogy. In G. M. Jacobs (Ed.), *Language classrooms of tomorrow: Issues and responses* (pp. 230–237). Singapore: SEAMEO Regional Language Centre.

Saunders, G. (1994). *A history of Brunei.* Kuala Lumpur, Malaysia: Oxford University Press.

Sercombe, P. G. (1996). Ethnolinguistic change among the Penan of Brunei: Some initial observations. *Bijdragen, 152–11*, 257–274.

Sercombe, P. G. (2000, June 10–14). Language and identity regarding the Penan in Brunei. In M. Leigh (Ed.), *Language, Management, and Tourism: Proceedings of the Biennial Conference of the Borneo Research Council* (pp. 21–33). Kuching, Malaysia. Kuching: Institute of South East Asian Studies, Universiti Malaysia Sarawak & Sarawak Development Institute.

Warschauer, M. (2000). The changing global economy and the future of English teaching. *TESOL Quarterly, 34*, 511–535.

# Chapter 11

# Voicing the "Self" Through an "Other" Language: Exploring Communicative Language Teaching for Global Communication

Jasmine C. M. Luk
*Hong Kong Institute of Education*

## INTRODUCTION

The global nature of the Communicative Approach to Language Teaching (CLT) is in many respects similar to the global nature of the English language. Like English, CLT emanates from the West. CLT methods are viewed as having embraced the principles of success, being "synonymous with progress, modernisation, and access to wealth" (Kramsch & Sullivan, 1996, p. 200). They are, therefore, revered as the ideal model in places outside its origin where "appropriate" methodologies for teaching and learning English as a second or international language (ESL–EIL) are much sought after. Experts of the method who are usually native English speakers from the British-Australia-North American group (BANA group, in Holliday's, 1994, term) are recruited by the ESL–EIL countries, particularly in the Far Eastern regions, to help make the method grow and take root.

However, an increasing number of Second Language Acquisition (SLA) studies have pointed out the unlikely success of a direct transplanting of

CLT methodology to places outside the Anglo-Saxon contexts due to incongruent sociocultural and institutional connotations. These refer to ideologies embodied in the instructional principles, activity types and teacher–student role expectations of the "guest" method which may be totally foreign or contradictory to those experienced and enacted by learners and language teaching practitioners in the "host" country (Canagarajah, 1999; Ellis, 1996; Pennycook, 1994; Sullivan, 2000). To avoid "tissue rejection" (Holliday, 1994), it is essential that CLT methodology of a global nature should be sensitive to local sociocultural conditions.

In this chapter, I intend to investigate an important aspect affecting an effective implementation of CLT, the students' *communicative intent* in communicative activities. Against a backdrop of research findings showing "mediation" as a promising factor leading to a more successful implementation of CLT in non-Western countries (Ellis, 1996; Kramsch & Sullivan, 1996; Sullivan, 2000), I show, through two contrasting classroom excerpts from two secondary schools in Hong Kong, how student's communicative intent could be promoted or demoted through the presence or absence of a genuine opportunity for students to express their *selves*. It is argued that people communicate (irrespective of whether it is their first or second language) mainly for the purpose of asserting their *local* identity, interests, and values. Without the provision of such opportunities, anything said by the students will only be empty noises. In the following sections, I begin by providing a brief overview of how CLT has been practiced in Hong Kong. I then explore the management of "self" and "communication" in my data, before discussing the implications for a locally relevant pedagogical practice.

## THE PRACTICE OF CLT IN HONG KONG

Hong Kong, a former colony of Britain, and a current Special Administrative Region of China, has practiced CLT since the early 1980s (Curriculum Development Council, 1983). Until recently, the principal theories of the communicative approach still underpin the latest English Language Syllabus, F.1 to F.5 (Curriculum Development Council, 1999), although the main thrust of the syllabus lies in its introduction of the task-based approach.

Almost 20 years of implementation of CLT in Hong Kong does not seem to have yielded the desired effects on the development of learners' communicative competence. Talks of declining English standards of Hong Kong's younger generations still prevail as ever in the public and academic discourses (Evans, 1996). Two rather extreme English classroom scenarios have recently been covered in academic works. One type of classroom is characterized by great student anxiety and reticence, with little student initiation and responses in the target language (Tsui, 1996); whereas the other type is one dominated by students' lively, but often impish verbal play in their first language (L1), Cantonese (Kwan, 2000; Lin, 2000; Pennington, 1999a, 1999b). Both types of students' classroom demeanor, by themselves, as pointed out by the authors, do not seem to be conducive to the second language (L2) development of the students.

Reasons for these undesirable classroom behaviors are manifold. Some people ascribe the reasons to the lack of a favorable language environment in the society to support the implementation of the communicative approach in the classroom. It is a well-known fact that though English is one of the official languages and enjoys second language status in Hong Kong, up to 98% of the population in Hong Kong is ethnically and linguistically homogenous. Cantonese remains the dominant language in the street. English is seldom used for intracommunity communication. As pointed out by Lin (2000), the majority of students in Hong Kong are closely attached to a Cantonese-dominated life world which is culturally and linguistically insulated from that represented by the English language.

A survey study on over 400 secondary school students conducted by Lai (1994) establishes learners' confidence level and self-esteem as major factors undermining a successful implementation of CLT. Her findings also reveal that insufficient provision of communication opportunities by the teachers is also a crucial factor. Similar findings showing a close relation between teachers' perceptions of language teaching and the implementation of CLT have been reported by Evans (1997), using similar research methods. His study indicates that the communicative curriculum has had a minimal impact on the Hong Kong English language classroom because "[p]ower, authority and control continue to be in the hands of the teacher. Teachers still appear to favor a didactic, transmission style, and text-book based type of teaching, while the students' main classroom role seems to involve listening to the teacher and working individually on examination-focused exercises" (Evans, 1997, p. 43). The increasingly frequent playful and sometimes disruptive L1 verbal behavior of the students mentioned earlier is perhaps a response in the form of *resistance* to such kind of unequal power structure between the teacher and students, and to the uninteresting and unstimulating classroom activities (Kwan, 2000).

Besides, the roguish verbal behaviors of the students in the classrooms coincide in many ways with the adolescents' discourse behaviors in the streets. In a study to investigate how adolescents who are at risk of joining gangs in Hong Kong use discursive choices to negotiate and construct identities, Candlin, Lin, and Lo (2000) found that the adolescents were using a rich and dynamic variety of discourse features that would not be allowed in Hong Kong classrooms such as ignoring the authorities' instructions, talking among themselves, and self-selecting to speak. It seems that more and more Hong Kong adolescents are trying to assert their identities constructed in noninstitutional social settings in the more institutional school and classroom settings. As pointed out by Candlin et al. (2000), such communicative behavior, if transposed into English, might be conducive to language learning.

What could be done to enable students to transpose their dynamic communication behaviors from L1 to L2? The Hong Kong Government introduced the Expatriate English Language Teacher Scheme toward the end of the 1980s (renamed Native English-Speaking Teachers Scheme and introduced on a wider scale in 1995; see Boyle, 1997, for a detailed documentation of the history of the Scheme), with a major underlying purpose to create "opportunities for students to interact with non-Chinese, non-Cantonese-speaking members of staff outside as well as inside the classroom" (Johnson & Tang, 1993, p. 206). It is also believed that teachers from a Western cultural background may be less transmission-oriented than local Hong Kong teachers (Evans, 1997, citing Young & Lee, 1987). At present, almost every secondary school in Hong Kong has up to two native English-speaking teachers. Have they all brought with them the appropriate methodology to implement CLT in Hong Kong?

## APPROPRIATE CLT PEDAGOGY IN EIL CONTEXTS

What exactly is "the" appropriate CLT methodology? As has been mentioned in the introduction, the appropriateness of a BANA-based CLT methodology in EIL countries is being questioned. Language teaching researchers have begun to look for ways through which CLT curriculum could be made more *socioculturally sensitive* and *appropriate* (Breen,1986; Holliday, 1994; Savignon, 1991). Kramsch and Sullivan (1996) call for language pedagogy of both *global* appropriacy and *local* appropriation. A pedagogy of *appropriation* is viewed as a promising method by Canagarajah (1999) to "enable students to appropriate the dominant codes and discourses according to their needs and interests" (p. 186). It is a pedagogy that would encourage students to "cross cultural and discursive borders" (Canagarajah, 1999, p. 186).

In this connection, the need for language learning to be "mediated" is apparent. Although Canagarajah (1999, quoting Kramsch, 1993) claims that the "bridge" to cross the border cannot be taught by teachers, in my opinion, they could certainly assist students to construct this bridge by ensuring the presence of proper mediation. The notion of mediation is one of the basic tenets of Vygotsky's sociocultural theory. In Vygotsky's perspective, mediation is essential in promoting learning as a higher human mental activity (Wertsch, 1991). Apart from the more traditional tools of mediation such as verbal and nonverbal texts, certain types of teaching and classroom discourse practices have been considered to be effective means of mediation. Ellis (1996) discusses how the teacher should act as a "cultural mediator" and demonstrate an "awareness of other culture identities" (p. 217) for the communicative approach to be culturally appropriate in Far Eastern countries. Sullivan (2000) has reported how lively and personally meaningful communication in L2 is promoted in the class of a Vietnamese teacher and students through a playful classroom discourse as a form of mediation even without the implementation of the principal concepts of CLT such as independent pair or group work, or an information gap. "Wordplay, one-upmanship and oral impromptu playfulness are, in fact, a part of the Vietnamese cultural heritage" (Sullivan, 2000, p. 126) and an adoption of this form of mediation reflects a cultural sensitivity on the part of the teacher.

In this chapter, I attempt to further develop the argument along the issue of socioculturally sensitive mediation to show that students' *self* could also be an essential form of mediation in their learning of a target language that represents an "other" world.

## THE CONCEPT OF SELF AND COMMUNICATION

Ivanic (1998) has provided a useful synthesis and elaboration of several related but different concepts of "self," which include "person," "role," and "identity." In her interpretation, "self" refers to "aspects of identity associated with an individual's feeling (or 'affect')" whereas identity is socially constructed from "a complex of interweaving positionings" (p. 10). Due to the multiplicity, hybridity and fluidity of identity from these interweaving positionings, Ivanic prefers the term *multiple identity* instead of the singular term *identity*. However, she adds that the noun *identity* sometimes seems too abstract for talking about specific people and their self-representations and she suggests using the word "self" for this purpose. This connection between "self" and "identity" seems to imply that although in most cases, our identities draw meanings from our "selves," there may be occasions in which our outward display of identities does not involve any inward representation of self.

The notion that our sense of self and identities are constructed and renegotiated through talk is not a novel idea (see, for example, Le Page, 1986). What I would like to extend further in this chapter is that in the process of constructing our sense of self and identities through interaction, our desire to assert our*selves* may also enhance our urge to communicate and the value of meaning of our utterances. As suggested by Belay (1996) and Canagarajah (1999), our sense of self and the act to construct and negotiate different identities seem most robust and dynamic in contacts with people and ideologies from other discourse communities, or other cultures. It may be this urge to represent ourselves in front of "other" people that has facilitated our development of communicative competence.

I also see a close relation of "self" with the sociocultural notion of "voice" developed by Bakhtin (1981). In intermental dialogic situations and intramental psychological processes, I perceive "self" as usually the primary source that gives meaning to the "voice," or "the speaking personality, the speaking consciousness" (Holquist & Emerson, 1981, p. 434; quoted in Wertsch, 1991, p. 51). "Voice" in Bakhtin's configuration is concerned with "the broader issues of a speaking subject's perspective, conceptual horizon, intention, and world view" (Wertsch, 1991, p. 51), implying that there is a presence of "self" of the interlocutors. However, a "voice" is never solely responsible for creating an utterance or its meaning because "every utterance must be regarded primarily as a *response* to preceding utterances of the given sphere" (Bakhtin, 1986, p. 91; quoted in Wertsch, 1991, p. 53, italics in original). Thus, an utterance carries with it not just the voice of the speaker, but also the voices of the addressees, or other people from the sociohistorical contexts. Therefore, as suggested before, there may be occasions when "voices" released from a speaker assuming a certain identity may not come from the speaking "self." He or she may be made to speak in a way that is of somebody else's desire. These cases would be quite the same as being the "animator" but not the "author" or "principal" of an utterance in Goffman's (1981) configuration of speaking roles.

Kramsch (2000) shows the importance of allowing learners not just to make voices (for example, by playing the narrative role), but to put their "'true' self on the line" (p. 151, quotation marks in original), which simply means giving one's own opinions on the issues. Our "self" is often the major factor driving us to speak, but more often, not to speak. Under circumstances when we are made to speak without mediation of the "self," our utterances are no more than mere sounds. The essential place of self in communicative activities, thus, lies in its direct relation with the emergence of communicative intent, the absence or presence of which will determine whether an activity will lead to genuine communication of the participants. As argued by Bakhtin (1981, pp. 293–294), words become "one's own only when the speaker populates [them] with his own intention, his own accent, when he appropriates the word, adapting it to his own semantic and expressive intention." In appropriating global discourse, it is essential for learners to be able to assert their selves in cross-cultural global interactions so that multiple, or pluralistic, language user identities could be constructed.

## TWO CLT CASES IN HONG KONG

In the following sections of this chapter, I discuss, through presenting EIL classroom teaching excerpts from two contrasting cases of native English-speaking teachers in Hong Kong, how students' communicative intent can be *promoted* or *demoted* by the presence or absence of opportunities for students to assert and represent their "selves." I show in Excerpt 1 how sometimes students utter words in the target language that are void of their own semantic and expressive intention and accent even in a seemingly CLT task setting. I then show, in Excerpts 2a and 2b, contrasting situations in which students have been successfully engaged in genuine communication in L2 although the discourse structure is basically teacher-dominated.

The classroom excerpts reported in this chapter came from a larger pool of data collected for my doctoral study in which the two native English-speaking teachers were participants. They are addressed by the pseudonyms of Mr. Hood and Miss Heron. Both teachers are British by nationality. Both were recruited under the Enhanced Native English-Speaking Teacher Scheme introduced in September 1998. Both had relevant qualifications in teaching English as a second language. Neither spoke any Cantonese at the time of the study. Both asserted that they were practicing CLT in their teaching. Both were teaching in Chinese medium secondary schools that admitted academically average to below-average students, the majority of whom came from districts populated by families belonging to a lower socioeconomic status group.

## Case 1

In the excerpt that follows, I show how Miss Heron's F.2 students (ages 13 to 14) participated in a communicative activity. The students were in the best class at their year level.[1] The excerpt took place in an oral English lesson.

***Excerpt 1.*** The F.2 students are supposed to be playing a language game called "Finding Grandma's False Teeth." After the teacher has presented relevant language structures and vocabulary items, the students are to work in pairs. They share a picture showing different rooms in a house. Student A first imagines that he or she is hiding Grandma's false teeth somewhere in the house. Student B then asks Student A the whereabouts of grandma's teeth with the structure, "Are they + (prepositional phrases indicating location)?" and Student A answers yes or no until the teeth are found. Excerpt 1 shows the conversation of two girls who were sitting near the recorder. Please refer to the Appendix for the Transcription Conventions.

1   GS1: (looking at the picture and talking to herself or GS2) **dim gaai keoi go ci suo gam daai ge?**

2   <*Why is her toilet so big?*>

---

[1] In most Hong Kong secondary schools, students are streamed into "good" and "average" classes to minimize the problem of mixed abilities.

3      **NT**: (talking to the whole class) I'm going to walk around, shhh, and I only want to hear
        English. Are they de de de, are they under de de de, are they in the ^ okay?

4      Are you ready? Okay, so start now,

5      English only.

6      **GS1**: Are they? (to GS2) **Nei zi jiu zou me aa?** <*You know what to do?*>

7      **GS2**: **Nei wan je** <*you're looking for something*>, **aa maa pang ngaa hai bin dou** <*Where are*

8      Grandma's teeth?>, **gan zu ngo man nei hai m hai hai** toilet **go dou** <*Then I ask*

9      **you if they are in the toilet.**>, **nei waa m hai** (???) <*You say it's not (???).*>

10     **GS1**: **man me aa?** <*Ask what?*>

11     **GS2**: Are the::[sic] [under the toilet?

12     **GS1**:            [Are THEY- (..) I give up

13     (Off-task talk in Cantonese for 5 seconds.)

14     **GS2**: **pang ngaa hai bin aa?** <*Where are the teeth?*>

15     (Inaudible speech)

16     **GS1**: No **aa** (a Cantonese particle usually attached at the end of a statement for emphatic
        purpose)

17     **GS2**: Under the mat **lo** (a Cantonese particle showing 'taken-for-granted' attitude)

18     **GS1**: (sounds rude) NO, NO NO NO NO (chuckling at the end)

19     **GS2**: under the television **lo** (4 seconds pause) Are the [sic] in the bath?

20     **GS1**: NO, NO

21     **GS2**: under the chair **lo**

22     **GS1**: NO, NO

23     **GS2**: (chuckling) in the XXX (a name, probably one of their classmates) **go hau** <*in XXX's*
        *mouth*>

24     (GS2 keeps asking and GS1 keeps saying 'no'.)

25     **GS2**: Are they under the ma:::t? Are- **hai maai hai li dou** ? <*Is it here?*>

26     **GS1**: **cuo** <*Wrong!*>

27     **GS2**: (chuckling) **hai mai hai li dou?** <*Is it here?*>

28     **GS1**: **cuo** <*Wrong!*>

29     **GS2**: **hai mai hai li dou?** <*Is it here?*>

30     **GS1**: **cuo cuo cuo cuo cuo** <*wrong wrong wrong wrong wrong!!!!*>

31     (Such exchange in Cantonese repeats eight times. From the laughter of both students,
        they are not doing the task seriously. GS1 sometimes says the Cantonese word meaning
        'wrong' many times non-stop.)

32     **GS2**: **hai mai hai li dou?** <*Is it here?*>

33     **GS1**: (sounds rude and annoyed) **m hai aa** <*It's NOT!*>

34     **GS2**: **faai di gong** <*Tell me immediately!*> (sounds very annoyed) **bin DOU aa?!** <*Where*
        *are they?!*>

35     **GS1**: **hai bun shu sheung min lo** <*They are on the book.*>

36     **GS2**: (sounds annoyed) **ngo mai waa hai mai hai li dou lo** <*I have asked if they were there*
        *before.*>

The activity illustrated in Excerpt 1 exemplifies some of the principles of functional communication activities in Littlewood (1981) by establishing a pair participation structure and introducing an information gap. Communicative games of such design are often found in reference materials[2] which claim to be elucidating the communicative approach. In a series of videos produced by the Government with an objective to illustrate different English Language Teaching (ELT) approaches, a similar kind of information-sharing task through controlled asking and answering sequences was introduced to teachers as communicative activities.[3] Being an experienced English teacher and teacher educator, I remember having used similar kinds of activities before and often find student teachers adopt similar activities during their teaching practice. Besides, the design of the activity characterizes the weak version (see, for example, Howatt, 1984, quoted in Holliday, 1994) of the CLT approach. As interpreted by Holliday (1994), the weak version of CLT focuses on "the practice of language use, with the basic lesson input as presentation of language models" (p. 170). Students are expected to practice using the target language through interaction with peers. However, I believe most experienced language teachers will feel that there is something wrong with the design and implementation of the activity after reading the transcript. The students should not be carrying out the task like this. The question–answer sequences were done as if they were police interrogations. There was also too much Cantonese. In the end, the task, finding Grandma's teeth, was accomplished without using any L2 at all.

Students' behavior in Excerpt 1 reveals some problems with the design and implementation of the communication game. These problems have prevented the students from fully engaging themselves in the communicative situation. Between the students and the expected L2 productions, there is a lack of proper mediation. The communication context illuminated by the picture (rooms in a house) and the information gap (the whereabouts of Grandma's teeth) are traditionally taken to be crucial forms of mediation in many CLT activities. However, evidence in Excerpt 1 shows that a detachment from the students' local sociocultural life-world would render these CLT elements ineffective.

---

[2]The task materials mentioned in Excerpt 1 are taken from a communication practice task reference book with photocopiable pictures published by a very famous local textbook publisher. The book was a personal copy of the teacher.

[3]The series of videos were produced by the former Colleges of Education in collaboration with the Education Department for teachers on the Retraining Course for Primary School Teachers in the early 1990s.

The purpose of the task reveals a basic sociocultural incongruity. The communicative context that presents the need to hide and find Grandma's false teeth is rather inauthentic to most local students. Given the small size of flats in Hong Kong, it is highly unlikely that students would live with their Grandma. Even if they do, their Grandma's false teeth are seldom young people's choice of objects with which to make fun. Even if they do, they may have chosen to hide Grandma's teeth in an object which may not be available on the pictures. In realistic situations, hiding a set of teeth under the television or on a book is highly ridiculous and impossible. It might have explained why the two girls seem to have problems understanding how to perform such a seemingly simple task. GS1's "I give up" (line 12) reveals her frustration at not being able to make sense of the meaning and purpose of the activity because the communication setup did not allow any *space* for any form of self-representation. Anything said remains as "noises" rather than "voices."

The repetitive nature of the question and answer sequence has probably created unbearable boredom which has resulted in GS1's hysterical "no" in English and Cantonese starting at line 18. The students' use of Cantonese to perform the task (line 25 onward) should not be taken simply as an inability to use English to fulfill the task (most of the names of the vocabulary items on the picture have been pretaught by the teacher), but more probably an inability to see why this has to be done in "an other" language. With an activity like this, perhaps only a passively conforming student such as GS2 would care to implement the task as instructed. However, with a nonconforming partner and a pointless task, GS2 has no choice but to do it *her* way—using Cantonese to perform the task and inserting an insider's joke (line 23) to make fun. The pair achieved the purpose of finding Grandma's teeth, but it is doubtful how much L2 they have acquired from this communication experience.

## Case 2

Let's now turn to look at Mr. Hood's F.4 class (ages 16–17). Contrary to Miss Heron's F.2 class, Mr. Hood's class was the weakest in the year level. Students in that class had lower self-esteem than their counterparts in other classes because they knew that only students with weaker academic performances joined this class. According to Mr. Hood, a number of students were rather rebellious. Although they knew the importance of education and to study well in school, few were prepared to work hard. Their motivation to learn English largely came from the desire to pass examinations, but their determination to make an effort was low.

*Excerpt 2a.* In the excerpt that follows, the teacher asks his students to show their agreement, disagreement, or uncertainty about some statements by standing in different parts of the classroom and giving reasons for their decisions. This forms part of the language preparation task for an interclass debate.

1  **NT:**  . . . . . Okay ⌃ so I'm going to read out the statements and you stand near, you stand near the, err,

2  (. .) you stand shuu, stand near the paper that represent your point of view=okay first statement

3  (. . .) shu shu, listen, first statement, Mr Hood is the best teacher=

4  **BS:**  (Loudly) =ye::s=

5  **NT:**  = (???) Mr Hood -, no no no, stand up, stand up, stand up, stand up (???) stand in the right place.

6  (Students move around, producing a lot of noise, talking to each other in Cantonese.)

7  **NT:**  Now listen, listen. (. . .) Okay the question is (???) shu shu shu, shu shu shu. It's not a question.

8  it's a statement. it's- (loudly) SHUT UP, dear ME (..) Mr Hood is the best teacher, best,

9  [best, Mr Hood is the best teacher at YKT[4]

10  **BS:**  [bad, bad, bad=

11  **NT:**  =Okay now everybody must stand in the right place=

12  **BS:**  =YES

13  **NT:**  (???) right okay, now lets- shu shu shu shu (???) let's find out (..) shu shu shu, let's find out (??)

14  shuuuuuu, let's find out some (???). As I said, you MUST HAVE one reason why, you must have one reason why.

15  If you don't tell me ⌃ (..) and if, and if you don't tell me your reason,

16  you can't go back to your seat.

17  **Ss:**  (showing great surprise) WAAAAA=

18  **NT:**  =you have to stay there a::ll LESSON. Stand up (???) Right okay (???) Mr Hood is

19  the best teacher in YKT, you disagree, why?

20  **BS:**  Err (.) only play silly games (other Ss laugh) but, but er he is a only one can say

21  English, er, only one err English teacher can (?)

22  **NT:**  Fantastic (???) Right okay now, can't decide, why?

23  **GS:**  (asking each other) **dim gaai aa, dim gaai aa** <*Why? Why?*>
      (. . . . . . .)

24  **NT:**  shuuuuuu, everybody must have a reason why. Carol. Carol. (????) (. . .) Right, okay, Carol, okay,

25  you stand there, tell me. Annie ⌃ why, why you disagree? Why do you disagree?

26  **GS:**  Because (.) in our class, there are many people sleeping.

27  **NT:**  Okay, great, that's fine. Carol, I (??) (. . .) Carol, you have to stand there and (???) (. . .) Carol ⌃

28  **GS:**  (???)

---

[4]YKT is a pseudo-acronym for the secondary school in which Mr. Hood was teaching at the time of the study.

29   **NT**:  Right okay. Okay that's fine. Sometimes very funny and interesting ⌐ sometimes
           very boring,
30          Okay that's fine. Mr Hood, (…) Mr Hood—
31   **Ss**:  shuuuu
32   **NT**:  Mr Hood is fat.
33          (Ss move again, some laughing, making lots of noise.)
34   **NT**:  Okay, okay, shushushu. (…) Patrick, you strongly agree, you strongly agree, why?
35   **BS**:  Because you are fat.
36   **NT**:  Because I am fat= (Many Ss laugh.)
37   **BS**:  Like a pig.
38   **NT**:  Like a PIG. Thank you very much. I'll remember that when I mark your
           homework.
39   (Many students laugh loudly.)

Polling students' opinions on whether the teacher is the best is only the appetizer, the attention-getter. In the rest of the lesson, the discussion moved from individuals, to the school, then to society. Most topics that came later were of a serious and formal nature, including "Hong Kong is a good place to live," "Violent Japanese comic books should not be sold to children," and "Hong Kong students cannot enjoy their youth because they have too much homework." These topics were chosen, according to the teacher, because of their high degree of relevance to adolescents in Hong Kong. He was sure that students at this age group would have lots of opinions about these topics. Due to the length of the transcripts, I cannot present them all here. But it is important to point out that from commenting on their teacher, to their peers, then their school, and then society, students were given ample opportunities to make their voices heard. Excerpt 2b shows how the teacher elicited opinions from the students on issues related to study and work in a highly engaged interaction.

### Excerpt 2b.

40   **NT**:  Why do you want to pass your exams?
41   **BS**:  Find a good job
42   **NT**:  Good jobs, so all you people here do want a good job? Is that right?
43   **NT**:  So aah if you go to uh United States, do the students do as much school work as you?
44   **BS**:  (very softly) No
45   **NT**:  If you go to Australia, do the students do as much school work as you?
46   **Ss**:  No, no.
47   **NT**:  Right, so their standard is lower?

| 48 | **Ss**: | (very softly) Higher |
| 49 | **BS**: | No, (??) |
| 50 | **NT**: | How does that work? (..) If you, you all work very hard, so your standard must be higher, than theirs. |
| | | (.....) |
| 51 | **BS**: | Maybe not. |
| 52 | **NT**: | Maybe not, why maybe? |
| 53 | **BS**: | Maybe they are clever. |
| 54 | **NT**: | SO this is the answer then. Hong Kong students have to work hard because they |
| 55 | | are stupid. (Some Ss laugh.) Is that the answer? |
| 56 | **BS**: | (sounding very sure) [NO |
| 57 | **BS**: | [some of them |

## DISCUSSION

On the surface, compared to Excerpt 1, the activity in Excerpt 2 (a & b) does not contain those dominant principles highly regarded by some CLT practitioners. Although most questions raised by the teacher, being "why" questions, were referential, the whole lesson was teacher-led and teacher-controlled. There was no pair work or group work. Students were not encouraged to talk with one another. Talking turns were mostly assigned by the teacher. Students were always shushed by the teacher to keep quiet. However, students' behaviors in Excerpts 2a and 2b showed that students were using English to express themselves. So what promoted the students' communication intent in Excerpt 2 which was absent in Excerpt 1?

Even from an outsider's point of view, Mr. Hood's class was a difficult one because the majority of the students were extremely passive whereas a few male students who were responsive displayed rebellious behavior and showed resistance to the teachers' instructions. On the few days of my visit, those male students always talked back to the teacher in an unruly manner, usually in Cantonese, and sometimes in bad language, even when the teacher was instructing. Frequent and long shushing was always heard from the teacher when he tried to focus the students' attention. Before doing this opinion-polling activity, most students were very reluctant to follow the teacher's instructions to put down on a piece of paper different expressions to show agreement or disagreement that they learned on the previous day. When the teacher asked them what they had put down, many were uncooperative and just said "zero." A couple of boys were making paper airplanes with the pieces of paper. Even at the beginning of the opinion-polling activity, many students were chatting in Cantonese when the teacher was giving instructions.

However, the whole scenario was changed when the first statement was given (line 8). Most students' attention was captured. The direct reference made to the quality of the teacher himself seems to have generated some impact on the students. Traditionally, Chinese students are taught to respect their teachers. Commenting on their teachers verbally in public, no matter whether the comments are positive or negative, is a very rare behavior (Biggs & Watkins, 1996). However, that does not mean students do not have any opinions about their teachers. Their desire to express may have been suppressed by certain socioculturally established behavior expectations. Now, under the encouragement of the teacher himself, all students can express their opinions about the teacher in front of him. From my experience as a local teacher, such an activity is unimaginable. Mr. Hood himself also admitted in the postobservation interview that it was a bold attempt. He had expected some unfriendly comments from the students. He knew that a few male students whose English was relatively better than that of others in the class always showed resistance to learning English by saying something in Cantonese which made the whole class laugh. He suspected that it was some kind of jeering and possibly insulting remarks about him. Instead of feeling angry, he saw it as psychological bait to motivate them to speak up in English. He wanted to build up their confidence and establish a kind of trust between himself and the students by showing his eagerness to listen to the students' voices. It is evident from Excerpt 2 that Mr. Hood's bold attempt afforded the students an opportunity to bring to surface suppressed forms of their self, and construct or renegotiate identities contrary to the institutionally expected one.

Obvious evidence showing students' behavioral changes could be found in Excerpt 2a (line 31) when it was the students, not the teacher, who were doing the shushing. The reason is simple. They were eager to participate in the activity and the first step of which involved listening to what the teacher was going to say. Their captivated attention is also evident in Excerpt 2b when all the student-response turns were self-selected by the students, whereas at the beginning of Excerpt 2a they were passively nominated by the teacher.

The interaction practice between Mr. Hood and his students (particularly the male ones) was in many ways illustrative of a kind of language play called "verbal duelling" (Cook, 2000). Although the language used was not conventionalized as in many typical cases of verbal dueling, the bantering back and forth between the teachers and students with witty and intricate insults and boasts, some of which were beyond the capturing of Excerpts 2a and 2b, were frequently in evidence during my visits. The defiant nature of some of the students' comments in Excerpt 2a (lines 20, 35, 37) mirrors those reported in Candlin et al.'s (2000) study. It is revealed in the study that adolescent participants tend to construct their identities through nonconforming behaviors. These include ignoring or giving dispreferred answers, joking, teasing, and swearing. Such desire to express themselves has often resulted in dynamic interaction behaviors. In Excerpt 2a, evidence is found showing how some of these discursive behaviors are transposed into English, which, according to Candlin et al. (2000), might be conducive to language learning.

As pointed out by Straehle (1993), teasing and playful barbs in an intimate behavior created alliances which reflect existing friendship, and "these same alliances enhance relationships by affording speakers 'safe' opportunities for showing conversational involvement and rapport" (p. 228). I would, therefore, claim that the opinion-polling exercise in Mr. Hood's F.4 class has allowed students an opportunity to develop a communicative intent which led to a genuine self-representation on the part of the students. In a postobservation interview with some of the most vocal and "nonconforming" students, they told me that they liked the discussion lesson very much because it was the first time in their secondary school life that they were allowed to express themselves so freely. Some said that they felt more confident in using English after the lesson because they had experienced success in genuinely interacting with a non-Cantonese-speaking person.

Although the class size is large (over 35 students) and students did not do a lot of speaking probably due to their limited English proficiency and lack of sufficient preparation, the sense of *active participation* in a discussion conducted in English is strong. The importance of participation in second language learning has been asserted by Pavlenko and Lantolf (2000). The metaphor of participation, as developed by Sfard (1998; quoted in Pavlenko & Lantolf, 2000), stresses the importance of membership as against the input–output conduit metaphor on the development of communication ability. To Pavlenko and Lantolf, participation and (re)construction of selves are mutually influenced. They argue that "A self is a coherent dynamic system that is in 'continuous production', and which emerges as the individual participates in the (most especially, verbal) practices of a culture. Thus, for children, growing up culturally is about engaging in activities" (p. 163). In turn, the desire to assert "self" has also motivated learners' active participation.

To many Hong Kong English teachers, the biggest challenge in their teaching is to motivate students to participate in L2 communication activities in the classroom. Excerpts 2a and 2b show how students' communicative intent has been successfully promoted, leading to active participation in the communicative activity. Although Mr. Hood's opinion-polling activity was basically teacher-led and conducted in lock-step style, students were observed having ample opportunities to make their voices and represent their selves. Although students still invariably used Cantonese to discuss the statements with their peers beyond the capturing of the microphone, whenever there was a need to address the teacher who was non-Cantonese-speaking, English (no matter how broken) had to be used. The experience students gained from participating in an L2 activity like this would have an impact on the (re)construction of their selves or identity as potential "multicompetent language users" (Cook, 1999). As evident in Excerpt 2, such multicompetence includes the ability to manifest multilingual and multicultural identities for global communication while maintaining one's local perspectives.

A closer look at Excerpts 2a and 2b enables us to discover the multiple identities the students were negotiating, constructing, and displaying. Following is a list of several identities:

*ID1–Learners of an international language*—Students displayed this identity by responding to the teacher's initiation in the target language. From the postobservation interview, students perceived this to be their *institutional* role. It should be noted that not all students displayed this identity (ID) conformingly. Some showed resistance to the institutional expectation on the fulfillment of this role. For example, many students refused to speak to their peers in English (the L2) and disregarded the teacher's pedagogical instructions.

*ID2–"Native" speakers of a language belonging to the local dominant social ethnic group*—This identity is felt to be the most deep-seated in the students. The local language (the students' L1) has planted the sociohistorical roots of the students' immediate life-world and contributed to students' selves, or local perspectives. It was confirmed from the interview that students almost invariably conducted their cognitive thinking in Cantonese and Cantonese was always the language for intimate talk with their peers. The sociocognitive functions of L1 in the L2 classroom and the positive impacts of these critical functions of L1 have been thoroughly discussed in literature (Anton & DiCamilla, 1998; Hancock, 1997).

*ID3–Interlocutors in a conversation that involves cross-cultural and interethnic elements*—The teacher, being a non-Cantonese-speaker who had newly arrived from a Western country, inevitably brought with him sociocultural perceptions about how things should be done which were likely to be different from members of the local community, including the students. Conversations of this kind between members of two distinct sociocultural life-worlds often involve the need to confront, and hopefully, resolve, conflicting ideologies from their counterparts. This is evident in Excerpt 2b when the teacher challenged the students' longstanding concepts of the purpose and methods of studying in school by making reference to how adolescents handled school work in the West. Such ability to participate in cross-cultural communication is growing in importance in view of the increasing opportunities for communication to be conducted globally and transnationally.

*ID4–Adolescents developing into adults who are capable of independent thinking*—This involves a development of cognitive ability to do critical thinking and the linguistic ability of adolescents to express opinions of their own. From my observation, although some students tended to follow their peers in choosing their own stances, quite a few were bold enough to be the odd ones out. The teacher, as expected, liked pursuing the thinking of these "odd" ones. It is interesting to note that on a few occasions, these "odd" ones changed their standpoints after some enquiries by the teacher. This is crucial evidence showing how identities are negotiable and constantly changing.

All the identities mentioned earlier do not contradict with each other. Instead, they seem to intertwine with, reinforce, and draw out the best from each other. Compared with the identities of the students in Excerpts 2a and 2b, those displayed by the two girls in Excerpt 1 were more limiting. Only identities 1 and 2 have been displayed. Despite this, due to the lack of sociocultural sensitivity of the task in Excerpt 1, the girls abandoned their ID1 shortly after the beginning of the activity. Their competence as native Cantonese speakers did not seem to have contributed to the advancement of their sociocognitive intellectual development either because of the controlled nature of the task. The lack of opportunities to construct ID3 and ID4 has also weakened the emergence of communication intent and undermined the development of the students concerned into multicompetent language users.

## IMPLICATIONS

### CLT and Global Communication

The contrasting students' behaviors in Excerpts 1 and 2 problematize many teachers' general beliefs about communicative language activities and point to the need for locally and socioculturally sensitive CLT methodology, particularly in view of the changing global communication structure and requirements. Evidence from the two contrasting excerpts supports that a prerequisite to communicate is the emergence of communicative intent. However, a communicative situation, one with a group of people and an information gap that needs to be bridged through communication, does not necessarily lead to *genuine* communication without the mediation of communicative space for the students to enter into with a need to express their selves. No doubt, an eagerness to speak for oneself is the prime origin of communicative intent. "Self" mediates between the speaking persons and the communicative situations. Students' awareness of their institutional identities as second language learners may have motivated them to take up speaking roles in activities such as the one presented in Excerpt 1. However, verbalizing voices does not necessarily equal communicating, which involves genuine expressions of thoughts, feelings, and intentions which are meaningful and relevant to the speakers.

## The Role of "Native" English-Speaking Teachers

As evident from Mr. Hood's lessons, the teacher often plays the role of a *linguistic mediator*, in addition to being the "cultural mediator" (Kramsch & Sullivan, 1996). In a basically monolingual society like Hong Kong with large monolingual classes in schools, such kind of linguistic and cultural mediation from L1 to L2 is almost always missing in peer-managed pair and group work. Apart from revisiting the desirability of relying on pair and group work as a means of engaging students in the use of target language for developing communicative competence (problems with the weak version of CLT suggested by Holliday, 1994), the role of the native-English-speaking teachers in CLT should also be reconsidered. Although both Miss Heron and Mr. Hood are native-English speakers, not both of them had experienced success with CLT. That means the target language nativeness of the teacher is not necessarily a promising factor in the promotion of students' communicative competence. Unexamined practice of dominant universal principles without relevant sensitivity to local subjectivities will not bring the expected success.

All the aforementioned discoveries point to the need for CLT practitioners in places like Hong Kong to reexamine their practices, particularly in the light of the recent boom in information technology, the globalization of the world economy, changes in economic and employment trends, and new requirements of literacy. The need to master English as a global language is all too obvious and in the process of appropriating the global discourse, we need language learning curricula that are not only based strictly on tasks which offer practice on narrowly defined and controlled syntactic or functional elements. We need curricula that could enable EIL learners to develop their global discourse competence by manifesting their pluralistic cultural and linguistic identities. Native-English speakers such as Miss

Heron and Mr. Hood have an important role to play in promoting ID3 of the students, that is, as creative interlocutors in cross-cultural and interethnic interactions. Their role in the English language curriculum should not be confined to providing a more "standard" language model for students to appropriate, but in providing the students live experiences in using English (the target language) for globalized communication.

## CONCLUSION

By presenting two contrasting classroom excerpts of CLT practices by native-English-speaking teachers in Hong Kong, I have shown how different CLT practices have resulted in different impacts on the learners' target language development. I have shown how the availability of a communicative space for learners to express in the target language with a localized self has facilitated the development of discourse competence for global communication. The prospect of being able to project, assert, and represent the self in interaction not only constitutes an important mediation in communication, but also enables the learners to situate themselves in and benefit from the global networks of human and economic resources through a possession of local knowledge and localized cultural and linguistic identities. Such discourse competence involves the ability to participate in intercultural and interethnic communications which are a distinct part of global interactions. The increased opportunities for conducting global communication in English point to the need for EIL teachers to develop in students the awareness of a plurality of cultures, identities, and perspectives of "other" EIL interlocutors in different parts of the world. The ability to negotiate self-relevant local perspectives in response to the linguistic and ideological challenges of other EIL speakers, therefore, seems to be a crucial skill to develop in learners of English as an international language.

## REFERENCES

Anton, M., & DiCamilla, F. (1998). Socio-cognitive functions of L1 collaborative interaction in the L2 classroom. *The Canadian Modern Language Review, 54,* 315–342.

Bakhtin, M. M. (1981). The dialogic imagination: Four essays by M. M. Bakhtin. In C. Emerson (Ed.), (C. Emerson & M. Holquist, Trans.). Austin: University of Texas Press.

Belay, G. (1996). The (re)construction and negotiation of cultural identities in the age of globalization. In H. B. Mokros (Ed.), *Interaction & Identity* (Vol. 5, pp. 319–346). New Brunswick, NJ: Transaction Publishers.

Biggs, J., & Watkins, D. (1996). The Chinese learners in retrospect. In D. Watkins & J. B. Biggs (Eds.), *The Chinese learner: Cultural, psychological and contextual influences*. Hong Kong, China: Comparative Education Research Center.

Boyle, J. (1997). Native-speaker teachers of English in Hong Kong. *Language and Education, 11,* 163–181.

Breen, M. P. (1986). The social context for language learning—A neglected situation? *Studies of Second Language Acquisition, 7,* 135–158.

Canagarajah, A. S. (1999). *Resisting linguistic imperialism in English teaching*: Oxford, England: Oxford University Press.

Candlin, C. N., Lin, A. M. Y., & Lo, T. W. (2000). *The discourse of adolescents in Hong Kong* (City University of Hong Kong Strategic Research Grant No. 7000707). Hong Kong, China: City University of Hong Kong.

Cook, G. (2000). *Language Play, Language Learning.* Oxford University Press.

Cook, V. (1999). Going beyond the native speaker in language teaching. *TESOL Quarterly, 33,* 185–209.

Curriculum Development Council. (1983). *Syllabus for English (Forms 1–5).* Hong Kong, China: The Education Department.

Curriculum Development Council. (1999). *Syllabuses for Secondary Schools: English Language Secondary 1–5.* Hong Kong, China: The Education Department.

Ellis, G. (1996). How culturally appropriate is the communicative approach? *ELT Journal, 50,* 213–218.

Evans, S. (1996). The context of English language education: The case of Hong Kong. *RELC Journal, 27,* 30–55.

Evans, S. (1997). Teacher and learner roles in the Hong Kong English language classroom. *Education Journal, 25,* 43–61.

Goffman, E. (1981). *Forms of talk.* Oxford, England: Basil Blackwell.

Hancock, M. (1997). Behind classroom code switching: Layering and language choice in L2 learner interaction. *TESOL Quarterly, 31,* 217–235.

Holliday, A. (1994). *Appropriate methodology and social context.* Cambridge, England: Cambridge University Press

Ivanic, R. (1998). *Writing and identity*: Amsterdam: Benjamins.

Johnson, K., & Tang, G. (1993). Engineering a shift to English in Hong Kong schools. In T. Boswood, R. Hoffman, & P. Tung (Eds.), *Perspectives on English for professional communication* (pp. 203–216). Hong Kong, China: City Polytechnic of Hong Kong.

Kramsch, C. (2000). Social discursive constructions of self in L2 learning. In J. P. Lantolf (Ed.), *Sociocultural theory and second language learning* (pp. 133–154). Oxford, England: Oxford University Press.

Kramsch, C., & Sullivan, P. (1996). Appropriate pedagogy. *ELT Journal, 50,* 199–212.

Kwan, M. H. Y. (2000). Reconsidering language learners' needs: A critical look at classroom verbal play of a reading lesson in Hong Kong. In D. C. S. Li, A. Lin, & W. K. Tsang (Eds.), *Language and education in postcolonial Hong Kong* (pp. 297–316). Hong Kong, China: Linguistic Society of Hong Kong.

Lai, C. (1994). Communication failure in the language classroom: An exploration of causes. *RELC Journal, 25,* 99–129.

Le Page, R. (1986). Acts of identity. *English Today, 8,* 21–24.

Lin, A. M. Y. (2000). Lively children trapped in an island of disadvantage: Verbal play of Cantonese working-class schoolboys in Hong Kong. *International Journal of Sociology and Language, 143,* 63–83.

Littlewood, W. (1981). *Communicative language teaching: An introduction.* Cambridge, England: Cambridge University Press.

Pavlenko, A., & Lantolf, J. P. (2000). Second language learning as participation and the (re)construction of selves. In J. P. Lantolf (Ed.), *Sociocultural theory and second language learning* (pp. 155–178). Oxford, England: Oxford University Press.

Pennington, M. C. (1999a). Bringing off-stage 'noise' to centre stage: A lesson in developing bilingual classroom discourse data. *Language Teaching Research, 3,* 85–116.

Pennington, M. C. (1999b). Framing bilingual classroom discourse: Lessons from Hong Kong secondary school English classes. *International Journal of Bilingual Education and Bilingualism, 2,* 53–73.

Pennycook, A. (1994). *The cultural politics of English as an International language.* London: Longman.

Savignon, S. J. (1991). Communicative language teaching: State of the art. *TESOL Quarterly, 25,* 261–295.

Straehle, C. A. (1993). "Samuel?" "Yes, dear?" Teasing and conversational rapport. In D. Tannen (Ed.), *Framing in discourse* (pp. 210–230). New York: Oxford University Press.

Sullivan, P. N. (2000). Playfulness as mediation in communicative language teaching in a Vietnamese classroom. In J. P. Lantolf (Ed.), *Sociocultural theory and second language learning* (pp. 115–132). Oxford, England: Oxford University Press.

Tsui, A. B. M. (1996). Reticence and anxiety in second language learning. In K. M. Bailey & D. Nunan (Eds.), *Voices from the language classroom* (pp. 145–167). Cambridge, England: Cambridge University Press.

Wertsch, J. V. (1991). *Voices of the mind.* Cambridge, MA: Harvard University Press.

Young, R., & Lee, S. (1987). EFL curriculum innovation and teachers' attitudes. In R. Lord & H. Cheng (Eds.), *Language education in Hong Kong* (pp. 83–97). Hong Kong, China: Chinese University Press.

# APPENDIX

## Transcription Conventions

| | |
|---|---|
| GS | • Girl student |
| BS | • Boy student |
| Ss | • Students |
| NT | • The native English teacher |
| **Bold print** | • Romanised transcriptions of Cantonese |
| *<Italics>* | • free translation of the Cantonese into English |
| Comma | • sense group boundary |
| Period | • falling intonation |
| Carat | • slightly rising intonation |
| Question mark | • slightly rising intonation |
| = | • latching |
| [ | • the beginning of overlapping speech |
| ( ) | • the fieldworker/author's commentary |
| CAPITALS | • Strongly stressed words |
| (???) | • inaudible utterances |
| - | • discontinued speech |
| (…) | • pausing (the more dots there are, the longer the pauses) |
| a::ll | • elongated vowels |

# Chapter 12

# Local Knowledge and Global Citizenship: Languages and Literatures of the United States– Mexico Borderlands

Elisabeth Mermann-Jozwiak
Nancy Sullivan
*Texas A&M University–Corpus Christi*

## INTRODUCTION

The issue of globalization has spawned numerous debates in English Studies, resulting in a search for new pedagogies, theories, and methodologies that reflect the new sociocultural, political, and economic realities. It has led to the publication of monographs, essays, and special issues of journals on the subject, most recently the *PMLA* (January 2001) and the *TESOL Quarterly* (Autumn 2000). Globalization, the interconnectedness of the world in a single global marketplace, which shapes politics and international relations, is seen by many as an essentially liberating phenomenon that aids in the democratization of societies and individuals (Friedman, 1999; Markee, 2000; Warschauer, 2000). Although the United States is at the forefront of the globalization process, social inequities concerning unequal access to important resources such as education *within* the United States remain disquieting. At a university heavily supported by an infusion of funds as a result of a Mexican American Legal Defense Fund suit—a law-

269

suit against the state of Texas for its lack of facilities of higher education for underrepresented populations—we need to be more cautious in our celebration of globalization and instead foreground the problems of access and academic success.

One of the recurring issues that emerge in discussions of globalization is the difficulty of negotiating "local diversity and global connectedness" (New London Group, 1996, p. 61; see also Warschauer, 2000). This chapter attempts to outline ways in which "local diversity" can be a valuable tool in fostering citizenship that is attuned to and skilled to deal with "global connectedness." We argue that a focus on local knowledges, specifically of Mexican American languages, literacies, literatures, and cultures, can foster what the New London Group (1996) has termed *multiliteracies*. The New London Group argues that whereas traditional literacy pedagogy means "teaching and learning how to read and write in page-bound, official, standard forms of the national language" (p. 61), "multiliteracies" represent the ability of "negotiating a multiplicity of discourses" (p. 61); of "interact[ing] effectively using multiple languages, multiple Englishes, and communication patterns that more frequently cross cultures, community, and national boundaries" (p. 64). These skills are indicative, we believe, of a global citizenship defined through exposure to and knowledge of various cultures, languages, and subcultures, which enable a flexibility that allows individuals to function adequately in different contexts.

Such multiliteracies were the focus of a course on Chicana language and literature that the authors, a Sociolinguist and an Americanist, team-taught at Texas A&M University–Corpus Christi. The course was designed to expose graduate and undergraduate students, most of whom were teaching in local schools or were studying to become teachers, to texts by authors such as Gloria Anzaldúa, Ana Castillo, Pat Mora, and Helena María Viramontes. Highlighting the interrelationships among language, culture, and identity, this noncanonical literature is reflective of knowledges and practices common to our local environment. It engages in various forms of syncretism: linguistically, by combining English and Spanish, mirroring the locally widespread uses of nonstandard English and of code-switching between English–Spanish; epistemologically, by bringing together elements from Meso-American and European spiritual and religious worlds; and ontologically, by juxtaposing worldviews that are rooted in rationalist assumptions with those that endorse nonrational elements as expressed in folklore, superstitions, and myths—a blending of views that finds expression in literary mode of "Magical Realism." These texts further confront students with nonofficial histories, focusing on knowledge and experiences of Mexican Americans and revolving around migrant farm work, land dispossession, legal and illegal border crossings, and bilingualism and biculturalism, all issues that rarely find entry into educational institutions. Through examining noncanonical texts such as these, current and future teachers interact with and negotiate the culturally constructed imagery, knowledges, languages, and world-views of many in the Mexican American community, activities which are essential in understanding minority students' home cultures.

In a study the authors conducted (Sullivan & Mermann-Jozwiak, 2000), we found that high school and college curricula do not pay as much attention to local, noncanonical writers and histories as they could to help ensure student success. Although Corpus Christi has a majority minority population of Mexican Americans, the school system places more value on European American traditions and culture. Students in the discipline of English are traditionally enculturated into canonical literature (read the masters!) and into standard language use (adopt correct English syntactical, lexical, and phonological patterns!). This assimilationist model of success asks students to leave behind language and culture only to adopt the dominant language and culture. One consequence of this model is that language minority students are often viewed from a deficit perspective (Bartolome & Trueba, 2000). The model further creates a hierarchical binary according to which everything that is not in the center is relegated to the periphery. Theorists of globalization have shown that this model of learning, a very authoritative one, is outmoded. For example, it does not take into account the emergence of multiple Englishes or "english," the numerous varieties of nonstandard English, and it also does not build on minority students' experiences to ensure success (Ashcroft, Griffiths, & Tiffin, 1989; Warschauer, 2000). The role of teachers is crucial in bridging cultural barriers. Teachers "can create a climate of warmth and acceptance for language minority children, supporting the home language ..." or "they can allow policies of the school to benefit only the language majority students by accepting the exclusive use of the dominant language, permitting majority language students to gain through the social and cultural reward system at the expense of those students who speak minority languages" (Díaz-Rico & Weed, 1995, p. 261). Similarly, Trueba (1999) claims that school activities must be perceived by students as supportive of their culture and home values to promote their success in the classroom. Our argument is twofold: first, that teachers need to acquire the skills that help them understand minority students' home cultures; that is, they need to be versed in local knowledges and become global citizens themselves. Second, we argue that, in a geographic area such as South Texas, where minority school failure is endemic, curricular inclusions of the language and the literatures produced by Mexican American writers in the Southwestern United States help bridge cultural and linguistic discontinuities present in the current educational system by tapping into and validating students' experiences.

**Theories of Failure**

The quest to explain minority school failure has produced multiple and diverse theories (for an excellent review of these issues, with a focus on Chicanos, see Valencia, 2002). Some propose genetic or environmental influences (Dunn, 1987; Eysenck, 1971; Herrnstein & Murray, 1994; Jensen, 1972, Stein, 1985), cultural deprivation (Bloom, Davis, & Hess, 1965; Heller, 1966; Valentine, 1968; see also Gibson, 1997, for review), language and cultural differences (Carter & Segura, 1979; Erickson, 1994; Laosa, 1984; Mehan, 1992; Trueba, 1991), and socioeconomic factors (Chapa, 1991; Valencia & Suzuki, 2001). In addition, schooling inequalities have been traced to discriminatory testing practices (Valencia & Aburto, 1991) as well as teacher attitudes and beliefs (August & Hakuta, 1997; Díaz-Rico & Weed, 1995; Ford, 1984; Richardson, 1997; Williams, 1976), teacher–student interaction (Padilla & Alva, 1988; Stevenson & Ellsworth, 1993), and institutionalized discrimination (Ogbu, 1992; Suarez-Orozco & Suarez-Orozco, 1995a, 1995b).

Many of the aforementioned models address pieces of the complex identity and language issues found in South Texas schools. However, if all languages and cultures are equally salient, a center–periphery model that favors European American culture along with a standard variety dialect and that devalues minority cultures and languages is untenable. The model that more convincingly begins to address the situation in the South Texas borderlands advances *cultural discontinuities* rather than cultural deficiencies as a crucial factor in school success or failure. The cultural discontinuity model considers, among other things, how majority and minority populations differ in language, cultural experiences, and value orientation (Carter & Segura, 1979; Trueba, 1989a, 1989b, 1993; Trueba, Rodriguez, Zou, & Cintron, 1993). These discontinuities, if left unaddressed by the education system, can lead to inequality of opportunity and empowerment. Zentella (1997) states that "The pull between what is rewarded in school and expected at home, and the stress occasioned by learning to speak and act appropriately in both worlds, make most Latino children true 'border children' ..." (p. 127). Currently, preservice teachers are mostly European American, female, and middle class (Bartolome & Trueba, 2000). In public schools, teachers traditionally draw on the assimilation model, which values middle-class European American culture and language. These teachers, consciously or unconsciously, are biased in favor of students who already speak the standard dialect. The resulting lack of continuity between home and school can lead, not surprisingly, to grave scholastic problems for minority students. For example, verbal interactions can be problematic. Heath (1983) illustrates this by showing how indirect commands used as verbal directives by middle-class European American teachers (e.g., "Would you like to clean off your desk now?") can be misunderstood by African American working-class children as questions rather than commands.

The cultural discontinuities model proposes that a learning environment that values the students' cultures and languages, that allows students to engage in activities where they can show their expertise, and that capitalizes on the students' linguistic and cultural experiences and knowledges, will foster academic success. In this model, the role of teachers and their willingness to include relevant learning experiences is crucial in determining the success or failure of minority children. Unacceptably large numbers of Corpus Christi's minority students are failing; in turn, it was not surprising to find that out of 139 undergraduate students surveyed at Texas A&M University–Corpus Christi, only 28% had been exposed to any Chicano or Chicana literature at the elementary or secondary school level (Sullivan & Mermann-Jozwiak, 2000). Additionally, the majority of those who had read such literature reported doing so in their Spanish classes—another indication of how the students' experiences and knowledges are often ignored in the core courses.

As with other proposed theories, the cultural discontinuity model does not address all the important and complex factors responsible for academic success or failure. For example, Ogbu (1987, 1991) argues that one limitation of the model is that it does not take into account the different types of minorities, some of whom gain academic success more easily than others (a voluntary immigrant or involuntary minority distinction). We claim that it also does not account for the negative attitudes faced by Mexican Americans and other minorities in South Texas and elsewhere in the United States (see Galindo, 1996, and Zentella, 1997, for a discussion of negative attitudes toward language use). Following, we return to the issue of language attitudes, as they pertain to South Texas.

## Educational Failure and Success in the Borderlands

Corpus Christi is located in South Texas, 2 hours north of the Mexican border, and has a "majority minority" population (50% Mexican American, 43% European American). The Mexican American (MA) community is by no means homogeneous in its linguistic and cultural practices. Some are recent immigrants from Mexico who use Spanish as the home language. Others have lived in Texas for generations and, within their bilingual community, Spanish–English code-switching (referred to locally as Tex–Mex) is the unmarked (i.e., the expected or normal) discourse code. For many, MA culture and language are at odds with the school language and culture, setting up students for educational problems if the discontinuity remains unaddressed.

In the Corpus Christi public school district, MA children make up 69% of the student body (24% European American, 6% African American, and 1%

Other). Educators in the area are concerned about the school dropout rate. In the district's senior high school classes (1998–1999), 30% of the MA students were classified as being at risk of dropping out of school, compared to 14% of the European Americans (EA). The 4-year dropout rate for MAs was 13.2% compared to 5.8% for EAs in the class of 1999. An additional 17% of the MA students did not graduate with their class but had to continue taking high school classes to receive their diplomas (Caballero, 2001). Local educators interviewed in a March 2001 series, "Left Behind: School Dropouts," in *The Corpus Christi Caller Times*, (http://wwwcaller2.com/dropouts/) attribute a number of causes to the high dropout rate, including low socioeconomic status, the social pressure to leave school and earn easy money on the street or to hang out with friends, the sense of not "fitting in" in an academic setting, the perception that nobody at school cares about them, a family background that does not support academics, poor academic achievement in school (Schwartz, 2001), and lack of English language skills (Caballero, 2001).

Interestingly, local educators failed to cite discrimination or the marginalization of the MA community as a possible cause for the high number of MA dropouts; however, previous research strongly suggests that these factors should be considered as components of any theory that tries to account for minority children's school failure in the city. In two studies conducted in Corpus Christi on attitudes toward English language legislation (ELL), Sullivan and Schatz (1999) found not only strong support for ELL, but also enmity toward the MA population and Spanish language use. When the respondents, who were university students (many of them education majors), were asked to provide reasons for their support of ELL, hostile statements were not uncommon (e.g., "Mexicans should go to Mexico if they want to speak Spanish," "immigrants are taking advantage of Americans," "I'm tired of seeing billboard advertisements in Spanish," "I can't stand it when two or more people are conversing in a foreign language right in front of me," etc.). Eleven percent of the responses were overtly hostile, and others seemed driven by antiforeigner sentiments (e.g., "People are coming into our country of their own free will, and they should adapt to us, not us to them."). As the minority population of the United States increases, there is a concomitant increase in anti-immigrant, antiminority, antibilingual education and pro-English legislation policies (see also Ray & Tinsley, 1995, on findings of a Texas Harte–Hanks poll on "English-Only" and immigration).

Language restriction laws intersect with minority rights and the place of cultural diversity in schools (King, 1997). The support in Corpus Christi for making English the official language of the United States clearly shows the implication of language in structures of domination. For example, the MA students' cultural and linguistic knowledge may be ignored or not fully utilized as an academic springboard to success; in fact, it appears that the cultural background of MAs and the Spanish dialect of the border are considered hindrances or deficiencies by the school system. Texans of Mexican descent in their 40s, 50s, and older report having had their names anglicized and undergoing physical punishment for speaking Spanish in elementary and high school. San Antonio poet Diana Montejano reported that, when she was in school, speaking Spanish was considered an "infraction," punishable by a slap with a ruler (Mermann-Jozwiak & Sullivan, 2000; see also Anzaldúa, 1999). Currently, students are asked to refrain from speaking Spanish in school with their friends, and local Corpus Christi employees have been reprimanded for speaking Spanish at work. As recently as 1995, a judge in Amarillo, Texas, demanded that a mother speak only English to her 5-year-old daughter, as speaking Spanish was a form of child abuse. The judge believed that the mother would be relegating the girl to a life as a maid if she spoke Spanish to her (Ray & Tinsley, 1995). These sentiments indicate the urgent need for dialogue and for education, particularly on the part of teachers. They are rarely trained to examine or identify their own beliefs about language minority students, and it is precisely these beliefs that can impact their students (Cutri, 2000).

## THE CHICANA LITERATURE AND LANGUAGE COURSE

### The Role of Literature and Language Studies

In South Texas, MA students' linguistic and cultural knowledge can be easily drawn on by including a Chicano and Chicana literature component in the curriculum. By emphasizing the historical, sociological, cultural, and linguistic conditions that set the stage for such literature, students are then able to examine more critically the existing constructs of language and culture and of domination and subordination—an essential undertaking for *all* students. Moreover, students who are engaged in relevant learning activities are provided opportunities to demonstrate their competence, which opens up the possibility of building self-confidence and academic motivation. Our college-level Chicana Language and Literature (CLL) course was designed to model these assumptions for future public-school teachers. Thirty-one students enrolled; eighteen were graduate students, and thirteen undergraduates. Fourteen considered themselves MA, thirteen EA, one Native American, and three African American.

*Course Goals.*     A team-taught class is ideally situated to show the interconnectedness and interdisciplinary nature of knowledge. In the language component of the class, our goal was to expose CLL students to the multiple discourses of the community, to the well-documented and negative attitudes toward nonstandard uses of English, the negative attitudes toward the use of Spanish and code-switching in Corpus Christi, to the rule-governed and domain-specific nature of code-switching, and to the history and politics of Spanish use in the Southwestern United States. As language "is the culturally constructed, conventional, and mutually presupposed imagery of worldview" (Palmer, 1996, p. 6), examination of the aforementioned linguistic issues allows students to negotiate the different local knowledges and ideologies often found in conflict in South Texas.

In the literature section of the course, we sought to introduce these current and future teachers to literature written by Chicanas. As a noncanonical literature, works by Chicanos and Chicanas do not adequately find representation in most high school textbooks used in the city due to traditional constructions of the English curriculum which place little value in local knowledges (DePaolo, 2000). We sought to foster an understanding of this literature as part of a distinct tradition with recurring historical and cultural references, distinctive use of genres, tropes and motifs such as the stories of *la llorona* or *la Malinche*, as well as its use of border Spanish and code-switching. Our goal was to provide tools for critical analysis of these texts by connecting the textual and the contextual dimensions of Chicana language and literature through a series of guest lectures by speakers from a variety of disciplines, including linguistics, art, anthropology, history, and sociology. Chicana critic Sánchez (1985) stresses the contextual and interlingual nature of Chicana poetry as well as its dialogue with and participation in history. She argues that it "exhibits a political, social, and cultural self-consciousness" (Sánchez, 1985, p. 1). Much Chicana poetry, then, is political in nature, focusing on issues of individual and collective identity, highlighting the culture of MA communities, the history of Chicano struggles, and issues of social justice. The political nature of this poetry may therefore elicit strong reactions from students with different conceptions of what poetry ought to be and may force them to confront issues they are unwilling to face.

## Pedagogical Elements of the Course

Three classroom assignments were designed to model one of the tenets of Critical Pedagogy to our CLL students, namely how teachers can involve students in becoming agents in their own learning processes (Aronowitz & Giroux, 1985; Freire, 1989; Weiler, 1988). In Aronowitz and Giroux's (1985) articulations of critical pedagogy, it

> would focus on the study of curriculum not merely as a matter of self-cultivation or the mimicry of specific forms of language and knowledge. On the contrary, it would stress forms of learning and knowledge aimed at providing a critical understanding of how social reality works, it would focus on how certain dimensions of such a reality are sustained, it would focus on the na-

ture of its formative processes, and it would also focus on how those aspects of it that are related to the logic of domination can be changed. (p. 217)

Kathleen Weiler (1988) elaborates that "critical pedagogy needs to make these conflicts themselves part of the text of critical teaching" (p. 150), and she continues, "the empowerment of students means encouraging them to explore and analyze the forces acting upon their lives" (p. 152). What educators need to understand is the large-scale implications of findings such as these, and, even more importantly, they must realize that teaching is never a politically and culturally neutral activity.

Although this was not a teacher education course, many of our students were teachers or studying to become teachers; therefore, we were deliberate in modeling for them pedagogical practices that we felt enhanced student learning. The class projects focused on the CLL students' local environment and, in essence, required them to become field workers, exploring the (dis)connections between this body of literature and the local community. Student projects were crucial in enhancing the learning process and became themselves topics of discussion.

**Examining the Language and Literature**

For the first exercise, each CLL student selected a Chicana poem and conducted a discussion section with participants from outside the class. The goal was to examine respondents' attitudes toward the literature and the language used in the poem. Most chose poetry by Anzaldúa or Mora that they had previously studied in class, but one, Victoria García,[1] chose a self-authored poem entitled "Homemade tortillas" for the exercise. Prior to speaking with respondents, CLL students were to examine their own biases and expectations. Students met with small groups of respondents outside of class where they wrote about and then discussed their reactions to the poem. The CLL students presented written project reports, which were used as the basis for our follow-up class discussion.

The students found a surprising (given our location) lack of previous exposure to MA literature and lack of knowledge about MA culture. They also found a whole gamut of identifications of MAs with MA culture, reflecting the heterogeneity of the MA population in South Texas and suggesting that although social identity is an important category, it is not a reliable indicator of attitudes. The MA responses to the poem ranged from "these poets are just whining," or "they overemphasize difference," with respondents finding no points of identification, to "yes, this poet expresses how I feel." In the latter category, the poetry frequently prompted respondents to share

---

[1]Names of students and respondents have all been changed.

their own life stories. "Jorge," for example, student Sandra Villarreal reported, was inspired to write his own poetry. Victoria García concluded that she needed to share more of her creative work. Others recognized the function of poetry in the transmission of culture, which can forge important connections among people. Student Jackie Perez stated that her MA respondents appreciated the poetry's ability to facilitate a process of (re)discovery of parts of their heritage and of realizing the importance "of telling stories of our history."

Code-switching was seen by some of the respondents as appropriate and reflective of MA culture—it was perceived as adding authenticity to the poetic expressions—whereas others disapproved of Tex–Mex, found it irritating, exclusive or even divisive, interfering with understanding, and suggesting a lack of education. Nonetheless, the two CLL students, Kate Davis and Chris Reese, who were secondary English teachers and used their own high school classrooms as fora for the exercise, both reported that the MA students in their classes found the exercise engaging and that many of the normally quiet students spoke up in class for the first time. During a minilecture on Chicano history to provide context for a reading, Reese observed that students "sat up in their seats and eagerly awaited the next bits of information." By conducting this poetry exercise with their students, Davis and Reese both learned about the kinds of issues and materials that help involve high school students in their own learning. Their findings are indicative of the positive processes that can occur in the classroom when including this literature.

The EA respondents reacted with empathy for the experiences the poetry portrayed, but also frequently with frustration when encountering the literature because of its inaccessibility; the use of different techniques, images, and languages all created discomfort and an increased awareness of cultural barriers and differences. Such lack of knowledge of MA culture produced significant misreadings due to the imposition of one cultural framework onto the other in the analysis of themes, techniques, images, and symbols. For example, a frequent symbol in MA literature, the serpent, was seen from a Judeo-Christian context as symptomatic of evil, and not from a Nahua framework where it signifies a connection to the earth and refers to Coatlicue, Aztec mother of the gods. Such cultural barriers often created a sense of alienation from the poetry. These CLL student findings indicate the need for further education, which can lead to greater appreciation for diversity and dispel stereotypes (for similar misreadings, see Saldívar-Hull, 2000, p. 22). As CLL student Heather Norton said, "being able to look at life through Chicana literature is one way to reach a better understanding of what it is like to live in the borderlands." Her response underscores the importance for all students to explore the social contexts of local literature to promote an understanding of the communities in which we live.

The exercise benefitted all learners in that it used difference as a productive resource in the classroom, which, after all, functions as a microcosmic reflection of society (New London Group, 1996). Although some MA students saw their culture and knowledge validated, EA students, in essence, were asked to learn a new language, a new variety of "nonstandard" literature. As the New London group argues, in a global world, "the most important skill students need to learn is to negotiate regional, ethnic, or class-based dialects; variations in register that occur according to social context; hybrid cross-cultural discourses; the code-switching often to be found within a text among different languages ..." (p. 69). With this assignment, CLL students in effect became teachers of the poetry, facilitators of the discussion, listening to and learning from the respondents who frequently reacted with stories of their own. They got the groups writing, reading, and thinking about a wide range of issues and facilitated dialogues on race relations, racial and cultural identity, culture clashes, the roles of literature in society, language and cultural barriers, biculturalism, and bilingualism. Their findings further underscore the potential of Chicana poetry to serve as an educational tool whose content provides insight into diverse local values and cultural practices and whose form can elicit discussion that may help to dispel negative attitudes toward uses of nonstandard languages.

## Examining Communicative Events

The second assignment required the CLL students to reflect, observe, and write an ethnography of communication—a report on a communicative event in their community (see Saville-Troike, 1989, for framework). The goal of the exercise was to create an awareness of the different communities and cultures in South Texas and to enhance intercultural understanding. The exercise at first proved challenging as the CLL students were asked to critically examine a "normal" event in their community, defined as family, neighborhood, ethnic group, and so forth, in terms of message forms, participant roles, rules for interaction, and norms of interpretation. Some of the situations students chose to describe included a traditional Mexican hog slaughter, rituals of a Mexican funeral, a marriage proposal in a MA family, a reunion of a EA family, the singing of "Spirit of Aggieland" at a Midnight Yell Practice (a long-standing Texas A&M University-College Station tradition), a Catholic confession, the interaction in an African American "beauty-shoppe," the gender roles at a MA dinner, and Dine (Navajo) dining customs. We collected students' ethnographies in a book and asked them to read several and respond to one in the reading journals they kept during the semester.

The first and second assignments used the ethnographic method of listening to and learning from informants and from each other. Through both the poetry and the ethnographic study, students increased awareness of cultural and linguistic values, practices, religion, gender divisions, and attitudes in their local community.

## Surveying Language Attitudes

The third assignment prompted students to design, conduct, and analyze a survey on language use and language legislation. Students developed a 7-item questionnaire in class with prompts concerning people's attitudes about making English the official language of Texas and about using Spanish in private and public domains in Corpus Christi. The survey also included a demographic section. On a 5-point Likert-type scale (1—*strongly disagree* to 5—*strongly agree*), respondents evaluated a variety of statements such as "it is appropriate for students to speak to one another or their teachers in Spanish in public schools" (question 1), "it bothers me when a Spanish language advertisement is aired on an English language channel" (question 5), "Spanish-speaking parents should teach their children Spanish" (question 4), or "English should be made the official language of Texas" (question 7). Students were responsible for distributing 20 to 25 surveys, analyzing the results, and summarizing their findings. Although exposing students to research methodology was important, what we considered even more meaningful was the experience of taking the pulse of the community and discovering firsthand what some of the class readings had sought to transmit: that language is a contested site in the Texas–Mexico borderlands and that there is strong disagreement within and across ethnic lines about the proper uses of language (see, for example, Galindo, 1996; Lippi-Green, 1997; and Zentella, 1997).

All three assignments focused on the students' interaction with their local community, that is, on the linguistic and cultural practices and on the prevailing *perceptions* of those practices, which are often regarded as parochial and peripheral. Student products and class discussions revealed that the issues raised by the literature led to manifold negotiations of identity and difference, particularly on the part of the MA students. Although we had expected a certain degree of resistance to the materials from EA students, most made an honest effort to view class readings and materials sympathetically—the self-selective nature of a group that *chose* to enroll in the course may account for this. It was the four other minority students who most unequivocally identified with the struggles the authors describe and who added their own similar experiences. In turn, we were surprised to find MA students sharply divided. Most made use of the opportunity our class sought to provide for them to help educate others about their heritage. However, there was a very vocal minority for whom the materials raised serious issues. Although these MA students learned about the heterogeneity of their own community as well as the multiple identities found within it, they were confronted with the question of how to position themselves vis-à-vis the Chicanas about whom they were reading. They rejected a hyphenated identity, insisted on calling themselves "Americans," and, in some cases, didn't speak Spanish. Their eagerness to move into or to remain in the American mainstream may be due to the fact that they had already achieved a considerable degree of academic success (they had made it through high school and were seniors or graduate students in college). Their desire to be part of that mainstream was expressed in frequent statements that echo dominant ideology, such as "everyone can achieve the American Dream if only they try hard enough."

It was in the first exercise and subsequent poetry discussions, completed at the beginning of the semester, that these patterns of negotiation became most obvious. Although three EA students "played it safe" and deliberately stayed away from controversy by choosing a formalist approach for their poetry reading groups, focusing exclusively on the poem's language or imagery, an overwhelming majority presented one of the very provocative readings by Anzaldúa to their reading circles. Because we had asked students to articulate their expectations before they discussed their findings, many elaborated on their learning processes, and reflected on their own subject positions. Several of the MA students described their initial reactions to her poetry. Ana Romero, for example, quite clearly stated that Anzaldúa "made her angry." Klara Ortiz asked, "how dare she [Anzaldúa] speak for all MAs?" She argued, "we have to move on and see past the tragedy of history."

Several of these students, however, were led by their discussion participants to revise their initial judgments and moved from a rejection of alternative histories and realities to more complex reflections. One poem by Anzaldúa, "El Sonovabitche," triggered particularly intense discussion. It describes, from the perspective of MA migrant farm workers, what historian David Montejano (1987, p. 197) has identified as part of "coercive labor relations," the practice of calling the border patrol on workers on or right before payday. Linda Castillo, who worried about being seen by friends and family as a "sell out" because she teaches in the composition program at the university, reported her own disbelief in the events narrated: "I suspected," she explains, that "Anzaldúa might have exaggerated some of the details." She found it inconceivable that people would act so "low." After inviting a former migrant worker into her poetry circle, she revised her judgment. The participant insisted on the poem's historical accuracy, and as a result, she concluded, "I recognize that I might be much too naive to believe that such horrible situations exist in the world." Linda's experience shows that the literature may confront readers with alternative histories and alternate ways of interpreting social realities. However, the texts alone do not necessarily lead to new insights. Instead, for those insights to occur, the role of the students' interaction with the non-campus community as well as the other class participants are crucial. Through these interactions, students began to see what Yaeger (2000, p. 88) in a different context has called "knowledges unknown," in other words, they gained insight into Texas history and social relations that is are not admitted into official textbooks. Furthermore, we were able to show that these invisible and unacknowledged realities, although counted as "local experiences," are nonetheless enmeshed in global politics, in this case the movement of labor across borders as a result of transnational capitalism. Global citizenship, for all students, then, entails gaining a "geopolitical literacy,"—that is, an ongoing successive realizations of how local practices are connected to global processes.

On the one hand, EA students learned through interaction with class-mates, the Corpus Christi Community, readings, and other materials, how to work against biases and beliefs such as the corruption of English if they are to become global citizens. We found that actively engaging them in the community and researching community literacy issues helped students put their own attitudes and ideologies into context. For example, student Kim Jennings wrote that before taking this course, she had always considered MAs who substituted "b's" for "v's" in their speech as "ignorant." Biases such as these can, as we have seen, be detrimental to minority student success. Although EA students learned from MA participants, they also helped educate the EA public. Stacey Johnson and Jennifer Hale, for example, chose Anzaldúa's poem, "La curandera," about a Mexican American faith healer, as the subject for discussion and encountered distinctly negative reactions by native Corpus Christians (EA). The respondents unambiguously called the curanderas "dangerous quacks" and followed up with the question, "Why read this stuff at the university?" Although initially uncomfortable in her role, Hale nonetheless managed to direct the conversation in a way that focused on the spiritual significance of a curandera's work within her cultural context.

## CONCLUSION

If it is true that academic success can be fostered through educational and cultural continuities, the research conducted by our CLL students demonstrates that our community has not begun to redress the educational issues of our MA students. We are not systematically providing our students with the multiliteracies required by the rapid globalization process where "local" and "global" have become less distinct. They are not learning the flexibility and adaptability that define global citizenship (New London Group, 1996). Although students no longer have to anglicize their names, their cultural and linguistic heritage is still marginalized or devalued. Although they are no longer being physically punished for speaking Spanish, we are not building on their cultural and linguistic strengths. And this should be more than a local concern. The MA population in Texas is expected to be the majority within the next 10 years, and similar demographic changes are taking place nationally. The number of EA school children in the United States is expected to decrease over the next few years whereas the number of MAs will continue to increase. By 2020 it is predicted that 25% of all school children in the United States will be Hispanic (Trueba, 1999). By the mid-21st century, minorities (Hispanics, Blacks, and Asians) will constitute half of the U.S. population. Nationwide, the dropout rate for Hispanic students in the United States was 30% in 1994, compared to 7.7% for EAs and 12.6% for African Americans (National Center for Education Statistics, 1996). Trueba (1999) argues that the future economical, technological, and military strength of the United States will depend on teachers' abilities and skills to humanize the learning experience for minority students. Changes must be made in the education system and in teacher preparation programs to address the issues responsible for the unacceptably high dropout rates. Not surprisingly, it has been found that "attention to how teachers' beliefs and attitudes influence their individual classroom language policies and interactions with language minority students is not widespread at either the pre-service or in-service levels of teacher education" (Cutri, 2000, p. 179).

The traditional curriculum still works on the assumption of what Paolo Freire (1989) has called "the banking model of education" where teachers (and state agencies, one might add) know best. Students are expected to gain competency in standard English and become conversant in canonical literature. In contrast, the CLL class encouraged reflection on nonstandard communicative practices in conjunction with exposure to and training in noncanonical literary texts that suggested culture-specific pedagogical initiatives and innovations. Our own as well as the students' research indicated that there are numerous linguistic and cultural barriers between educational agents and students, and between students of different ethnicities. Overcoming these barriers is one step toward educating global citizens, students who are aware of the world outside their own social, economic, and political milieu. From a geopolitical perspective, in an area so closely located on the United States–Mexico border as South Texas, where two national languages and cultures intersect, local knowledge leads to more effective global citizenship for both the minority and majority communities.

## REFERENCES

Anzaldúa, A. (1999). *Borderlands/ La Frontera: The new mestiza* (2nd ed.). San Francisco: Aunt Lute Books.

Aronowitz, S., & Giroux, H. (1985). *Education under siege: The conservative, liberal and radical debate over schooling.* South Hadley, MA: Bergin & Garvey.

Ashcroft, B., Griffiths, G., & Tiffin, H. (1989). *The empire writes back: Theory and practice in post-colonial literatures.* London: Routledge.

August, D., & Hakuta, K. (Eds.). (1997). *Improving schooling for language-minority children: Research agenda.* Washington, DC: National Academy Press.

Bartolome, L., & Trueba, H. T. (2000). Beyond the politics of schools and the rhetoric of fashionable pedagogies: The significance of teacher ideology. In H. T. Trueba & L. Bartolome (Eds.), *Immigrant voices* (pp. 277–292). Lanham, MD: Rowman & Littlefield.

Bloom, B. S., Davis, A., & Hess, R. (1965). *Compensatory education for cultural deprivation.* New York: Holt, Rinehart & Winston.

Caballero, P. (2001, March 27). For many Hispanics, future must wait. *Corpus Christi Caller Times,* pp. A1, A4.

Carter, T., & Segura, R. (1979). *Mexican Americans in school: Decade of change.* New York: College Entrance Examination Board.

Chapa, J. (1991). Hispanic demographics and educational trends. In D. Carter & R. Wilson (Eds.), *Ninth annual status report on minorities in higher education* (pp. 11–17). Washington, DC: American Council on Education.

Cutri, R. M. (2000). Exploring the spiritual moral dimensions of teachers' classroom language policies. In J. Kelly Hall & W. G. Eggington (Eds.), *The sociopolitics of English language teaching* (pp. 165–177). Clevedon, England: Multilingual Matters.

DePaolo, D. (2000). *Teaching Mexican American literature in high schools.* Unpublished manuscript, Texas A&M University at Corpus Christi.

Díaz-Rico, L. T., & Weed, K. Z. (1995). *The crosscultural, language, and academic development handbook: A complete K–12 reference guide.* Boston: Allyn & Bacon.

Dunn, L. M. (1987). *Bilingual Hispanic children in the U.S. mainland: A review of research on their cognitive, linguistic and scholastic development.* Circle Pines, MN: American Guidance Service.

Erickson, F. (1994). Transformation and school success: The politics and culture of educational achievement. In J. Kretovics & E. J. Nussel (Eds.), *Transforming urban education* (pp. 375–395). Boston: Allyn & Bacon.

Eysenck, H. (1971). *The IQ argument: Race, intelligence and education.* New York: The Library Press.

Ford, C. (1984). The influence of speech variety on teacher's evaluation of students with comparable academic ability. *TESOL Quarterly, 18,* 25–40.

Freire, P. (1989). *Pedagogy of the oppressed* (M. Bergman Ramos, Trans.). New York: Continuum.

Friedman, T. L. (1999). *The lexus and the olive tree.* New York: Farrar, Straus & Giroux.

Galindo, L. (1996). Language use and language attitudes: A study of border women. *Bilingual Review/La Revista Bilingüe, 21*(1), 5–17.

Gibson, M. (1997). Complicating the immigrant/involuntary minority typology. *Anthropology and Education Quarterly, 28*(3), 431–454.

Heath, S. B. (1983). *Ways with words.* Cambridge, England: Cambridge University Press.

Heller, C. (1966). *Mexican American youth: The forgotten youth at the crossroads.* New York: Random House.

Herrnstein, R. J., & Murray, C. (1994). *The bell curve: Intelligence and class structure in American life.* New York: Simon & Schuster.

Jensen, A. (1972). *Genetics and education.* London: Methuen.

King, R. (1997, April). Should English be the law? *The Atlantic Monthly, 4,* 55–64.

Laosa, L. M. (1984). Ethnic, socioeconomic, and home language influences upon early performance on measures of abilities. *Journal of Educational Psychology, 76,* 1178–1198.

Lippi-Green, R. (1997). *English with an accent.* New York: Routledge.

Markee, N. (2000). Some thoughts on globalization: A response to Warschauer. *TESOL Quarterly, 34,* 569–574.

Mehan, H. (1992). Understanding inequality in schools: The contribution of interpretive studies. *Sociology of Education, 65,* 1–20.

Mermann-Jozwiak, E., & Sullivan, N. (2000). *Braiding languages, weaving cultures: An interview with Diana Montejano.* Unpublished manuscript.

Montejano, D. (1987). *Anglos and Mexicans in the making of Texas, 1836–1986.* Austin: University of Texas Press.

National Center for Education Statistics. (1996). *Dropout rates in the United States: 1994.* Washington, DC: U.S. Department of Education.

New London Group. (1996). A pedagogy of multiliteracies: Designing social futures. *Harvard Educational Review, 66,* 60–92.

Ogbu, J. U. (1987, December). Variability in minority school performance. *Anthropology and Education Quarterly, 18,* 312–334.

Obgu, J. U. (1991). Immigrant and involuntary minorities in comparative perspective. In M. Gibson & J. Ogbu (Eds.), *Minority status and schooling* (pp. 3–36). New York: Garland.

Ogbu, J. U. (1992, November). Understanding cultural diversity and learning. *Educational Researcher, 21,* 5–14.

Padilla, A. M., & Alva, S. A. (1988, April). *Academic performance of Mexican American students: The importance of academic accountability and acculturative stress.* Paper presented at the annual meeting of the American Educational Research Association, New Orleans, LA.

Palmer, G. B. (1996). *Toward a theory of cultural linguistics.* Austin: University of Texas Press.

Ray, S., & Tinsley, M. (1995, November 4). Poll: English-only divides Texans. *Corpus Christi Caller Times,* pp. A1, A8.

Richardson, V. (Ed.). (1997). *Constructivist teacher education: Building new understanding.* Washington, DC: Falmer.

Saldívar-Hull, S. (2000). *Feminism on the border: Chicana gender politics and literature.* Berkeley: University of California Press.

Sánchez, M. E. (1985). *Contemporary Chicana poetry: A critical approach to an emerging literature.* Berkeley: University of California Press.

Saville-Troike, M. (1989). *The ethnography of communication: An introduction.* New York: Blackwell.

Schwartz, J. (2001, March 25). Confronting our dropout problem. *Corpus Christi Caller Times,* pp. A1, A12.

Stein, C. B. (1985). Hispanic students in the sink or swim era, 1900–1960. *Urban Education, 20,* 189–198.

Stevenson, R. B., & Ellsworth, J. (1993). Dropouts and the silencing of critical voices. In L. Weis & M. Fine (Eds.), *Beyond silenced voices: Class, race, and gender in United States schools* (pp. 259–271). Albany: State University of New York Press.

Suarez-Orozco, M., & Suarez-Orozco, C. (1995a). *Transformations: Immigration, family life and achievement motivation among Latino adolescents.* Stanford, CA: Stanford University Press.

Suarez-Orozco, M., & Suarez-Orozco, C. (1995b). Migration: Generational discontinuities and the making of Latino identities. In L. Romanucci-Ross, & G. DeVos

(Eds.), *Ethnic identity: Creation, conflict, and accommodation* (3rd ed., pp. 321–347). Walnut Creek, CA: Alta Mira Press.

Sullivan, N., & Mermann-Jozwiak, E. (2000). *Chicano/a literature in public schools.* Manuscript in preparation. Texas A&M University at Corpus Christi.

Sullivan, N., & Schatz, R. (1999). When cultures collide: The official language debate. *Language & Communication, 19,* 261–275.

Trueba, H. T. (1989a). *Raising silent voices: Educating the linguistic minorities for the 21st century.* Cambridge, MA: Newbury House.

Trueba, H. T. (1989b). Rethinking dropouts: Culture and literacy for minority empowerment. In H. T. Trueba, G. Spindler, & L. Spindler (Eds.), *What do anthropologists have to say about dropouts?* (pp. 27–42). New York: Falmer.

Trueba, H. T. (1991). From failure to success: The roles of culture and cultural conflict in academic achievement of Chicano students. In R. R. Valencia (Ed.), *Chicano school failure and success: Research and policy agendas for the 1990s* (pp. 151–163). New York: Falmer.

Trueba, H. T. (1993). Race and ethnicity: The role of universities in healing multicultural American. *Educational Theory 43,* 41–45.

Trueba, H. T. (1999). *Latinos unidos.* Lanham, MD: Rowman & Littlefield.

Trueba, H. T., Rodriguez, C., Zou, Y., & Cintron, H. (1993). *Healing multicultural American: Mexican immigrants rise to power in rural California.* London: Falmer.

Valencia, R. R. (Ed.). (2002). *Chicano school failure and success* (2nd ed.). New York: Routledge Falmer.

Valencia, R. R., & Aburto, S. (1991). The uses and abuses of educational testing: Chicanos as a case in point. In R. R. Valencia (Ed.), *Chicano school failure and success: Research and policy agendas for the 1990s* (pp. 203–251). New York: Falmer.

Valencia, R. R., & Suzuki, L. (2001). *Intelligence testing and minority students: Foundations, performance factors, and assessment issues.* Thousand Oaks, CA: Sage.

Valentine, C. (1968). *Culture and poverty.* Chicago: University of Chicago Press.

Warschauer, M. (2000). The changing global economy and the future of English teaching. *TESOL Quarterly, 34,* 511–535.

Weiler, K. (1988). *Women teaching for change: Gender, class and power.* New York: Bergin & Garvey.

Williams, F. (1976). *Explorations in the linguistic attitudes of teachers.* Rowley, MA: Newbury House.

Yaeger, P. (2000). *Dirt and desire: Reconstructing southern women's writing, 1930–1990.* Chicago: University of Chicago Press.

Zentella, A. C. (1997). The Hispanophobia of the official English movement in the U.S. *International Journal of the Sociology of Language, 127,* 71–86.

# Author Index

# Subject Index

## A

Affirmative action, 130
Agency, 212
Ambilingualism, 31
Anthropology, xvii, 56, 60
    cultures, xvii, 79
Assimilation, 62–67

## B

Barbarian theorizing, 73–75, 93
Bilingualism, 34–37, 42, 62

## C

Case studies,
    Brazil, 75–79, 81–93, 105–109,
        118–120
    Brunei, 225–244
    Cajun French, 55–69
    Dominicans, 149–160
    England, 173–174, 187–191
    Hong Kong, 248–250, 252–263
    India, 25–28, 32–35, 39–47
    Malaysia, 124–142
    Mexico borderlands, 270–283
Coevalness, 74
Communication, 279
    and the "self", 251–252, 261, 264
Communicative language teaching (CLT),
    175–177, 247–248, 255, 265
    and global communication, 263–264
    in Hong Kong, 248–250, 252–263
    pedagogy, 250–251
Creolization, 15
Cultural discontinuities, 272–273
Cultures, xvii, 79, *see also* Indigenous
    cultures

## D

Didacts, 33–37

## E

ELT (English Language Teaching), xiv–xv,
    xxiii, xxv–xxvi, xxix, 20, 31, 49,
    255
English "threat", 105–109
Ethnogenesis, 74, 90–92
Ethnography, 279–280
Expert discourses, 57–60, *see also*
    Venerable discourses
Expert knowledge, 99–102

## F

Fetishization, 15
Foreignisms, 106
Fossilization, 31

## G

Global communication, 263–264